Period House

Collins

Period House

Albert Jackson & David Day

IN ASSOCIATION WITH ENGLISH HERITAGE

COLLINS PERIOD HOUSE

was created exclusively for HarperCollins Publishers by
Albert Jackson, David Day and Simon Jennings
trading as Inklink

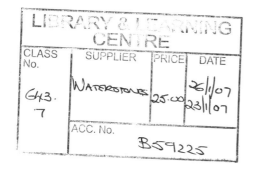

Authors
Albert Jackson
David Day

Design
Simon Jennings
Alan Marshall
Elizabeth Standley

Editor
Peter Leek

Illustrators
Robin Harris
David Day

Location photographer
Shona Wood

Studio photographers
Neil Waving
Ben Jennings

Indexer and proofreader
Mary Morton

Originally published as
Collins Complete Home Restoration Manual in 1992, then as
Collins Care & Repair of Period Houses in 1998 and
Collins Period House in 2002

This edition first published in 2005
by HarperCollins Publishers, London
in association with English Heritage

For HarperCollins
Senior Managing Editor – Angela Newton
Production Controller – Chris Gurney
Jacket Designer – Sarah Christie

For English Heritage
David Pickles

**The CIP catalogue record for this book is available from
the British Library**

ISBN 000-7192754

Printed by
Printing Express Ltd, Hong Kong

Copyright © 2005
HarperCollins Publishers

CONTENTS

INTRODUCTION

FROM THE STATELY HOME TO THE HUMBLE COTTAGE, there is a growing interest in the care and protection of historic buildings. Every old house has its own individual character and, despite the potential problems, more and more people are attracted to owning and living in period properties.

Before the boom in house prices in the 1960s, many people rented their homes – partly because houses were frequently built for renting, but also because owning a house was considered to be a liability. Since there was no incentive to invest money in aesthetic improvements when house prices were static, landlords in particular tended to sanction only repairs that were necessary in order to prevent a building deteriorating to the point where it would begin to depreciate. One consequence of this was that old houses tended to remain more or less as built, albeit often in a somewhat dilapidated condition. Subsequently, rising prosperity engendered new confidence in the long-term benefits of home ownership. This led to a profound change of attitude, and we now take it for granted that sympathetic improvements to a house are likely to be financially advantageous. However, people are now more mobile and houses change hands more frequently – and a succession of different owners, each eager to make their own mark and each making alterations, can quickly erode the character of a house. The patina of age is a subtle feature, and one that is only too easily destroyed.

Many of us dream of buying and refurbishing an old house. Making that dream a reality can often be a struggle, but the rewards are many. Not only can you take pride in what you have achieved, but there is also the satisfaction of helping to save part of the country's heritage. Even so, finding sufficient finance to undertake the work can be daunting, and sustained patience is needed to see the project through without being tempted by short cuts – which could result in inappropriate work and so accelerate deterioration. An old house complete with its period fixtures and fittings can be regarded as a composite work of art and document of history. Despite the best of intentions, it is easy to impair the integrity of your house by misguided alterations – but often, by analysing and understanding its special qualities, such mistakes can be avoided.

Sometimes damage can occur through removing too much historic fabric, so that the building loses some of its appeal. It is better to have a worn and carefully patched old door than a modern replica, however faithfully copied. Old buildings vary greatly in the extent to which they are able to accommodate change without loss of character. Some are sensitive to even seemingly minor alterations, particularly externally or if they retain original interior fixtures, fittings and details. Others may have been modified to such an extent that putting them back to a previous state is not a feasible or sensible option. A conservative approach is fundamental to good conservation – so retaining as much of the original fabric and keeping changes to a minimum are of key importance when carrying out work on a period house.

Serious damage can result from the use of inappropriate or incompatible materials. Where possible, materials matching the original should therefore always be used. Also, old houses are often damaged by lack of care. Regular maintenance is both cost-effective and an important part of looking after an old building. Often, prompt action can prevent decay and avoid the need for major repairs.

Period buildings constitute a precious non-renewable legacy that needs to be sustained. Owning one implies responsibility – in the history of a 300-year-old cottage an individual's residency is but a short event. We are looking after these buildings for our children and their children, so that they will have something worthwhile to inherit. William Morris, who founded the Society for the Protection of Ancient Buildings, urged his contemporaries to 'hand them down instructive and venerable to those that come after us'. That is no less true today. The stock of old buildings is finite, and every loss or instance of serious damage is significant.

This book provides practical guidance about maintaining and repairing the older house and how to reinstate missing features authentically. It explains what you need to consider before embarking on any work, and when necessary how to obtain expert advice. It also indicates which tasks you may be able to tackle yourself, and gives information about techniques and materials so you can discuss aspects of repairs or restoration in detail when briefing professionals to do work for you.

PHOTOGRAPHS & ILLUSTRATIONS

The authors are grateful to the following companies and individuals for additional photographs and illustrations:

Photographs

Peter Aprahamian/Traditional Homes Magazine
Pages 201BR; 204C

Chris Challis/Traditional Homes Magazines
Page 202

Paul Chave
Pages 16R; 157B

Crown Berger Ltd
Page 172T

Edifice
Pages 10T, CL; 11; 25; 27CR, BL; 41BL; 47TL; 58CL; 59BR; 61CL; 64C; 75BR; 76BR; 89TL; 91; 102; 103BR; 104CL; 175TL, CL, BL, C, TR; 180TL

English Heritage Photographic Library
Pages 18; 19; 22; 23TL, BL; 24; 27TC; 28CL, CR; 64TR, CR, BR; 65; 105TR; 224; 228; 229TL, BR

Tony Herbert
Pages 153BR; 156CR; 157TL

John Heseltine/Traditional Homes Magazine
Pages 152CL; 184T; 205BL

Hugh Howard
Page 211L

Inklink
Pages 27TR, BR; 28TR, CL, C, BL; 29TL, TC, TR, C, BL, BR; 57BR; 176CR

Albert Jackson
Pages 13C, BL, BR; 14; 15; 17CR; 23TR, B; 31BL, C, TR; 32; 33R; 34; 35; 36L; 39TR, BR; 40; 42BL; 46CR; 48C, BL; 50; 61BC, BR; 62; 66CL

Simon Jennings
Pages 16T; 17TL; 25TL; 33TR; 63TR; 66CR, B; 68; 89TC; 92CR; 114; 120BR; 122B; 195L

Richard Littlewood/Traditional Homes Magazine
Page 184B

Alan Marshall
Page 158

Ian Parry/Traditional Homes Magazine
Pages 36R; 152C, CR; 154; 183; 189; 204BL, BR; 212BR; 214T

Rentokil Ltd
Pages 28BC, BR; 29CR; 227

Traditional Homes Magazine
Page 153TL

Adele Bishop/Carolyn Warrender Stencil Designs
Page 190

Neil Waving
Pages 9R; 125BR; 146; 162; 195

Historical illustrations

B. T. Batsford Ltd
Pages 9T; 12B

Bexley Library & Museums Department
Pages 17CL; 20CR

Chiswick Library
Pages 9BL; 20T, B

Mary Evans Picture Library
Pages 12T; 38TL; 61T; 151T; 152T

Ironbridge Gorge Museum Trust
Pages 31T; 32CL; 41T; 45TL; 62TL; 75T; 111CL, TR; 113TR; 131TR; 141; 159T; 191T; 200L

Warwick Leadlay
Page 12C

Marflex International Ltd
Pages 211T; 212T; 213T

KEY TO CREDITS
T=TOP, B=BOTTOM, L=LEFT, R=RIGHT, TL=TOP LEFT, TR=TOP RIGHT, C=CENTRE, TC=TOP CENTRE, CL=CENTRE LEFT, CR=CENTRE RIGHT, BL=BOTTOM LEFT, BR=BOTTOM RIGHT, BC=BOTTOM CENTRE.

MATERIALS

The authors are indebted to the following companies and individuals who generously supplied samples or products for photography:

Stonework

The Carving Workshop

Doors & windows

The Antique Hardware Store
Ball & Ball
Clayton-Munroe Ltd
Comyn Ching Ltd
Peter Cornish
Dorset Restoration
GKN Crompton Ltd
Joseph Tipper Ltd

Ornamental glass

Lamont Antiques Ltd
Sam Towers

Plasterwork

E. J. Harmer & Co.

Decorative woodwork

Cumberland Woodcraft Co. Inc.

Wall panelling

Desfab
Winther Browne & Co. Ltd

Tiling

Chris Blanchett
H. & R. Johnson Tiles Ltd
Dennis Ruabon Ltd

Decorative metal

R. Bleasdale (Spirals)
Britannia Architectural Metalwork & Restoration
County Forge Ltd

Fireplaces

Westcombe Antiques

CONSULTANTS AND CONTRIBUTORS

The authors are grateful to the following experts who generously contributed their time and expertise:

Chimneys & fireplaces

Christian Pederson,
Marflex International Ltd
Eddie Gidding,
Stoneage

Ornamental glass

Peter McDonnell,
Gray & McDonnell Ltd
Sam Towers

Plasterwork & stucco

Ernest Millar,
E. G. Millar (Plastering) Ltd
Karl Walters,
British Gypsum Ltd

CHAPTER ONE

ARCHITECTURAL STYLES

WE ARE BECOMING MORE SENSITIVE to the importance of protecting our heritage. Yet in the not so distant past many old houses were subjected to indiscriminate assault, with relatively little protest.

During that period many house owners would simply discard what were thought of as unfashionable fittings and decoration in the belief that by 'modernization' they were increasing the market value of their homes. But attitudes have changed. Today, period houses retaining all their original features are highly marketable, and those of us who own old houses that have not been ruined by ill-considered alterations now make every effort to repair and maintain them.

Often these houses require extensive repairs and improvements, such as new wiring and plumbing or the installation of full central heating. But such considerations seldom dissuade the eager house hunter from acquiring a period home that attracts them.

What they find irresistible are those elegant façades with their perfectly proportioned windows, the carved wood and stonework, the delightful moulded plasterwork, the colourful stained glass and floor tiles – all those decorative elements that our forebears were able to fashion with such consummate skill and confidence, and which give every old house its distinctive appeal. The process of preserving, re-creating or repairing such features can provide a great deal of satisfaction.

By describing the development of house construction over the centuries, this chapter aims to help you understand the way your house is built and give you a fuller appreciation of what you have and how it may have changed over time.

A lithograph of 1882 depicting the Victorian suburb of Bedford Park

Thoughtful conservation has preserved Bedford Park for over 100 years

EARLY BRITISH HOUSES
Timber frames to masonry

Jettied wealden house

HOUSES CAME INTO BEING *as soon as people begin to settle into communities and cultivate the land. The development of domestic architecture reflects their increasing desire for comfort and privacy. In Britain, Roman housing eventually reached a high state of sophistication, based on classical ideas. Then, following the departure of the Romans, the standard of domestic building declined until after the Norman conquest, when the invaders, with their passion for masonry, introduced stone houses.*

EARLY TIMBER HOUSES

From earliest times, houses have been constructed from a series of prefabricated timber frames (cross frames, wall frames, floor and roof frames) that were joined, one to another, dividing the building into bays. One type of cross frame is known as a cruck, which comprises a pair of long curved timbers joined by tie beams or 'collars'. In some places it is still possible to find examples of cruck houses, which display the distinctive frame prominently on the outside.

Cruck-house timber construction

MEDIEVAL AND VERNACULAR HOUSES

Few, if any, examples of humble housing have survived from the twelfth and thirteenth centuries, as the peasants' simple wattle-and-daub houses and outbuildings have now largely perished. But by the beginning of the fourteenth century the timber-frame house had become established, and this form of construction continued to be widely used for the next 300 years.

The medieval house was generally divided into three sections. At its nucleus was the hall, usually with an entrance at one end and a dais at the other. At the upper end of the hall was the 'master's' accommodation; and at the lower end, beyond the through passage,

or 'screens passage', were the servants' quarters and household services. Hall houses, which were normally rectangular in plan, were constructed with a series of wooden trusses that divided the building into bays.

One of the most distinctive types of timber-frame house to develop during the fourteenth century was the wealden house. This type of dwelling, which was particularly common in the south-eastern counties of England, continued to be built until the late sixteenth

century. The chief characteristic of the wealden house is the 'jettied' (overhanging) upper storey of the end bays of the house. In towns the jetties often continued round the sides of the house and sometimes round the back as well – a feature less common in rural houses. The entrance, opening into the through passage formed by screens, was at the lower end of the hall.

In early hall houses the hearth had been in the centre of the hall, with the smoke escaping through open timber

The timber-frame house has developed over hundreds of years

Attractive raised pargeting

louvres in the roof. The fourteenth century witnessed the advent of wall fireplaces, but external chimneys built of brick or stone were not a common feature until the sixteenth century.

The changes in living habits in early Tudor times can be seen in the alterations that were made to hall houses – because the great hall had ceased to be a vital centre of daily life, it began to change. During the sixteenth and seventeenth centuries, in many houses upper floors were built into the hall and over a period of time other changes were introduced, too. Bay windows were often added to the dais end of the hall, making a small space that could be screened off for dining. Oriels and bays became popular stylistic features, and windows and doorways imitated the prevailing style of church architecture. During the sixteenth century, houses were still predominantly made of timber, but brick began to be used, particularly as infilling for the timber framework.

By the seventeenth century, the desire for improved comfort and weatherproofing began to change the way houses were constructed. Windows were glazed and interior walls plastered. Externally, plaster was often used to cover the frame and frequently it was ornamented with incised or raised patterns, known as pargeting. The plaster was usually limewashed, with the addition of a pigment to provide colour. But plastering was not the only method of covering the timber frame. In Kent and Sussex, hung tiles became a common feature, mainly on the upper storey. In some counties wooden weatherboarding was popular, often disguising the presence of an earlier house.

The plan of the vernacular house remained much the same – seldom more than one room deep and two storeys high. Additional rooms were accommodated by extending the slope of the main roof or in wings built at right angles to the main part of the house.

THE IMPACT OF THE RENAISSANCE

During the seventeenth century, building gradually passed out of the hands of carpenters into the hands of masons and bricklayers. Improved transport began to make bricks more accessible, especially when canal systems were introduced. Much of the once plentiful supply of timber was being reserved for the navy, and during the latter part of the century legislation on fire prevention began to have an impact.

The spread of Renaissance style to the smaller house was slow, and traditional building methods continued to be used in the north and west of the country long after they had declined in the south. However, the growth of classical ideas gradually began to impact on vernacular building. This usually manifested itself in the introduction of a symmetrical show front when houses were altered internally. The hierarchy of the house now began to shift away from the end-to-end plan of the medieval house, with its hall as the main living space, to the deeper front-and-back arrangement – which is still how most houses are organized.

Timber frame infilled with brick

Relatively small town house, exhibiting the impact of Renaissance style

THE GEORGIAN PERIOD
Classicism & elegant proportion

Inigo Jones, architect, 1573–1652

THE STYLE OF ENGLISH HOUSES *when George I came to the throne in 1714 was largely derived from classically inspired architects, particularly the sixteenth-century Venetian, Andrea Palladio.*

The English Palladian movement began with Inigo Jones, who built the nation's first Palladian mansion, the Queen's House in Greenwich, in the early seventeenth century. But the most formative influence on early-Georgian architecture was probably Palladio's QUATTRO LIBRI DELL' ARCHITETTURA, *which was translated into English in 1715. This was a detailed study of the ruins of ancient Rome, interpreting building style and proportion in terms of the five classical orders of architecture – Tuscan, Doric, Ionic, Corinthian and Composite.*

PALLADIANISM AND PROPORTION

The classical orders embodied a set of guidelines and rules that enabled an architect or builder to determine the proportions of a building with confidence. Once the key dimensions were established, the rest could be calculated with ease. An early-Georgian building or terrace was conceived like an ancient Graeco-Roman façade. The ground floor, which was often rusticated to give an impression of solidity, represented a plinth

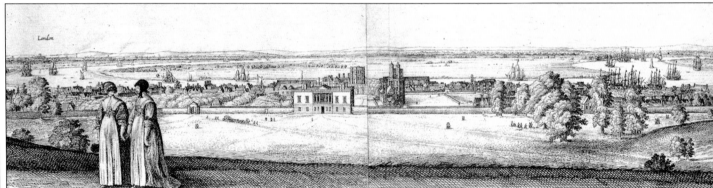

A detail from an engraving by Wenceslaus Hollar, showing the newly built Queen's House, Greenwich

The classical orders of architecture

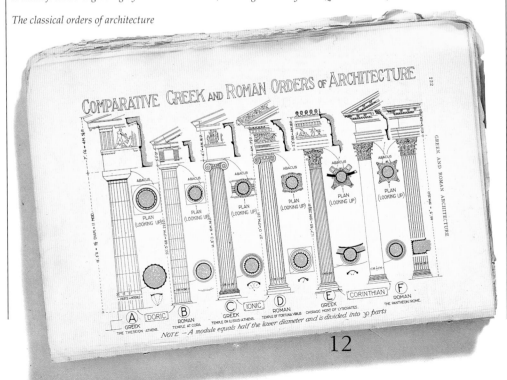

upon which was constructed a row of columns or pilasters extending through perhaps two storeys to a classical entablature incorporating a cornice, frieze and architrave. Some façades were even capped with a pedimented gable reminiscent of an ancient temple.

This literal interpretation, which was acceptable for large public buildings and grand mansions, was too much for the average house built on a smaller scale. Yet the same principles of proportion were applied – the line of the plinth, capitals and entablature being defined by simple stone courses and by the placing of the windows, in what was otherwise a simple unadorned brick or stone

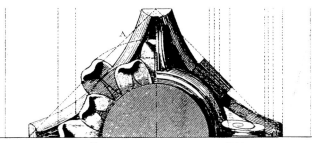

façade. Recognizable references to the classical orders were largely restricted to window and door surrounds – especially doorcases comprising pilasters or engaged columns in one of the accepted styles, surmounted by a pediment enclosing a semi-circular fanlight. Classically inspired motifs are to be found inside houses of the period, too, particularly in the form of plaster ceiling cornices incorporating dentils, modillions, rosettes or paterae.

NEO-CLASSICISM

The followers of Palladianism were convinced to the point of dogmatism that the tenets of the movement were based on irrefutable principles. But Palladianism itself was derived from yet another revival movement, a Romanized version of ancient-Greek architecture. By the middle of the eighteenth century, a passion for foreign travel and research into ancient cultures had led to a rediscovery of the Greek originals. This inevitably brought about a reassessment of accepted principles, which in turn led to the movement known as Neo-classicism and eventually to the stricter Greek revival. Proponents of the Greek revival rejected the Tuscan and Composite orders as Roman interlopers, and defined a purer Greek form of the Doric, Ionic and Corinthian orders.

Neo-classicism supplemented the existing Palladian repertoire with a delightful range of new ornamental motifs, including scrolling, foliage, strings of husks, classical urns, mythical beasts, abstract enrichments, such as the Greek key pattern, and the ubiquitous anthemion motifs, most commonly based on honeysuckle flowers and leaves.

THE REGENCY PERIOD

Historically the Regency period is defined as those few years between 1811 and 1820 when the future George IV ruled as Prince Regent in place of his deranged father. However, the architectural style of the first 30 years of the nineteenth century is generally known as Regency.

The lingering influence of Neo-classicism, particularly the Greek-revival movement, is discernible in typical late-Georgian bow-fronted houses, which sometimes boast rusticated-stucco ground floors. However, the taste for painted stucco led to bright, colourful urban vistas, which began to reflect more flamboyant influences brought from the Far East – particularly the passion in fashionable circles for so-called chinoiserie. Perhaps the most famous example of Regency whimsy is the Royal Pavilion in Brighton, with its domes, minarets and elaborate pseudo-oriental interior decoration. The more ordinary houses of the period show little trace of these extravagant flights of fancy, apart from occasional references – such as canopies over porches or balconies with a hint of oriental style.

Grand stone-built façade based on Graeco-Roman architectural concepts

C18th terrace embodying simple yet precise Georgian proportions

Bow-fronted Regency houses

Regency adaptation of exotic style

THE VICTORIAN PERIOD
Confident opulence

ASPIRATIONS AND TASTE *do not change automatically with the death of a monarch. Early-Victorian buildings were no different from late-Georgian ones. Some conservative institutions, for example, continued to opt for time-honoured classical styles and ornamentation throughout the nineteenth century, presumably to proclaim their permanence and dependability; and the popular stuccoed Italianate villas of the early nineteenth century, which were inspired by Renaissance architecture, still reflected classical themes. However, many Victorians were eventually to reject the classically inspired homogeneity and traditionalism of the eighteenth century and boldly adopted new forms that were more in step with the endemic confidence of the era.*

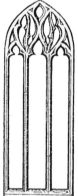

A large family house with Gothic-revival features

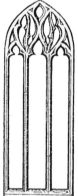

This splendid house epitomizes the sombre romanticism of the Gothic revival

THE GOTHIC REVIVAL
The Victorians were intensely nationalistic in their attitudes and aspirations, and many architects and designers of the era consistently strived to develop a distinctive British style. However, just what that style should be was vigorously debated and contested. If there was ever a victor in the early days of what is sometimes called 'the battle of the styles', it was the Gothic-revival movement, which exerted a dominant influence on Victorian architecture until the latter part of the nineteenth century.

Although the epitome of high-Victorian taste and ideals, the Gothic-revival movement had its roots in the mid eighteenth century. The architects of that time had experimented with romantic Gothic symbolism, but always as a fairly light-hearted parody of medieval style. The Victorians were to take Gothic architecture much more seriously. The Palace of Westminster had been destroyed by fire in 1834. When two years later it was decided to rebuild it in Gothic-revival style, the movement gained respectability and it was adopted enthusiastically for important public buildings – especially churches, for which the Victorians considered the style more appropriate than pagan classicism.

Based as it was on medieval church architecture, pure Gothic revivalism did not translate easily for the mass of smaller houses built in the Victorian era. Very often these were built by speculators who adopted vaguely Gothic forms to give their houses a fashionable appearance. Lancet windows, stained glass, battened doors in oak, and bay windows with elegant medieval-style pillars are all typical features of speculative Victorian housing.

Less austere references were inspired by the publication in 1851 of *The Stones of Venice*, John Ruskin's studies of Italian Gothic architecture. Among other developments, the book led to widespread use of polychromatic and patterned brickwork, which were ideally suited to the average-size house.

Although the Gothic-revival movement attracted its share of dedicated purists, Victorian architecture in general was self-indulgent compared with the disciplined practices of the eighteenth century. Indeed, houses were frequently an amalgam of styles and motifs borrowed from different ages and cultures, simply because an architect, builder or client found them attractive. To some extent this eclectic approach to design is what gives mid-Victorian architecture its peculiar charm – although that is not the way it was viewed by some contemporary critics.

An archetypal Victorian terrace of polychromatic-brick houses

THE DOMESTIC REVIVAL

Some artists, designers and architects disapproved of the more obvious mid-Victorian excesses in the decorative arts. From the late 1860s onwards, a number of groups began to form in an attempt to shift the emphasis away from eclecticism and mass production towards a revival of vernacular architectural forms and traditional craftsmanship. It can be argued that the fruits of such movements were as derivative as those they sought to replace. Although it had a strong appeal to Victorian middle-class romantics, the idealized image of rural life in the sixteenth and seventeenth centuries was far from historical truth. But what cannot be faulted was the earnest endeavour to promote materials and workmanship of the highest quality.

Groups such as the Arts and Crafts movement, led by William Morris, and the Aesthetic movement were influential in furthering their cause in every aspect of the visual arts, from architecture and interior decoration to wallcoverings and carpets. Among the popular motifs of the period were exotic birds (such as peacocks and cranes), traditional Japanese themes (such as cherry and apple blossom), medieval symbolism, and botanical subjects (especially lilies and sunflowers).

Several architectural styles were spawned at about this time, all of them reminiscent of Tudor or Stuart England. One of the most potent yet unpretentious fashions, the Queen Anne revival, seemed ideally suited to the smaller town house. Simple red brick became popular again, sometimes accented with stone mouldings. There were

A charming Queen-Anne-revival house built in the late 1870s

Craftsman-built Victorian house in the Old English style

distinctive Flemish gables, decorative stucco or pargeting, and a return to sash windows with thick white-painted glazing bars and small panes of glass.

Some considered the 'Old English' style to be the rural equivalent of the rather more mannered Queen Anne style, which was perhaps better suited to urban settings. Inspired by Elizabethan or Jacobean architecture, 'Old English' houses frequently combined motifs and forms from both periods, with little consideration for historical verisimilitude. Some houses were tasteful fusions of half-timbering and roughcast, tile-hung gables and leaded-light casements. Others included even more overt references to the past, such as diaper-pattern brickwork and tall chimneys, carved bargeboards and linenfold panelling, stone mullions, and drip mouldings over the windows.

Such houses, invariably set in delightful surroundings, marked a return to a human scale of domestic architecture. People felt comfortable with the so-called Domestic-revival movement. As a result, it became an enduring influence, lasting well into the twentieth century.

TWENTIETH CENTURY
Art Nouveau & Art Deco

E ARLY TWENTIETH-CENTURY HOUSES, *especially those built for the middle classes during Edward VII's short reign, were often similar in style to their Victorian precursors, though generally smaller in scale and with less decoration. However, the Edwardians themselves would probably have considered their houses to be relatively sophisticated compared with the highly ornate, even ostentatious, fashions of the previous era, and much of the architecture of the early twentieth century is epitomized by styles and forms that broke new ground – styles that owed little to the past and which appealed to the more avant-garde Edwardian architects and designers.*

Art Deco architecture seemed extraordinarily avant-garde in the 1930s

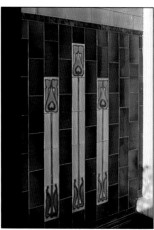

Art Nouveau ceramic porch tiles

Art Deco interiors relied on bold shapes and simple fittings for their impact

ART NOUVEAU
Art Nouveau, which is one of the most distinctive design styles, originated in France in the 1880s. Although it was adopted in Europe with some enthusiasm, it made hardly any impact in Britain until the turn of the century – and even then only for furnishings and decorative detail rather than as a full-blown architectural style.

Art Nouveau is characterized by sinuous lines, especially the so-called whiplash curves that frequently appear in compositions. Subjects such as luxuriant foliage and young women with long flowing hair were consciously chosen in order to exploit their linear qualities. Asymmetry was the other conspicuous trademark of the Art Nouveau movement – one that demanded considerable skill on the part of an artist or a designer in order to achieve a composition that was both pleasing and balanced.

It was clearly a style that the average builder would have had some difficulty in mastering. As a result, perhaps, Art Nouveau rarely features as an architectural style in British housing. However, being an idiom that appealed to artists and professional designers, it appears not infrequently in the form of stained glass, cast-iron fire surrounds, light fittings and, above all, wallcovering patterns.

ART DECO
The other remarkable innovative movement of the early twentieth century was also of European origin. Art Deco took its name from the *Exposition Internationale des Arts Décoratifs et Industriels Modernes* held in Paris in 1925. Uncompromisingly modern in its approach, Art Deco was ideally suited to the contemporary passion for homes that were clean, simple and full of light. The style is notable for bold geometric shapes and highly stylized natural forms. Typically, touches of intense colour, in the form of ornamental glass, tiles or paint, are used to accentuate larger white or pale-coloured textured surfaces or to contrast with natural materials such as marble and wood. Built-in furniture became a coveted feature, often constructed from bent or moulded plywood to create striking curvilinear forms.

During the 1920s and 1930s, Art Deco percolated through all strata of society and various types of edifice, from the modernist homes of the fashionable elite to public buildings such as underground-railway stations and cinemas. Sometimes one can even discern a passing reference to Art Deco ideas in local-authority housing projects of the time.

Semi-detached dream homes were built in their thousands between the two world wars

New Ideal Homesteads

•Sidcup
Albany
Park Estate

Some Edwardian garden-city developments were highly sophisticated

Village charm was the model for this estate on the outskirts of London

SEMI-DETACHED SUBURBIA

The late-Victorian ideal of the village-style cottage estate was no doubt the inspiration for the county-council garden-suburb developments built just before and after the First World War. These schemes were designed to alleviate the pressure on chronically outdated housing by demolishing the Victorian slums of the major cities and transposing their inhabitants to the outskirts.

The better developments were highly successful, with the houses built to a modest budget yet with an emphasis on individuality. In place of the straight terraces of identical houses, there were meandering avenues and small squares or courts lined with vaguely 'Old English' style cottages, each seemingly built to a slightly different specification.

Between the two world wars, the housing boom continued at an unprecedented rate. Improved transport systems and new-found prosperity led to a doubling of Britain's housing stock, largely by extending city-suburb developments in all directions. These comprised the now familiar semi-detached mock-Tudor houses, with their bay windows at the front and French windows at the rear. Built to a formula that was enormously popular, such houses embodied everything that would appeal to the aspiring home owner. They were easy to

clean and heat (they included the latest labour-saving appliances), and had indoor toilets and tiled bathrooms as standard. These were thoroughly desirable and up-to-date residences, with no small measure of prestige.

The suburban 'semi' has been much maligned for its image of dreariness and stuffy conservatism. Such houses have probably suffered most from the ravages of modernization, not the least because they have been considered unworthy of conservation. An unspoilt example of a 1930s semi-detached house has now become almost as difficult to find as a Victorian or Georgian house in similar condition.

However, the undoubted qualities of these soundly built houses are now at long last being appreciated. Thanks to their somewhat unsophisticated charm and the fact that they can be restored comparatively cheaply, they are one of the more recent additions to the catalogue of desirable period homes.

THE POSTWAR PERIOD
Prefabs to high-rise blocks

Temporary accommodation built in the 1940s is still in use today

I N THE AUTUMN OF 1939 *the outbreak of war inter-rupted building in Britain, and for the next six years only airfields and other military installations were built. With the cessation of hostilities the government's first priority was to house people who had lost their homes to bombing, and simple prefabricated dwellings were erected on waste ground in many towns and cities. Surprisingly, some of these 'prefabs' survive to this day and many are now legally protected.*

Simple forms are a feature of 1950s housing

High-rise flats are now desirable residences

Architects delighted in designing one-off houses

THE FESTIVAL OF BRITAIN
Rebuilding on a large scale presented architects with many new and exciting opportunities. One of the most important single factors to influence contemporary design was the Festival of Britain, an international showcase for British culture, described as a 'tonic to the nation', held in 1951. However, this celebration of the new era was set against a backdrop of post-war austerity, with a system of building licences in force due to the shortages of building materials. Despite these constraints, the 1950s saw a burst of creative thinking in Britain. Advances in construction and the use of a wide variety of materials – timber, plastics, steel and concrete – were the major influences on the form of postwar buildings. Simplicity combined with a variety of surface finish and texture became a feature of house design during the 1950s.

HIGH-RISE DEVELOPMENTS
Most of the building work in the period immediately after the war was publicly funded. The need for schools and public housing had drawn many talented architects to work for local authorities. Several new towns had been designated soon after the war ended, and Britain continued to play a pioneering role in the design and planning of suburban housing. At the same time, much publicly funded housing in towns and cities was being built in the form of 'high-rise' blocks of flats. Although many of the high-rise blocks became – and remain – objects of hatred and derision, some of them are now viewed as desirable residences and are legally protected.

ONE-OFF DESIGNS
As the 1960s approached, shortages of money and materials eased. Throughout this decade many new ideas were explored in the building of small 'one-off' private houses alongside public-sector architecture. No single overall style or movement emerged, but the chance to build a completely original house provided an attractive alternative to the then unfashionable houses of the Victorian and Edwardian eras, which at that time were often remodelled internally to create a more 'contemporary' ambience. The fundamental elements of house design were being questioned, both in the way the house functioned and in how it looked.

By the 1970s, house design had moved on from large-scale redevelopment schemes. There was growing interest in the rehabilitation of old buildings, alongside new ecological concerns and a search for a more humane environment born out of a new pragmatism that respected place and local materials.

CHAPTER TWO

TAKING STOCK

WE ALL HAVE OUR REASONS *for wanting to find out more about older houses. Maybe you are actively looking for a period house or already have a property in mind and are wondering whether you're making the right decision in taking on what could be a long-term refurbishment project. Or perhaps you live in an old house or have inherited the family home, and are concerned about how to go about putting the building in good order. In any of these situations, you may be asking yourself whether it is going to be worth the time and effort involved. With so many important considerations to weigh up, the worst possible course of action is to make hasty decisions that you might have cause to regret in the future.*

When you are caught up in the excitement and anticipation of buying a house, there are strong pressures to make a snap decision before somebody else gets there first or the price of the property escalates out of your reach. But before buying any house, especially an old one, it is essential to have it surveyed professionally in order to ascertain its true value and ensure that there are no unforeseen problems.

Even when you are over these initial hurdles and you have actually moved into the house, it is worth living in it for a while before deciding how to adapt, renovate or modernize your new home. Getting to know your house more intimately will give you an opportunity to discover and appreciate its best attributes, and also to identify aspects of the house you cannot live with. It may be difficult to curb your enthusiasm, but a period of careful reflection will help you take stock of the situation and then move forward confidently.

Old houses should be surveyed to ensure there are no unexpected problems

Living in a house for a while helps you appreciate its best attributes

GETTING TO KNOW YOUR HOUSE

Original plans may be available

HAVING RECENTLY PURCHASED *or inherited an old house, you probably can't wait to turn it into your dream home. But do you really know enough about the house to make the most of what you now own, and to avoid costly mistakes? Naturally there are going to be practical considerations with regard to the structural condition of the building – but putting those aside for the moment, try to find out all you can about the history of your house. What was it like when it was built, and what changes has it gone through? Answers to these questions will provide valuable clues as to how you can best preserve the essential qualities of the house, while modifying it for a contemporary lifestyle.*

HISTORICAL RESEARCH

Discovering the history of your house and, in particular, how it has evolved over time will help you identify the important features that should be preserved or reinstated. Similarly, understanding how the house was constructed or has been modified may shed light on some of the problems that exist today.

You could engage the services of a professional architectural historian, who will be familiar with all the relevant sources of information and who may be able to spot clues that are not obvious to an untrained eye.

However, there's a great deal of research you can do yourself. For example, there are numerous books on domestic architecture, including some that are aimed specifically at helping house owners research the history of their homes.

Once you have a general idea of what you are looking for, you can begin to broaden your search. Original plans, site maps and deeds may still exist, and there may be other valuable documentary evidence, such as old letters, legal transactions, electoral registers and census returns, that could tell you something about the people who built your house or lived there before you. Ask around to see if there are people living in your neighbourhood who can give you a first-hand account of how things have changed over the years.

The local reference library might have an archive of photographs and paintings, which may include pictures of your house. Estate agents' advertisements that appear in old newspapers are another source of detailed information.

Visit your local-authority planning department to see if they have records and plans of work carried out on your house, including applications for planning permission and listed-building consent.

The National Monuments Record contains brief descriptions of listed buildings and, in some cases, photographs of older properties.

Old advertisements are informative

Though not entirely reliable, a contemporary painting will give some idea of what your street may have looked like

ORIGINAL FEATURES

One of the pleasures of first-hand investigation is discovering delightful features, such as walled-up fireplaces or nicely proportioned panelled doors, hidden beneath sheets of painted hardboard. But too

Original Victorian tiled panel

often the owner of an old house is left wondering what the original windows or plaster mouldings might have looked like.

You may come across pictures or perhaps written descriptions, but more direct evidence can often be found by studying neighbouring houses of similar design to your own. On the outside, see if attractive brickwork, stonework and, especially, stuccowork could have been covered over or removed at some time in the past. Carved or fretted woodwork might have been discarded as a cost-saving exercise or in a misguided attempt at modernization. Internal features such as decorated plaster surfaces, window shutters, doors and doorcases, and finger plates might all have suffered a similar fate. If features such as these have survived, it is worth making an effort to repair and preserve them.

Neighbouring buildings may hold valuable clues

ALTERATIONS AND EXTENSIONS

As you consult various plans and records, try to establish the changes that have occurred over the life of the building. Have walls been removed or added? Perhaps internal partitioning has been rearranged.

There may well be clues in the house itself, such as interruptions to the run of ceiling cornices, picture rails and dadoes. Similarly, you may be able to detect a change in floor levels or floorcoverings. Blocked doorways could provide a clue to how rooms or passages were laid out in the past. Perhaps you will discover a simple

way to reinstate the original interior, or you may perhaps decide that the present arrangement is a distinct improvement.

An extension is usually easy to identify. There may be a case for dismantling a poorly designed or badly constructed extension that spoils the appearance of the house, but not every extension is detrimental. A well-designed extension not only reflects the way previous owners used and adapted the house, but can be seen as integral to the building and part of its architectural history.

Even simple unadorned features contribute to the appeal of an old house

Reinstate items that have survived

21

WORTHWHILE IMPROVEMENTS

THE GENERAL LEVEL OF PROSPERITY *in this country engenders confidence in the long-term benefits of home ownership. For the most part, we take it for granted that improving a house can be financially advantageous. Nevertheless, opinion is divided as to precisely what kind of improvements are worthwhile.*

GETTING IT RIGHT

It is generally preferable to buy a house that has not been completely modernized, even if it is in poor condition. You will have the satisfaction of owning an authentic, unspoilt period house, and will find that repairing dilapidated features is usually cheaper than having to locate and install suitable replacements. It also avoids having to pay for previous 'improvements' that can unduly inflate the purchase price of a house.

However, basically sound, untouched period houses have become scarce, and most people in search of an old house have to settle for one that is not only in need of some repair but has also been stripped of at least some of its original features. In today's market it often makes financial sense to reinstate them, provided you resist the temptation to spend more on refurbishments than is warranted by the house's market value. To attempt to enhance its status by introducing uncharacteristically ornate fittings or decorative elements is as inappropriate as ripping out original features in the name of modernization.

Each type of house within a given locality has a maximum value and no one, especially an experienced estate agent, is going to be fooled into accepting an inflated price for a house that is pretending to be something it isn't. A shrewd investor will put back only what was there in the first place, while ensuring that all repairs and restoration work are done to the highest standard. That way, the house will command the best price in return for the minimum investment.

Don't embark on extensive refurbishments until you have a clear idea of what you want to achieve and what it is going to cost. From the start, work out how much you can realistically afford and, if you are on a limited budget, spend money first on essential repairs that will keep the building watertight and structurally sound. Also, make sure the water, gas and electrical services are operating efficiently and are in a safe condition. Don't forget to put aside money for ongoing maintenance.

New work and modernization

If you need to extend the building or feel you want to install new fixtures or fittings, there's no need to copy slavishly the original style of the house. In these circumstances, it is often best to consult an architect (or an experienced builder) who is sensitive enough to reflect the character and qualities of your house without creating a second-rate pastiche. This is also an opportunity to establish which elements of the building are structural and cannot be removed without substituting some other means of support. This type of information is vital to formulating realistic plans for redesigning the interior of your house.

Unless you are intent on creating a living museum, it makes perfect sense to take advantage of modern technology. In theory, we might enjoy the romance of candlelight, but few of us would seriously contemplate forgoing modern lighting or hesitate to install labour-saving laundry and kitchen appliances. And although accommodating radiators discreetly in an old house may take ingenuity, central heating has become a welcome and universally accepted advance.

Nowadays we consider hygienic functional bathrooms plumbed with hot and cold water a necessity, and would scarcely entertain the notion of doing without an indoor toilet.

When making repairs, retain as much original material as possible

It is worth making every effort to reinstate original features

Stone cladding destroys the integrity of a terrace

Drastic refurbishments have all but obliterated the character of these Victorian houses

GETTING IT WRONG

Provided the work is carried out tastefully and to a good standard, genuine improvements not only add to our comfort and wellbeing but also have a positive effect on the value of the property. On the other hand, it pays to think twice before spending large sums of money on what are at best fashionable whims that ultimately could detract from the sale price of your house.

Don't buy a house unless you are prepared to accept what it has to offer. Most old cottages, for example, are built with small rooms and low ceilings, often with modest windows that were never meant to flood the interior with daylight. The doors may be made from rough boards and fitted with worn iron latches and hinges. But that's what makes these houses special.

Replacing original windows and doors not only destroys the character of the building, but also makes little financial sense when they can be repaired and reinstated at no extra cost. No future buyer is likely to object to authentic windows and doors in good condition – the same cannot necessarily be said of PVCu or aluminium replacements.

Cladding the exterior of a house with colourful fake stone, or pebble-dashing what was supposed to be exposed brickwork are irreversible measures that have limited appeal. Apart from the visual disruption they cause to a terrace or group of buildings, the costs involved are unlikely to be recoverable when it comes to selling the house after such treatments have fallen from favour. Similarly, garish paint schemes may dissuade a potential buyer, particularly when the bricks or stonework are painted in bright colours and the pointing is picked out with white or black paint. Restoring painted masonry to its original condition is likely to be expensive.

Every old house has a unique quality, or at least it shares that quality with its immediate neighbours. It is important to recognize and respect those aspects of older houses that distinguish them from run-of-the-mill modern homes and to refrain from transforming them into something that was never intended.

Painting brickwork is a mistake

Colourful but inappropriate paintwork may not appeal to prospective buyers

23

SURVEYING YOUR HOUSE

H OW YOU GO ABOUT SURVEYING *your house depends on the condition of the building and also on whether you already own the house or intend to buy it. If you have lived in the house for some time and know it sufficiently well to be sure there are no serious defects, you could draw up a schedule of repairs, making a note of which jobs you can tackle yourself and which are best left to professionals.*

If, on the other hand, you are thinking about purchasing a property, then it is advisable to have it surveyed professionally before making up your mind.

Peeling wallpaper is often the first indication of damp in an old building

PROFESSIONAL SURVEYS

If you are applying for a mortgage, the initial survey will probably be carried out by a mortgage-valuation surveyor. A basic valuation survey simply gives the lender a guide as to whether the property is worth the amount of money you have requested. The valuation survey is unlikely to be very detailed and may not even mention certain serious defects. Even if the surveyor finds signs of damp or infestation, the valuation report is unlikely to provide any detailed diagnosis or recommendations, but will probably suggest that the building be inspected by a damp-proofing company or a firm that specializes in spraying to eradicate woodboring insects. Surveyors and valuers undertaking a mortgage valuation of an old house usually refer to what is known as the 'Red Book' (the RICS/ISBA Appraisal and Valuation Manual), which provides guidance on what valuers should look for when inspecting listed or historic buildings.

Another type of survey is the 'Home Buyers' Survey and Valuation Report', which follows a standard format set out by the Royal Institute of Chartered Surveyors (RICS). This is suitable for properties that are in reasonable condition and no more than 150 years old.

In the long run, it is worth investing in an independent full-condition survey, often referred to as a 'building survey'. This

Commission a comprehensive survey

should be undertaken by an expert who is fully conversant with the problems associated with older buildings and who can accurately diagnose defects and make recommendations for correcting them. This type of survey provides a detailed guide to long-term refurbishment and may even furnish ammunition to enable you to negotiate a fair purchase price. A thorough survey is a sound basis for establishing what repairs are necessary, and it should help you devise a realistic timetable for carrying out the work.

UNDERSTANDING A SURVEY

A building survey, which can cover everything from the state of the foundations to the condition of the interior decoration, can at first sight make depressing reading – until you can put it all into perspective. Your first step is to decide which faults are serious and require urgent attention, and which ones can be tackled as part of a long-term strategy.

If you are applying for a mortgage, a building society or bank may insist that you carry out essential repairs highlighted in the surveyor's report before they advance the entire sum you have applied for. And they will almost certainly demand that the repairs are carried out by a contractor who is prepared to furnish guarantees. However, depending on who has carried out the survey, it may be worth getting a second opinion to make sure the defects highlighted in the report are a genuine cause for concern.

Dilapidation and its causes

Weathering is a fundamental cause for dilapidation in all houses, regardless of their age. The combined effects of wind, rain, frost and sunshine create stresses that cause paint to flake, wood to split, masonry to spall, and roofcoverings to fall off. The list of possible defects caused by weathering is long. However, most can be eradicated without too much trouble and can even be prevented by regular maintenance. Indeed, lack of maintenance can be the root cause of a number of problems. A blocked gutter that allows rainwater to spill over and soak the wall below can lead to blown internal plaster or, worse still, an outbreak of dry rot. An airbrick blocked with moss or leaves could be the reason why your floor joists are suffering from fungal attack or mould is growing in your bathroom.

Ill-considered measures carried out in the past can be the cause of your problems today. If earth is piled up against the walls or paving has been laid above recommended levels, water may saturate the masonry, eventually rotting structural timbers below the floor. Poorly executed repairs, including the use of hard cement renders and mortar, can allow moisture to penetrate the structure with similar results.

Though potentially ruinous, none of these problems is insoluble. However, one should be aware that houses subjected to problems such as severe rising damp for prolonged periods can take a long time to recover, even after the initial cause has been identified and remedied.

Why is your house damp?
Damp is high up on the list of concerns for owners of period houses, and it features in a great many surveys. However, the causes of damp are often misunderstood and, as a result, the measures taken to eradicate it are frequently ineffective or un-necessary. There are three main categories of damp – rising damp, penetrating damp and condensation – and each can be mistaken for the others.

Condensation is caused by warm saturated air coming into contact with a cold surface. If that happens to be a windowpane, the nature of the problem is easy to diagnose. But if it happens to be an external wall, a great deal of money can be spent on damp-proofing measures when all that's required is better ventilation, heating and possibly insulation.

Any defect that allows water to make its way through to the inside of the building can be the reason why damp patches or stains are appearing on the inside of your walls and ceilings. Defective seals around doors and windows, missing roof slates or broken flashings, damaged masonry and defec-tive gutters or downpipes are among the most common reasons why there's wide-spread penetrating damp in your home.

If, however, signs of damp are restricted to an area that extends no more than about 1m (3ft) above skirting level, there's a strong possibility that moisture is being drawn up from the ground below. From the mid 1870s, houses were built with impervious damp-proof courses to pre-vent moisture rising above critical levels. At later stages, damp-proof membranes were included in concrete floors, for similar reasons. If either a DPC or a DPM has been breached, the simple answer is to have it repaired or replaced – but before opting for such drastic action, you would want to make sure that the surrounding ground level is at least 150mm (6in) below the DPC. Similarly, check that external render that extends below the level of a DPC is not acting as a bridge for rising damp.

Distinguishing one form of damp from another is not always as straightforward as you might imagine. If you are in any doubt, you should consult a professional who has in-depth knowledge of damp in old houses.

Is a DPC necessary?
Before the Public Health Act of 1875, houses were built without damp-proof courses. Moisture rising from the ground into the walls and floors simply evaporated, often without causing the kinds of problems we see today. This was because the materials used in construct-ing these older buildings were more permeable than their modern equivalents and the structure could 'breathe' more effectively.

Problems tend to occur when attempts are made to upgrade these old houses with modern building standards – walls are covered with impervious paints and renders, lime mortars are replaced with cement-rich mortars, and floors get sealed with DPMs. This all tends to trap moisture within the fabric of the building, and the damp is driven further up the walls. Rising damp usually contains salts that have been carried up from lower levels and, being highly absorbent, the salts exacerbate the problem.

The installation of a DPC may be an appropriate measure to correct rising damp in your home – but before you make a decision, obtain independent expert advice from someone other than a damp-proofing contractor, who may have vested interests (see PRO-FESSIONAL HELP and ROT & INFESTATION). Dampness is one of the most damaging problems associated with period buildings, and accu-rate diagnosis is vital to finding the right solution.

Structural movement
Alarm bells start ringing whenever the term subsid-ence is mentioned in a building survey. Structural movement in old houses can be attributed to a number of causes. It could be the result of rot or infestation, or possibly distortion caused by the movement of materials that react differently to changes in temperature and humidity. Bad practice and ineptitude also contribute to structural instability – partly dismantled chimney breasts, overloaded floors, and poorly supported door and window openings are the sorts of problems often highlighted in survey reports. Period houses were frequently built on shallow foundations, which are not always capable of accommodating natural expansion and contraction of the ground beneath them.

These are all potentially serious defects that could threaten the stability of the building, but in reality a great many old houses move to some degree without it ever becoming a problem. In some cases, settlement has occurred in the past but at some point the building has stabilized again. Only when

Subsidence may need expert attention

Movement may have stabilized

Get expert advice from a surveyor

movement is ongoing and threatens the safety of the structure should the owner be concerned. To reassure yourself, seek the advice of a structural engineer who is familiar with the construction and behaviour of old houses (see PROFESSIONAL HELP).

MAINTENANCE & REPAIR

COMMISSIONING A PROFESSIONAL SURVEY *is merely the first step in getting your house in good order. You now have to act on that advice and draw up a schedule of repairs. Following your survey point by point, make an inspection yourself to ascertain which tasks you can tackle personally and make notes of those jobs you will put out to professionals. Even if you have been living in your house for years, a similar exercise will help you plan a programme of regular maintenance.*

REGULAR MAINTENANCE

On founding the Society for the Protection of Ancient Buildings in 1877, William Morris spoke of the need to 'stave off decay by daily care, to prop a perilous wall or mend a leaky roof'. Morris was stressing the importance of tending to minor defects before they get out of hand and become expensive repairs.

Routine maintenance is designed to tackle the defects that occur during the life of any building – it is a form of insurance against more serious problems and, as such, should be adopted by every home owner. It may seem like a tedious chore, but a building that is looked after properly retains its maximum value and enriches the neighbourhood. At the same time, you avoid the stress and expense of dealing with unexpected emergency repairs and may prevent accidents to your family and members of the public.

It is convenient to divide a programme of maintenance into three parts:
● Inspection – assessing the condition of the building and checking that the services are working satisfactorily.
● Remedial action – drawing up a list of minor repairs and specific tasks, such as clearing leaves and debris from blocked gutters, that you are able to undertake yourself.
● Instituting long-term repairs – undertaking work needed in order to rectify more serious defects that will return the building to good condition. You may decide to employ professionals for this type of work, which falls outside your programme of day-to-day maintenance.

Inspecting the property

Ideally you should inspect your house twice a year: in the autumn, to safeguard the house throughout the winter, and again in spring to see what maintenance can be done outside when the weather is more favourable. Take a look at the building after heavy rain, when defective gutters, downpipes and leaky roofs are going to be easier to spot.

Work safely. If you have to climb a ladder to check the roof or look into the loft, make sure that the ladder is propped at a safe angle and is secured on firm ground. Where access is particularly difficult, consider employing a professional.

You will need some basic equipment to help you inspect your house and note defects: binoculars that will enable you to inspect the roof and chimneys from the ground, a penknife for probing timber to see if it is hard or spongy, a pocket notebook, a torch, and a compact camera to record defects, especially those you want to show to a professional.

It is worth starting a log in which you can make a record of your inspection and then document all the repairs you make to your house. Any professional surveys can be filed together with your personal log. You could store the information and scanned photographs on a personal computer, but a scrapbook serves the same purpose and will no doubt prove to be a fascinating document in years to come, perhaps even being handed over to the next occupier.

No two houses are ever exactly the same, but knowing where to look and what to look for may help you spot potential problems. The illustrated check list on the following pages will serve as a guide to analysing the condition of your house and preparing a plan of action.

DOING IT YOURSELF

Fees for professional labour often constitute the largest proportion of the costs involved in repairing an old house. It is therefore not surprising that the DIY trade has mushroomed dramatically in order to serve the ever growing numbers of amateur builders, decorators and plumbers. But no matter how enterprising you are, there will always be some aspects of the work where it is expedient to hire contractors, simply because they can do the job better, faster and more safely than someone who is not a skilled tradesperson.

To help you decide on the most appropriate approach to maintaining and repairing your house, keyed illustrations are included, both in the pages that follow and throughout the book, suggesting which jobs are so straightforward that even a beginner can achieve satisfactory results, which ones require a reasonable level of competence, and which are best left to a professional contractor.

DRAWING UP A CHECK LIST

OLD HOUSES ARE BUILT *primarily from three kinds of material – wood, stone and brick – with a variety of roof coverings. In addition, some are rendered and many are plastered internally. Each of these materials deteriorates in a particular way, and this determines how well a house is able to stand up to natural weathering. Being able to recognize the various forms of decay and dilapidation is the key to instigating an effective programme of regular maintenance.*

Be systematic when inspecting your house, so you don't miss anything. It is often best to start at the top, making a note of any roof or chimney defects, then gradually work down through the structure, inside and out. Once you have inspected the building itself, lift the manhole covers to see whether there are any blockages within the drainage system, and clean out debris and leaves from the gullies at the foot of your rainwater downpipes. At the same time, cut back any plant growth that is causing physical damage or encouraging damp conditions. Finally, check the condition of boundary walls and fences.

ROOF AND CHIMNEYS

Check your roof regularly, especially after storms or strong winds. If you notice slate or tile fragments on the ground, inspect your roof from all angles (including from inside the roof space) for indications of damage. Be sure to inspect the gutters and downpipes, to make sure they are not leaking and saturating the wall below.

ASSESSING REPAIRS
● Easy even for beginners.
■ Fairly difficult. Good practical skills required.
▲ Difficult. Hire a professional.
◆ Various levels of skill required.

Unstable chimney
An unstable chimney should be repaired before it topples, causing extensive damage and possibly injuries to pedestrians.
▲ Exposed masonry is susceptible to weathering. Repair or rebuild (pages 72–3).

Climbers out of control
Ivy and other climbing plants left to grow unchecked can block gutters and damage roof coverings and chimneys.
● Cut back climbers at least once a year, making sure you have a safe platform to work from.

Moss growing on the roof
On a thatched roof, moss indicates moisture retention. Get expert advice.
▲ Have the roof inspected by a master thatcher (page 65).
● Scrape moss from other roofcoverings before it blocks the gutters.

Broken downpipe
Staining and algae are often signs of a leaking downpipe.
■ Have corroded downpipes repaired or replaced. Clean and repaint stained walls. Check inside the house for signs of damp (page 25).

Damaged gutters
Broken or blocked gutters cause penetrating damp when rainwater soaks the wall.
■ Repair the gutter and check for signs of damp (page 25).
● Check the condition of parapet and valley gutters.

Loose slates or tiles
Corroded fixings allow slates and tiles to slip out of place.
◆ Reinstate or replace slates or tiles (pages 67–9).

Poorly maintained flashing
Inappropriate repairs are likely to deteriorate rapidly.
▲ Have an expert replicate the original flashing (page 70).
● Check all lead flashings and mortar fillets for signs of dilapidation.

WALLS

Masonry in good condition stands up well to weathering, and will usually dry out quickly after heavy rain. However, as soon as defects are allowed to go unattended, water begins to seep into the structure and serious deterioration can develop. Check for signs of damage outside, and for damp patches and stains on internal plasterwork.

ASSESSING REPAIRS
● Easy even for beginners.
■ Fairly difficult. Good practical skills required.
▲ Difficult. Hire a professional.
◆ Various levels of skill required.

Eroded pointing
Mortar can deteriorate and fall out of the joints.
■ Repoint the wall (pages 36–7).

Cracked pointing
Brittle cement mortar tends to crack and allow moisture to penetrate the wall.
◆ Cut out the cracked mortar and repoint (pages 36–7).

Spalled brickwork
Low-strength bricks are susceptible to frost damage.
■ Insert replacements in severe cases (page 38). Repoint with lime mortar (page 37).

Cracked masonry
This may not be serious.
■ Replace individual cracked bricks (page 38).
▲ Have extensive cracking checked (pages 24–5, 230).

Damaged wattle and daub
Carry out prompt repairs where daub is missing and wattle framework exposed.
▲ Seek expert advice on suitable repair materials.

Delaminating stone
Poorly laid stone can flake.
▲ Consolidate serious flaking with epoxy resin (page 50).
▲ Have badly damaged stone replaced by a contractor.

Broken render
Cracked and loose render can fall from the wall.
■ Patch damaged render before damp develops (page 52).

Mould growth
Organic growth proliferates in damp conditions.
● Scrape off the mould and try to determine why the wall is damp. If necessary, treat the wall with a biocide (page 34).

STRUCTURAL TIMBERS AND WOODWORK

Old houses incorporate a great many timber components, ranging from structural beams and joists to decorative woodwork. Like wooden windows and doors, these components suffer from the effects of weathering and rot. Because carved and fretted woodwork can be expensive to replace, decorative features are often in poor condition or have been discarded.

Dry rot
Timber that is allowed to get wet in poorly ventilated areas of a building is subject to fungal attack.
▲ Get expert advice on remedial treatment (pages 24–5, 227).

Woodworm
Woodboring insects consume house timbers.
● Treat minor outbreaks with preservative (page 226).
▲ Have seriously infested timber treated by experts (page 226).

DOORS AND WINDOWS

Because they are vulnerable to decay and corrosion, doors and windows require special attention. Not only should you attend to any defects in the wood or metalwork, but make sure the seals around the frames and doorcases are well maintained, in order to prevent penetrating damp and wood rot.

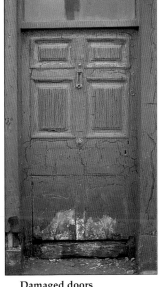

Overpainted woodwork
Layers of old paint can obscure fine details.
● Before you strip and repaint the wood, make sure you are not erasing historical evidence (pages 81–2).

Damaged doors
Weathering affects wooden doors that have not been painted regularly.
■ Repair loose joints (page 83).
■ Bottom rails are particularly prone to rot (page 85, 114).

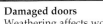

Poorly maintained joinery
Often, doors and windows are in need of attention. Expect to redecorate every three to five years.
■ Repair and repaint (pages 81–91, 109–15, 118).

Corroded metal frames
Rust sheds paint from metal casements.
◆ Treat and repaint (page 118).

Wet rot
Neglect causes water to rot wooden frames and sills.
■ Repair or replace rotted wood (pages 114–15).

SERVICES

Serious water damage can occur if pipes burst after freezing, so check that cold-water pipes are insulated. Employ a qualified contractor to service your boiler and other appliances annually.

Mains electrical installations are dangerous if they have not been updated and are not kept in good working order.

Old wiring and equipment
Unsafe wiring and electrical equipment must be replaced at the earliest opportunity.
▲ Get a competent electrician to test your circuits and fuse board.

FENCES AND BOUNDARY WALLS

Fences and garden walls are an integral part of your property. Wooden components can be replaced and treated for rot, and masonry repointed. Many of the problems associated with metalwork you can tackle yourself, and there are plenty of skilled contractors able to carry out more major repairs or reinstate missing components.

Rusty or broken metalwork
Corrosion is the most common cause of metal deterioration.
◆ Paint, repair or replace shabby metalwork (pages 191–200).

LEGAL PROTECTION FOR OLD HOUSES

LEGISLATION EXISTS TO PROTECT BUILDINGS *of special interest and to control building development and the methods and materials used for construction. The relevant items of legislation tend to be complex, and they are often amended and reviewed. The information given here should not be taken as an* authoritative interpretation of the law, and you should always check with the relevant authorities for information and clarification. Most householders sensibly employ a professional to make the necessary applications, including the preparation of the drawings that are often required for the various forms of consent.

LISTED BUILDINGS

Since the nineteenth century, amenity societies such as the Society for the Protection of Ancient Buildings have existed to encourage the preservation of old houses and other structures. However, it was not until 1947 that significant numbers of houses were given legal protection. Part of the purpose of the legislation was to ensure that buildings of special architectural or historical interest could not be demolished or altered without consent.

In England and Wales, there are three main grades: Grade I (the highest grade), Grade II* (known as two-star listing), and Grade II. In Scotland and Northern Ireland, there are slightly different grades.

Listed status does not just cover features mentioned in the listing description. It covers the entire building, inside and out, and may also include other structures that are attached or close by.

If your house is listed, it does not mean that all alterations are precluded, but you must apply to your local planning authority for listed-building consent before making any alterations. To proceed without consent is a criminal offence. If you are in any doubt as to whether the work you propose may require consent, contact the Conservation Officer at your local authority.

If the owner of a listed building neglects to keep it in good condition, the local authority can serve a repairs notice to enforce proper upkeep; and if the owner then continues to ignore legitimate requests, the local authority may issue a compulsory-purchase order.

Grants are sometimes available to help owners of listed buildings meet the costs of necessary repairs (see PROFESSIONAL HELP).

CONSERVATION AREAS

Regardless of whether or not it contains listed buildings, a locality that merits preservation can be designated a conservation area by a local authority. A conservation area has additional planning protection to safeguard the area's special character. This ranges from protection of trees to consent for demolition, new developments and alterations to buildings. The authority is required to pay special attention to preserving the character and appearance of the area. With a few minor exceptions, it is illegal to demolish any building within such an area or to alter the external appearance of the building without consent from the local planning authority. In some cases, the local authority may use an 'Article 4 Direction' to remove permitted development rights; this enables it to control alterations that affect the character of the area, such as the removal or alteration of doors or windows.

National Parks also have special consent procedures.

PLANNING PERMISSION

Planning permission is needed before you carry out any alteration that affects the use or siting of a building or other structure. In addition, any development that does not blend sympathetically with its surroundings may require consent. However, your proposed development may fall within permitted development rights, for which planning consent is not required. Extensions and conversions generally require planning permission – but even building a garden wall can be subject to approval if, for example, it blocks a right of way. Therefore, it pays to contact the planning department at the outset, before making detailed plans.

Having submitted your application, you can expect a decision within eight weeks. Once granted, planning permission remains valid for five years. If permission is refused, the authority has to give you a full explanation – so that, if you wish to do so, you can amend your plans and resubmit them for further consideration. Alternatively, you can submit an appeal against the decision, using a form obtainable from the planning authority. Should you proceed without consent, the planning authority can insist you restore the building to its previous state.

BUILDING REGULATIONS

Even if planning permission or listed-building consent is not needed, you will have to obtain Building Regulations approval (Building Standards in Scotland) for structural alterations and for any other alterations that fall within the scope of the regulations. The applicability of Building Regulations depends on the extent and type of changes proposed and on considerations such as whether the property is a single dwelling and whether the work may affect neighbouring properties. The regulations are designed to implement adequate construction and health-and-safety standards, and also govern issues such as access to buildings. If you are unsure about the need for approval, speak to your local Building Control Officer. If your building is listed or in a conservation area, you may be able to obtain special concessions from Building Control in order not to compromise historic features.

You are obliged either to supply 'full plans' showing all constructional details or to complete a form called a 'building notice', which you can obtain from your local Building Control Office. Scale drawings have to accompany a building notice, but they need not be as detailed as the ones required for a full-plans application.

Apply for approval well in advance, so you have time to discuss your proposals with the Building Control Officer. He or she will also advise on relevant local legislation and tell you whether you need to approach other authorities concerning sanitation, fire escapes and so on. So that the Building Control Officer can arrange an inspection, you must give at least 48 hours' notice before starting work and 24 hours' notice before covering foundations or laying drains. You must also let the officer know when the work has been finished.

PARTY-WALL AWARDS

If you plan to carry out work on or near to a wall shared with neighbours, a party-wall agreement may be required. A booklet explaining the provisions of the Party Wall Act 1996 is available on the website of the Office of the Deputy Prime Minister under 'Building Regulations'.

CHAPTER THREE

BRICKWORK

URING THE LATE EIGHTEENTH CENTURY towns expanded rapidly as builders constructed acres of densely packed terraces to house the thousands drawn from the countryside by the promise of employment in factories, mills and workshops. Brick was frequently the material chosen to satisfy this demand for housing that could be built quickly and cheaply. The result was often rows of overcrowded houses lacking basic amenities. These became the notorious Victorian slums, many of which were cleared for the rebuilding schemes of the 1950s and 1960s.

However, brick was by no means an exclusively working-class material. On the other side of town, the

merchants and industrialists who had prospered from the new technology erected luxurious villas. In parts of the country where good local building stone was lacking, brick was just as likely to have been used for these houses built by the new middle class.

The better-quality houses boasted fine ornamental brickwork, with moulded terracotta tiles, decorative coursing and finely gauged arches. Yet with its subtle colours and texture enhanced by age and weathering, even plain bonded brickwork is often a delight to the eye. These are qualities well worth preserving, especially as shaped and decorative bricks and terracotta panels can be replicated easily by specialist suppliers.

The warm glow of London stocks

Victorian moulded-brick tiles

Care and attention was often lavished on the smallest of brick houses

Beautifully detailed brick almshouse

Fine early C18th rubbed brickwork

COLOURS & TEXTURES

BEFORE INDUSTRIAL CHANGES *made mass production feasible and transport easier, bricks were produced for a particular locality, using the clays occurring in that part of the country. Local clays lent a distinctive colour to the brickwork of the region.*

When improved transportation systems were introduced in the nineteenth century, it became possible to buy bricks made at the other end of the country. Often bricks were named after the town or district in which they were made. The list must once have been extremely long and included evocative names such as Accrington Bloods, Staffordshire Blues and Leicester Reds. The ready availability of a variety of coloured bricks helped to bring to an end clearly defined regional characteristics. It also contributed to the spread of the spectacular polychrome brickwork much loved by the Victorians.

BRICK MANUFACTURING

Although the local clay gave a brick its distinctive colour, the subtleties of shape and hue were to a large extent determined by the method of manufacture.

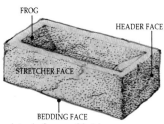

A typical pressed brick

Hand-moulded bricks

Although there were early attempts at mechanization, before the mid nineteenth century all bricks were made by hand in individual wooden moulds. The clay was 'pugged' (mixed with water and kneaded to a smooth consistency), often in a horse-driven pug mill.

Sand, or sometimes water, was sprinkled into open-top moulds to prevent the clay sticking to them. Then the moulds were filled, and the clay levelled with a steel or wooden straightedge. After the 'green' bricks had been turned out of the moulds, they were often stacked on layers of straw to dry naturally before being fired.

Pressed bricks

Bricks with sharper arrises (edges) and a smoother surface texture were produced mechanically by pressing semi-dry clay into moulds. Since they were dense and hard-wearing, pressed bricks were frequently employed as facing bricks for façades.

Wire-cut bricks

The other common mechanized method of production was to extrude a long bar of clay and use wires to slice it into bricks. Wire-cut bricks do not have the distinctive recesses known as 'frogs' often found on pressed bricks. The frog fills up with mortar, thus keying the brick into the wall, and also reduces the weight of the brick.

Some pressed bricks have a recess in the top face only; others have a frog in the bedding face as well. Wire-cut bricks are sometimes made with holes passing through them that perform a similar function.

The mottled colours of old handmade bricks

Patterned polychromatic brickwork

Colourful brickwork incorporating projecting headers

CLEANING & WEATHERPROOFING

An impressive Gothic-revival façade built from coloured bricks and stone

BEFORE EMBARKING *on an ambitious and irreversible cleaning programme, it is worth pausing to consider why you should want to clean the brickwork of your house at all. There's every reason to remove stains, spilled paint and graffiti, but it would be disastrous to lose the mellow character of nicely weathered brickwork in the pursuit of total renovation. Harsh methods of cleaning that involve sandblasting or powerful chemicals have the most detrimental effects and they tend to leave brickwork looking unpleasantly raw.*

An overcleaned detached house looks bad enough. It is even worse to spoil the appearance of a lovely old terrace by cleaning or stripping individual dwellings.

Yellow London stocks show the dramatic results of cleaning brickwork

Firing bricks

Once the clay had dried out, the bricks had to be baked to make them hard enough for building purposes. The earliest method of firing bricks was to pile them in rows in a stack or 'clamp'. Channels left between the rows were filled with timber (or, later, with coal or coke), and the entire stack was surrounded with previously fired bricks daubed with clay. The whole clamp was then set alight and was left to burn, sometimes for weeks. The method produced unevenly fired bricks that varied in colour according to their position within the clamp. Hand-made bricks were fired in clamps until the process was industrialized, at which point firing in brick-built kilns became the preferred method of production, as it produced bricks of a more consistent hardness and colour. The early kilns were tiny compared with modern continuous kilns, normally consisting of a simple brick chamber with an opening at one end that was sealed before firing.

BRICK CLASSIFICATION

Modern firing techniques are designed to produce bricks with specific characteristics – but with earlier methods the bricks from a single firing varied in quality and had to be sorted according to their properties.

The most regular bricks (the ones that were most evenly fired) were classified as 'facings' or face bricks. These attractive weather-resistant bricks were generally used for building exposed exterior walls. The less uniform, poorly fired bricks were designated as common or place bricks and were normally used for constructing walls that were to be covered with plaster or stucco. Overburnt bricks, from the hottest parts of the clamp or kiln, were reserved for flue linings or for headers in diaper-pattern brickwork.

WASHING BRICKWORK

An old brick house in any environment will eventually develop a patina due to airborne dirt and pollution. This 'natural' weathering simply reflects the history of the building. However, if you are really bothered by the appearance of your brick-work, it is often possible to wash off surface grime with water.

Starting at the top of the wall, wet an area of bricks with a garden hose and scrub the brickwork with a stiff-bristle brush. Never use a wire brush, which can damage the surface of the bricks. Clean the wall in horizontal bands, gradually working your way down to the bottom.

Heavy deposits that have combined with the brick surface chemically can usually only be removed by professional masonry-cleaning contractors, using hydrofluoric acid.

STRIPPING A PAINTED WALL

Brickwork in good condition does not need painting, rendering or any other form of weatherproofing – but sadly there are plenty of houses with once beautiful brickwork hidden beneath layers of paint.

Probably unnecessary in the first place, the paint is now expensive to remove. There are professionals who will undertake this work for you, but before proceeding consult your local Conservation Officer to ensure that it won't have adverse effects on the brickwork.

Stripping painted brickwork

There are several reasons why it may be advisable to hire a reliable professional company to strip old paint from brickwork. First of all, it is usually necessary to erect scaffolding, perhaps around an entire building that may be several storeys high. Also, experience of applying and removing chemical stripper is essential in order to remove every trace of paint from a deeply textured surface. In addition, paint stripping on this sort of scale can be a time-consuming and messy business, involving the use of toxic materials that have to be handled with care and disposed of safely. Most oil-based paints, for example, can be softened using a methylene-chloride paint stripper applied as a thick paste, or by applying other proprietary pastes that contain sodium hydroxide. Thick coatings of paint may require several applications of a stripper. This type of treatment can leave harmful salts in the mortar joints if paint stripper is not washed away adequately.

To determine whether the outcome is likely to be satisfactory, ask the company or contractor you are thinking of hiring to strip a small inconspicuous patch of brickwork, using the chemicals they recommend for the job. In certain cases the results may indicate that it is better to repaint, in which case you should use a paint suitable for masonry (see PAINT FOR PERIOD HOUSES).

Alternatives to painting

Once the old paint has been removed (or if you want to preserve unpainted brickwork), your best option is to prevent moisture permeating the wall by repointing or by repairing or replacing cracked and spalled bricks. But there are situations where a whole wall has become porous due to natural erosion, or because the brickwork has been subjected to abrasive cleaning. Blasting with sand or grit should be avoided, as it tears and pits the surface of the brickwork, accelerating decay.

Water ingress is usually through poor pointing, and rarely through the bricks themselves. Consequently, it is nearly always more appropriate and effective to repoint the wall than to coat it with a water repellent. Some repellents can trap moisture within the walls, and can also exacerbate salt damage to soft bricks. After a while, repellents cease to be effective and can attract dirt. In the rare cases where water repellents can be justified, the wall should be coated after repointing with porous lime mortar, which allows salts and moisture to escape through the joints. Brick walls should never be coated with a water repellent immediately after chemical paint stripping or cleaning with water, as this risks trapping moisture in the masonry.

Heavy organic growth on brickwork should be treated with a biocide

REMOVING STAINS

Tar, grease and oil can often be softened by applying white spirit, paraffin or a proprietary grease solvent. Since there is a slight risk that the softened stain will be spread further if you attempt to wash it from the surface, apply a poultice to absorb the oil or grease. To make a poultice, saturate an absorbent material (such as whiting, fuller's earth, sawdust, or even talcum powder) with solvent. Follow the maker's recommendations when handling and disposing of solvents. Also, always wear protective gloves and goggles.

Dampen the stain with the solvent, then cover it immediately with a layer of poultice about 12mm (½in) thick. Tape a sheet of plastic over the poultice, and leave it to dry out and absorb the stain. When the poultice is dry, use a wooden or plastic spatula to lift it off the wall. Finally, scrub the bricks with water and a bristle brush.

EFFLORESCENCE

A white crystalline deposit that commonly appears on new and old brickwork, efflorescence is caused by soluble salts within the masonry migrating to the surface. This occurs as saturated masonry dries out. Efflorescence can also occur within the bricks – the salt crystals damage the surface of the brickwork, particularly if the bricks are underfired. Locate and cure the cause of the dampness within the wall (such as a failed damp-proof course), then brush the crystals from the bricks with a stiff-bristle brush. You may also have to brush the wall periodically as the masonry dries out.

ORGANIC GROWTH

Since moulds and lichens tend to grow in moist conditions, their presence may indicate a source of damp that needs to be eradicated before any surface treatment is considered.

To remove heavy organic growth from a wall, scrape it from the bricks with a non-metallic spatula; then apply a clear proprietary biocide specifically formulated for masonry. Paint on a generous application of the biocide, starting at the top of the wall. After a couple of days, when the wall has dried, brush off the dead growth and treat the wall a second time.

BRICK BONDS

ORTAR, *though strong under compression, has practically no tensile strength. If a wall was built by stacking bricks one directly above the other, creating continuous vertical joints, movement within the wall would tend to pull the joints apart and seriously weaken the structure. Bonding (staggering the vertical joints) ties the bricks together and spreads any load over a wide area. Brick bonding is primarily functional and the patterns created by staggering the joints can be most attractive.*

TRADITIONAL BRICK BONDS

Modern cavity walls consist of two individual leaves of masonry that are separated by a gap spanned by metal or plastic ties. Most frequently, the outer leaf consists of brickwork built with a stretcher bond. In contrast, up to at least the end of the nineteenth century, since most brick walls were solid, they were constructed with a variety of traditional bonding patterns that utilized different combinations of stretchers and headers. Stretchers are the bricks that run parallel with the face of the wall; headers run from front to back, tying the stretcher courses together.

In the eighteenth century, façades were frequently only one brick thick. These façades were tied to the structural brickwork of the building with true headers in every fifth or sixth course; the rest of the 'headers' were simply half-bricks.

There is no real evidence to suggest that one bond is significantly stronger than another. It must therefore be assumed that the popularity of any particular style was primarily due to its visual appeal. English bond, Flemish bond and English garden-wall bond were all developed in the fifteenth and sixteenth centuries, and have been used for solid-brick walls ever since. The Flemish bond was especially popular in Georgian times.

DECORATIVE BONDS

Purely decorative bonds were used to relieve large areas of unbroken brick-work, typically in the form of basket-weave or herring-bone panels.

Traditional diaper work (which used dark headers to produce diamond patterns against paler brickwork) is just one example of how bricks of contrasting colour or tone were incorporated into a decorative bond. Similar patterns were also created by allowing headers to project slightly from a wall so that they would cast attractive shadows.

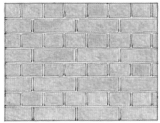

English bond

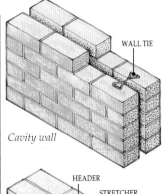
Cavity wall

WALL TIE

Flemish bond

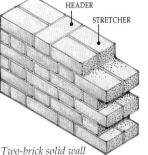
HEADER
STRETCHER
Two-brick solid wall

English garden-wall bond

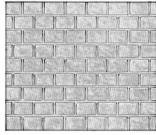
Header bond

Three-brick solid wall

C19th diaper-pattern brickwork

Combination of basket-weave and herring-bone panels

REPOINTING BRICKWORK

S KILLED BRICKLAYERS *have always taken pride in their ability to build regular bonds with precise joints. Much relies on the consistency of the mortar. It must neither be so firm that it prevents the bricklayer tapping each course into alignment nor so soft that it slumps under the weight of the bricks. In addition, each mortar joint must be shaped to complement the style of the building and the type of bricks used in its construction. The collective name for these shaped joints is pointing.*

Early-C19th tuck pointing used to simulate rubbed brickwork

Eroded pointing weakens the wall

Cement-rich mortar is liable to crack

WHEN TO REPOINT

Repointing is a laborious job that is expensive if you hire a bricklayer to do the work and time-consuming if you do it yourself. Consequently, it is advisable only to repoint when necessary and to limit repairs to as small an area as possible, matching the old pointing in shape, colour and texture. Within a fairly short time, the new and old pointing will be practically indistinguishable, provided the work is done properly. But if say three-quarters of the pointing has decayed, then it makes sense to rake out what's left and repoint the entire wall – or, if need be, the whole building.

If recent repointing is too unsightly to ignore, there may be a case for raking out the mortar and starting again. Otherwise, look for signs of deterioration likely to lead to penetrating damp or to the disintegration of the bricks themselves.

Natural erosion

Under the combined assault of wind and driving rain, soft mortar tends to erode, especially on the windward side of exposed buildings. Erosion can lead to deep crevices in the pointing that not only allow rainwater to soak deeply into the wall but may eventually lead to loose brickwork.

Damp and frost

Excessive damp caused by leaking gutters and downpipes can exacerbate the effects of erosion, and the action of frost tends to make matters even worse.

Cracked mortar

As often as not, cracked mortar is the result of using an inflexible cement-rich mortar that is unable to absorb the slightest movement within the masonry. In a relatively short time, cracked mortar falls out, leaving vulnerable open joints.

JOINT STYLES

Unless it is leading to deterioration of the brickwork, it is best to copy the existing style of joint when repointing a small area of wall. However, if complete repointing seems inevitable, choose the style most appropriate for the age of the house and the condition of the brickwork.

The joints described below are probably those most often used for the brickwork of old houses. If you have walls pointed with one of the less common styles (such as beaded or V-shaped pointing) that may be original, then it is worth finding a bricklayer able to replicate them.

Flush joint

Before the second half of the nineteenth century most brickwork was pointed with flush joints. In practice, many so-called flush joints are slightly recessed or concave to allow for the rounded arrises of old handmade or worn bricks.

Weatherstruck joint

This joint has only been in use since the 1850s or 1860s. It sheds water efficiently and enhances the appearance of bricks with sharp arrises. It is not suitable for repointing very old brickwork.

Tuck pointing

Tuck pointing was used, in the eighteenth century especially, to simulate the exactness of rubbed brickwork (see OPENINGS IN BRICKWORK).

The joints were filled flush, using mortar coloured to match the brickwork. Fine grooves, scored along the centres of the joints, were filled with a slightly projecting strip of lime putty. This was normally white and was sometimes mixed with silver sand. Less commonly, soot was used to stain it black. When repairs are necessary, it pays to hire a bricklayer with experience of replacing tuck pointing.

Penny-round pointing

As proper tuck pointing was expensive, bricklayers were sometimes persuaded to substitute penny-round pointing. Although a narrow groove was scored along each joint (presumably with a coin), to save money the lime putty was omitted.

1 Flush joint

2 Weatherstruck

3 Tuck pointing

4 Penny-round

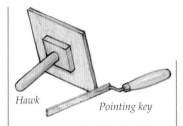

Hawk   *Pointing key*

PREPARING THE WALL

Rake out the old mortar to a depth at least twice the width of the joint, using a piece of wood shaped to fit the joints. If necessary, chop out hard mortar with a mason's quirk (plugging chisel) – a special tool that you can rent from a tool-hire company. Take care not to damage the edges of the bricks. Never use a power tool, such as a chain saw or an angle grinder.

Brush out all loose material, then hose the wall lightly so that the new mortar will not dry too quickly.

Chop out hard pointing

FILLING AND SHAPING THE JOINTS

Many builders use a small pointing trowel to push mortar into the open joints, but a better method is to use a tool called a pointing key or jointer that fits between the bricks. Carry a small quantity of mortar to the wall on a hawk (a hand-held board with a wooden handle underneath). Holding the hawk against the wall, fill each joint flush with mortar, compacting it with the pointing key (1). Try not to smear mortar onto the faces of the bricks. Leave the mortar to stiffen until it will retain a clear impression of your thumb, then shape the joints as appropriate. As soon as the pointing has set, use a dry scrubbing brush to clean any specks of mortar from the faces of the bricks.

Flush joints
Flush joints need no further shaping; but if the finish left by the tool looks smoother than the old mortar, you can stipple the joints with a stiff-bristle brush to expose the sand aggregate (2).

Weatherstruck joints
Use the pointing key to shape the mortar, leaving each joint with a sloping profile. The vertical joints, which should be shaped first, can slope to either right or left – look at the original pointing and make the new joints consistent.

Bricklayers remove excess mortar from the base of the joints with a tool called a Frenchman that has a blade with a right-angled tip. You can make one from a narrow strip of thin metal.

Use a wood straightedge to guide the Frenchman's blade. Nail plywood scraps to the straightedge to serve as spacers, so there's a gap through which the excess mortar can drop as you draw the tool along the joints.

1 Use a pointing key to fill joints

2 Stipple flush joints with a brush

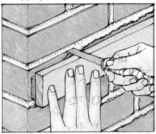

Scrape off mortar with a Frenchman

MORTAR

Old brickwork was usually built using lime mortar. Even when set, this mortar is flexible enough to withstand slight movement in a wall without cracking. Also, lime-based mortar allows moisture within the wall to evaporate harmlessly. When cement-based mortar is used to repoint soft brickwork, it prevents evaporation except through the bricks themselves. This can result in the surfaces of the bricks spalling (flaking).

Lime for mortar
Lime is classified as either hydraulic or non-hydraulic, and is sold in various forms.

Non-hydraulic or 'fat lime' hardens slowly when exposed to the air. Nowadays it is available as lime putty in sealed tubs and can also be obtained premixed with sand.

Hydrated or 'bagged lime' is non-hydraulic lime, the water having been removed. It is sold as a powder in bags at builders' merchants. It needs to be soaked in water for 24 to 48 hours to 'fatten up' to a putty with the consistency of yoghurt before it is ready to be used for mortar.

Naturally hydraulic lime, also supplied as a powder, sets by chemical reaction with water. It sets faster than non-hydraulic lime and is not so entirely dependent on contact with the air. Naturally hydraulic lime is available in various strengths.

Matching colour and texture
To match original pointing, choose the ingredients of the new mortar carefully. Sand varies a great deal in colour, and grade. A mortar made with a relatively coarse grade of sharp sand usually matches the appearance of old weathered pointing.

Even with the correct materials, it is difficult to get a precise match unless you prepare some test samples of mortar and let them dry. However, the only way to determine the make-up of the old mortar exactly is to have it analysed by a specialist.

Mixing mortar
Of all the mixes available, the one you might consider using is a weak naturally hydraulic lime supplied as a powder for mixing with water and sand. Mix the mortar in the proportions of 1 part lime to 2.5 parts sand, and add water until the mixture has the consistency of cottage cheese. As lime is caustic, always wear gloves and goggles when mixing and handling it.

Don't apply lime mortars in either freezing, very wet, very dry or windy conditions. Once applied, lime mortar should be protected from wet weather with plastic sheeting for 2 or 3 days. In a hot dry atmosphere use dampened hessian sacking instead.

REPAIRING BRICKWORK

EXTENSIVELY CRACKED BRICKWORK *and bulging walls should be inspected by a surveyor, architect or structural engineer (see* PROFESSIONAL HELP*) to ascertain the cause of the damage and to determine whether the structure has stabilized. Even serious faults such as defective foundations, broken lintels or detached bonding can be corrected, but the remedial work should always be carried out by an experienced contractor.*

You may find the professional's report indicates that there has been minimal movement, and it is always possible that the movement may have been arrested by a previous owner. In such cases, you will probably be able to repoint or replace the damaged bricks yourself.

REPLACING SPALLED BRICKS

In freezing conditions the expansion of water trapped just below the surface of bricks often causes spalling (flaking) since the moisture cannot evaporate evenly.

If spalling is widespread, hard cement pointing may have cracked, allowing moisture to penetrate. Or there could be drainage problems at the base of the wall, or a defective damp-proof course allowing rising damp. These defects should be eradicated before further treatment is considered.

More often, spalling affects only a small area of the wall, and individual bricks can be cut out and replaced. There's a limit to the number of bricks you can take out without destabilizing the structure of the wall. If more than two or three bricks have to be removed at a time, hire a builder.

POINTING WORN BRICKS

As soft mortar is eroded the corners and arrises (edges) of the bricks are exposed to the elements, and eventually they will become worn and rounded. If worn bricks are pointed so that the mortar is flush with their stretcher faces, the joints look much wider than intended. Also, the mortar presents weak feathered edges that quickly deteriorate **(1)**.

When you are repointing worn bricks, recess the joints to retain their original width. Recessed joints look best if they are flat or slightly concave **(2)**. Special tools are made for shaping concave joints, but you can improvise with a short length of bent copper tubing. Finally, stipple the mortar with a brush to match weathered pointing.

1 Flush joint with weak edges

2 Recessed joint is preferable

Cutting out a spalled brick
Rake out the mortar joints around the spalled brick. If need be, loosen the mortar by boring into it with a masonry drill **(1)** and chop out what remains with a quirk (plugging chisel). After you have removed the brick, brush dust from the cavity and dampen the inside.

1 Loosen mortar with a drill

Inserting a replacement
Spread mortar on the bottom of the cavity and up one side. Wet the replacement brick, spread mortar on top of the brick and on one end, then insert it into the cavity **(2)**. Compact the mortar and, once it begins to get firm, shape the joints to match the rest of the pointing.

2 Insert a mortared brick

FINDING REPLACEMENT BRICKS

Finding replacement bricks that will blend with period brickwork is not easy. With their clean, sharp edges, mass-produced bricks are usually too perfect; they are also unlikely to be the same size as the ones you are replacing. On the other hand, you can have hand-moulded bricks made to any specification you require, although you will need to track down a specialist brick manufacturer operating in your part of the country.

Most people restoring old brickwork try to acquire some second-hand bricks (seconds) from a building of a similar age and style that has undergone alterations or partial demolition. Whenever possible, avoid buying seconds that have been repointed with cement-rich mortar. It usually has to be hacked off with a cold chisel, which often results in bricks being broken.

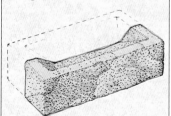
Cut bricks lengthwise for economy

If you are repairing a small area of brickwork, you can make your supply of second-hand replacement bricks go twice as far by cutting them in half with an angle grinder fitted with a stone-cutting disc. This provides you with two brick 'slips' that you can back up with mortar and fit into the wall with their good face outwards.

Similarly, if you are able to remove a spalled brick without breaking it, you can turn the brick round, so the flaking face is hidden and the intact face exposed, and then mortar it back in place.

OPENINGS IN BRICKWORK

THE BRICKWORK *above windows and doors has to be supported in some way, otherwise the wall would collapse. Very often this is achieved by the insertion of a stone or wooden lintel, but frequently a brick arch is used instead. The two methods are also sometimes combined, a lintel being concealed behind a brick arch.*

Brick arches are invariably carefully designed and constructed, and they contribute significantly to the character of terraces and individual façades. The effect is further enhanced if openings are given additional embellishment in the form of coloured-brick jambs.

Late C18th semi-circular brick arch

Exquisite elliptical-arched doorway

BRICK ARCHES

A true arch is composed of a number of bricks that support each other as weight is applied from above, transmitting the load to the brickwork on each side of the door or window opening. Purpose-made shaped bricks are now used to construct arches, but better-quality structures were once made from soft bricks that were individually cut and rubbed (ground to shape on an abrasive stone). A skilled bricklayer could shape these 'rubbers' so accurately that the joints between them were no more than 2–3mm (⅛in) wide. Superior-quality 'gauged' (rubbed-brick) arches were pointed either with 'fat' lime putty or with a mixture of lime putty and silver sand (which is very fine). For cheaper work, ordinary bricks were sometimes cut to a tapered shape or uncut bricks were built into an arch, using tapered mortar joints.

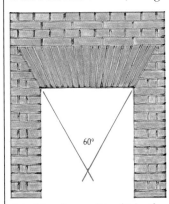

1 *Arch based on equilateral triangle*

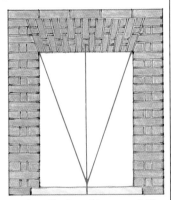

2 *Joints aligning with centre of sill*

Flat gauged arch

An elegantly constructed flat gauged arch is a pleasing feature of classic Georgian straight-head windows.

The lower edge of this type of arch has to be raised with a slight curve in order to counteract an optical illusion – if it was perfectly straight, the arch would appear to sag in the middle.

Each brick in each half of a flat gauged arch is a different shape. The joints radiate from the apex of an imaginary inverted equilateral triangle plotted below the arch (**1**). Alternatively, they may align with a point in the centre of the window sill (**2**).

Segmental arch

A segmental arch is built with identical tapering bricks, known as voussoirs, once again centred on the apex of an equilateral triangle. Although there are notable exceptions, few segmental arches seem to have been built with the same care lavished on most flat gauged arches and they are often constructed with whole or crudely cut bricks.

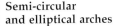

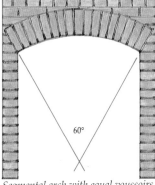

Segmental arch with equal voussoirs

Semi-circular and elliptical arches

Semi-circular arches were used for spanning not only windows but also doorways with fanlights. The elliptical arch is more subtle in shape and consequently requires a variety of accurately made rubbed voussoirs for its construction. It is mostly used to span fairly wide openings.

Pointed arch

Pointed arches, sometimes picked out in soft red bricks, became popular during the Gothic-revival period.

Soldier arch

The soldier arch (or 'brick lintel') is nothing more than a row of upright standard bricks. This structure, which is inherently weak, is usually supported from below by a sturdy steel angle or flat metal bar.

Classic Gothic-revival pointed arch

POINTING RUBBED BRICKWORK

The extremely fine joints in rubbed brickwork cannot be repointed in the usual way. The process described below demands patience and care, but it will ensure that the bricks are not smeared with lime putty.

Ready-made lime putty is sold in tubs, and if need be it can be mixed with fine silver sand (about 1 part lime putty to 3 parts sand) to make a mortar matching the texture of the original pointing.

Sometimes in gauged work the joints are so narrow that the blade of a pointing key is too wide to enter the joint, so you may have to improvise with something like a steel ruler that fits snugly between the bricks.

Rake out loose pointing with a hacksaw blade – taking care not to damage the edges of the very soft bricks – then dampen the open joints.

To keep the bricks clean, apply strips of heavy-duty adhesive tape over the joints and then cut a slit along the centre of each joint, using a sharp knife. Introduce the lime putty/mortar, through the slits in the tape, into the joints and compress it with the pointing tool. Then carefully peel away the tape.

Flat gauged arches composed of soft red rubbed bricks

REPAIRING BRICK ARCHES

Whenever there is a structural failure of a building's foundations, cracks tend to develop at the corners of window and door openings. If this happens, the integrity of the window or door arch is compromised and there is a danger that the voussoirs will fall out. This is a situation that must be remedied without delay.

Get an experienced builder to correct the original cause of the collapse. It will then be possible to insert a beam through the wall above the arch to support the brickwork while the arch itself is dismantled. Rubbers should be handled with care, as they are easily chipped or broken.

The builder will erect a timber-and-plywood former to support the arch while it is being rebuilt. This should not be removed until the mortar or lime putty has set hard.

SHAPED BRICKS & TERRACOTTA

BRICKLAYERS *were adept at constructing decorative detailing from ordinary bricks. Dentil courses beneath the eaves or dogtooth brickwork created by laying bricks at an angle to the face of the wall are typical of the ornamentation found on even the humblest of Victorian workers' cottages. However, much more elaborate embellishments were possible using special-purpose shaped or moulded bricks and terracotta tiles or panels.*

Special-purpose brick voussoirs

Doorway with terracotta panels

SPECIAL BRICKS

Rubbed brickwork, which was extremely laborious to produce, gradually gave way to factory-made shaped bricks. By the second half of the nineteenth century, brick manufacturers were offering a vast selection of profiles and 'specials' for creating all manner of plinths, cornices, arches, chamfered borders and moulded jambs.

There is still a wide range of special-purpose bricks in production, from which you may be able to select suitable replacements for damaged originals. But if you are unable to find appropriate substitutes, then it is generally preferable to live with ornamentation that is in less than perfect condition, rather than allow a builder to cut away or render over original decorative brickwork.

MOULDED BRICKWORK

The Victorians frequently used moulded-brick tiles or slips to make cornices, string courses and other classical-style mouldings. Much of the detailing was extremely elaborate, making it possible to create extravagant ornamentation that was previously only possible with expensive hand carving.

Purely decorative panels composed of soft pinkish-red abstract or figurative brick tiles are a familiar feature of better-quality Victorian and Edwardian housing. If such decorative tiles have been hacked away in the course of insensitive refurbishment, it is very often possible to find modern reproductions of moulded brickwork that will enable you to re-create perfectly acceptable period-style panelling.

CHAPTER FOUR

STONEWORK

BECAUSE WE ARE ACCUSTOMED to seeing impressive public buildings and gentrified houses constructed from dressed stone, many of us tend to equate stonework with quality and wealth. And yet to someone living in an area where stone is plentiful, it is a commonplace material used for practically every house, cottage, workshop and barn in the vicinity. But this in no way diminishes the importance of stone as a building material. Being built from indigenous stone, using local methods of construction, vernacular architecture becomes virtually part of the landscape – a quality which we cannot help but admire.

Houses that are built from limestone, sandstone or granite reflect the local geology, and are most commonly found in areas where such stone predominates. A relatively small number of houses incorporate cobble and knapped flint, which can be found near the coast and on chalk downlands. Generally, vernacular buildings are built of rubble masonry, sometimes plastered or rendered in lime; more refined buildings are of dressed ashlar and often of imported stone. Native and imported marbles are costly, so tend to have been reserved for decorative floor tiles, fireplaces and other features.

Dressed and carved stone has always been expensive, and builders would often substitute cast imitation stone. Some early examples look so authentic that only an expert can tell them from the real thing.

A charming rubble-built cottage

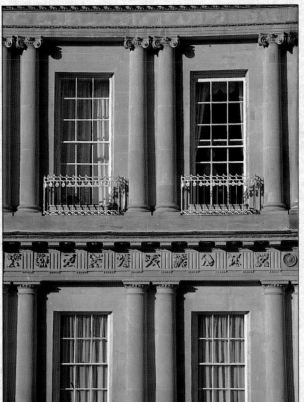

Mellowed limestone ashlar masonry in the neo-classical manner

Squared rubble makes for precision

Sophisticated carved stone doorway

C19th surround with transom lights

RUBBLE & DRESSED STONE

NOWADAYS MACHINERY AND POWER TOOLS *take much of the hard labour out of the quarrying of stone. Until the mid nineteenth century, however, quarrying had hardly changed since ancient times. Although the harder building stones would have been extracted by controlled blasting, huge slabs of softer stratified rocks were still being split from the bed using metal wedges driven into the rock. These slabs were then split or sawn into building blocks, which perhaps received a surface dressing, depending on the requirements of the builder or mason.*

Beautifully proportioned cottages built with squared rubblework

FLINT WALLING

For centuries, nodules of flint have been dug out from soft chalk deposits or collected from seashores or river beds for this delightful form of rubble walling. When quarried, a nodule is covered with a pale-grey crust of lime. It's only when the stone is split that the glassy black or brown-coloured flint core is revealed.

Relatively smooth flint cobbles are selected for building purposes and are laid in courses with their rounded ends projecting from the face of the wall. Alternatively, the cobbles are snapped in half to expose the core. For better-quality work, snapped cobbles are then knapped (dressed) on all four sides to make building blocks, approximately 100mm (4in) square, which are laid in bonded courses with relatively fine joints.

Although a flint facing is extremely hard-wearing, an all-flint wall is not particularly strong and it's impossible to build one with accurate square corners. Consequently, most flint buildings have brick or stone quoins at each corner, usually tied together at regular intervals with narrow lacing courses and piers of brick, stone or tiles. As a result, flint-built houses are a delightful blend of colours and textures, with the various structural elements creating attractive geometric patterns.

Typical flint and brick combination

Square-knapped flintwork

RUBBLEWORK

Although the name might suggest otherwise, rubble walls are not shoddy structures. Even with random rubblework **(1)**, the irregular stones must be carefully selected and arranged to build stable masonry walls with staggered joints. In addition, transverse stones that extend for at least two-thirds of the thickness of a wall are incorporated to bond the masonry securely. For slightly better-quality work, the stones are laid in courses **(2)**, creating a level bed every 450mm (1ft 6in) or so. Random-rubble walling is frequently finished at the corners with quoins constructed from blocks of dressed stone.

Random rubblework is most often found in rural areas, but the better-quality housing, particularly in villages and country towns, tends to be constructed from squared rubble **(3)**. This type of rubblework is composed of split blocks, which are sometimes roughly dressed with a hammer or steel chisel. With squared rubble, it was possible to construct masonry with regular courses **(4)** that are constant in height, although the stones themselves vary in length.

1 Random rubblework

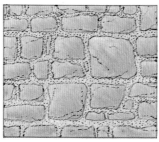

2 Coursed random rubble

3 Squared rubblework

4 Regular-coursed squared rubble

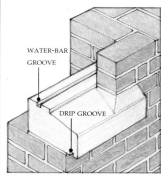

Weathered stone subsill

Sills

A stone sill (or, strictly speaking, subsill) is used to cap the section of wall at the base of a window. The wooden window frame sits directly on the stone sill and the joint is weatherproofed with a metal water bar fitted into a groove in each component. The ends of a stone sill are normally built into the brick or stone wall on both sides of the window. The top surface is weathered (sloped) to drain water away from the wooden window frame. In addition, a drip groove cut along the underside causes rainwater to drop to the ground before it can run back to soak the wall behind. Drip grooves should be raked out periodically to ensure that they do not become bridged by paint, moss or lichen.

Jambs

The stone jambs flanking door and window openings are usually constructed from quoins (alternate headers and stretchers of dressed stone). These are particularly obvious when they are built into rubble walls or when picked out with distinctive surface dressings.

The jambs in ashlar walls, in particular, are sometimes lined with narrow dressed stones that form reveals. Known as upstarts, these stones often project slightly from the face of the wall and are carved to create decorative architraves.

Jambs may be splayed to provide more natural light.

Mullions and piers

Stone mullions are used to divide a window opening in order to accommodate two or more individual windows and provide additional support to the lintel above. Larger vertical supports, such as those at the corners of a bay window, are called piers. Piers and mullions are frequently decorated with ornamental carvings.

Carved stone door surround

Stone courses contrast with brick

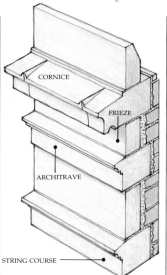

Painted stone arch with keystone and capitals

STONE COURSES

Many stone-built or brick façades are broken by horizontal moulded bands of stone that project beyond the face of the wall. As well as dividing a building into aesthetically pleasing proportions, these stone courses have a more prosaic function. Like a window sill, stone courses are weathered so they shed rainwater, which would otherwise saturate or stain the wall.

Cornices

A cornice is normally situated just below the parapet at the top of a house. Often the junctions between the individual blocks of stone were saddled (raised) to encourage water to flow away from the actual joints; alternatively, the top of the entire cornice was protected with a lead flashing.

Architraves

An architrave is a similar but smaller moulding situated just below the cornice. The section of wall between the two is known as a frieze.

String courses

A string course is a narrow horizontal band of moulded stones. A square-faced one is called a band course.

CORNICE

FRIEZE

ARCHITRAVE

STRING COURSE

Horizontal stone courses

COPINGS

A coping is a row of capping stones designed to shed rainwater from the top of a brick or stone wall. Coping stones, which may be either saddled or weathered, are wider than the wall itself and have drip grooves on the underside.

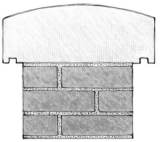

Coping stone with drip grooves

47

ARTIFICIAL STONE

W E TEND TO REGARD IMITATIVE MASONRY *as a relatively modern phenomenon restricted to garden paving and cast-concrete walling. However, by the beginning of the nineteenth century artIficial cast stonework was already fairly commonplace as a cheaper alternative to hand carving, and the earliest experiments in processing artificial stone were carried out perhaps a century earlier.*

In the eighteenth century the public was intrigued by artificial-stone products, not just because of their convincing natural appearance but also because of the mystery surrounding their manufacture. Richard Holt, who took out a patent for artificial stone in 1722, went so far as to claim that he had succeeded in rediscovering a lost formula possessed by our ancestors long ago, who used it for manufacturing building materials for such well-known monuments as the pyramids of ancient Egypt and the megaliths of Stonehenge.

COADE STONE

The artificial-stone market was potentially so lucrative that processes and exact compositions were jealously guarded secrets. However, recent scientific analysis has revealed that Coade stone, perhaps the most famous of all artificial stones, was composed of nothing more exotic than china clay mixed with finely ground aggregates and linseed oil.

Founded in the 1760s, the Coade Company established a reputation for manufacturing artificial stonework of the highest quality, and time has proved the durability of their products. Coade's output included copies of well-known classical stonework, but most of their products were designed specially for their catalogue. The company produced a vast range of cast architectural features, including their now familiar door surrounds complete with masked keystone and vermiculated quoins. Even though Coade-stone artifacts were made in quantity, the more intricate castings were finished by hand – which is perhaps why it is sometimes difficult to tell Coade-stone castings from genuine stone.

The Coade family together with their various associates traded successfully for about seventy years, eventually exporting their products as far afield as America and the West Indies.

A Coade-stone door surround incorporating quoins and masked keystone

Vermiculated window opening

Terracotta is rich and colourful

TERRACOTTA

Terracotta arguably has more in common with brick so far as its composition and manufacture are concerned. Nevertheless, for architectural purposes it is generally classified as an artificial stone. It had already been in use for centuries when the Victorians, with their characteristic enthusiasm for ornamentation, took to terracotta and its glazed version 'faience', exploiting the potential of industrial production to full advantage.

We are perhaps used to thinking of terracotta as a decorative facing for large public buildings and department stores, but it was also used in better-quality houses to embellish entrances and for sculptured panels, cornices and other mouldings. Manufacturers experimented with different colours, but castings for both commercial and domestic buildings were mostly brick red or beige.

Normally made as hollow blocks, terracotta and faience in particular are extremely durable unless water is able to seep behind them, rusting steel or iron fixings, which eventually expand and crack the castings. It is possible to order replacement castings, although the cost is likely to be prohibitive. However, depending on the nature of the damage, you may be able to repair cracked terracotta with epoxy adhesive.

REPAIRING DEFECTIVE STONE

DESPITE ITS REPUTATION FOR DURABILITY, *stone is surprisingly susceptible to wear and decay. In addition to the more obvious defects resulting from accidental breakages, stonework can be eaten away by atmospheric impurities caused by the coal fires and furnaces of the past or today's acid rain. Occasionally the erosion is very gradual and may be acceptable, even attractive, but when stone begins to flake, the disintegration can be rapid and urgent treatment may be essential.*

In most cases, especially when you are dealing with carved stonework or ashlar, professional skills are required to produce a sound and inconspicuous repair. However, most of the better-known stone-restoration companies are used to working on public buildings, such as city halls or churches, and are usually not geared to small-scale work. There are both individual masons and carvers and small groups that are happy to undertake domestic commissions, but they are not always easy to find. The best way to track down suitable repairers is to consult a directory such as the Building Conservation Directory, which lists skilled contractors.

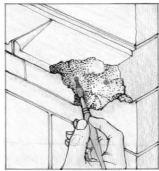

1 Mark pin positions with paint

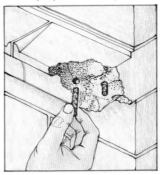

2 Insert keyed and glued pins

MECHANICAL REPAIRS

If a small fragment of stone breaks away – from a carving or moulded course, for example – you can glue it back in place with epoxy adhesive. This type of adhesive only begins to set once its constituents have been mixed. Low-viscosity epoxy glues are available from specialists, but most DIY shops stock a standard two-part adhesive that can be thinned sufficiently by warming the tubes on a radiator. Large pieces of stone need to be reinforced with non-ferrous metal pins.

Reinforcing a repair

Make the reinforcing pins by cutting stainless-steel or brass rod into short lengths. File notches along each pin to form keys for the adhesive. Mark the position of the pins on one half of the repair with small spots of paint (**1**). Reposition the broken piece of stone to transfer the spots.

Dismantle the repair again and use a masonry drill to bore holes in each half of the repair that are slightly larger in diameter than the pins. Make a dry assembly, with the pins in place, to ensure that the joint fits snugly.

Scrub the mating surfaces with acetone (nail-varnish remover), then glue the pins into one half (**2**). Spread a thin layer of adhesive on the other half, and also onto the projecting pins. Assemble the joint, rocking the stone slightly to squeeze out excess adhesive, then wipe it off immediately with cotton-wool buds wetted with acetone. If possible, bind the repair with string or self-adhesive parcel tape until the adhesive has set hard.

THE EFFECTS OF INCORRECT BEDDING

Sedimentary rocks, such as sandstone and limestone, are the products of materials that have been deposited in geological beds (strata) by water or wind. As a result, when cut or split blocks are laid, their erosion may be exacerbated if the mason fails to allow for the effect of this bedding.

When a block of stone is laid with its strata horizontal (**1**), the weight of subsequent masonry prevents the block from delaminating. Laying stones in this way is known as 'natural bedding'. It is the method that should be used in most situations.

When a stone block is face-bedded (**2**), with the strata on edge and parallel to the face of the wall, the action of spalling tends to shear flakes from the

surface of the stone – rather like shedding individual playing cards from a deck. Gradually the disintegration eats deeper and deeper into the wall until it seriously compromises the stability of the masonry.

Courses, such as cornices, that project from a wall should be constructed from edge-bedded stones (**3**) in order to prevent delamination. For the same reason, stone lintels above window and door openings should also be edge-bedded.

Even skilled stonemasons sometimes have difficulty in identifying the direction of the bedding on a newly cut block. The direction is therefore normally marked on the stone itself, either at the quarry or once the block has been sawn roughly to size.

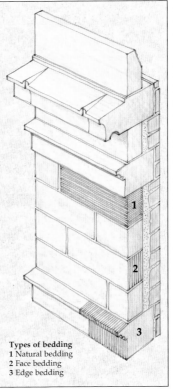

Types of bedding
1 Natural bedding
2 Face bedding
3 Edge bedding

Face-bedded stone that begins to delaminate can be consolidated by an expert

REPAIRING WITH MORTAR

Patching stonework with mortar is simpler and cheaper than having to cut out and replace damaged stones. In fact, as long ago as the early nineteenth century builders used Roman cement (see INGREDIENTS OF RENDER AND STUCCO) for such repairs. Provided that the damaged stones have a simple profile, it is possible to undertake 'plastic' repairs yourself – however, since it is difficult to obtain an exact match, you may prefer to hire a professional mason unless the stonework is painted.

Depending on the nature and colour of the original stonework, a mason will probably select silver sand or even crushed stone as the aggregate for a suitable repair mortar. Some masons include cement in the mortar, but you might consider using a weak naturally hydraulic lime or a fat lime-putty mix instead of the cement. If necessary, consult your district Conservation Officer or an experienced architect or surveyor practising in your area.

Gluing delaminating stone

It is possible to consolidate flaking face-bedded stones by injecting a thin epoxy adhesive into holes drilled through the laminations. Reinforcing pins are then introduced into the same holes. However, this is a skilled repair best left to a professional conservator.

Injecting adhesive for reinforcing pins

Indenting

Replacing damaged stone blocks with new ones is known as indenting. Since it is difficult even for an experienced mason to guarantee an exact match of colour and texture, it may be preferable to live with slightly blemished stone-work rather than risk having a repair done that could prove more noticeable than the blemish itself.

One stone at a time can be cut out and replaced without propping, but if a number of adjacent blocks are affected, the surround-ing masonry should be supported while the work is in progress.

An entire facing stone can be removed with a hammer and chisel, but it is often only necessary to cut back the stone by a minimum of 100mm (4in) in order to make sufficient room for a shallow block to be mortared in place.

Unless the stonework has been face-bedded, it may be possible to dismantle an eroded section of the wall and then turn the blocks round so as to expose the undamaged faces.

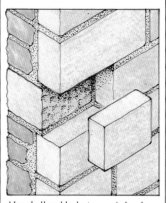

Use shallow blocks to repair headers

Preparing the masonry

The decayed stone should be cut back by at least 25mm (1in) to sound material. Cut a regular shape with under-cut edges, except for the bottom edge which should be left square **(1)**. Treat each individual stone separately, using strips of wood to form appropriate joints in the mortar until it has set (the strips are then removed and the joints repointed in the usual way).

Reinforce the repair by gluing non-ferrous pins or wire into holes drilled in the stone **(2)**. Brush off loose material and wet the stone to reduce suction.

Applying the mortar

Apply a coat of mortar 12 to 18mm (½ to ¾in) thick and scratch the surface to provide a key. Two to four hours later, apply a second coat and smooth its surface with a wooden float. Once the top coat has begun to get firm, stipple it with a damp sponge or a bristle brush in order to expose the aggregate.

When repairing cornices and other moulded courses, you can use a running mould to shape them (see STUCCO MOULDINGS).

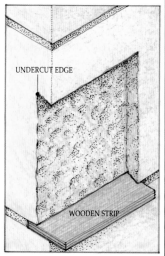

1 Cut a recess in the worn stone

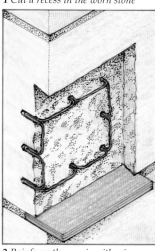

2 Reinforce the repair with wire

CHAPTER FIVE

RENDER & STUCCO

RENDER USUALLY DENOTES *a plain external-wall coating. It has been in use from the very earliest times. Renders used for the walls of old houses range from single low-strength lime coat-ings applied over wattle or lath to high-strength cement-based renders applied to brickwork.*

The term stucco encompasses many different applications – from covering exterior walls in imitation stone to fine plaster applied to interior walls or ceilings and the creation of all manner of decorative mouldings. The term is now often employed to describe the high-quality renders used to provide a cheap yet convincing substitute for stonework – brick or rubble masonry being coated to look like best-quality ashlar, complete with mouldings, quoins and cornices.

Stucco became highly fashionable in the late eight-eenth century and was to remain popular throughout

the Victorian era, being widely used for decorative window and door surrounds. Although the illusion was frequently reinforced by painting to resemble nicely weathered masonry, there was keen competition to produce stuccos that would dry naturally to match the colours of building stones. The materials used for stucco varied considerably, but in England in the early nineteenth century stucco finishes were generally lime-based renders applied as either two-part or three-part coatings to façades.

Towards the end of the nineteenth century a very different type of render, known as roughcast, became fashionable for mock-Tudor houses. The top coat of this coarsely textured rustic-looking render is mixed with gravel. Pebble dash, a slightly later type of render, is similar in composition but a dry aggregate is thrown onto the wet render so that the aggregate remains exposed on the surface.

Painted stucco contrasts with brick

Plain-rendered seaside terrace

Fully stuccoed early-C19th house with rusticated ground floor

Unpainted stucco with white details

Semi-rusticated Regency façade

REPAIRING RENDER

BEFORE EMBARKING ON REPAIRS, *it's important to establish whether the old render is lime-based or cement-based.*

Cement renders are generally hard and impervious, whereas lime renders are normally weaker and can accommodate slight movement. It is essential to make repairs with a compatible material.

Before starting work, try to establish why the render has failed. An unsuitable material may have been used to repair the wall, or damp may be causing the render to detach itself from the background masonry.

FILLING CRACKS

Rake out large cracks – 2mm (⅛in) wide or more – with a cold chisel, undercutting the edges to form a key. If you discover that the brickwork behind is cracked too, seek professional advice. Clean out loose debris with a stiff-bristle brush, then wet the crack and fill it flush with new lime-based or cement mortar to match the rest of the render.

PATCHING HOLES

If you neglect to repair damaged render (particularly cement-based render), rainwater penetrates and soaks the wall behind, leading to damp and decay internally. The wetting and drying cycle may cause efflorescence. Also, trapped moisture expands during frosty weather, causing the render to break away.

Preparing the wall

Tap the wall in the vicinity of obvious damage with a wooden mallet, listening for the hollow sound that indicates loose render.

Use a bolster chisel and a heavy hammer to hack off loose render. Cut the edges straight, to avoid a patchy appearance, and try to align them with features of the building that will disguise joins between old and new stucco. Undercut all but the bottom edge, which should be left square. Rake out the mortar joints between bricks to a depth of about 16mm (⅝in), then brush all loose material from the wall.

Applying the render

Thoroughly wet the area that is to be patched and use a plasterer's trowel to apply the first layer of render. Sweep the render onto the wall with upward strokes of the trowel, using fairly firm pressure **(1)**, then smooth it out to a depth of between 10 and 12mm (⅜ and ½in). As the render begins to set firm, scratch the surface to form a key for the next coat and leave it till the following day to set.

Depending on the thickness of the original render, repeat the procedure – adding a second layer of render approximately 10mm (⅜in) thick – before applying a 6mm (¼in) finishing coat.

Before you trowel on the finishing coat, wet the keyed surface of the previous layer. Use a wooden straightedge to scrape the render flush **(2)**, working with a zigzag action from the bottom upwards, then fill any low spots with fresh render.

Finally, smooth the finishing coat with a wooden float, using circular and figure-of-eight strokes.

INGREDIENTS OF RENDER AND STUCCO

Before the latter part of the eighteenth century, most exterior render was a mixture of lime and sand, sometimes reinforced with chopped animal hair. It set slowly, drying out over a period of days while the lime absorbed carbon dioxide from the atmosphere. During the eighteenth and nineteenth centuries, other ingredients were used in an attempt to create a high-quality but inexpensive material. These stuccos or 'mastics' were made using fine aggregates (limestone, various sands, crushed pottery, glass) bound with linseed oil and other additives.

Experiments aimed at making faster-setting renders, led to the development of more durable and water-resistant materials. One of these was called Roman cement. Used as a render material from the 1790s, it was a form of natural cement that dried to a distinctive pink/brown colour. These developments culminated with the patenting in 1824 of Portland cement. Cement sets by a chemical reaction that begins as soon as it is mixed with water. As a result, render containing cement sets hard in a matter of hours and continues to gain strength over a period of weeks.

Depending on the strength of the render to be repaired, there are a number of mixes you might consider. For lime/cement-based renders, mix the undercoats using 1 part cement, 2 parts lime, and 9 parts sand. For the top coat, a weaker mix of 1:3:12 is suitable. When repairing a lime-based render, you can use either a naturally hydraulic lime mixed with sand or a lime-putty/sand mix. For the hydraulic-lime mix, use 2 parts lime mixed with 5 parts well-graded sharp sand as an undercoat, with 1 part lime and 3 parts soft sand for the top coat. When using lime putty, make the undercoat of 1:2.5 lime putty and sand; and for the top coat, use a mix of 1:3.5.

Mixing the ingredients

If you are preparing render from dry ingredients, mix them thoroughly first, then form a well in the centre of the pile and pour in some water. Shovel the ingredients from around the edges of the well into the water until it has been absorbed, then gradually turn the mixture over until the consistency is even – the render should retain marks left by the shovel without slumping or crumbling. When handling lime, wear a face mask, goggles and gloves.

1 Trowel on first layer of render

2 Scrape level with a straightedge

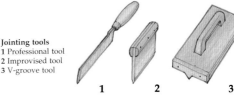

RUSTICATION

Late-Victorian roughcast

PATCHING PEBBLE DASH AND ROUGHCAST

The method for patching a hole in a pebble-dash wall is the same as for plain stucco – but while the top coat is still soft, pick up some 6mm (¼in) washed pebbles on the toe of your plasterer's trowel and flick them onto the render **(1)**. Spread a dust-sheet at the foot of the wall to catch fallen pebbles. When you have filled the patch evenly, tap the pebbles lightly with a float to bed them into the render **(2)**.

When patching roughcast, mix equal parts of sand and 6mm (¼in) crushed-stone aggregate into the top-coat render, using slightly more water than normal. Soak the keyed undercoat and flick the roughcast mixture onto it, covering the patched area evenly so as to match the surrounding wall.

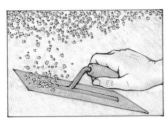

1 Flinging pebbles with a trowel

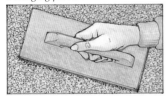

2 Bed them in with a float

O N CLOSER EXAMINATION, *what appear to be ashlar (dressed stone) blocks making up the ground floor of an early-nineteenth-century house often prove to be nothing more than an illusion created by a plasterer drawing a tool through wet stucco in an attempt to disguise cheap brickwork.*

The horizontal and vertical joints of closely fitting ashlar blocks are frequently represented in the stucco-work of the period. Alternatively, pronounced grooves are incised – often as banded rustication, which does not include vertical joints. When executed by a skilled plasterer, it is difficult to distinguish rusticated stucco from genuine stonework unless part of the render has broken away to reveal a telltale brick background.

VERMICULATION

Some plasterers went to even greater lengths to deceive the eye by reproducing vermiculation – a deep irregular texture, similar in appearance to worm tracks, which was a traditional stonemason's surface dressing. Vermiculation was most commonly used to decorate door or window surrounds and to create fake quoins on the corners of buildings.

Half-stuccoed late-Georgian houses with banded rustication

RE-CREATING VERMICULATION

If you are sufficiently skilled, it is possible to cut vermiculation by hand in wet stucco, using modelling tools or old chisels. However, it is easier to take an impression from an identical 'stone' and to cast vermiculated blocks in sand-and-cement render (see CASTING VERMICULATION).

Cutting vermiculation by hand

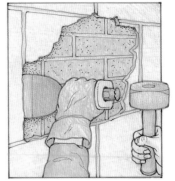

1 Chop back to nearest joint lines

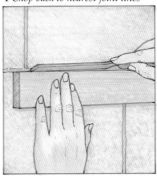

2 Rule lines with a jointing tool

RESTORING RUSTICATION

Square-cut ashlar rustication was created by marking stucco with a steel jointing tool, but there's no need to buy special tools. You can make a jointing tool of your own from wood; and to re-create deep V-grooves you can screw an improvised wooden template to the end of a float.

Use a bolster chisel and hammer to cut loose rusticated stucco back to the nearest joint lines in sound render **(1)**. Fill flush with fresh stucco and finish the surface with a wooden float.

Using a straight batten as a guide, slowly draw a jointing tool through the stucco **(2)**. For the time being leave any specks of render that are dragged out onto the surface, then carefully rub them off with a float when the stucco begins to harden.

STUCCO MOULDINGS

STUCCO REALLY COMES INTO ITS OWN *when it is used to simulate the mouldings and other enrichments associated with carved stonework. In Georgian times entire façades were often covered with ornamental stucco, whereas the Victorians tended to favour the contrast of brickwork with stucco details.*

Classically inspired stucco cornice and string course

Decorative moulding and pediment   *Stucco architrave with keystone*

RESTORING MOULDINGS

Classically inspired cornice mouldings running just below the parapet of a house or near the top of a porch are design-ed to shed water clear of the face of the wall. Their top surfaces are therefore 'weathered' (sloped) to ensure that rainwater drains away from the masonry. Similar, though smaller, mouldings known as string courses are used to provide horizontal emphasis and improve the visual propor-tions of a façade. Architraves in stucco often surround window openings, and many a doorway is flanked with stucco pilasters.

Mouldings were either fabricated directly on the wall or cast on a bench then fixed to the building once they had set. As with internal plasterwork, stucco mouldings frequently include beds for accommodating separately moulded decorative features.

RUNNING MOULDINGS ON THE WALL

It is normally easier to work on a horizontal bench than on the vertical surface of a wall. However, there are times when it makes more sense to repair mouldings *in situ* – for example, when a moulding is built around an integral support of brick or tile corbelling (1), or only a short section of a long moulding is damaged, or a moulding is simply too large to be lifted into place.

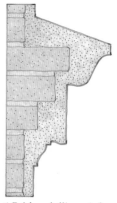

1 Brick-corbelling reinforcement

The running mould

A stucco moulding is shaped by using a zinc template screwed to a running mould. This is made in a similar way to the moulds used for making interior plaster cornices (see RUNNING A PLAIN CORNICE). Wooden battens, known as rules, are nailed to the masonry to guide the running mould (2).

2 Running mould with fixed rules

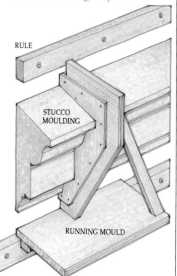

RULE

STUCCO MOULDING

RULE   RUNNING MOULD

EMPLOYING PROFESSIONALS

You should seriously consider whether it is worth attempting to restore stucco mouldings yourself or whether it is advisable to employ a professional plasterer. Considerable skill is needed to restore some mouldings, especially those that have to be run *in situ*. Also, there are inherent risks in working at the height at which some of these features are located, and mouldings installed high up on a building constitute a safety risk unless they are securely attached. Scaffolding is normally required to provide a safe working platform for the duration of the work – and as you are likely to take longer to complete the job than a professional, the saving on scaffold hire makes at least some contribution towards the cost of paying a plasterer.

However, there is a degree of satisfaction in restoring one's own house – and provided that you can reach damaged stucco from a low platform constructed from hired slot-together scaffold frames, there is no practical reason why you shouldn't tackle the work.

Fabricating a moulding

If you are fabricating mouldings that form part of a larger area of stucco, you should use a mix for the mouldings that is compatible with the rest of the render. For separate mouldings, a mix of 1 part Portland cement, 1 part hydrated lime and 2.5 parts plasterer's sand might be suitable.

After the masonry background has been wetted, the approximate shape of the moulding is built in stucco. A professional plasterer would use a gauging trowel – a tool shaped like a bricklayer's trowel but with a round-tip blade. However, a pointing trowel can be used instead. The running mould is then slid along the rules, scraping the stucco to create the profile of the finished moulding (1). Any slight blemishes are smoothed out with a wooden float. All

mitres and returns must be shaped by hand as the work progresses.

Deep mouldings are built up gradually in layers approximately 12mm (½in) thick by making 'muffle' runs. A muffle is a smaller template that is run in advance of a finished-profile one. Several muffles, each increasing in size, may be needed in order to build a large moulding.

Each layer is scratched to provide a key for the next (which is normally applied about 24 hours later), the keyed surface having first been dampened with water.

Some plasterers prefer to apply a subsequent coat while the previous one is slightly wet – when it's still 'green'. This is possible if you make one run early in the morning and a second run sometime after lunch.

Creating a stonelike texture

To create a stucco moulding with a convincing stonelike texture, mix roughly equal proportions of dry sand and cement together – then while the finished moulding is still wet, flick the dry mixture onto the surface of the stucco with a plasterer's trowel. When you see the mixture change colour as it absorbs moisture from the moulding, make one final pass with the running mould.

Including reinforcement

Repairs to deep mouldings are sometimes reinforced with metal rod and wire bent into a suitable armature (2). Choose non-ferrous metal and use an epoxy adhesive to glue the rods into holes drilled in the masonry. Before gluing them, file the ends of the reinforcement rods in order to provide a key for the adhesive.

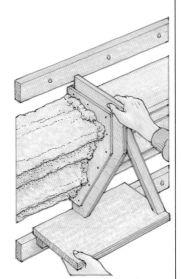

1 Slide the running mould sideways

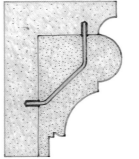

2 Bent-metal reinforcement

MAKING MOULDINGS ON A BENCH

The alternative method for making mouldings was to cast them on site then apply them to the walls. The same procedure can be used when replacing damaged sections, or to re-create entire cornices or other mouldings. When installing replacement mouldings, it pays to attach them to the wall with fixings such as non-ferrous expanding-anchor screws.

Making a reverse mould.

A replacement moulding is cast in a reverse mould (1) run in plaster of Paris (see RUNNING A PLAIN CORNICE).

Traditionally once the plaster of Paris has set, the reverse mould is sealed with three coats of shellac.

However, to produce a casting with a better surface finish, seal the mould with a coat of PVA bonding agent then paint a film of cooking oil over it. If the bonding agent sticks to the stucco, it will peel off easily, due to the presence of the oil, without harming the surface of the casting.

Casting the moulding

Make a semi-dry mixture of 1 part cement and 3 parts sand. Add just enough water for a ball of stucco squeezed in your hand to retain the impression of your fingers.

Evenly cover the inside of the mould with stucco to a depth of about 25mm (1in), then use a piece of wood to tamp it into all the crevices. Lay longitudinal reinforcement in the mould (such as galvanized-metal rods or non-ferrous expanded-metal strips), then fill the mould with more stucco.

Push lengths of wooden dowel through the stucco to

form clearance holes for wall fixings (2). Next day, lift the casting out of the mould and leave it on the bench for 48 hours or so to harden. Spray it with water from time to time to prevent cracking.

Installing the moulding

You will probably need at least one assistant when installing a stucco moulding. It also helps if you nail a wooden batten to the wall to support the moulding (3).

Countersink the clearance holes, then drill through them into the wall behind. Insert and tighten the fixings before removing the batten.

Depending on the style of stuccowork, either render up to the moulding or fill gaps between the moulding and the wall with a mortar paste. Also, cover the screwheads with mortar.

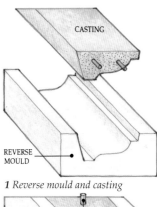

1 Reverse mould and casting

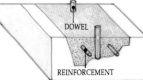

2 Make clearance holes for fixings

3 Support the moulding on a batten

CASTING ORNAMENTS IN STUCCO

BROKEN OR MISSING CONSOLES, *scrolls and other ornaments cast in stucco can be reproduced by taking an 'impression' from an original that is still intact. A flexible mould made from cold-cure silicone rubber is normally used – but it is possible to reproduce simple textures, such as vermiculation, using plaster of Paris alone.*

USING A FLEXIBLE MOULD

Brush loose dust off the original ornament and spray it with the release agent supplied. Mix the silicone rubber following the manufacturer's directions, including a thixotropic additive that enables the material to cling to vertical surfaces without slumping. Build a 3mm (⅛in) layer of silicone rubber, embed a light scrim and then add a further layer of rubber about 3 to 6mm (⅛in to ¼in) thick. Leave it to set for 12 hours or so.

An unsupported silicone-rubber mould is often too flexible and tends to distort when filled with stucco. Consequently, you usually need to apply a fairly thick layer of reinforced plaster of Paris to the outside of the flexible mould while it is still in place. Remove the plaster backing once it has set hard, then peel the flexible mould off the wall.

Making the casting

Reunite the flexible mould with its plaster backing and lay them on a workbench. Brush a fairly liquid mixture of 1 part cement to 3 parts sand onto the inside face of the mould, then fill it to the brim with more stucco.

Heavy castings may need reinforcing with non-ferrous expanded metal, and they should be attached to the wall with screws or expanding bolts. Disguise the wall fixings with mortar.

Decorative painted-stucco gable

Ornamental lintel in painted stucco

Classical pilasters with ornate capitals

CASTING VERMICULATION

To re-create vermiculation, first brush the original clean then paint it with a cooking-oil release agent. Coat the stone with a 30mm (1¼in) layer of plaster of Paris, including some jute scrim to reinforce it. When the plaster has set, ease the mould off the wall and lay it flat on a bench. Coat the inside of the mould with cooking oil.

Half-fill the mould with stucco. Place a strip of non-ferrous expanded metal on top and cover it with stucco, filling the mould to the brim. Leave the stucco to set hard, then remove the casting and screw it to the wall. Finally, fill the edges and cover the screwheads with mortar.

Impeccably restored vermiculated arches and dentil cornice

PAINTING STUCCO

New stucco must be dry before it's painted. Non-hydraulic-lime stuccos will require between 7 and 21 days, depending on the type of mix, the ambient temperature and level of humidity. Stucco based on hydraulic lime dries faster – perhaps in a few days. New stucco should be protected with plastic sheets to stop it drying too quickly in hot, dry weather. Use damp hessian to prevent it drying too slowly if humidity is high.

Most lime-based stucco was painted with limewash or lead paint. Limewash is still used, as it allows the building fabric to 'breathe'. Masonry paint is suitable for most cement-based renders.

CHAPTER SIX

TIMBER CLADDING

TIMBER-FRAME HOUSES *are among the earliest buildings still standing. The familiar picturesque 'half-timbered' house is often constructed with a stout oak framework infilled with wattle and daub or sometimes with bricks.*

From the sixteenth century, it became fashionable to cover timber frames with lime render, which also provided additional weatherproofing. At around the same time, some houses, particularly in south-east England, were clad with planks of wood known as weatherboarding. The boards were usually cut from oak or elm, but by the late eighteenth century sawn softwood boards were increasingly being imported from the Baltic and North America. Gradually weatherboarding became less widely used in Britain, except for the decorative cladding of gable ends and bay windows.

Early cladding in oak or elm may have been left unfinished, but the poorer-quality softwood needed protection in the form of wood tar or limewash mixed with pigments. In the early nineteenth century, coal tar was sometimes used, although mainly for agricultural buildings. Up to the 1950s, weatherboarding was often finished with white lead paint.

When repairing weatherboarding, disturb as few boards as possible. Old boards are likely to be of a better-quality timber and should be reused where possible. Replacing slightly irregular older boards with modern machine-cut ones may detract from the character of a building.

Early weatherboarded house that has been maintained in perfect condition

Partially clad timber-frame cottage

WEATHERBOARDING

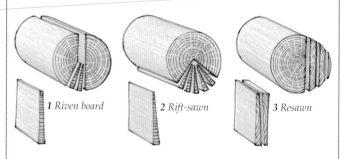

1 Riven board   *2 Rift-sawn*   *3 Resawn*

WEATHERBOARDING *is essentially a means of cladding a building effectively against the weather – and perhaps it is this honest 'no frills' appearance, with its neat horizontal shadow lines, that we find so appealing. There are plenty of examples of houses totally clad in weatherboarding, from eaves to ground level, but in certain areas it was a common practice to use timber cladding for the first floor only, which was supported by a lower storey of brick or stone; also, cladding is sometimes nailed to battens to protect substandard brickwork. This combination of painted weatherboarding and natural-coloured masonry is particularly handsome.*

From the earliest times, softwoods such as white pine, hemlock and spruce were used for weatherboarding. But it was not until the start of the twentieth century that red cedar – perhaps today's most fashionable timber for exterior cladding – became widely available.

Rare unpainted weatherboarding

Typical combination of painted weatherboarding and red bricks

BOARD PROFILES

The earliest boards were wedge-shape planks, riven from logs like slicing a cake. The result was a more-or-less symmetrical feather-edged board **(1)** with the grain running directly across its thickness. By the late nineteenth century similar boards were being produced by machine. Turned logs, suspended above a circular saw, were rotated fractionally between cuts, producing rift-sawn boards **(2)**.

Due to the orientation of the grain, riven and rift-sawn boards are relatively stable and are rarely susceptible to the splitting and warping that often results from shrinkage. Riven boards were seldom more than about 100mm (4in) in width, whereas much wider boards could be cut by machine. Typically, rift-sawn boards were 125 to 150mm (5 to 6in) wide, but widths of 225mm (9in) or more were available.

Another method for producing feather-edged boards was to saw logs into thick planks, which in turn were resawn to make two bevelled boards **(3)**. With this type of board, the grain direction varies and the worst effects of shrinkage are common.

Riven and sawn boards were usually planed on one face. At the same time, some boards were machined with a moulding along their bottom edges **(4)**.

Shiplap boarding **(5)** has been popular since the late nineteenth century and is still in use today. Tongue-and-groove boards **(6)**, used since the 1920s, were often machined with a profile that made a wide board look like two narrower ones, thus halving the time it took to clad a house.

4 Machined   *5 Shiplap*   *6 T & G board*

NAILS FOR WEATHERBOARDING

In the eighteenth century, weatherboarding would have been fixed in place with handmade iron nails with large raised heads. Although most iron nails will have rusted away by now, it is preferable when replacing boards to use nails made in the traditional manner by a blacksmith specializing in the production of wrought-iron door fittings. However, it is generally more practical to use modern galvanized nails for repairs, or other non-ferrous nails that will not corrode. With their superior grip, ring-shank nails are good for fixing weatherboarding, too.

FIXING WEATHERBOARDING

There is some debate about the best way to fix weatherboarding. Traditionalists follow the time-honoured method, whereas others favour an approach that is designed to cope with modern mass-produced boards.

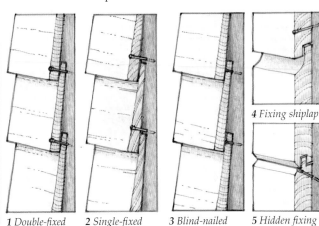

1 Double-fixed   *2 Single-fixed*   *3 Blind-nailed*   *4 Fixing shiplap*   *5 Hidden fixing*

CORNERS AND EDGE DETAILS

In theory it is possible to mitre the ends of boards where they meet at a corner, but such detailing requires skilful carpentry. And even when boards are fitted perfectly, the joints are likely to open up in time – which is not only unsightly but exposes the vulnerable end grain to wet rot.

Corner posts

The most common method of finishing weatherboarding at corners, both internal and external, is to butt the ends of the boards against a vertical wooden corner post nailed to the underlying framework. An internal-corner post is simply a square batten **(1)**. Two strips of wood are nailed together at right angles to cap an external corner **(2)**.

Nailing procedures

Feather-edged boards overlap by about 25 to 38mm (1 to 1½in). Traditionally, nails were driven right through the overlap, pinning both boards to the framework **(1)**. Because riven and rift-sawn boards tend to shrink and swell across their thickness only, fixing them rigidly in this manner leads to few problems.

The modern practice is to hammer each nail through one board only, just missing the board below **(2)**. This permits the boards to move unrestrictedly and prevents splitting if the timber shrinks across its width. However, even some professional installers are of the opinion that driving nails in this way is likely to cause a board to cup (bend across its width), which is in itself sufficient to promote a split.

With 'blind' nailing, each board is nailed along the top edge only, so that the overlap hides the fixings **(3)**. This method has the advantage of being neat in appearance, but there's nothing to stop the lower edges of the boards bowing or twisting.

It is normal to fix shiplap cladding with a single row of nails for each board **(4)**.

When nailing tongue-and-groove boards, hidden fixings are more usual **(5)**.

Drip mouldings

Some early boarded houses have cladding running right down to the ground – an unsatisfactory solution that inevitably leads to rotting timber. The weatherboarding on later houses, which were normally built on masonry foundations, begins just above the ground with some kind of drip moulding to shed rainwater. This may be nothing more than a wooden starter strip nailed under the first board to hold the bottom edge away from the wall **(3)**, but better-quality houses often have purpose-made drip mouldings **(4)**.

Fascia boards

At the eaves, the cladding is lapped by a flat fascia board. Occasionally, the top board is tucked into a rebate planed along the bottom edge of the fascia board.

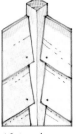

1 Internal

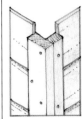

2 External

Boards bent around a corner

3 Starter strip

4 Purpose-made

Drip moulding fixed above windows

Conjunction of boards and hung tiles

REPAIRING WEATHERBOARDING

EXPERIENCE HAS PROVED *that provided a timber-clad house is maintained regularly it can last for centuries. What is perhaps even more encouraging is the fact that few if any of the repairs that may be necessary are beyond the skills of any reasonably competent carpenter. The repairs described below refer mainly to feather-edged weatherboarding, but you can adapt the techniques for other varieties of horizontal timber cladding.*

ROUTINE MAINTENANCE

You will find it pays to inspect weatherboarding at least once a year, and also immediately after periods of storms or high winds. If you are able to spot potential problems early enough, they need never develop into costly or time-consuming repairs.

Old iron nails are bound to corrode, until eventually they are too weak to hold the boards securely. Look out for loose boards and, before the wind does further damage, tap back and renail any that have dropped. Check to see if it's time to recaulk around window and door frames and along the butt joints between boards and corner posts.

REPLACING A ROTTED SECTION

The end grain of any piece of timber is particularly prone to wet rot. As a result, it is quite common to find that an otherwise sound length of weatherboarding has rotted at one or both ends. Rather than discard perfectly serviceable boards, replace only the rotten sections with new wood.

Prise up the bottom edge of the board above the one that has rotted, then make a sawcut over the nearest stud, so you can remove the rotten section (1). Keep the saw upright and make the last few strokes with the point of the blade, in order to avoid damaging the board below.

Use a chisel to split out the decayed wood (2), which you can remove piece by piece. Don't drive the chisel too deep, or you will tear the building paper that may lie beneath timber cladding.

A strip of wood still held by the nails under the edge of the board above is now all that remains of the rotted section. Slide a hacksaw blade up behind the board to cut through the nails, then prise out this last piece of wood. If necessary, patch any building paper that is

1 Open split and apply adhesive

2 Clamp glued split with nailed block

REPAIRING SPLIT BOARDS

A crack running along the centre of a board can be caulked or filled to prevent water getting in behind the cladding, but if a split occurs near the end of a board it is best to repair it with glue. Prise the split apart carefully (1) and apply an exterior wood glue to the exposed edge. To clamp the split together, temporarily nail a block of wood against the underside of the damaged board (2). You may have to slip a hacksaw blade up behind the board to cut the nails, so that the section below is free to move. Wipe excess glue from the surface of the cladding. Then, once the glue has set, remove the block and if necessary renail the repaired board.

torn. Next, cut a new piece of board to length. Treat both sides of the board with preservative, coating the end grain thoroughly, before you tap the new piece into place, using a block of wood to protect the edge (3). Since you will have to nail very close to the ends of the new piece of board, drill pilot holes first to avoid splitting the wood. If the rest of the siding is fixed with hidden nails, drive the new fixings just below the surface and cover their heads with either exterior wood filler or putty before painting the timber.

PAINTING BOARDS

If you fail to paint a timber-clad house regularly, sooner or later you will be faced with serious deterioration – wet rot and split timbers that may have to be replaced.

When repainting the boards, you need to match the existing finish. If it is tar, then this can still be obtained from specialist suppliers, but you will need to check that it is compatible with the old finish.

When exterior paintwork deteriorates, it tends to dry out and flake – so, before redecorating, all you need do is scrape it off and rub down the woodwork with abrasive paper.

Areas of sound paintwork may simply need washing down with a solution of sugar soap to remove the dirt and grease that would prevent new paint adhering. Cladding should be finished with a compatible paint or with limewash.

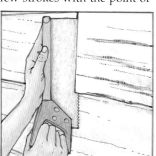

1 Cut off the rotted section

2 Split out decayed wood with chisel

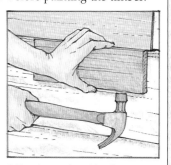

3 Tap the new board in place

CHAPTER SEVEN

ROOF COVERINGS

IN THE DAYS OF RUDIMENTARY TRANSPORT *heavy building materials such as masonry were not usually taken great distances, so roofs and walls had a distinctive local character.*

This changed with the spread of cheaper machine-made materials made possible by the Industrial Revolution and the growth of the railways and canal systems. Nor was this diversification of materials restricted to just one or two nations, or to the products of machines alone – for, as well as architectural styles, European settlers spread their craft skills and manufacturing methods around the world.

Most roofs are pitched in order to shed water efficiently and have a large surface area, which makes them a prominent feature. The type of roof covering is therefore important to the character of the building. Like brickwork, most roof coverings are made up from small units that together form an aesthetically pleasing pattern. And the majority of traditional coverings have a naturally attractive quality of colour and texture which, like other building materials, mellow with age to enhance the appearance of a period house.

Roofs require sympathetic maintenance to preserve their original character. With the resurgence of interest in older buildings, many trade manufacturers are able to supply traditional roof coverings, such as handmade clay tiles. As a result, it is usually possible to repair or recover an old roof in the appropriate style.

The thatched roof enhances this charming half-timbered house

An impressive 1920s hipped and gabled plain-tiled roof

Plain-tiled roof with dormer window

Slate roofing harmonizes with stone and rendered walls

Gable roof with tile-hung walls

TYPES OF ROOF

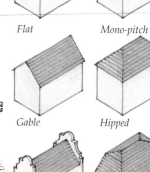

Flat   *Mono-pitch*

Gable   *Hipped*

Dutch gable   *Mansard*

T HE FUNCTION OF THE ROOF *is to shelter the fabric and contents of a building from the weather. The shape of the roof and the type of material used to cover it are largely determined by historical precedents evolved over the centuries to meet local conditions and architectural fashion and style.*

ROOF SHAPES

The shape of a roof is important not only to its function but also to the architectural style of the house. A flat roof affords good shelter from wind and sun, but is not very efficient for shedding rain. Pitched roofs are more common, as they are better able to withstand rain or snow. The pitch can vary considerably, depending on the type of covering used and the complexity of the roof shape.

The simplest form of pitched roof is the mono-pitched type, but the most common is the duo-pitched or gable roof. Hipped roofs, which are a variant of the latter, have one or both ends pitched as well as the front and rear slopes. Various combinations of these two types are frequently used.

The Mansard roof, which originated in France, is a variation of the pitched roof incorporating two angles on each side in order to create a greater volume of habitable space within the roof area.

Conical, hexagonal or octagonal roofs are all used for capping decorative turrets. Some pitched roofs have dormers, projecting structures that usually include a window to allow light into the attic space.

Victorian mechanized tile production

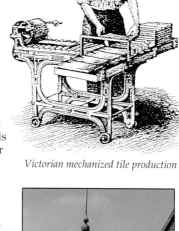

Decorative slate-covered tower

Functional needs

The design of a roof has to take into account the exposure of the site, the architectural style of the building, and the loading on the structure. The roof load is not restricted to the static load of the covering alone. Wind forces apply pressure on the windward side and suction on the lee side, so adequate covering and fixings are important. Weight of snow may need to be taken into account, and also thermal movement caused by extremes of temperature in different seasons. The fire resistance of some coverings may be a consideration.

When it comes to repairing or renewing an existing roof, most of these factors will already have been established by the original design and the performance of the roofing materials over the years. However, if you are planning modifications or a change of roof covering, then it is best to obtain advice from an experienced roofing specialist. Also, get advice from your local planning authority as to whether any consent is required. A new roof or major alterations have to comply with building regulations and may require consent if your house is listed or in a conservation area. Regular maintenance of an old roof is not subject to controls.

Components of a pitched roof

The terminology used to describe the individual parts of a roof can become quite complex when different elements are combined in its construction. The principal terms used in the roofing trade are illustrated here.

ASSESSING REPAIRS

● Easy even for beginners.
■ Fairly difficult. Good practical skills required.
▲ Difficult. Hire a professional.

Tiled roofs
Tiles can fracture, spall, or suffer from weak fixings.
● Check the condition of the fixings (page 66)
■ Replace damaged or dislodged tiles (page 67).

Thatched roofs
Thatching deteriorates over time.
▲ Check for slipped or thinning thatch (page 65)
▲ Look for eroded abutments with chimneys or gables (page 65)
▲ Complete renewal may be your only option (page 65).

Slate roofs
Cracked or missing slates can allow water to enter.
■ Remove and replace broken slates (page 69).
▲ If fixings fail, have slates in good condition stripped and relaid (page 68).

Ornamental features
Damaged or missing details mar the integrity of a roof.
■ Refix or replace damaged or loose ridge tiles (page 69).
▲ Have damaged or missing details replaced (page 69).

Metal roofing
Corrosion and thermal movement can weaken sheet-metal roofs.
● Keep the roof clear of debris and moss (page 70).
● Check condition of flashings regularly (page 70).
▲ Get a specialist to carry out repairs promptly (page 70).

Roof terminology
1 Roof covering
2 Ridge
3 Gable end
4 Verge
5 Bargeboard
6 Eaves
7 Fascia
8 Soffit
9 Hip
10 Hipped end
11 Valley
12 Stepped flashing
13 Back gutter
14 Apron
15 Dormer window
16 Flat roof
17 Parapet

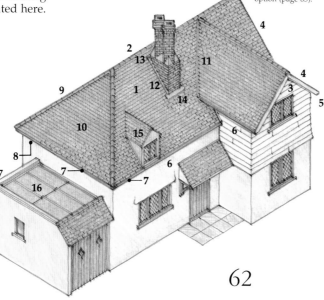

ROOF COVERINGS

Traditional roof coverings still in use today include clay tiles, slates, thatch and, to a lesser extent, metal sheeting. Their durability, cost-effectiveness, and fitness for purpose have been responsible for their continued use. Appearance, too, has played a part in their survival, particularly in the case of thatching. This centuries-old craft, using straw or reeds as a roof covering, is much appreciated for its charm and character. Although its use has been restricted in the past (it was banned in London in 1212 as a fire hazard), thatch is now enjoying a revival. Thatching follows regional styles and needs to be undertaken by a skilled thatcher experienced in the appropriate local traditions.

Steep-pitched plain-tiled roof c.1911

Beautifully crafted thatched roof

Weathered terracotta pantiles complement the old stone walls

Thick natural-stone roof slates

Roof pitch

The type of covering must be suitable for the pitch of the roof, which is determined by the exposure of the site and the local weather conditions.

The pitch of tiled and slate roofs depends on the size and overlap of the individual tiles or slates. Small plain tiles or slates are typically pitched at 40 to 45 degrees, though they can be used on steeper slopes and even on vertical surfaces. Roofs covered with large slates or profiled single-lap tiles need a pitch of no more than 30 degrees. Thatch needs a steeper angle (at least 50 degrees), so that it will shed rainwater quickly.

Flat roofs or ones with a shallow pitch require a continuous covering, such as metal or asphalt.

Double-lap coverings

Shingles, slates and plain tiles are known as double-lap coverings. They are laid in 'broken-bond' courses – staggered so that, with a slate roof, for example, the vertical joints between slates are centred over the slates in the row below. As a result, the 'head' of each slate is partly overlapped by the two courses above. In this way, the nail fixings are covered and the gaps between the exposed parts of the slates are always backed up by a whole slate, thus rendering the covering waterproof.

Double-lap roof coverings are fairly expensive, since a lot of material is involved and installing them is labour-intensive, particularly if the roof shape is complex.

HEAD LAP · SIDE LAP

Double-lap covering

HEAD LAP · SIDE LAP

Single-lap covering

Single-lap coverings

Single-lap roof coverings are made of specially shaped tiles. The profile of each tile is designed to overlap or interlock at the sides to stop rainwater penetrating the vertical joints. Some tiles are made to interlock at the head and tail in order to provide a barrier between the courses.

Each course only has to lap the one below, and in most cases the vertical joints are not staggered. Single-lap coverings are relatively quick to lay, compared with double-lap roofing.

Single-lap coverings were traditionally made of clay pantiles, but there are also modern types made of concrete and finished in various colours.

Spacing of battens determines lap

Lap and gauge

If double-lap and single-lap coverings are to perform properly, the head lap must fall within certain limits. The minimum lap dimensions that suppliers recommend depend on the size of the unit, the pitch of the roof and the degree of exposure.

The lap is adjusted by the spacing or 'gauge' of the battens to which the roof covering is fixed. With modern materials, the maximum specified gauge is usually given in the manufacturer's literature. The exposed part of the tile or slate is called the margin and is the same dimension as the gauge.

SAFETY

- Roof work is hazardous, so every care must be taken to ensure that safe working platforms are erected and barriers provided to prevent tools and materials falling or being knocked off the work area.
- For routine repair work, use a stable scaffold tower and a roof ladder – a special lightweight ladder that hooks over the ridge.
- For major work, have full scaffolding erected by an independent installer. Roofing contractors are required by law to provide safe working platforms and will either put up scaffolding themselves or arrange for it to be erected by a scaffolding firm.

THATCHED ROOFS

THE COTTAGE OR FARMHOUSE *with a thatched roof is one of the most enduring images of our countryside. Indeed, Britain probably has the greatest concentration of thatched buildings anywhere in the world: an estimated 50,000, half of which are listed buildings. Until the end of the Middle Ages, nearly all smaller houses were thatched. But the use of thatch gradually declined with the growth of industrialization and the increasing availability of other building materials, such as slate, brought about by cheap transport. Thatch is usually made from straw or water reed, though in parts of Britain other materials, such as heather and bracken, are used. Being an organic material, it is truly sustainable.*

One of the most enduring images of the English countryside

CHOOSING THATCH

When repairing thatch, the first problem is deciding which type to use. Over the centuries a house may have been thatched with a variety of different materials, which can make the decision difficult.

Your local planning authority may well have a policy concerning which type of thatch is appropriate, and if your building is listed or in a conservation area you may need consent to change from one type of thatch to another. It is therefore important to speak to their Conservation Officer at the outset, not least because the lower layers of thatch – which can date back hundreds of years – may provide valuable historical information, such as medieval smoke blackening on the underside of the thatch. Consent may also be required for any change in the external appearance of the roof or a change to another material.

Types of thatch

The three main types of thatch all consist of plant stems laid sloping downwards, towards the outer edge of the thatch. Water is therefore shed from the surface of the roof as quickly and directly as possible, minimizing the rotting process to which all thatch is eventually prone. The overall pitch of the roof, the pitch of the stems and the design of the roof should work together to achieve this end.

Water reed is a wetland plant. By the nineteenth century it was being used in Norfolk, the Fens, parts of south Dorset, and some other areas. Nowadays a lot of water reed is imported.

Combed wheat reed is a variety of thatching straw, sometimes grown specially for thatching. The straw is combed mechanically to remove the grain and other waste material without crushing the stems.

Long straw was at one time the commonest form of thatching in most parts of England. As with combed wheat reed the basic material is wheat straw, but long straw retains the heads and butts.

With some materials, patching is a viable option

ROOF VENTILATION

MANY PERIOD HOUSES *are made of porous materials that tend to absorb more moisture than modern building materials do. It is therefore important that the whole building is allowed to 'breathe', so the moisture can evaporate. A crucial part of this process occurs within the roof space, where moisture can easily accumulate – which is why ventilation is an important characteristic of traditionally detailed tile and slate roofs. In modern times, the performance of many roofs has been compromised by the use of inappropriate roofing felts and by badly placed insulation. Until recently most roofing felt was impervious – but over the past few years vapour-permeable membranes have been introduced, which help disperse moisture.*

REPAIRING THATCH

Recognizing when rethatching is essential and judging whether to repair or replace are not easy decisions and require an expert inspection from a master thatcher. To find one in your area, contact the Thatching Information Service.

Your thatcher will be able to assess how much of the top surface of the thatch has eroded. This tends be most evident at abutments with chimneys or gables. He or she will also be able to tell whether some of the thatch has slipped, determine the thickness of covering left over the fixings, and gauge the condition of the fixings and the tightness of the thatch.

Repair methods differ from one type of thatch to another. With long straw and combed wheat reed, successive coats are often added when the top layer wears down. With water reed, the thatch is usually taken back to the rafters.

Unlike water reed, straw thatches are often repaired by patching, rather than replacing the entire thatch. Patching particular areas in need of repair can substantially extend the life of the main coat.

In all cases, the ridge and the areas around chimneys, where the thatch tends to sink after a time, are the most vulnerable parts of the roof and are likely to require replacement sooner than the main coat (they usually need replacing every 15 to 20 years). Only when partial repairs become uneconomic should complete rethatching be considered. Endeavour to retain as much of the existing thatch as possible, while ensuring that the building remains watertight. It may be possible to extend the life of a thatched roof by reridging and redressing plus some localized repair work.

Thatching is a job for an expert

When the thatch does eventually need complete renewal, it is worth laying a fire-resistant barrier between the rafters – but be sure to provide a ventilated gap, in order to allow ventilation to the thatch. Also, consult your house insurers, as they may have specific guidelines to reduce the risk of fire.

Unlike other forms of roofing material, thatched roofs have wide eaves that shed water clear of the building, so gutters and downpipes are not required. However, it is important to provide adequate drainage, so that rainwater does not saturate the base of the walls.

ROOFING FELT

Roofing felt was first used in the 1930s, in the form of a thin building paper laid beneath the slates or tiles. It acted as a secondary barrier, to keep out wind-driven rain and snow. Not long after, bitumen and plastic felts were introduced. These types of roofing felt provide a high level of resistance to the passage of water vapour and constitute a cold contact surface upon which warm moist air can condense. In severe cases, this can cause decay to the roof rafters.

More modern roofing felts permit the passage of some water vapour. However, in order to install vapour-permeable felt, the roof needs to be stripped of its slates or tiles – so it is most conveniently fitted when the roof needs to be re-covered.

You can install proprietary roof ventilators that allow the passage of air between the overlapping sheets of underlay without intruding above the roofline. Ideally, the airflow should be from the top to the bottom of the roof, which may necessitate counterbattening. Ventilators that protrude above the roofline are not recommended for period houses.

INSULATING THE ROOF

The insulation of roof spaces started to become widespread in the 1970s. The placing of insulation within a roof space requires some careful thought. When it is laid just above the ceiling, it may make the roof space colder and increase the risk of condensation, particularly if there is no ventilation. Care also has to be taken to ensure that the insulation doesn't inhibit the passage of air at the eaves. If insulation installed between the rafters is next to an impervious roofing felt, condensation can make the insulation damp. Many modern insulation quilts retain moisture and do not dry out readily – which may cause decay to the tile battens and roof timbers.

As an alternative to the many types of manufactured roof insulation, you can use natural sheep's wool. If it is used in conjunction with a vapour-permeable felt, the risk of decay induced by condensation is thought to be significantly less.

To reduce the amount of water vapour in your home, consider providing mechanical ventilation, particularly in the kitchen and bathrooms.

TILED ROOFS

Glazed coloured profile tiles on a C20th hipped roof

CLAY TILES, *which have been in use for centuries, had their origins in the great civilizations of the East and the Mediterranean. The latter had the greater influence in the countries of Europe, and subsequently in their colonies.*

Until labour-saving mechanization was introduced in the nineteenth century, plain and profiled tiles were made by hand. Today there is a resurgence of interest in the qualities of the original materials – and, though they never completely died out, handmade tiles are once more available for those who can afford them.

PLAIN TILES

Plain tiles make up a double-lap covering that produces a pleasing overall texture similar to that of a slated roof. The colour, character and durability of clay tiles soon came to be appreciated, and they began to be used as a fireproof alternative in areas where thatched roofs had predominated.

The small size and overall regular pattern of the tiles, albeit with some variation due to their handmade nature, produced an attractive covering that mellowed with age. Plain tiles look equally at home on rural houses and barns and on sophisticated town houses.

Decorative tiled gable roof

Verge detail of swept valley

Handmade   Machine-made

Types of plain tile

Made from processed clay, plain tiles are mostly made to a standard size of 265mm (10½in) by 165mm (6½in) by 12mm (½in). These dimensions were established by Edward IV in the fifteenth century. Nowadays, larger plain tiles and specials are also available.

The tiles are simple rectangles moulded with a slight curve or 'camber' from head to tail. Early handmade tiles also had a cross-camber that gave the roof an attractive texture and a measure of ventilation, while shedding rainwater efficiently. Modern machine-made tiles are produced without a cross-camber, but it is still possible to obtain handmade cross-cambered clay tiles.

Fixing methods

Early handmade plain tiles were punctured with two holes close to the top edge or head, through which oak pegs were fitted. The pegs hooked over riven tiling battens, and the tiles were generally known as peg tiles **(1)**. Later versions had nibs of clay formed in the top edge **(2)**, although nail holes were provided for extra security in exposed situations. Sometimes the head laps were sealed on the inside with lime mortar known as 'torching'.

Tile-hung walls, for which ordinary or shaped plain tiles were often used **(3)**, also required nail fixings. In this case, every tile was twice-nailed, whereas in roof work it was usual only to nail the perimeter tiles at the eaves, verge and ridge and at every fourth course.

Shaped tiles

During the earlier part of the nineteenth century, shaped versions of the simple plain tile began to appear. These were used to create attractive repeat-pattern tile-hung walling as well as decorative roof coverings.

On walls, as with some ornamental roofs, shaped tiles were often laid with alternating courses of plain tiles or tiles of a different colour to produce interesting decorative treatments.

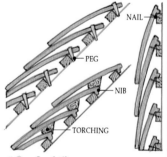

1 Peg-fixed tiles
2 Nibbed tiles with torching
3 Nail-fixed wall-hung tiles

Coloured tiles

Although red-toned tiles are the most common in many parts of the country, other colours, such as blues and beige, were produced from clays of different regions. These were sometimes combined to create diaper patterns or other polychrome designs. If you are fortunate to own such a feature, take reference photographs of it in case it should have to be stripped for renovation purposes in the future.

Decorative tile-hung walling

Hips and valleys

Tiled roofs have the benefit of specially shaped tiles for hips and valleys which are laid to bond neatly with each course. However, one of the most attractive features of a plain-tiled roof is the swept valley, where the tiles are cut to a tapered shape so the courses can be run round in a curve (1). A less expensive alternative is the laced valley, where the tiles are not cut but laid to butt up to wide tile-and-a-half tiles set diagonally (2). Although even a laced valley is quite costly to reproduce, it is worth the expense in order to preserve the style of an old tiled roof. Hire the services of a specialist roofing company familiar with historic craft practices to help maintain the roof's original features.

REPLACING TILES

Although clay tiles are very durable, they can fracture if struck or undue pressure is applied to them; and if they become porous, they may suffer frost damage. Also, it's inevitable that with time the nail fixings will fail.

Traditional peg-tiled roofs are unusual. Should the pegs break or perish, they can be replaced and the tiles refitted.

If nibbed tiles are broken, replacements can be hooked onto the tile battens. Use copper, aluminium-alloy or silicon-bronze roofing nails to fix those that can be nailed. Slide the tiles of the last course into position, while using wooden wedges to lift the course above. If the tiles do not have nibs, use a wire or sheet-metal hook (see FITTING A SLATE).

A modern fixing method for old roof coverings, involves spraying a foam onto the underside of the slates or tiles, where it sets into a hard layer. Much is claimed for these foams. They are said to improve insulation and weatherproofing, stop tiles or slates slipping and prevent condensation, but they can cause problems in old buildings. Since the tiling battens and the upper parts of the rafters are covered with foam, normal airflow into the roof space is restricted and rotting can occur. Also, you can't salvage the slates or tiles when you want to reroof the property.

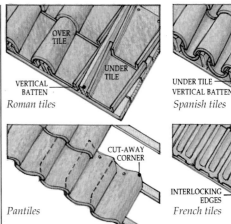

1 Swept valley

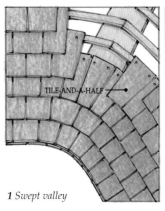
2 Laced valley

Use wooden wedges to lift the tiles

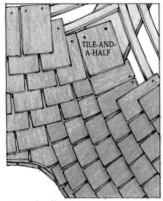

Roman tiles

VERTICAL BATTEN — OVER TILE — UNDER TILE

Spanish tiles

UNDER TILE — VERTICAL BATTEN — OVER TILE

Pantiles

CUT-AWAY CORNER

French tiles

INTERLOCKING EDGES

PROFILED TILES

Profiled tiles are single-lap coverings that are shaped to overlap or interlock with one another. The principal traditional types are Roman tiles, Spanish or mission tiles, pantiles, and French or Marseilles tiles. These coverings, which in most cases are laid in unbonded courses, produce a boldly textured roof.

Roman tiles

Roman-tiled roofs are made up of flat 'under tiles' and half-round barrel-shaped 'over tiles'. Most are tapered from head or tail so that they nest together along their side edges and between courses. The under tiles are nailed flat on tiling battens or close boarding, while the over tiles are nailed to vertical battens run between them.

Spanish tiles

Spanish or 'mission' tiles (so called because they were introduced into the southern states of America by Spanish missionaries) are similar in principle to the Roman type. The main difference is that the under tile of the Spanish type is concave. The under tiles are nailed sideways into the vertical battens on each side, and the over tiles are single-nailed to the top of the battens.

Pantiles

The pantile is a simpler variation of the Spanish tile, the trough of the under tile being combined with the curve of the over tile to produce an S-shaped profile. The opposite diagonal corners are cut away to allow

Multi-coloured Spanish tiles

the tiles to fit together in the same plane where the head and tail meet between courses. The tiles are located on tiling battens by a single wide nib at the head and are fixed with a single nail.

French tiles

The French tile is one of many machine-made interlocking tiles that became widely used in the early part of the twentieth century. It provides an efficient and visually pleasing roof covering that is fairly easy to install.

Most French tiles were a natural terracotta red, but some were coloured and glazed. They were hung on tile battens and rarely nailed, as their interlocking shape helped keep them in place.

SLATE ROOFS

Traditional slate roof laid in diminishing courses

SLATE ROOFING *provides a highly durable and relatively maintenance-free roof covering. This type of roofing uses naturally occurring fissile stone that can be converted into thin slabs or sheets.*

True slate – as opposed to the sedimentary limestone or sandstone slabs used in some regions – is a hard metamorphic rock formed from clay sediments. Due to immense pressure millions of years ago, it has a laminated structure that enables it to be readily split into sheets. This type of stone has been quarried or mined for centuries.

Smooth blue-grey slate from Wales is perhaps the best known, because with the advent of industrialization it was produced in great quantities and transported to all parts of the country and exported abroad. Its fine grain meant it could be split into thin, even thicknesses and mass-produced in uniform sizes, which made it particularly suitable for roofing the houses of the rapidly developing towns and cities.

As well as Welsh slate, there are many other types of regional slates, such as Collyweston, Horsham, Pennine and Delabole. Although the slate industry has diminished in recent times, natural slates are still available for renovation work if you are unable to reuse your own slates.

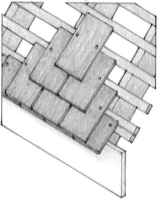

1 *Centre-nailed slates*

2 *Counterbattens on boarded roof*

SHAPED SLATES

After splitting, the edges of each slate are cropped to bring the slate to the finished length and width. This process is known as dressing. The dressed edge gives the characteristic bevelled finish to the face of natural-slate roofing. Slates were cut and dressed by hand but are now mostly machine-processed.

Most are cut to standard rectangular sizes, although sometimes the tail of the slate is shaped to form a decorative pattern when laid.

Slates that cannot readily be worked and thick stone slates are sold as 'random sizes' for thickness grading and sorting by the roofer. This type of roofing is laid with the largest slates at the eaves and the smallest at the ridge. As it takes skill to install, it is expensive.

COLOUR AND TEXTURE

The colour and texture of slate varies according to its origin. The surface of some slates is smooth; others have a distinct riven texture to the face. The colours can vary from cool greens, blues and greys to warmer purples and russet reds in a range of tones. Some are variegated, with stripes or mottled patterns, while others are plain. In most cases just one type of slate was used, giving a pleasing natural colour and texture to the roof. However, in the mid nineteenth century different-coloured slates were sometimes combined to create a decorative effect.

If you need to replace old slates, take a sample slate or fragment to a supplier of roofing materials to help you match the colour and size.

FIXING METHODS

Slate roofing is a double-lap covering laid in bonded courses. Usually each slate is fixed with two nails, though sometimes old stone slates were simply located on battens with wooden pegs.

The holes for the nails are punched through by hand or machine from the underside. This produces countersunk holes on the face of the slate in which the nailheads sit. Slates are sometimes head-nailed, but are more commonly centre-nailed to prevent them being lifted by the wind (1).

Slates may be fixed to battens or to close boarding. If the roof is boarded, the current practice is to lay roofing felt then fix vertical counterbattens up the slope of the roof to raise the horizontal battens clear of the surface (2). This allows any penetrating moisture to drain down freely.

Many old slate roofs were fixed with iron nails, though more durable copper nails were used on better-quality houses. Good slates will last for generations, but a slate roof covering can fail due to corroded fixings.

Whenever carrying out repairs, or if you have your roof re-covered, make sure stainless-steel or copper roofing nails are used. The nails should be 20mm (¾in) to 25mm (1in) longer than the thickness of the slate. Galvanized nails can be used for the battens. If the fixings perish but the slates are still in good condition, have the roof stripped and re-laid with the original slates rather than new ones.

1 Cut fixing nails

2 Nail strip to batten

3 Bend tail of strip

Perfectly matched group of slated buildings

REPAIRING A SLATE ROOF

Before tackling the work, you will need to find a supply of matching slates with which to make the repairs. If they are to function properly and look right, the thickness of the slates must be the same as that of the original. If they are too thick, the overlapping courses will not lie flat.

The overall size is less of a problem, because new slates are available in a wide variety of sizes. If individual slates are too large, you can cut them down to the required dimensions. The width should allow a gap of about 3mm (⅛in) between each vertical joint.

Removing a broken slate

Nail-fixed slate roofing is laid in such a way that each course covers the fixings of the course below. In order to remove an individual slate it is necessary to release the hidden fixing. This is done with a special tool called a slater's ripper.

Slide the end of the tool under the damaged slate and hook it onto one of the nails. Give the hilt of the handle a sharp tap with a hammer to cut or pull out the nail (1). Remove the second nail in the same way. If you aren't able to hire a slater's ripper, try cutting the nails with a hacksaw blade. You should now be able to pull the broken part of the slate free.

Fitting a slate

Cut a strip of lead about 25mm (1in) wide. The strip should be 50mm (2in) or so longer than the head lap of the roofing. Nail the strip to the slate-fixing battens or boarding between the slates of the course below, just clearing the head of the next course down (2). Slide the new slate into place and then bend the tail of the strip over the edge to form a hook (3).

Cutting to size

Provided it is not too thick, you can cut a slate to a smaller size. Hold it face down on a straight board, with the edge of the slate overhanging by the amount that is to be trimmed off. Use the edge of a bricklayer's trowel to chop off the waste, working towards you and using the edge of the board as a guide (4).

4 Cut slate with a trowel

ORNAMENTAL FEATURES

The roofs of many Victorian and Edwardian houses were embellished with decorative metal cresting and terracotta ridge tiles and finials. Unfortunately, as a result of poor maintenance, many of these are now missing – but you can buy suitable replicas from roofing-tile manufacturers.

For any major repairs to an ornamental cresting, call in a roofing company. If you are used to working at heights, you may be able to fix loose ridge tiles yourself. First, lift off the loose tiles and chisel off the weak old mortar. Mix a bedding mortar of 1 part lime, 1 part

Lay mortar carefully in bands

cement and 6 parts sand. Lay a band of mortar on each side of the ridge and at each end. Carefully set the tiles into the mortar and bed them down. Remove excess mortar with a trowel, taking care not to smear the roof tiles or slates.

Decorative terracotta ridge tiles and finials

METAL ROOFS

LEAD AND COPPER SHEETING *have been used as roof coverings for generations. Both metals are soft, malleable and highly durable, and were principally used for important public buildings.*

In the domestic context, lead was most commonly used for covering roofs, doorhoods and porch or balcony canopies where other traditional coverings were unsuitable because of the pitch or shape of the roof. Lead sheeting is manufactured by a rolling or casting process. Cast lead is considered to be the best, but is more expensive than rolled-sheet lead.

TYPES OF METAL ROOFING

Metal expands and contracts with changes in temperature. To overcome movement problems, sheet roofing is made up from panels of metal. Where the panels meet on vertical edges, they are joined by weathertight rolled or flat seams; on horizontal edges, they are joined by lapped or drip joints. In both cases, the joints are formed by hand.

Sheet iron began to be used for roofing in the eighteenth century. Corrugated iron, patented in England in the early nineteenth century, was in common use for commercial buildings by the middle of the century. It was also used for colonial domestic buildings and outhouses.

Lightweight tin-plate roofing was in use in the eighteenth century, and became popular in the United States towards the end of the nineteenth century with the introduction of interlocking embossed machine-made tin-plate tiles.

FLASHINGS

Flashings are used to weatherproof the junctions between the roof covering and wall abutments, chimneys, or other elements that interrupt the roof surface. These junctions, which may be either mortar fillets or strips of metal, are often the most vulnerable part of the roof. They therefore require regular inspection, and prompt attention if repairs are needed. Metal flashings are superior and mostly made *in situ* to suit the type of roof covering. If they are beyond repair, get a specialist to replicate the original pattern.

Double-lap covering

The abutment flashings for double-lap coverings, such as tiles, slates or shingles, are made up with 'soakers' and stepped cover flashing **(1)**. Soakers are thin sheets of metal that are turned up at right angles and fitted under each tile. The top edge generally hooks over the head of the tile to keep the soaker securely in place.

The step flashing is made from a 150mm (6in) strip of lead, no more than 1.5m (5ft) long. This is cut into a stepped shape to follow the pitch of the roof and is tucked into the mortar joints. Lead wedges are used to fix the flashing, and the joints are then pointed with mortar.

Single-lap covering

Flashings for single-lap coverings, such as profiled tiles, are made without soakers. A wide step-and-cover flashing is used instead, the extra width being formed into the contour of the roofing **(2)**.

MAINTAINING METAL ROOFING

In time all metal roofing deteriorates, mainly due to fatigue or chemical action. The latter may occur as a result of atmospheric pollution or contact with corrosive substances in other materials or in organic matter. Corrosion can also take place when dissimilar metals are used together (for example, when copper sheeting is fixed with iron nails). It is therefore advisable to use compatible materials – such as copper nails for fixing copper or lead sheeting, and galvanized fixings for galvanized iron.

Repairs to lead and copper sheeting require the services of a metal-roofing specialist. Pinholes in lead caused by corrosion can be patch-repaired; so can splits caused by thermal movement. It is not usually necessary to have the entire covering stripped and replaced. Splits can be welded successfully using oxyacetylene (known as lead burning); or a patch of matching material can be let in using the same technique.

Lead burning allows the repair to expand and contract at the same rate. Stringent fire precautions must be followed when this process is being used.

Mastics and repair tapes are rarely successful, even as a temporary repair, and can make a permanent repair to metal roofing more difficult.

Always keep flat roofs free from debris and build-up of mosses – both can reduce water flow, and the latter causes corrosion. If organic growth is a persistent problem on a lead roof, apply a chemical treatment available from builders' merchants. Copper will not sustain organic growth. Wear soft shoes when walking over a flat roof, and take care not to damage the surface when brushing or scraping the surface of the covering.

Iron-based roof coverings will rust if the protective galvanizing or tin plating breaks down, so keep them well painted to prolong their working life.

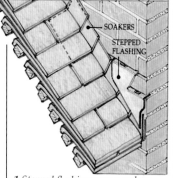

1 Stepped flashing covers soakers

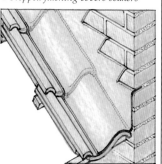

2 Step-and-cover single-lap flashing

CHIMNEY FLASHING

A flashing round a chimney is more complex than other roof flashings, as it has to be waterproof on four sides. This is done with an apron flashing at the front **(1)**, step flashing at the sides **(2)**, and a back gutter at the rear **(3)**.

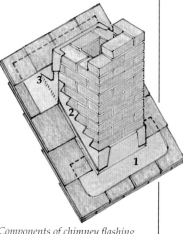

Components of chimney flashing

CHAPTER EIGHT

CHIMNEYS

Before chimneys existed *the smoke from fires simply escaped through a central covered hole in the roof. Funnel-shaped hoods of lime-plastered timber were used in houses when fireplaces began to be sited against walls. Eventually the hood evolved into the brick or stone chimney, either built onto the outside of the wall or projecting inside the room to form a chimney breast. In some houses the centrally placed fire continued with the introduction of massive brick or stone fireplaces, either single or back-to-back, that divided the house.*

The chimney became an important feature of domestic architecture from early medieval times, when the roofs of houses were graced with magnificent moulded-brick examples. But by the early eighteenth century the imposing chimney stack had lost its importance, thanks to the influence of classical architectural styles. The chimney, along with the low-pitched roof, was now set back and hidden or masked by the parapet of the symmetrical façade. Whereas formerly chimneys had been built separately, although often set in groups, they were now combined into a relatively plain rectangular mass of brick or stone. However, the reintroduction of steeply pitched roofs and decorative chimneys, along with the vogue for fancy terracotta chimney pots, gave added interest to the rooflines of Victorian houses.

Simple well-proportioned stone chimney

Imposing pair of brick-built chimneys with decorative coursing

CHIMNEY STYLES

CHIMNEYS *are generally constructed of brick, although stone was used for grand houses and in areas where it was a common local material. In most cases, the only visible part of a chimney is the chimney stack protruding from the roof. However, some chimneys show as imposing monoliths, rising majestically on the outside of the house.*

Stone chimneys are usually built of smooth ashlar (dressed-stone) blocks, although rusticated and rubble stone with ashlar quoins are also used. More often than not, the upper part is moulded in the manner of a plain column; or sometimes the top is castellated.

Brick chimneys, like stone ones, may be square, octagonal, rectangular or round in plan, although the brick types tend to be more ornamental. The Victorian revival movements produced some impressive decorative structures based on Tudor models. The flanks of towering brick-built chimneys were often relieved by recessed brick panels and brick strapwork, while oversailing courses added decorative relief at the top. If this was not enough, coloured-brickwork patterns were sometimes included, too.

Castellated dressed-stone stacks

Decorative brickwork chimney

CHIMNEY CONSTRUCTION

Single-storey dwellings require only a simple chimney. In early country houses this took the form of a massive fireplace with a proportionally large straight flue. The chimneys of houses with more than one floor were more complex. The plan of Georgian and Victorian town houses had the fireplaces of individual rooms built against the side walls so the flues could be grouped into single chimney structures.

The interior masonry of each chimney was corbelled or 'gathered over' above the fireplace to form a funnel shape leading into the flue. In order for the flue of the lower fireplace to circumvent the fireplace in the room above, it had to be bent to one side. Although theoretically a long straight flue is the most efficient, it was found that the bend stopped rain falling on the

fire. It was also, erroneously, believed that bends reduced down draughts. Even flues that had no need to avoid obstacles above were therefore built with bends, too.

Where the flues converged in the chimney stack, they were separated by brick or stone divisions known as withes or midfeathers. The insides of the flues were 'pargeted' or rendered with a 12mm (½in) lining of mortar. This helped to seal each flue and make a smoother passage for the smoke.

At the point where the chimney stack emerged through the roof, a fillet of mortar or a dressed-lead flashing provided a waterproof seal around the base. The top of the stack may be finished with shaped brickwork or stone, or each flue may terminate with a chimney pot bedded in an angled fillet of mortar known as a flaunching.

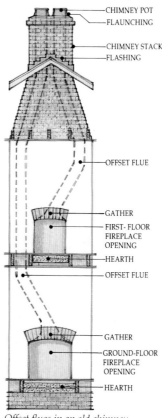

CHIMNEY POT
FLAUNCHING
CHIMNEY STACK
FLASHING
OFFSET FLUE
GATHER
FIRST-FLOOR FIREPLACE OPENING
HEARTH
OFFSET FLUE
GATHER
GROUND-FLOOR FIREPLACE OPENING
HEARTH

Offset flues in an old chimney

CHIMNEY REPAIRS

Because of their exposed position, chimneys are particularly susceptible to the effects of wind, rain and frost – including exfoliated stonework or brickwork, eroded pointing, cracked flaunching, damaged pots and perished flashing.

They are also susceptible to sulphate attack from inside. Water vapour, given off as a by-product of burning fuel, condenses on the cooler upper regions of the flue and combines with other products of the combustion process to form sulphuric acid and other corrosive chemicals. These acids cause masonry, mortar joints and pargeting to decay.

In some cases the condensation is concentrated on the windward side of the flue, resulting in uneven erosion of the lining and mortar joints – which makes the chimney lean in the direction of the prevailing wind. Repointing may arrest the problem, or it may be possible to stabilize the structure by reinforcing it with a concrete liner. Failing this, the chimney can be rebuilt, using the original masonry plus a new liner – which is often the best solution.

Acid attack also causes erosion of the withes, leading to cracks in the structure or bulging, or poor draught due to leakage between the flues.

Erosion of masonry

Badly exfoliated bricks or stone blocks may have to be cut out and replaced. Try to match the original material, and point new brickwork in the appropriate style. If you have difficulty finding suitable replacement material, use a colour-matched mortar to fill the surface (see REPAIRING DEFECTIVE STONE).

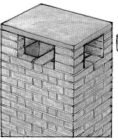

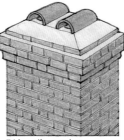

Wire binding   *Stone-slab capping*   *Ridge-tile capping*

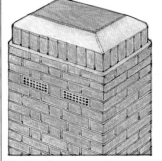

Flush roofing-slate capping   *Terracotta chimney-pot inserts*

CHIMNEY POTS

CHIMNEY POTS *generally started to transform the appearance of chimneys in the eighteenth century, although earlier examples existed. However, a wide range of decorative patterns did not become available until the nineteenth century. Made of terracotta, an unglazed fired clay that has excellent durability and resistance to heat, they were used to improve the efficiency of the chimney.*

You can still buy chimney pots made using traditional methods and patterns. The shapes are produced either by hand on a potter's wheel or by pressing kneaded clay into plaster moulds. The moulding is removed while the clay is still workable, then finished by hand and left to dry out before being fired in a kiln.

CHIMNEY POT REPAIRS

Although terracotta is fairly durable, it can decay (especially if underfired in manufacture) and, being relatively brittle, it cracks quite easily. However, it is worth trying to preserve old chimney pots, even on a chimney that is disused.

Chimney pots are surprisingly large when seen close up, and need careful handling. Although it may be feasible to carry out repairs *in situ*, it is often safer to remove the pot from the stack and either work on it on a securely constructed scaffold platform or lower the pot by rope to the ground.

Cracks in brickwork

Differential settlement or erosion of the mortar joints may result in cracks opening up in the stack. Where these follow the joints, they can be raked out and repointed. If the bricks themselves are cracked, have them replaced.

Small brick-built chimneys that have suffered cracking can be reinforced by binding them with stainless-steel wire. This entails raking out the horizontal joints around the upper part of the chimney in order to receive the wire, which is then discreetly hidden with new pointing.

If the old lime mortar is badly perished and the brickwork is in a poor state, you may have to have the chimney rebuilt. Should that be necessary, it is important that the original details are recorded before the stack is dismantled, so they can be reproduced. Have reusable bricks re-laid, preferably with the weathered face showing, using a 1:2:9 mortar mix of sulphate-resistant cement, lime and sand. Use a 1:1:6 mix for the flaunching around replaced chimney pots and the top edges of oversailing courses.

Damp chimneys

Since chimneys are open to the elements, rain is able to enter them. When the chimney is in use, the heat from the fire normally keeps the system relatively dry. So, to some extent, does the through draught when the fire is not alight.

A stone slab set on brick piers is a traditional form of capping for a large working stack that provides ventilation when the chimney is not in use. Disused chimneys should be capped in a way that prevents the ingress of water while allowing ventilation. Half-round ridge tiles bedded in mortar can be used. Where the chimney would look better with a flush top, roofing slates can be mortared in place and an airbrick built into opposite sides of the stack to provide the necessary ventilation. A variety of terracotta tops and hood inserts are available that provide ventilated covering for chimney pots.

In all cases, air must be allowed to enter at fireplace level to provide a through draught. If the fireplace opening has been sealed off, fit a vent in the form of an airbrick or grille.

Repairing cracks

Fix cracks with a two-part epoxy-resin adhesive. Reinforce the repair by binding the pot with fine stainless-steel wire. Twist the ends of the wire together with pliers to tighten it, and fold the twisted end back against the face. Position the wire to lie in a groove or under a bead to disguise its presence.

Weathered pots

You may be able to prolong the life of a decaying pot by refitting it so the eroded side faces in a sheltered direction. If it has to be replaced, try to match the style and colour. Architectural-salvage firms generally have a variety of pots in stock, and you may be lucky enough to find one that is naturally weathered.

Otherwise, try a company that sells new pots; or if you are really dedicated, have a replica made to order.

Fitting pots

Chimney pots must be well seated and securely fitted. The method will depend on the size of the pot and the shape of the base. Tall pots should be set into the top courses of the brickwork, to make them less vulnerable to high winds. The top of the stack is then finished with a mortar flaunching sloped to shed water. Although short pots are very often set in the flaunching, they are better built into the brickwork, too.

Terminals and inserts

A selection of terminals and inserts is available today, mostly in terracotta or metal. They are designed to assist performance or prevent rainwater entering the flue. Bird guards are available, too.

When fitting a pot or an insert, check with the supplier that the design won't restrict flow of smoke from the flue.

FLUE LINERS

I F A FLUE IS INEFFICIENT, *that can lead to erosion of the mortar joints, causing potentially dangerous fumes and tars to escape. It also boosts the build-up of soot and so increases the risk of fire.*

All new chimneys now have to be built with a flue lining to protect the masonry from harmful flue gases. The lining is usually made of refractory concrete or impervious clay. It has long been realized that a flue lining improves the flow of combustion gases, and it was not uncommon for old flues to be pargeted (lined) with lime-mortar as the chimney was erected. However, many were not lined at all.

A modern flue liner can replace perished pargeting in an old flue, reduce the size of the flue in order to make it more efficient, or add stability to a frail chimney structure. A specialist installer will advise you about the most suitable and cost-effective type of liner.

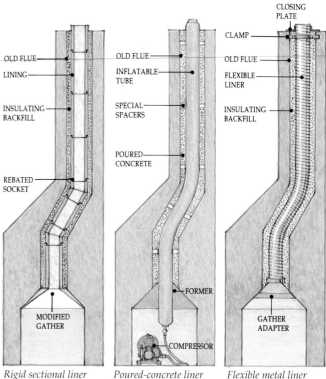

Rigid sectional liner   *Poured-concrete liner*   *Flexible metal liner*

RIGID SECTIONAL LINERS

This type of liner, which may be made of ceramic, lightweight pumice or refractory concrete, is well established because of its durability and is commonly used for new installations. It is suitable for all types of fuel.

Manufactured in short round or square lengths of various sizes, these liners are installed in sections, which are then mortared together. Ideal for straight flues, they can be adapted to offset ones either by cutting the ends to an angle or using standard elbow sections. Usually the meeting edges of the parts simply interlock, the rebated socket always being placed uppermost, but some types have a locating collar too.

The chimney pot has to be removed in order to reline a flue using this method. Also, holes have to be made at key points in the chimney wall, particularly at bends, in order to gain access to the flue. For a straight chimney this may only be at the bottom of the flue, where a support is needed for the liner and insulating backfill.

The sections are lowered down the flue from the top of the chimney. The top joint of each piece is coated with mortar to receive the next section as it is lowered down the flue. Once the openings have been rebuilt, the void around the new liners is usually backfilled with lightweight concrete – although this is not always needed, as sectional liners have good insulation properties. The chimney pot and capping are finished in the normal way.

POURED CONCRETE

This fairly recent innovation for lining old chimneys uses a lightweight concrete that is pumped into the flue around an inflatable tube. The concrete is specially formulated to provide a fire-resistant insulative lining that seals the old brickwork while re-inforcing the structure.

First of all, the contractors will clean and inspect the chimney. Where bends are located, an opening is made so the former can be centred using special spacers. The toughened-rubber former is passed down the flue and inflated to suit the size of the appliance or fireplace. Then, after all the openings have been sealed, the concrete mix is pumped into the chimney from the top to fill the void around the tube.

When the mix has set, the former is removed, leaving a smooth, efficient cylindrical flue that can be used for all types of fuel. Once installed, it is virtually permanent. It is a good lining for single flues but may not be suitable for a multi-flued system, as the dividing masonry may be too weak to bear the weight of the poured concrete.

FLEXIBLE METAL LINERS

Of the three basic kinds of chimney lining, flexible stainless-steel liners are the simplest to install. The best of these is the spirally wound double-skinned type. Made of austenitic stainless steel, which is particularly resistant to corrosion as well as heat, it has a smooth inner surface and can be used for appliances that burn coal, wood, oil or gas, as well as for open fires. Made as a continuous length, it can be fitted easily to both straight and offset chimneys.

A rope, which is passed down the flue, is attached to the liner by a nose cone. The liner is then fed down the chimney and carefully pulled through from below. The bottom end is sealed and secured into a flue-pipe adaptor, for connecting to an appliance, or a gather-type adaptor (a funnel-shaped hood) for an open fire. At the top of the chimney, the liner is cut to length and fitted with a clamp and a closing plate, after backfilling the old flue with a lightweight insulation such as perlite or vermiculite. The closing plate is finished with a cement mortar flaunching, into which a chimney pot may be set. Gas boilers require an approved flue terminal, which can be set inside the chimney pot.

Single-skin flexible steel liners are usually designed for use with gas-fired boilers or room heaters only. They should never be used with solid-fuel or wood-burning fires or stoves.

CHAPTER NINE

DOORS

THE FRONT DOOR OF A HOUSE *is much more than a means of entry or a barrier against intrusion. The porch or doorway becomes the focus of attention as visitors approach the house, and the door itself creates a first impression of the building and its occupants. And while the visitor waits to be admitted, there's time to admire the decorative mouldings and ornamental glass or fine metalwork of the door and its surround.*

The front door is usually designed to impress and is singled out for special treatment. This may take the form of nothing more than a bold splash of colour in an otherwise plain façade. More often, even in comparatively modest houses, a great deal of money is lavished on embellishing the door and its surround.

Imposing columns and canopies, classically inspired pediments, and elaborate hoods and porches have all been used at one time or another to enhance the visual impact of the main entrance. To 'modernize' or remove such important features detracts from the character of a house and will probably reduce its monetary value as well.

Although interior doors are generally less ostentatious, they make an equally valuable contribution to the character of a building. Yet it is disturbingly common to find that they have been ruined or superficially disfigured by ill-advised attempts to modernize the décor. Fortunately, however, doors are sturdy pieces of joinery that are rarely prone to serious deterioration and they are relatively easy to repair.

Sturdy solid-oak door

Georgian taste and elegance

Victorian brick-built doorway

It is difficult to imagine a more impressive approach to any house

Exquisite Edwardian door and window

BATTENED DOORS

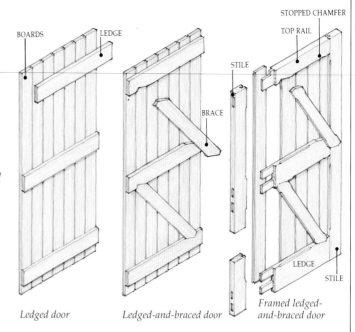

Ledged door   Ledged-and-braced door   *Framed ledged-and-braced door*

T HE BATTENED DOOR *dates from the Middle Ages, but the design is so practical that it has been employed in one form or another, especially in country houses and cottages, right up to the present day. Battened doors were fitted in internal as well as external doorways; at first oak and other hardwoods were used, but many of the later doors were made from softwoods.*

As more sophisticated designs became fashionable, a battened front door was sometimes relegated to the rear entrance of the house or cut down to fit an attic or cellar doorway. Consequently, some battened doors have been in continuous use for centuries.

LEDGED DOORS

The simplest and earliest type of battened door was made from vertical boards approximately 18 to 30mm (¾ to 1¼in) thick, nailed to three horizontal rails known as ledges.

Stronger doors, primarily for the main entrance of a house, were sometimes made with an internal skin of horizontal boards instead of the three ledges.

LEDGED-AND-BRACED DOORS

In the nineteenth century the construction of battened doors was improved by the addition of wooden braces, to prevent sagging. To be effective, a brace must run diagonally downwards towards the hinged edge of the door. Preferably, each end of the brace should be notched into the ledges and secured with a nail.

FRAMED LEDGED-AND-BRACED DOORS

An even more sophisticated form of construction was used for better-quality work, the facing boards being surrounded on three sides by substantial framing, so as to present a flush surface on the outside. The top rail is joined to the vertical stiles with haunched mortise-and-tenon joints, and the stiles and rail are rebated or grooved on the inner edges to hold the boards. Two ledges run behind the boards and are joined to the stiles with pairs of barefaced mortise-and-tenon joints. The braces, as on the simpler versions of the door, run diagonally downwards towards the hinged edge of the door. As a decorative feature, stopped chamfers were sometimes planed on the inside of the frame and along the ledges and braces.

BOARD JOINTS

On early battened doors square-edged vertical boards were simply butted together, the joints being covered on the outside with strips of wood to keep out draughts (**1**). Alternatively, the boards could be rebated to create weatherproof joints (**2**).

The Industrial Revolution was responsible for the introduction of machine-cut tongue-and-groove joints. Tongue-and-groove boards had both edges chamfered to form a V-joint (**3**), or a bead (**4**) was cut along one edge of the board. These details were designed to mask the effects of shrinkage, which could result in unsightly gaps opening up between the boards.

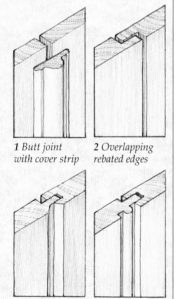

1 Butt joint with cover strip   *2 Overlapping rebated edges*

3 Tongue-and-groove joint   *4 Beaded edge disguises joint*

This battened door is a comfortable partner for a weathered-stone wall

PANELLED DOORS

P ANELLED DOORS, *constructed in a similar way to the wooden wall panelling of the time, were made, in relatively small numbers, as early as the sixteenth century. However, it took a further two hundred years for the style to gain widespread acceptance.*

By the middle of the eighteenth century the panelled door had become commonplace – and, although from time to time whims of fashion have resulted in changes in its appearance, its basic construction has remained unaltered to the present day.

C18th fielded-panel door

Typically simple Georgian door

An impressive combination of bevelled-glass lights and bolection mouldings

PANEL ARRANGEMENTS
The basic design comprises a frame of rails, stiles and muntins infilled with thin panels of solid wood. The classic Georgian front door had six rectangular panels (1), although various arrangements of five or seven panels were also used by Georgian architects.

Most Victorian doors, especially interior ones, were of the four-panel type (2) still widely used today. Panels were sometimes arched (3) or circular (4), in which case they were usually surrounded by heavy wooden mouldings.

After the First World War panelled doors became simpler in appearance, and there was a tendency to dispense with mouldings in favour of solid-wood or plywood panels (5).

1 Six-panel

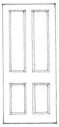
2 Four-panel

3 Arched

4 Circular

5 Plywood

Victorian studded entrance door

Panelled door of the 1920s or 1930s

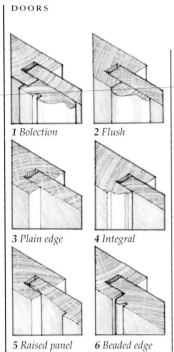

1 Bolection   *2 Flush*

3 Plain edge   *4 Integral*

5 Raised panel   *6 Beaded edge*

MOULDINGS AND PANELS

The joints between panels and the surrounding frame were masked with planted (separate) mouldings. These are nailed to the frame, never to the panels, and are always mitred at the corners.

Bolection mouldings were planted mouldings rebated to cover the edge of the frame **(1)** and disguise the effects of shrinkage. Flush mould-ings **(2)** that do not project beyond the face of the frame were also popular, especially for internal doors. The inside face of a door for a minor bedroom or for a cupboard was frequently left plain, without any mouldings **(3)**. Other doors were made with integral mouldings cut on the inside of the frame members **(4)**.

Door panels are usually flat on both sides, but some-times, particularly in the Georgian period, raised-and-fielded panels **(5)** were used. On entrance doors, the bottom panels were often made to be flush with the frame and were edged with a small bead moulding **(6)**. These relatively thick panels were stronger than the raised-and-fielded type and tended to shed rainwater more efficiently.

Springing hinges
Badly fitted hinges prevent the door closing properly.
● Fit correct-size screws (page 84).
● Pack out hinge leaf (page 84).

Creaking hinges
Hinges often creak loudly when dry or under strain.
● Apply oil (page 83).
■ Realign hinges (page 83).

Loose hinges
A door will drop if hinge screws work loose or knuckle joints wear.
● Renew screw fixings (page 82).
■ Swap hinges (page 83).

Bowed mouldings
Mouldings can bow because of uneven shrinkage, creating unsightly gaps.
● Renail mouldings (page 85).
■ Replace mouldings (page 85).

Wet rot
If rainwater can run under the door, the wood around the end grain rots.
● Treat with timber preservative (page 114).
■ Fit weatherboard (page 85).

Components of a panelled door
1 Stile
2 Top rail
3 Bottom rail
4 Lock rail
5 Frieze rail
6 Muntins
7 Mortise-and-tenon joint
8 Wedges
9 Panel
10 Groove
11 Moulding

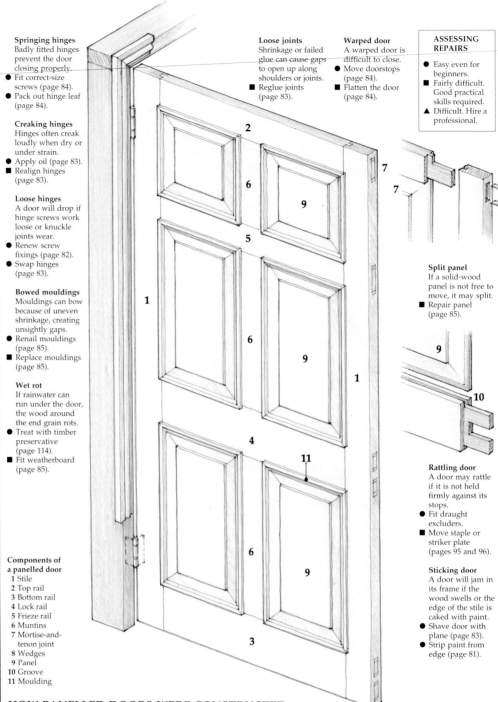

Loose joints
Shrinkage or failed glue can cause gaps to open up along shoulders or joints.
■ Reglue joints (page 83).

Warped door
A warped door is difficult to close.
● Move doorstops (page 84).
■ Flatten the door (page 84).

ASSESSING REPAIRS
● Easy even for beginners.
■ Fairly difficult. Good practical skills required.
▲ Difficult. Hire a professional.

Split panel
If a solid-wood panel is not free to move, it may split.
■ Repair panel (page 85).

Rattling door
A door may rattle if it is not held firmly against its stops.
● Fit draught excluders.
■ Move staple or striker plate (pages 95 and 96).

Sticking door
A door will jam in its frame if the wood swells or the edge of the stile is caked with paint.
● Shave door with plane (page 83).
● Strip paint from edge (page 81).

HOW PANELLED DOORS WERE CONSTRUCTED

Hardwoods such as oak and mahogany have been used at various times for making panelled doors. But they are more often constructed from softwood, which is almost invariably painted.

A typical panelled door has a vertical stile **(1)** on each side. The one that is hinged is known as the hanging stile, the other as the closing or lock stile.

Between the stiles are the top rail **(2)**, bottom rail **(3)** and middle or lock rail **(4)**. The fourth rail of a six-panel door is known as the frieze rail **(5)**. Running down the centre of the door are vert-ical muntins **(6)**.

The frame is constructed using mortise-and-tenon joints **(7)** throughout, and those that pass right through the stiles are secured with

wedges from outside **(8)**. The panels **(9)** are held loosely in grooves **(10)** cut along the inside edges of all the frame members. In order to avoid splitting when the wood shrinks, the panels are not glued or fixed in any way.

On most types of panelled door, mouldings **(11)** are used to cover the joints around the panels. They also disguise any shrinkage.

GLAZED DOORS

HE FANLIGHT *above the front door that became a delightful feature of Georgian architecture was designed to admit light to the hall. For the same reason, narrow windows were sometimes incorporated in the surround. But only rarely, if ever, was the front door itself glazed, although the two upper panels were sometimes subsequently replaced with glass.*

DECORATIVE GLASS PANELS

From Victorian times, glass panels became widely used for all sorts of doors and were especially popular for entrance doors, where acid-etched or stained glass could be employed to impressive decorative effect.

Glazing was generally restricted to the upper half of the door. Often it took the form of a single large panel; but sometimes several small panes were used, divided by wooden glazing bars. A common alternative was to insert glass instead of wood in one of the conventional door-panel arrangements.

Traditional battened doors were never glazed, but many of the country-style 'revival' houses that were popular after the First World War have a small rectangular or diamond-shape window placed centrally in the upper half of battened doors.

SAFE GLASS FOR DOORS

Before modern safety standards were introduced, doors were glazed using whatever thickness of glass suited the glazier or the client. However, for greater safety, if you have to replace glass in a door, you should comply with British Standards recommendations. (This does not mean you are obliged to replace old glass that is still intact – for example, when you remove a panel from a door in order to carry out extensive repairs to the woodwork.)

Provided that there is more than one pane of glass in the door or a single pane does not take up the greater part of the door's area, you can install ordinary (annealed) glass, which must be at least 6mm (¼in) thick. However, this stipulation regarding thickness does not apply to leaded lights, because even a large leaded window is constructed from relatively small pieces of glass held in a lead or copper lattice – and the lattice tends to buckle under impact, which reduces the risk of injury from shattered glass.

Recommendations regarding fully glazed doors are particularly stringent, and you may have to fit toughened glass. For more detailed advice, contact the Glass and Glazing Federation.

Glazed cottage door with side lights

Edwardian glazed entrance door

Glazed lobby doors admit light to a Victorian hallway

Glazed doors frequently incorporate painted lights

FLUSH DOORS

A GREAT MANY OLD HOUSES *have been spoilt by replacing original panelled doors with modern plywood or hardboard flush doors. But, thankfully, thoughtless vandalism of that kind is no longer encouraged and, apart from more modern uses, flush doors are now considered appropriate only for some of the flats and houses built in the 1920s and 1930s.*

When they made their first appearance, flush doors were considered extremely smart and fitted perfectly with fashionably stark Art Deco styling. The cheaper, plywood-faced doors were painted, but flush doors were also frequently finished with hardwood veneer.

HOW PANELLED DOORS WERE CONSTRUCTED

Earlier flush doors were often made by gluing strips of solid wood together **(1)** then applying a plywood sheet **(2)** to each face. Hardwood lipping **(3)** along the edges protected the surface veneer from damage.

Framed flush doors

Framed flush doors were developed in order to reduce the overall weight. The outer frame comprises softwood top **(1)** and bottom **(2)** rails joined to vertical stiles **(3)**. Narrow regularly spaced intermediate rails **(4)** form

the core, with heavier blocks of wood **(5)** inserted at strategic points in order to accommodate a mortise lock and, in the case of external doors, a letter plate. A plywood skin **(6)** on each side adds rigidity to the door. Slots **(7)** cut across the intermediate rails ventilate the core, to prevent changes of atmospheric pressure bowing the plywood skins, and disperse moisture-laden air. As on the earlier flush doors, hardwood lipping **(8)** protects the plywood veneer from wear and tear.

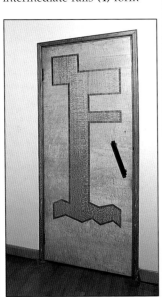

Veneered flush door from the 1930s

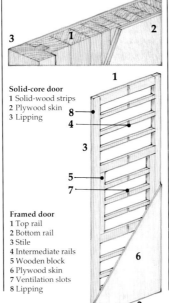

Solid-core door
1 Solid-wood strips
2 Plywood skin
3 Lipping

Framed door
1 Top rail
2 Bottom rail
3 Stile
4 Intermediate rails
5 Wooden block
6 Plywood skin
7 Ventilation slots
8 Lipping

HOW DOORS WERE FITTED

T RADITIONALLY THE DOOR OPENING *was lined with a wooden frame, within which the door was hung. Although the structure of the wall itself varied considerably, the construction of door linings was generally consistent.*

INTERNAL DOORS

The lining of an internal door opening is known as the casing. It comprises two vertical jambs **(1)** joined by barefaced housings to the soffit **(2)**, which runs across the top of the opening. The door hangs from one of the jambs. Sometimes the casing was rebated to create a doorstop, but more often the doorstop took the form of separate strips of wood nailed to the jambs and soffit **(3)**. An architrave **(4)** was nailed all round to cover the joints between the casing and the wall.

Door-casing components
1 Jamb
2 Soffit
3 Doorstop
4 Architrave

Architrave details

Victorian architraves usually take the form of tapered mouldings that extend down to the floor on each side of the door and are mitred at the top corners. The skirting boards butt against this type of moulding.

Frequently late-Georgian doorways were graced by fluted rectangular-section architraves. These had separate decorated square blocks nailed into the top corners. Skirting blocks were fitted each side of the door to finish the foot.

Wide door casings

Wide framed casings were used to line door openings in thick internal walls.

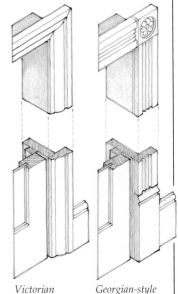

Victorian architrave   *Georgian-style architrave*

STRIPPING DOORS

EXTERNAL DOORS

Door-surround designs vary enormously, but in principle an external door was hung from a substantial wooden frame comprising a head **(1)** across the top, a post **(2)** on each side and, sometimes, a wooden threshold **(3)** at the bottom. A transom **(4)** was included if there was a fanlight above the door. The posts and head or transom were usually rebated to form a doorstop **(5)**. If the wooden threshold was omitted, a metal dowel was sometimes used to attach the bottom end of each post to the stone doorstep.

Usually, the frame was fixed to the surrounding structure by nailing through the posts into strips of wood or plugs built into the wall. Alternatively, bent metal lugs **(6)** screwed to the outside of the frame were bedded in mortar joints as the wall was being built. Like window frames, doorframes were often fitted in a recess built in the surrounding masonry.

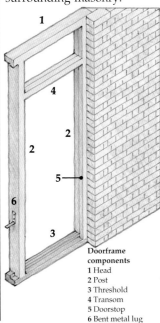

Doorframe components
1 Head
2 Post
3 Threshold
4 Transom
5 Doorstop
6 Bent metal lug

ATTRACTIVE DETAILS *such as mouldings and carving are often obscured by layers of old paint. Clumsy application can also spoil the appearance of woodwork, leaving unsightly runs and sagging paint. You may have to consider stripping the old paint and starting again – but stop and think before you go ahead. Sometimes, as well as destroying the door's character, stripping the paint will erase a record of all the finishes that have been applied since the house was built. And it is a mistake to imagine that stripped pine looks authentic, because most was painted from the outset. In some rare cases, you may require consent to remove historic paint from a listed building – so, before proceeding, speak to a Conservation Officer.*

Although this section focuses on doors, most of the information is relevant to stripping other items of woodwork, too. For industrial stripping, they need to be portable and small enough to be immersed in a tank.

USING HEAT TO STRIP PAINT

Burning the paint off with a blowlamp or propane torch used to be the normal way to strip wood, but apart from a few professional decorators hardly anyone uses this method today. Unless you are fairly experienced, it is easy to scorch areas of woodwork and there is always the risk of causing a fire. Also, blowlamps vaporize the lead contained in old paints, so you could find yourself breathing toxic fumes. A modern electric hot-air stripper is not only safer, it is also easier to handle and there is less risk of scorching. Although these strippers will lift paint while operating at a relatively low temperature, you should still wear a respirator when burning off old paint.

Hold the nozzle of a hot-air stripper about 50mm (2in) from the surface, and move it from side to side until the paint begins to blister. As soon as it does so, remove the softened paint with a flat scraper, or with a shavehook if you are stripping a moulding **(1)**. When working on a door, it is usually best to strip mouldings first then the flat areas. If you use a hot-air stripper close to a window, fit a heat deflector to avoid cracking the glass **(2)**.

If you plan to repaint a door, there's no need to extract the specks of paint trapped in the pores of the wood. Just rub down the stripped wood lightly with a medium-grade abrasive paper, then redecorate. If you intend to use a clear finish, however, remove the residue of paint with small balls of fine wire wool dipped in chemical stripper. Rub the wood in the direction of the grain only, then wash the surface with white spirit or water to neutralize the stripper.

STRIPPING WITH CHEMICALS

Chemical strippers soften old paint until it is liquid enough to be scraped and washed from the surface. Thick gel-like strippers are

1 Strip mouldings with a shavehook

2 Protect glass with a heat deflector

ideal for doors, because they are stiff enough to cling to vertical surfaces. The average chemical stripper will dissolve old oil-based and modern resin-based paints, but there are also specific varnish strippers that are formulated to remove tough polyurethane varnishes.

Chemical strippers are potentially hazardous, so they must be handled with caution and the maker's recommendations observed very carefully. Wear vinyl gloves and protect your eyes with safety spectacles or goggles. Many strippers emit unpleasant fumes – it is therefore essential to ventilate the area in which you are working and wear a face mask. Never smoke in the vicinity, and keep pets and children away from all chemical strippers. If you splash stripper on your skin, wash it immediately with plenty of cold water. If it gets in your eyes, rinse them thoroughly under running water and seek medical advice without delay.

CURING MINOR DOOR PROBLEMS

Safer all-purpose strippers have been developed that are fume-free and will not burn your skin, although they may take a little longer to soften the paint. Read the manufacturer's instructions before you buy one, to make sure it is not one of the more common caustic strippers.

Using chemical strippers
The procedure described below will serve as a guide to using chemical strippers safely and efficiently, but always follow the detailed recommendations supplied by the manufacturer.

Lay a polyethylene dust sheet under the door, then brush on a liberal coat of stripper. Stipple the gel into mouldings to make sure all surfaces are covered. Leave it for 10 to 15 minutes, then scrape a small section to see if the paint is soft enough to remove easily. If the paint is still resistant, apply more stripper – but this time stipple it onto the whole area, so the chemicals come into contact with all the still-unsoftened paint.

Five minutes later, scrape off the paint and wrap up the scraped-off paint in newspaper. Dispose of it carefully at a toxic-waste disposal point at your local council rubbish dump.

Unless the wood is oak, use wire-wool balls dipped in fresh stripper to remove stubborn patches of paint and clean up mouldings. For oak, use coarse sacking since wire wool can stain the wood and detract from its appearance.

Finally, wash the surface with water or white spirit, depending on the maker's recommendations. Allow the wood to dry thoroughly before rubbing down and repainting.

INDUSTRIAL STRIPPING
Most people derive great satisfaction from stripping paint from a beautiful door and revealing the natural wood beneath. But faced with the prospect of having to strip perhaps half a dozen doors, many people turn to industrial stripping.

The cheapest method involves dipping the door in a tank of hot caustic stripper, which then has to be washed off by hosing the wood with water. The combination of heat and water can be detrimental and, although most doors emerge from the process relatively unscathed, occasionally solid-wood panels split, joints open up, and mouldings distort.

Another drawback is that hot dipping always raises the grain, leaving a furry surface that has to be rubbed down with abrasive paper before you can proceed to refinish the wood.

To avoid most of these problems, you need to go to a company that dips wood in cold chemicals only. Cold dipping does not discolour the wood and it is ready for refinishing after 24 hours, whereas after hot dipping it may not be ready for weeks. With cold chemicals the grain may be raised slightly, but you are unlikely to be faced with the worst side effects of hot dipping. The only disadvantage is that, because the chemicals are expensive, you have to pay more for cold dipping.

Most firms will collect a door and deliver it back to you after stripping. If you're having a front door stripped, same-day service is essential. Never submit a veneered door to industrial stripping unless the company can guarantee that the veneers will not delaminate.

SOME DOORS *have to be shouldered open, others catch on the floor or doorframe whenever you use them. These irritating problems can occur for a number of reasons, so you need to check the door carefully to determine the appropriate course of action.*

CURING LOOSE HINGES
If the screws holding the top hinge work loose, the door sags and its top corner binds against the frame. Open the door partially and lift it by the closing stile. If you can see the hinge moving, examine it more closely.

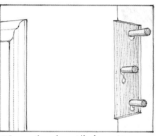

1 Leave dowels until glue sets

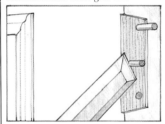

2 Then pare them flush with a chisel

Tightening loose screws
If the screw heads are protruding, try tightening them with a screwdriver; and if that's successful, check whether the screws in the other hinges need to be tightened, too.

You may find the screws are loose because repetitive movement has caused the screw threads to tear the wood and lose their grip. If the door has a substantial frame or the screws have worked loose from the door itself, it may be possible to substitute longer screws of the same gauge.

However, the jambs of most interior doorframes are too thin for this solution to work. In which case,

remove the screws and fold the hinge out of the way. Use a sharp knife to shape softwood strips into tapered dowels that will fit the screw holes. Glue the dowels and tap them into the holes. Leave them untrimmed **(1)** until the glue sets, then cut them off and pare them flush with a chisel **(2)**. Finally, fold the hinge back, then drill pilot holes for the screws and replace them.

Swapping worn hinges
The hinges may be screwed firmly in place, yet when you lift the closing stile you may still be able to detect movement. This is probably due to wear on the hinge pins and knuckles. Since the weight of the door puts uneven strain on the top and bottom hinges, it is sometimes possible to correct the fault by simply swapping the top and bottom hinges, thus reversing the wear on the pins.

REMOVING THICK PAINT
If the closing stile binds regularly against the frame, along its entire length, it is probably due to a build-up of paint over the years. If you are planning to strip the door entirely for some other reason, the problem will be solved in the process. Otherwise, use a hook scraper to remove paint from the edge of the door.

REPAIRING LOOSE JOINTS

Wood shrinks considerably during very dry hot spells, then swells again when wet weather returns. This movement can break down the glue in the joints of a door. If the mortise-and-tenon joints of a panelled door work loose and the securing wedges fall out, the joints can gradually open up until the door is fractionally too wide for its opening.

Check carefully for gaps along the shoulders of the joints (they may have been filled in the past). If necessary, strip the paint around the joints and rake out any debris lodged between the shoulders. Chop out any wedges that remain in through mortise-and-tenon joints. Inject PVA woodworking glue between the shoulders and into the ends of the joints (**1**). Tap the joints home, using a mallet and protective softwood block (**2**), or hire a large sash cramp to pull them together. Glue and insert overlength hardwood wedges, tapping them in with a hammer (**3**). When the glue has set, trim the wedges flush with a chisel.

If a door is made with stopped mortise-and-tenon joints, it may be impossible to inject sufficient glue between the shoulders to secure the joints. Having closed the glued joints with a cramp, insert a locking dowel (**4**) and trim it flush when the glue has set.

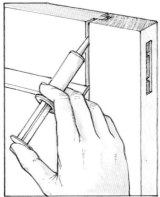
1 Inject glue into the joint

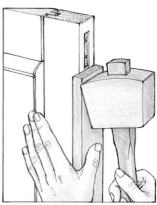
2 Tap the joint home with a mallet

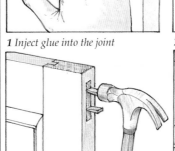
3 Glue and insert hardwood wedges

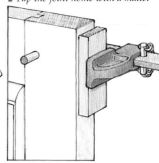
4 Secure stopped tenon with a dowel

CREAKING AND RATTLING DOORS

Most people find creaking doors annoying, and doors that rattle with the slightest draught can be positively infuriating to live with. As well as removing a source of constant irritation, it pays to rectify these relatively minor faults before wear on the door furniture increases.

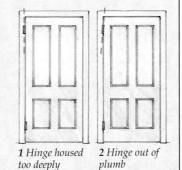
1 Hinge housed too deeply *2 Hinge out of plumb*

Stopping a door creaking

In most cases a creaking door can be cured with a drop of oil on the hinges. Place the oil on the top of the hinge pins, then swing the door gently back and forth so the lubricant works down into the hinge.

Occasionally, oiling fails to silence the creaking. In which case, examine both hinges carefully to see if their pins are out of line with each other. Use strips of thin card to pack out a hinge housed too deeply in the wood (**1**). To align a hinge pin that is out of plumb (**2**), pare the bottom of the hinge housing with a chisel.

Stopping a door rattling

The easiest way to cure a rattling door is to stick soft-plastic or foam draught-excluding strips to the doorstops. If fitting draught-excluding material would make the door difficult to close, you can prise off the stops and reposition them closer to the door. Alternatively, move the striker plate of the lock slightly so the latch fits snugly (see LOCKS).

DEALING WITH EXPANSION

If a door only sticks during humid weather or after a lot of rain, the cause of the problem is probably the swelling of the wood. The answer is to trim the edge of the closing stile while the weather is still wet. Don't wait for dry weather to return, or the door will shrink and you won't be able to judge how much wood to remove.

Take the door off its hinges and support it on edge, with the closing stile uppermost. Remove the latch or lock, and trim the edge of the door with a plane. You may find that it is necessary to adjust the fit of the lock when you replace it.

STOPPING A DOOR CATCHING

People often fit rising butt hinges (which lift the door as it swings open) to stop a door catching on an uneven floor or thick carpet. However, there are other causes that can make the bottom of a door catch – and other solutions worth considering before you go to the expense of fitting new hinges.

Detecting a loose bottom hinge

When a door normally opens and closes smoothly, you may well not suspect that it has a loose bottom hinge. However, once the door swings past a certain point, a loose bottom hinge tends to dislocate, allowing the bottom of the door to drag on the floor.

Check whether the screws are loose or the bottom hinge is worn – and if necessary, either tighten the screws or swap or replace the hinge (see opposite page).

Adjusting the bottom hinge

If the bottom edge of a door is jamming on a bump in the floor, you can sometimes overcome the problem by adjusting the position of the lowest hinge.

First, open the door and remove the screws from the hinge leaf fixed to the frame.

Move the leaf sideways, away from the doorstop, so that the hinge pin projects slightly further from the frame than the pin of the hinge above does. Replace the screws to hold the hinge in its new position. To prevent the door creaking, you may have to adjust the top hinge slightly, so that both hinge pins are at the same angle.

Trimming the bottom

You may have no option but to trim the bottom of a door that is catching, especially if it is already fitted with rising butt hinges.

Professional carpet layers use a special power saw with a horizontally mounted circular blade that can trim a specified amount off a door *in situ*. However, in order to do the job yourself, you will have to take the door off its hinges and either plane the bottom edge or trim it with an ordinary circular saw.

You can use a sharp bench plane, with the door held in the vice jaws of a folding workbench – but

there is a lot less effort with a portable power planer. Whichever type of plane you use, work from both ends towards the middle, to avoid splitting the end grain.

Trimming the top

You may find that a door fitted with rising butt hinges scrapes the frame above as it opens. To provide the necessary clearance, plane a shallow bevel on the corner of the door.

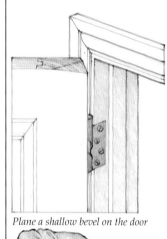

Plane a shallow bevel on the door

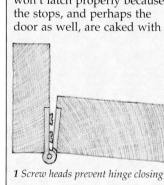

Support a door with a folding bench

ENSURING A DOOR CLOSES PROPERLY

You should be able to close a door without having to apply force. There are several problems that can make a door keep springing open, but they are mostly fairly easy to resolve.

Relieving springing hinges

A door that resists closing just before it latches is most probably 'hingebound'. As a result, it tends to spring open again as you release pressure against it. If that is happening, check whether the hinges are being levered out of their housings by the act of pressing on the door.

It may be that projecting screw heads are stopping the leaves of the hinges closing properly **(1)**. Try driving the screws home; or if someone has inserted screws that are too large, swap them for ones with smaller heads that nestle flush with each leaf.

Inaccurately fitted hinges are another possible cause. If one or more of the leaves have been housed too deeply in the wood **(2)**, unscrew them and place strips of thin card behind each hinge to pack it out flush.

If both the hinges appear to have been fitted correctly, try scraping or stripping any thick paint from the edge of the hanging stile and, if need be, from the doorframe too.

Easing tight doorstops

You may find that a door won't latch properly because the stops, and perhaps the door as well, are caked with

layers of paint. If scraping the closing face of the stops fails to cure the problem, strip the frame and, if need be, the door itself.

Firm draught-excluding strips sometimes prevent a door closing properly. In which case, either substitute soft-plastic or foam strips or move the doorstops slightly to accommodate the existing draught excluders.

Flattening a warped door

Temperature variation on each side of a door can dry the timber unevenly. As a result, the door may twist or warp so that it will no longer rest against its stops without being forced shut. Leaving a door to dry in the sun after industrial stripping can also cause warping.

Strip the paint from the warped door and soak both sides with water. To reverse the effects of warping, place the door on the floor with a block of wood under one corner then load the door with heavy weights. After 24 hours remove the block, but leave the weights in place for a similar period.

A much simpler, though less satisfactory, solution is to move the doorstops to accommodate the warping.

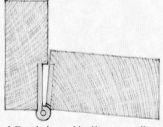

1 Screw heads prevent hinge closing   *2 Deeply housed leaf has same effect*

REPAIRING DOORS

R EPAIRING THE FABRIC OF A DOOR *often requires considerable exertion and skill, but the high cost of an authentic replacement or acceptable replica more than compensates for the effort involved.*

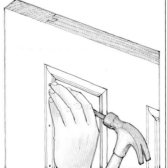

CORRECTING BOWED MOULDINGS
When the mouldings on a panelled door bow, unsightly gaps are left between the mouldings and the stiles, rails and muntins **(1)**.

To get rid of the gaps, nail the mouldings back against the framework, working from the middle of each length of moulding. Drive the nailheads below the surface with a nail set **(2)** and fill the holes before redecorating.

With luck, the mitre joints at the corners of each panel will close up as you renail the mouldings. If the mouldings have shrunk, leaving open mitres, you can buy replacement mouldings from a DIY store or builders' merchant. Alternatively, if you want something special, choose a moulding from the catalogue of a specialist joinery supplier or ask a joiner to make a replica of the original.

1 Bowed mouldings leave ugly gaps

2 Sink nailheads with a nail set

Settlement can distort a doorframe

REPLACING A WEATHERBOARD

Moulded weatherboards are frequently fixed to external doors to shed rainwater away from the threshold. A drip groove machined along the underside of the weatherboard prevents water running back to the base of the door and rotting the wood.

In the past, many a householder found it expedient to discard a damaged or rotted weatherboard rather than repair or replace it. But nowadays you can purchase stock weatherboard mouldings from many builders' merchants and timber suppliers.

Measure the width of the opening between the doorstops and cut the weatherboard moulding to this length. Plane the end near the latch side of the door to a slight angle, so that it clears the stop when the door swings open **(1)**.

To make a weatherproof seal between the moulding and the door, paint the back of the weatherboard with a thick coat of primer. While the paint is still wet, screw the weatherboard to the door **(2)**. Fill or plug the screw holes, then prime and paint the moulding.

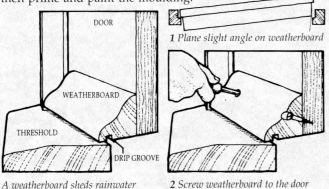

DOOR

1 Plane slight angle on weatherboard

WEATHERBOARD

THRESHOLD

DRIP GROOVE

A weatherboard sheds rainwater

2 Screw weatherboard to the door

REPAIRING SPLIT PANELS
If a solid-wood door panel has been fixed inadvertently with nails or glue, there's a chance that it will split if the wood shrinks. Incompetent industrial paint stripping can also cause splitting. You may be able to reglue a split panel *in situ* (see REPAIRING PANELLING). If not, you will have to dismantle the door to remove and repair the panel. Having chopped out any securing wedges, steam the door joints with a kettle to soften the glue. Then tap them apart with a hammer, using a block of softwood to protect the components from damage.

Fixed door panels tend to split

FILLING AN UNEVEN GAP
One characteristic indication of building settlement is the distortion of doorframes, resulting in a tapering gap between the top of the door and the head or soffit. If the settlement is recent, consult a professional who will be able to advise you on whether there's subsidence that requires remedial action (see PROFESSIONAL HELP).

However, an old house may have settled years ago then restabilized, albeit in a less-than-perfect condition. In which case, the simplest solution is to cut a softwood wedge to fill the gap and screw it to the top of the door. Plane the wedge flush with the door before painting.

DEALING WITH WET ROT
Doors are less susceptible than windows to wet rot attack. However, if a door is neglected and its finish is allowed to deteriorate, water can penetrate and soften the fibres, especially around areas of end grain.

For methods of treating wet rot, see DEALING WITH ROTTED WINDOWS.

REPLACING DOORS

WHATEVER *the cost of repair or maintenance, it pays to do everything you can to retain the doors that were installed when the house was built. They were made to fit openings that almost certainly do not conform to modern notions of standardization and they are, of course, authentic in style.*

However, not everyone holds the same opinion. For example, it was once fashionable to install a brand-new front door in the mistaken belief that it would increase the value of a property; and panelled doors, which were considered old-fashioned, were frequently replaced with mass-produced flush doors. As a result, many home owners are now faced with the task of reinstating old doors in order to restore the character of the building.

With luck, you may be be able to buy an old door from a local architectural-salvage company exactly like

one that once hung in your home, but the further afield you have to search the less chance there is of obtaining a perfect match. Alternatively, you may be able to find a similar door and plane or cut it to fit the opening, though there is a limit to the amount of wood you can remove without weakening the structure of the door or spoiling its proportions.

Another option is to buy a modern reproduction door, but it is extremely difficult to find a mass-produced door that is entirely suitable for an old house. However, there are joinery companies that specialize in making doors to order, using traditional methods and authentic styles, including external doors, interior room doors and a variety of doors with glazed panels. Although custom-made doors are relatively expensive, they are usually made to the highest standards.

REMOVING AN OLD DOOR

First, secure the door in an open position by driving a wedge under it **(1)**. If the doorframe is painted, uncover the screw heads that hold the hinges to the frame by scraping off the paint. It is important to dig out paint clogging screw slots before you attempt to turn the screws. Place a corner of a screwdriver tip at one end of each slot and tap the screwdriver sideways with a hammer to cut out the paint **(2)**. With the tip in position, tap the end of the handle with the hammer to break the paint seal around the screw head, then extract the screw. Remove all but one screw from each hinge, then get an assistant to support the door while you extract the last screws.

If a screw slot becomes so badly damaged that it is impossible to engage it with the blade of a screwdriver, drill out the head in stages, using progressively larger bits. Lift off the hinge and remove the remains of the screw by turning its shank with a plier wrench.

1 Drive a wedge under the door

2 Clear slots with a screwdriver

HANGING A NEW DOOR

New doors are sometimes supplied with extended stiles, known as horns, to ensure that the corners are not damaged during transportation. You need to saw off the horns before fitting the door in its opening.

A custom-made door may need nothing more than a light trimming with a plane, but other doors may have to

Saw the horns off a new door

be cut down with a saw in order to obtain a perfect fit. Ideally, there should be a 3mm (⅛in) clearance at the top and sides of a door, and a gap of at least 6mm (¼in) at the bottom. A gap of up to 12mm (½in) may be needed to accommodate a thick carpet. When planing the top or bottom of a door, always plane inwards towards the middle, to avoid splitting the end grain.

Mark the position of the hinges on the door, using the existing housings in the doorframe as a guide. Cut hinge housings in the door (see HINGES).

Hang the door with a single screw holding each hinge to the doorframe, and check the swing and fit of the door. Make any adjustments that may be needed, then insert the other screws. Finally, fit the lock and other hardware (see DOOR FURNITURE).

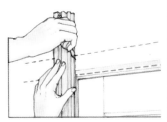

1 Draw alongside each component

2 Mark the positions of the mitres

REPLACING ARCHITRAVES

Replacing *door or window architraves that are damaged or unsightly is a very straightforward procedure. Standard architrave mouldings in softwood can be purchased from DIY stores and timber merchants. If you need to obtain a more elaborate or wider-than-average moulding, choose one from the stock of a specialist joinery supplier. A good joinery supplier will also make a replica of a moulding for you.*

1 Mark the height of the architrave

2 Mark the length of the top member

**REMOVING
AN ARCHITRAVE**

To remove a damaged architrave, drive a bolster chisel behind each piece until you can lever it off with a claw hammer. Pull out any nails left in the frame or casing.

Picture rails and skirting boards often butt against an architrave. If the new architrave is wider than the one you are replacing, trim the ends of the picture rail or skirting with a tenon saw. If you are unable to saw a skirting board *in situ*, you will need to lever it off the wall (see SKIRTING REPAIRS).

**INSTALLING
AN ARCHITRAVE**

Hold an upright in position about 6mm (¼in) from the face of the jamb. Mark its length with a pencil, allowing for the width of the top member and 6mm (¼in) clearance **(1)**. Cut a 45-degree mitre on the marked line; then, using a spirit level to keep the upright vertical, nail it to the casing every 300mm (1ft) or so with 50mm (2in) lost-head nails. Don't drive the nails all the way home at this stage, in case you have to move the architrave. Install the second upright using the same procedure.

Rest the top member upside down on the ends of the uprights and mark its length **(2)**. Cut a mitre at each end and nail the moulding between the uprights **(3)**. Drive a nail through the edge of the top member into the

mitre joints at each end **(4)**. Drive all nailheads below the surface, then fill the holes and joints before painting; if you plan to varnish the wood, use a coloured wood filler instead.

Composite architrave as seen below

**Fitting an architrave
to an out-of-square frame**

If your doorway is not quite square, 45-degree mitre joints will not fit snugly. Instead, hold each component in position against the wall and draw a pencil line against each edge where the joints will occur **(1)**. Mark the mitres where the lines cross **(2)**, then transfer these points onto the architrave members. Cut the mitres and fit the components as described left.

Wide decorative door architraves embellish a Victorian hallway

3 Nail the moulding to the casing

4 Drive a nail into the mitre joint

DOORCASES & DOORHOODS

MEDIEVAL BUILDERS *began the practice of setting dripstone mouldings into the masonry above doors and windows in order to divert rainwater to each side of the opening, where it could drip harmlessly to the ground.*

By the beginning of the eighteenth century the dripstone above the front door had been superseded by a cantilevered hood beneath which visitors could shelter while waiting to be admitted. But eventually practicality took second place to aesthetic considerations, and special emphasis was given to the front door by surrounding it completely with a decorative wooden doorcase. By Georgian times the demands of the shipbuilding industry had made oak a scarce commodity for the building trade. As a result, all but the earliest hoods and doorcases were made from imported softwoods.

Wooden doorcases are often extremely elaborate, mimicking styles originally intended for stonework. The restoration of masonry and stucco surrounds is described elsewhere in this book; only wooden hoods and doorcases are included here.

DOORHOODS

A doorhood consists of a wooden frame, often with a deep moulded edge, supported on two stout beams projecting from the wall. The exposed part of each beam was typically carved into a decorative scroll, creating what appears to be a bracket on each side of the door.

The shallow sloping 'roof' of the hood had a sheet-lead covering which, in order to prevent rainwater running behind the hood, was formed into a flashing against the wall. The lead was folded over the edges of the hood to protect the timber. The door opening below the hood was usually surrounded by a relatively simple wooden architrave.

Later, the supporting wooden beams were concealed within the structure of the doorhood itself. As a result, the brackets became purely decorative and were frequently made from separate, deeply carved elements.

CONSOLES

Eventually, Georgian doorcase brackets evolved into vertical wooden consoles that appeared to support narrow cornices or pointed classical-style pediments above the door. Consoles were often elaborately carved and even pierced.

PILASTERS AND COLUMNS

Narrow pilasters, running from bracket to ground level on each side of the opening, were frequently used to give consoled doorcases an impression of strength and solidity. Pilasters were to become increasingly complex, often resembling fluted piers that appeared to support classically inspired pediments or entablatures. A pilaster of this sort might include a carved capital and a moulded base.

Some doorcases had semi-circular staved-timber columns constructed the same way as a barrel. On larger houses, the canopy above the front door might project sufficiently to form a shallow porch supported by freestanding columns. A second pair of semi-circular columns would usually flank the door opening itself.

When painted, doorcases constructed from separate wooden elements nailed together could be difficult to distinguish from genuine stone surrounds.

Carved brackets support a doorhood   *Vertical wooden consoles*

SUFFOLK HOUSE

Beautifully proportioned doorcase with fluted Ionic columns

REPAIRING DOORCASES

O N A SURPRISING NUMBER *of eighteenth-century houses, what looks like a stone door surround is in fact a wooden doorcase.*

Any wooden structure that has stood in the open for a couple of centuries is bound to have suffered to some extent from the effects of weathering. Usually, the greatest harm is inflicted by the ingress of water, which can in turn lead to wet rot. Damaged flashings allow rainwater to run behind hoods and canopies; open joints between a doorcase and the wall or between wooden components also provide routes for water to penetrate; and rising damp in masonry walls can saturate the timbers from behind.

Carved stone door surround   *C18th engaged wooden columns*

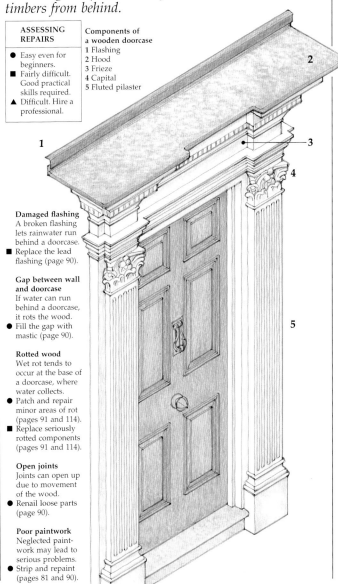

Freestanding staved columns support this substantial canopy

ASSESSING REPAIRS

● Easy even for beginners.
■ Fairly difficult. Good practical skills required.
▲ Difficult. Hire a professional.

Components of a wooden doorcase
1 Flashing
2 Hood
3 Frieze
4 Capital
5 Fluted pilaster

Damaged flashing
A broken flashing lets rainwater run behind a doorcase.
■ Replace the lead flashing (page 90).

Gap between wall and doorcase
If water can run behind a doorcase, it rots the wood.
● Fill the gap with mastic (page 90).

Rotted wood
Wet rot tends to occur at the base of a doorcase, where water collects.
● Patch and repair minor areas of rot (pages 91 and 114).
■ Replace seriously rotted components (pages 91 and 114).

Open joints
Joints can open up due to movement of the wood.
● Renail loose parts (page 90).

Poor paintwork
Neglected paint-work may lead to serious problems.
● Strip and repaint (pages 81 and 90).

REGULAR MAINTENANCE

If an old doorcase has survived unscathed, it has probably been maintained regularly throughout its life. If paintwork is beginning to flake, craze or crack, attend to it before it deteriorates further and lets in water to rot the timbers. Except for very minor blemishes that can be rubbed down then filled and repainted, you may have to strip the doorcase down to the bare wood – which will allow you to make good any defects and redecorate with a superior finish. However, there may be historic paint layers that are worth retaining, along with a beautiful old patina that is impossible to reproduce.

A partially stripped doorcase in the process of being restored

STRIPPING A DOORCASE

Most period doorcases are too elaborate to be stripped using a hot-air gun alone, so the only practicable solution is to use a chemical stripper. However, what looks like low-relief carving on panels, brackets and pilasters may in fact be moulded plaster, which could be damaged by the scrapers and wire wool used for removing softened paint from wood.

To be on the safe side, it's best to scrape a small area of paintwork with a very sharp blade. If you detect plaster below the paint, use the type of chemical stripper that is recommended for painted plaster ceilings.

Treating and painting the wood

Once you have exposed the wood, treat the whole doorcase with clear preservative in order to protect it from rot in the future. Then nail back any open joints or loose components. Before repainting the doorcase, sink the nailheads, using a nail set, and fill the holes.

WEATHERPROOFING A DOORCASE

Take whatever measures are required to prevent water saturating a wooden doorcase. Cure rising damp as a matter of priority, and if possible allow the doorcase to dry out thoroughly before further treatment.

Filling open joints

If nailing doesn't close up a joint satisfactorily, fill it with a flexible exterior wood filler before painting. Use flexible mastic to seal gaps between the doorcase and wall. You can buy it in cartridge form and inject it into the gap with a gun **(1)**, or as a strip sealant that you press into place with your fingers **(2)**.

Renewing the flashing

A doorhood or canopy has a sheet-lead covering, which is turned up against the wall. A strip of lead flashing is inserted in a mortar joint just above the canopy and bent down to cover the upstand, forming a weatherproof joint. It's common to see a damaged flashing replaced by a mortar fillet. However, over a period of time a fillet may shrink, leaving a gap between it and the wall. In the long run it therefore pays to renew the flashing.

Chop out the mortar joint to a depth of 25mm (1in) and remove any scraps of the old flashing that remain. Buy a strip of flashing lead 1.8mm (1/16in) thick from a builders' merchant. Use tinsnips to cut it to width so that it reaches from the canopy to the mortar joint, plus 25mm (1in).

Clamp the lead between two wooden battens, leaving a 25mm (1in) strip projecting **(1)**. Bend this over to form a right-angle lip and gently hammer it flat, using another batten to protect the lead **(2)**. Insert the lip in the mortar joint above the canopy and wedge it in place with small rolled strips of lead **(3)**. Use a soft hammer to tap the flashing against the upstand, shaping it to fit against the wall snugly. Finally, repoint the mortar joint.

Pointed pediments require stepped lead flashings that are best replaced by a skilled professional roofer.

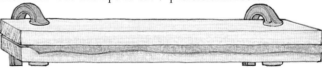

1 Clamp lead strip between battens

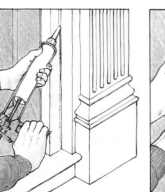

1 Inject mastic into the gap

2 Or introduce a strip sealant

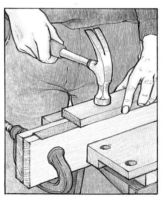

2 Hammer strip over to form a lip

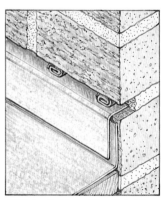

3 Wedge flashing with rolled strips

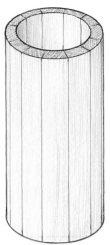

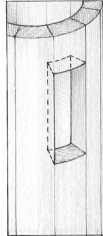

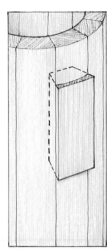

A wooden column is staved like a barrel

1 Cut a hole bevelled on all four sides

2 Tap an oversize plug into the hole

REPAIRING COLUMNS

Owing to their shape and construction, columns are particularly difficult to repair. Most of them are hollow, comprising a number of narrow strips of wood or staves with bevelled edges glued together then shaped on the outside. A staved column is fairly stable, but unless the joints are reinforced with splines they tend to open up as a result of glue failure or shrinkage.

Having supported a porch roof, it is possible to remove an entire column and close a reglued joint with heavy-duty strap cramps. However, this type of repair work is best left to a professional restorer who has the experience to judge whether clamping a joint is likely to create additional strains and splits in the column.

Filling a split column

A vertical split or gaping joint in a semi-circular doorcase column would be difficult to repair using the method described above, but provided the wood is relatively stable it is possible to fill a narrow gap with a sliver of softwood.

If necessary, open up the split with a power jigsaw. Shape the sliver with a sharp plane so that it will fill the gap. Plane a shallow bevel on both sides of the sliver to form a wedge, then glue it in place with waterproof exterior adhesive. Tap it home firmly with a hammer (but not too hard, or you may expand the column). Leave enough of the wedge projecting to plane once the glue has set, so that it will fit flush following the curve of the column.

Inserting a plug

An isolated patch of wet rot in a column can be cut out and replaced with a tapered plug of matching timber.

After drilling an insertion hole, insert the blade of a power jigsaw and cut out the rotted wood, leaving a rectangular hole bevelled on all four sides (1).

Make a plug of wood with the grain running vertically, shaping it so that it fits the hole but protrudes slightly from the column (2).

Apply waterproof exterior adhesive to the edges of the plug, then tap it into the hole with a hammer. Either use a strap cramp to hold the plug in place or nail it with long panel pins, driving them below the surface with a nail set. Once the glue has set, plane the plug to match the shape of the column.

TREATING WET ROT

Wet rot most frequently occurs near the end grain of timber, where water is able to penetrate more easily. It also often breaks out near the base of columns and pilasters, where water tends to collect. Check for wet rot by pressing the wood with the tip of a screwdriver. Rotted wood is soft and spongy when wet, and becomes dry and crumbly during warm weather.

To preserve, harden and fill areas of wet rot, see DEALING WITH ROTTED WINDOWS. Badly affected wood has to be cut out and replaced. Because a doorcase is an assembly of several pieces of wood, it is feasible to replace individual components with preservative-treated timber. It is also possible to splice wood onto a component to replace a short section of rotted timber.

Wooden columns constructed from narrow staves

REINSTATING DOORCASES AND COLUMNS

Don't be tempted to buy scaled-down mock-Georgian door surrounds designed to enhance modern town houses. A good specialist joiner is capable of making accurate replica doorcases and freestanding columns, using traditional materials and methods of construction. However, it is essential to employ a professional who is conversant with period proportion and detailing.

DOOR FURNITURE

DOOR FURNITURE *is the collective name used for hardware made for doors, both external and internal. Each piece of hardware is primarily functional – yet for the past 250 years or so, being specifically designed to enrich the main entrance and principal rooms of our homes, most door furniture has been extremely handsome. Attractive and sometimes costly materials were used for period door furniture, and as a rule it was expertly crafted and finished.*

Finding and renovating door furniture is perhaps one of the most pleasurable activities associated with restoring old houses. Antique hardware and good-quality reproductions are both widely available, and the level of skill required to fit, clean and finish just about any piece of door furniture is well within the capabilities of any householder with the slightest practical experience.

A pair of cast-iron knockers complements this ornate Victorian door

Suitably dignified brass fittings

Iron fittings are perfect for a cottage

CHOOSING DOOR FURNITURE

With such a wealth of products to choose from, it is not always easy to decide which is the right hardware for a particular door.

The heaviest (and usually most expensive) hardware was normally reserved for the main entrance of the house. However, one should always respect the age, style and character of a building and select the door furniture accordingly.

A country house with battened doors looks best with simple wrought-iron fittings, whereas a Victorian villa can take more elaborate cast-iron or brass door furniture without appearing overornamented. Similarly, it makes sense to reserve heavily ornate hardware for the principal rooms and install more modest fittings in what would perhaps have been the servants' quarters in earlier times.

You can learn a great deal about period styles from contemporary magazine advertisements and trade catalogues. However, it pays to exercise a little caution before replacing what at first sight appear to be historically inappropriate additions or modifications.

Whereas few would argue against replacing a 1950s plastic handle added to an Edwardian drawing-room door, it makes little sense to discard a good-quality Victorian mortise lock on an early-Georgian door simply because it is not 'authentic'.

Our predecessors were just as keen to improve their homes and take advantage of the latest advances in technology as we are – and, provided an item has been fitted properly, looks well and is still in working order, there's a great deal to be said for retaining it.

Authentic weathered door furniture

DOOR LATCHES AND HANDLES

When door handles, knobs and latches were replaced in the past, they frequently found their way into the second-hand market. As a result, it is possible to buy matching sets of original door knobs from architectural-salvage companies, market stalls, house-clearance sales and other antiques-trade outlets. And if you can't obtain an item of door furniture from any of these sources, there is a vast range of excellent reproduction hardware to choose from.

LATCHES

One of the earliest methods of keeping a door closed was with a short horizontal beam, pivoted at one end, that dropped onto a hook fixed to the doorframe. The beam, which in its crudest form was made from timber, would have been lifted by means of a length of string or leather thong that passed through a hole in the door to the outside.

More sophisticated latches based on the same principle were made in wrought iron by blacksmiths. The more successful versions were eventually mass-produced and are still to be found in manufacturers' catalogues. Handmade wrought latches that are perfect replicas of ones made by early blacksmiths can be obtained from specialist suppliers.

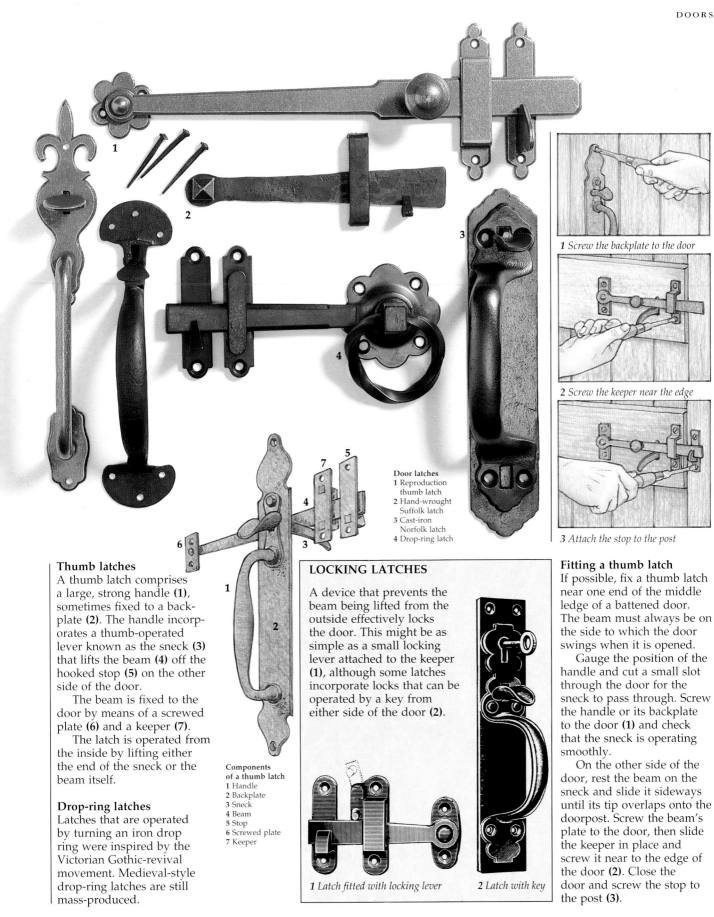

1 Screw the backplate to the door

2 Screw the keeper near the edge

3 Attach the stop to the post

Door latches
1 Reproduction thumb latch
2 Hand-wrought Suffolk latch
3 Cast-iron Norfolk latch
4 Drop-ring latch

Thumb latches

A thumb latch comprises a large, strong handle (1), sometimes fixed to a backplate (2). The handle incorporates a thumb-operated lever known as the sneck (3) that lifts the beam (4) off the hooked stop (5) on the other side of the door.

The beam is fixed to the door by means of a screwed plate (6) and a keeper (7).

The latch is operated from the inside by lifting either the end of the sneck or the beam itself.

Drop-ring latches

Latches that are operated by turning an iron drop ring were inspired by the Victorian Gothic-revival movement. Medieval-style drop-ring latches are still mass-produced.

Components of a thumb latch
1 Handle
2 Backplate
3 Sneck
4 Beam
5 Stop
6 Screwed plate
7 Keeper

LOCKING LATCHES

A device that prevents the beam being lifted from the outside effectively locks the door. This might be as simple as a small locking lever attached to the keeper (1), although some latches incorporate locks that can be operated by a key from either side of the door (2).

1 Latch fitted with locking lever

2 Latch with key

Fitting a thumb latch

If possible, fix a thumb latch near one end of the middle ledge of a battened door. The beam must always be on the side to which the door swings when it is opened.

Gauge the position of the handle and cut a small slot through the door for the sneck to pass through. Screw the handle or its backplate to the door (1) and check that the sneck is operating smoothly.

On the other side of the door, rest the beam on the sneck and slide it sideways until its tip overlaps onto the doorpost. Screw the beam's plate to the door, then slide the keeper in place and screw it near to the edge of the door (2). Close the door and screw the stop to the post (3).

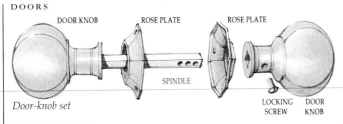

DOOR KNOB • ROSE PLATE • ROSE PLATE • SPINDLE • LOCKING SCREW • DOOR KNOB

Door-knob set

DOOR KNOBS

With the invention of rim locks and mortise locks, the latch was incorporated into the lock's mechanism in the form of a sliding latch bolt. A latch bolt is retracted by turning one of a pair of handles attached to each end of a square metal bar or spindle that passes through the lock.

From the Georgian period onwards, these handles usually took the form of door knobs that were roughly circular or oval in shape. A wide variety of materials was used in their manufacture, including brass, ceramic, glass, wood and even plastic, which was first used for door furniture in the early twentieth century. The principal rooms of a house, particularly throughout the Victorian period, were frequently furnished with impressive pairs of door knobs that were enhanced with cast or printed decoration.

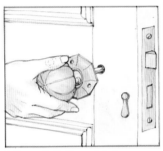

1 Pass spindle through lock

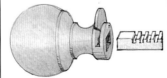

2 Locate second knob with screw

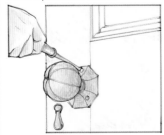

3 Some spindles are slotted

4 Fix rose plates with woodscrews

Fitting a door knob

Door knobs are normally sold in pairs, complete with either one or two rose plates (depending on whether they are intended for a door fitted with a rim lock or a mortise lock). A square spindle links the pair, and one of the knobs is usually fixed to the spindle. Slide this knob's rose plate up to it, then pass the spindle through the lock (1).

Slide the second knob and rose plate onto the other end of the spindle. In most cases the knob is secured by inserting a small machine screw through the neck of the knob into one of a series of threaded holes in the spindle (2).

Instead of screw holes, some spindles have a row of machined slots into which a pivoting 'key' on the knob locates (3).

Screw the rose plates to the door (4). Some knobs are made with integral rotating rose plates and fit onto each end of a plain spindle. Screwing both plates to the door is sufficient to hold the knobs onto the spindle. Since the fixing screws are very small, use a bradawl to make pilot holes in the wood so that it is easier to insert them without damaging the screw slots.

Door handles
1 Ceramic knob
2 Early-C20th copper lever handle
3 Copper-plated oval door knob
4 Cast-metal knob
5 Pressed-brass knob
6 Victorian door pull

DOOR PULLS

Door pulls for external doors are substantial iron or brass handles used to pull the door closed. Georgian and Victorian front doors were furnished with a single round or faceted knob or with a bar fixed to a backplate.

Fitting a door pull

Door pulls are invariably positioned centrally at about waist height and are fixed to the door with bolts. Round door pulls are often made with cast lugs on the back that are designed to bite into the wood and prevent the handle spinning and unscrewing itself. You will need to drill shallow holes in a hardwood door in order to accommodate the lugs.

LEVER HANDLES

Lever handles were not common in Georgian or Victorian homes except on double doors in the grander houses. However, chromed or bronzed lever handles became fashionable in the 1920s and 1930s, when they were fitted to flush and panelled doors of the period. Like door knobs, lever handles are attached to square spindles that operate sliding latch bolts.

Art Deco lever handle with spindle

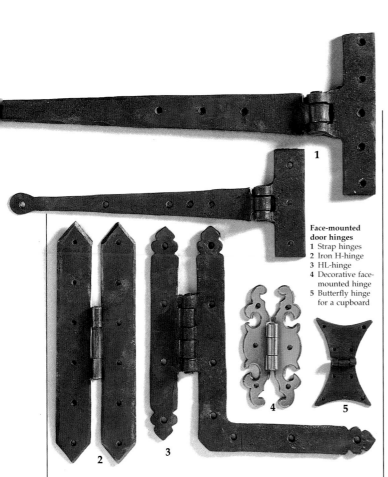

Face-mounted door hinges
1 Strap hinges
2 Iron H-hinge
3 HL-hinge
4 Decorative face-mounted hinge
5 Butterfly hinge for a cupboard

BUTT HINGES

The cast-metal butt hinge (1) was patented in 1775. This revolutionary hinge was designed to fit between the door stile and the jamb, so only the knuckle was visible when the door was closed. Not surprisingly its discreetness appealed to Georgian architects and builders, and by 1800 it was commonplace.

Early butt hinges were made of cast iron and were painted along with the door, but brass was used for more handsome hinges for showwood doors. By the middle of the nineteenth century, cheaper hinges were being made by stamping them from sheet metal. Decorative brass butt hinges (2) became popular later in the century.

Improvements in manufacturing led to the lift-off hinge that allowed the door to be removed without unscrewing the hinges (3).

The rising butt hinge (4) was a further development. The spiralling shoulders of this type of hinge cause the door to rise as it is opened, so it clears carpets and rugs. All butt hinges are screwed to the door and frame.

Fitting butt hinges

You will find two 100mm (4in) butt hinges are strong enough to hang the average panelled door. Add a third if the door is particularly heavy. Lightweight flush doors can be hung with two 75mm (3in) hinges.

First, wedge the door in its opening and mark the position of the hinges on the door stile and the jamb. The top hinge should be about 175mm (7in) from the top of the door and the bottom hinge about 250mm (10in) from the bottom edge. The recesses cut into the stile and jamb for each hinge must be an equal depth.

Support the door on edge and lay each hinge on the stile. With the knuckle overhanging, mark the position of the hinge by drawing round it (1). Mark the depth of each hinge recess on the side of the stile, using a marking gauge (2).

Make a series of shallow cuts with a chisel (3), then pare out the waste (4) to leave a shallow recess for each hinge leaf. Neaten the edges and corners of the recess with a bevel-edge chisel, then insert the hinge to check the fit.

Screw the hinges to the door and then wedge it in an open position with the hinges aligned with the marks on the jamb. Draw round the hinges (5). Mark the depth of the recesses and chop out the waste wood, as before.

Hang the door with one screw only in each leaf to check that the door swings and closes properly, then make any adjustments that are needed (see ENSURING A DOOR CLOSES PROPERLY). Once the door swings and latches to your satisfaction, insert the remaining screws.

1 Butt hinge   2 Decorative hinge   3 Lift-off hinge   4 Rising butt hinge

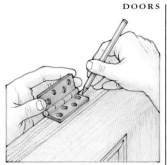

1 Mark the position of the hinge

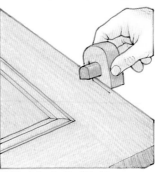

2 Mark the depth of the hinge recess

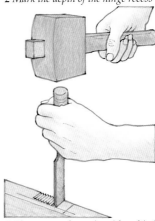

3 Chop across the grain with a chisel

4 Pare out the waste wood

5 Mark the hinge on the jamb

CLEANING & FINISHING DOOR FURNITURE

WHETHER DOOR FURNITURE *should be cleaned and polished is a matter of controversy. There is no question that metalware that is seriously corroded or disfigured by layers of paint needs to be restored, but some people argue that cleaning old brass is ill-advised since the metal loses the mellow patina built up over the years. However, there are no hard and fast rules and, provided you follow the maxim that in restoration one should never do anything that cannot be undone in the future, there is no reason why you should not follow your own inclination.*

STRIPPING PAINTED HARDWARE

Even if you intend to strip a door, it is best to remove the hardware, so that the door and its furniture can be treated more effectively.

Arrange the hardware in one or more metal-foil dishes and pour chemical paint stripper into them. Stipple the stripper onto each piece of door furniture with an old paintbrush to ensure that the chemicals penetrate all the crevices. Leave the stripper to do its work for 10 to 15 minutes, then check that the paint has begun to soften.

Wearing protective gloves, remove the softened paint from each item with fine wire wool. If there is still paint adhering to the fitting, return it to the dish and apply fresh stripper. Wash the stripped metal in hot water and dry it thoroughly with thick kitchen paper. If the fitting is hollow, stand it on a wad of newspaper to allow any water trapped inside to drain away.

STRIPPING METALWARE SAFELY

Follow the manufacturer's safety recommendations whenever you use chemical paint strippers.

Stipple stripper onto the fittings

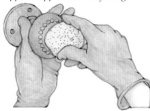
Soften corrosion with a salted lemon

CLEANING TARNISHED BRASS

Brass (which is an alloy of copper and zinc) develops a brown patina when left unprotected. It is a patina that does not lead to further corrosion, and many people find it attractive. Polishing brass door furniture that has been exposed to the elements for some time can be hard work, especially if it has begun to develop traces of green verdigris as a result of a higher-than-average copper content.

One traditional method for cleaning tarnished brass is to sprinkle some salt onto the cut surface of half a lemon and rub the metal vigorously with the fruit until the corrosion softens.

Another method is to make a cleaning solution of one level tablespoon of salt plus a tablespoon of vinegar in half a pint of hot water. Dip a pad of fine wire wool in the solution and use it to swab the corroded brass.

Before polishing, rinse the brass in clean water and dry it thoroughly.

POLISHING DOOR FURNITURE

Metal polishes are mildly abrasive cleaning agents that remove small amounts of metal along with the dirt and corrosion. They should therefore be used sparingly on plated door furniture, since frequent polishing will eventually wear through to the base metal. It is safer to clean items such as copper-plated finger plates by washing off greasy marks with lighter fluid, then buff them with a clean soft cloth.

Burnish brass door furniture with a 'long-term' brass polish that leaves an invisible chemical barrier on the metal and inhibits corrosion, so the metal needs polishing less frequently.

Clean grimy chromium-plated door furniture with lighter fluid, or wash it in warm soapy water containing a few drops of household ammonia. Then burnish the metal with a mild cream chrome polish.

Protecting the paintwork

Clearly, it would be too much of a chore to remove door furniture every time you want to polish it. To protect the surrounding paintwork from abrasive cleaners, cut a template from thin card to slip over each item of door furniture or stick low-adhesive masking tape over the paintwork.

If you don't want to remove door furniture with raised edges, such as a letter plate or the number of the house, you can leave the fittings *in situ* when you repaint the door. Allow the paint to coat the edges of the fittings, but wipe it from their surface, using a cloth dampened with white spirit.

Once the paint is dry, you can polish the exposed metal without spoiling the newly painted woodwork.

CLEANING RUSTY IRON

Remove rusty wrought-iron or cast-iron fittings from the door and soak them in paraffin for several hours to soften the corrosion, then clean them with fine wire wool. Dry the metal and treat it immediately with a chemical rust inhibitor before priming and painting.

FINISHING DOOR FURNITURE

You can protect polished brass with clear acrylic lacquer. Paint it on fairly quickly with a soft artist's brush. If you can't avoid leaving brush marks in the lacquer, stand the door furniture on a warm radiator before the lacquer sets really hard. The heat will soften the lacquer sufficiently for the brush marks to flow out naturally. If lacquer becomes discoloured or gets chipped, remove it with acetone then repolish the metal and apply fresh lacquer.

Iron door furniture is usually protected by applying a calcium-plumbate or zinc-phosphate primer followed by one or two coats of semi-matt black paint. However, some restorers prefer to keep wrought-iron hinges free from rust by wiping them occasionally with an oily rag.

CHAPTER TEN

WINDOWS

BY THE EIGHTEENTH CENTURY *there were two designs for domestic windows in common use. The side-hung casement – which swings open like a door – was probably of medieval origin and at the beginning of the century it was the chosen style for humble cottage and grand house alike. However, the last quarter of the seventeenth century saw the introduction of the sliding-sash window, which revolutionized building design and remained the most popular type of window, in Britain for the next two hundred years.*

Probably of British origin, although some maintain that the Dutch were the inventors, the sliding-sash window consists of two overlapping glazed frames, or 'sashes', that slide vertically. The earliest versions had a single sliding sash, which was held open with wedges or by inserting pegs in holes drilled in the wooden frame that lined the window opening. However, the double-hung sash window, which has two movable sashes, was to become the standard model within a few years of its invention. Save for a few minor variations, it has remained unchanged ever since.

A double-hung sash window is a sophisticated piece of design, the sliding sashes being suspended from pulleys on weighted cords or chains so that they will remain in any position required. Leaving the window open at top and bottom provides an ideal means of promoting efficient circulation of air within the room.

One notable variation on the sash window was the horizontally sliding version. Although its use was largely restricted to modest dwellings, it can be found in most parts of the country. This type of window generally had only one movable sash. Since it was horizontal, there was no need for counterweights or supports of any kind.

Metal-frame Modern-movement windows

C20th metal casements resemble earlier window styles

Simple unspoilt rural casements

Bowed sashes exhibit Georgian skill

Nicely proportioned fixed lights

GEORGIAN SASH WINDOWS

EARLY SASH WINDOWS *were divided by thick wooden glazing bars, or astragals, into anything from 16 to 24 almost-square panes. But as the eighteenth century progressed, the classic twelve-pane or 'six-over-six' sash window became a universally accepted norm.*

The classic six-over-six or twelve-pane sliding-sash window

PROPORTIONS

The shapes of window openings were based on simple geometric proportions that appealed to refined Georgian architects, builders and clients alike. The width and status of a particular window determined the height of the opening. A window on the main floor, or *piano nobile,* which was normally located at first-floor level in the grander houses, was usually a double square, being twice as high as it was wide. The height of a window on the 'chamber' or bedroom floor was often 1¼ times its width, while windows at attic level, where the majority of the servants' rooms were situated, tended to be square. These proportions are largely responsible for the elegant appearance of Georgian houses.

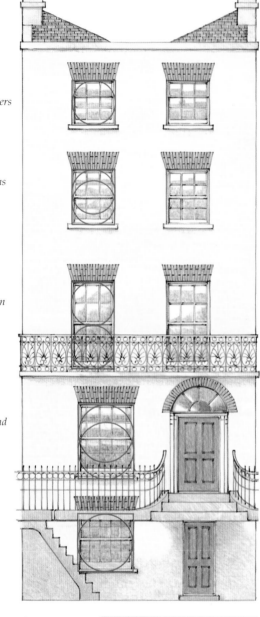

Attic level
Servants' quarters and nursery

Second floor
Family bedrooms

First floor
Formal reception rooms

Ground floor
Dining room and parlour

Cellar
Kitchen and scullery

Window proportions

The elevation of a typical late-Georgian house demonstrates the principles of geometry used to arrive at the proportions of the windows. These principles were not adhered to rigidly but served as useful rules of thumb. Wide windows were divided by extra vertical glazing bars to keep the size of the panes constant.

Tall windows need additional panes

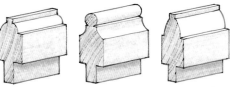

1 Ovolo   *2 Astragal and hollow*   *3 Sash ovolo*   *4 Lamb's tongue*

1 Basic straight-head sash window

2 C18th segmental-head window

3 Late-Georgian semi-circular head

4 Elliptical-head sash window

GLAZING BARS

The glazing bars, or astragals, that divide each sash are rebated on the exterior to support a pane of glass on each side. The putty that holds the glass in place is shaped to form simple bevels. Glazing bars are moulded on the inside and are perhaps the most decorative elements of the design. Although there were innumerable local variations, certain styles of glazing-bar moulding can be identified as typical for different stages in Georgian sash-window development.

Early Georgian windows were made with thick square-ovolo mouldings **(1)**. The number of glazing bars decreased when larger panes of glass became fashionable. At the same time, they became thinner and thinner, with more refined mouldings. The astragal and hollow **(2)** was popular from about the 1730s, followed in quick succession by the sash-ovolo **(3)** and lamb's-tongue **(4)** mouldings – all of them remaining in use well into the nineteenth century.

Although the majority of windows were made with a straightforward grid of glazing bars, late-Georgian windows were enhanced by rearranging the astragals to create narrow marginal lights, and semi-circular-head and elliptical-head windows afforded the opportunity for decorative radial and curved patterns of glazing bars.

VARIATIONS ON THE SASH WINDOW

Although one thinks of a typical Georgian house as having a more or less symmetrical façade with regularly placed individual windows, architects rang the changes by grouping sash windows, usually in combinations of three.

The Venetian or Palladian window is the most obvious example. A semi-circular-head sash window is flanked by narrow, slightly lower, sashes that are sometimes fixed. In order to keep the mullions between the windows as narrow as possible, the counterweight cords for the moving sashes in the middle often ran over the top of the flanking windows so that the weights could hang on each side of the group.

Bow and bay windows were often a combination of three separate windows, and in many cases all three of them were working sash windows.

WINDOW SHAPES

The basic rectangular straight-head window **(1)** is common-place in Georgian houses, but in the early eighteenth century windows with segmental heads were fashionable, too **(2)**. Late-Georgian houses were often built with semi-circular-head **(3)** or elliptical-head windows **(4)**.

BLIND WINDOWS

Fake sashes or plain recesses in the masonry are often found in Georgian houses where, from the outside, one would expect to see a genuine window. Some of these were, in fact, once real windows but were blocked up to avoid the infamous eighteenth-century window taxes, which were levied according to the number of windows in a house. More often, blind windows were inserted so as not to disturb the rhythm of a façade when a real window would have broken into a flue or some other internal feature. Although a blind window is often no more than a simple recess in the wall, sometimes part of the masonry is set back slightly to cast a shadow resembling a lower sash. More elaborate examples are constructed with glazed but non-working sashes in the recess and may even include a painted facsimile of a window blind to complete the illusion.

Early-eighteenth-century Venetian window

103

VICTORIAN & EDWARDIAN SASH WINDOWS

Windows styles *did not, of course, suddenly change as the Georgian period drew to a close. However, the prevailing feature that distinguished Victorian windows from Georgian ones was the larger panes of cheap mass-produced glass, supported by fewer and fewer glazing bars. Four-over-four, two-over-two, and eventually one-over-one are all typical Victorian windowpane arrangements. Earlier windows were frequently 'modernized' by removing the original glazing bars in order to install larger sheets of glass, which is why you find horned windows in some Georgian buildings.*

Four-over-four

Two-over-two

One-over-one

Edwardian sashes with original glass

Gothic-revival lancet window

Composite sashes admit more light

THE INTRODUCTION OF HORNED SASHES

The elimination of glazing bars put an additional strain on the relatively slim meeting rail of the upper sash, especially on the joint at each end of the rail. From about 1840 this joint was modified to include a wedged through tenon, and so the vertical stile had to be extended in order to reinforce the joint. This extension, known as the 'horn', was either bevelled or moulded.

Horns strengthen the meeting rail

VICTORIAN WINDOW SHAPES

The Victorians continued to employ semi-circular and segmental-head windows, and the Gothic-revival movement was responsible for the widespread use of the pointed-head or lancet window. However, since rectangular window openings were easier to build, these shapes were frequently incorporated within a rectangular sash, creating 'triangular' lights in the top corners of the window.

COMPOSITE SASH WINDOWS

The desire for larger areas of glass, which would admit more light, is reflected in Victorian and Edwardian housing by the combination of sash windows in pairs and groups of three. In the majority of cases, all the sashes slide and the counterweights are housed in the dividing mullions. Palladian windows feature regularly in more grandiose and ornate houses throughout the Victorian period.

BAY WINDOWS

Curved (bow), square and canted bay windows, often
running the full height of the house, up to the eaves, occur
so frequently that they are practically synonymous with
Victorian and Edwardian housing. Bay windows enrich the
seemingly endless rows of terraced houses built during both
periods. They also have the practical advantage of greatly
increasing the field of view from inside.

Oriel windows, cantilevered from the upper storeys, are
charming variations of the traditional bay. Square and canted
oriels with windows on three sides are used to light major
bedrooms. Small triangular oriels illuminate small bedrooms
and staircases. Oriel windows recur from time to time in
later revival styles, particularly in the neo-Tudor housing of
the 1920s and 1930s.

Canted bay window   *Stone-built oriel window*

Restricting glazing bars to the upper sash was a typically Victorian practice

The ubiquitous brick terrace with full-height square bays

GLAZING-BAR ARRANGEMENTS

With their characteristic enthusiasm for anything decorative,
the Victorians employed a much greater variety of glazing-
bar arrangements than their Georgian predecessors had
done, and they delighted in marginal lights incorporating
coloured glass. Often, however, decorative arrangements of
astragals were restricted to the upper sash, with a single
undivided pane of glass in the sash below. The Queen Anne
revival during the last quarter of the nineteenth century saw
the reintroduction of the early-Georgian-style multi-pane
sash with thick glazing bars.

Elegant glazing-bar arrangement   *Imaginative use of glazing bars*

HOW SASH WINDOWS WERE MADE

D OUBLE-HUNG SASH WINDOWS *vary in the details of their construction, but the basic principles described here are common to all windows of this type. A sash window is a complicated piece of joinery, yet is designed in such a way that it can be dismantled easily when it is necessary to carry out maintenance and repairs. Most windows are made from softwood, although oak and mahogany have been used for better-quality windows.*

CONSTRUCTION OF THE SLIDING SASHES

Each sash comprises two vertical stiles (1), a top rail (2) or bottom rail (3), and a meeting rail (4). The meeting rails oppose each other when the sashes are closed, and their adjoining faces are bevelled (5) so they close together relatively tightly in order to keep draughts and rattles to a minimum. They are sometimes bevel-rebated to prevent a knife blade or similar implement being slipped between the rails to open the window fastener from outside.

Sash rails are rebated on the outside (the lower-sash meeting rail is grooved) to accept the glass, and they are moulded on the inside. The glass is retained with sprigs (small nails) or glazing points (flat triangular metal fixings) and linseed-oil putty.

The top rail of the upper sash and the bottom rail of the lower sash are joined to the stiles with through mortise-and-tenon joints (6). Joints are glued and usually reinforced with wedges from the outside or with locking dowels through the sides of the joints.

Meeting rails are wider than stiles in order to close the gap between sliding sashes. They are joined to the stiles with a form of dovetailed bridle joint (7). Often a stronger mortise-and-tenon joint is used for the upper sash, and the stile is extended to form a 'horn' that strengthens the bottom of the mortise.

Glazing bars

Narrow wooden glazing bars (8) are used to hold relatively small panes of glass within the sashes. These are rebated for the glass and moulded on the inside. Vertical glazing bars are usually continuous, and are jointed into the rails (9) with mortise-and-tenon joints. The shorter horizontal bars are made with similar joints. Alternatively, all the glazing bars may be continuous, in which case they are joined with halving joints (10) where they cross. A single vertical glazing bar may be joined to the meeting rail of the upper sash with a wedged through tenon.

CONSTRUCTION OF THE WINDOW FRAME

The frame within which the sashes slide comprises two vertical jambs (one on each side), a head across the top and a sill across the bottom. Because a jamb needs to be hollow to house the sash weights, it is made in three parts – the inner lining (11), the outer lining (12) and the the pulley lining (13) – which together form a three-sided box. With better-quality work, a rough-sawn back lining (14), nailed to the inner and outer linings,

strengthens the jamb and prevents the sash weights getting caught on any projections from the wall behind. The weights are separated from each other by a narrow strip of wood, called a parting slip (15), which is housed in a slot in the head and suspended from a nail or peg. The parting slip stops about 100mm (4in) short of the sill.

The head is constructed in a similar way to a jamb, with inner and outer linings plus a soffit lining (16). Since there is no top lining, glued

triangular blocks (17) are used to strengthen the head.

The sill (18) is cut from a single piece of solid wood, and is shaped so that water flows away from the sashes to the outside.

A recess is formed for the upper sash by the projecting lips of the outer linings together with the two parting beads (19) that are nailed into grooves cut in the pulley stiles and a similar bead running across the soffit lining. Stop beads (20) nailed all round the frame hold the lower sash in place.

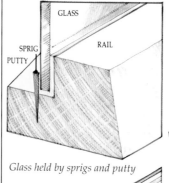

Glass held by sprigs and putty

Joint between bottom rail and stile

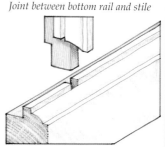

Halving joint for glazing bars

Joint between glazing bar and rail

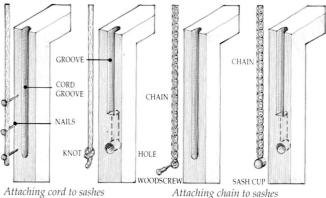

Attaching cord to sashes

Attaching chain to sashes

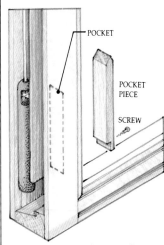

POCKET

POCKET
PIECE

SCREW

Access to sash weight via pocket

WEIGHTS AND PULLEYS

A pair of counterweights **(21)** is attached to each sash with waxed cords **(22)** or chains that pass over pulley wheels **(23)** screwed to the jambs. Cheap pulleys have plain axles, but better-quality ones are made with roller or ball bearings. Each cord is nailed into a groove cut in the sash stile or, alternatively, the knotted end of the cord may be located in a hole drilled into the stile. Chains are attached with woodscrews or by means of a metal lining (sash cup) for the hole in the stile.

Access to sash weights is by means of openings known as 'pockets' **(24)** cut through the pulley stiles. Each pocket is closed by a strip of wood, or 'pocket piece', which may be fixed by a single screw at the bottom – although often pocket pieces are simply held in place by the beads and lower sliding sash.

TAPE BALANCES

Tape balances have been used since the latter part of the nineteenth century as an alternative to the weight-and-cord method of hanging sliding sashes. A spring-loaded steel tape, wound into a metal drum, is hooked onto the sash stile. The drum is screwed into the pulley recess in the jamb.

ASSESSING REPAIRS

- ● Easy even for beginners.
- ■ Fairly difficult. Good practical skills required.
- ▲ Difficult. Hire a professional.

Broken glass
■ Try to find matching glass to replace broken windowpanes (page 112).

Damaged weatherseal
Mortar used to seal around the frame shrinks and falls out.
● Seal the joints as soon as possible (page 115).

Seized pulley wheel
Paint can jam a pulley, making a sash difficult to open and close.
● Lubricate or strip pulley (page 110).

Broken cords
■ It is worth replacing all the sash cords when one breaks (page 109).

Loose joints
Sash joints shrink and work loose.
■ Repair them before water penetrates and rots the wood (page 110).

Loose putty
Loose putty is a security risk and encourages wood rot.
● Replace it with fresh putty (page 113).

Dry rot
Dry rot can develop inside the jamb.
▲ Have it inspected and treated by an expert (page 114).

Tape balance

Rotted sill
Being the lowest horizontal member, the sill often rots.
■ Dig out and patch the rotten wood (page 114).
▲ Have the old sill replaced with a new hardwood sill.

Components of a sash window
1 Vertical stile
2 Top rail
3 Bottom rail
4 Meeting rail
5 Bevelled face
6 Through mortise-and-tenon joint
7 Dovetailed bridle joint
8 Glazing bar
9 Mortise-and-tenon joint
10 Halving joint
11 Inner lining
12 Outer lining
13 Pulley lining
14 Back lining
15 Parting slip
16 Soffit lining
17 Triangular block
18 Sill
19 Parting bead
20 Stop bead
21 Counterweight
22 Sash cord
23 Pulley wheel
24 Pocket

Bevelled meeting rails

Bevel-rebated meeting rails

Dovetailed bridle joint for meeting rail

HORN

Mortise-and-tenon with horn

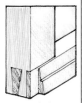

Sticking sashes
Swollen sashes or a build-up of paint can cause a wooden window to jam.
● Ease sash (page 110).

Rotted rails and glazing bars
Condensation and rainwater run down the glass and seep behind loose putty. Wet rot develops.
● Patch and preserve (page 114).
■ Replace the rotted wooden components (page 115).

An unusual sash in a wooden wall

SASH WINDOWS IN MASONRY WALLS

From the last quarter of the eighteenth century, wooden window frames were made to be a close fit in the window opening, and the jambs and head were recessed behind the brickwork on each side and behind a stone lintel or brick arch above. Sometimes wedges were inserted around the frame to centre it in the opening. The wooden sill sits on top of a stone subsill built into the wall. A metal strip forms a weatherproof joint between both sills. The head might be nailed to a wooden lintel that supports the masonry behind the stone lintel or brick arch. Once the internal wall is plastered and architraves (cover mouldings) are fitted, the window frame is firmly fixed in place.

SASH WINDOWS IN TIMBER-FRAME WALLS

When a sash window was fitted in a timber-frame wall, it was centred in the opening with wooden shims, then the soffit lining was nailed to a header or lintel and the sill similarly nailed to a subsill. The inner and outer linings form a casing that hides the joint between the window frame and the wall.

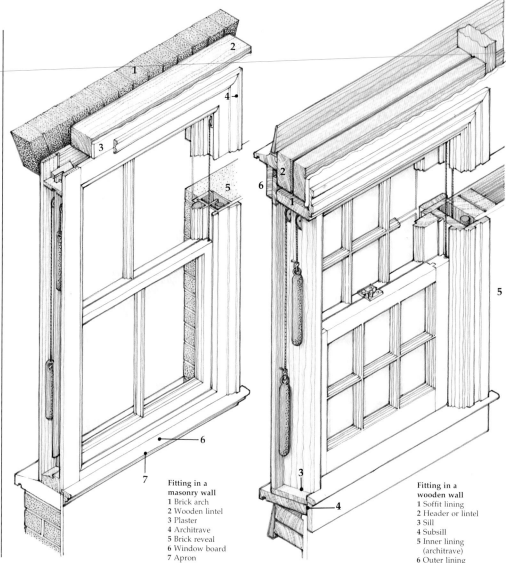

Fitting in a masonry wall
1 Brick arch
2 Wooden lintel
3 Plaster
4 Architrave
5 Brick reveal
6 Window board
7 Apron

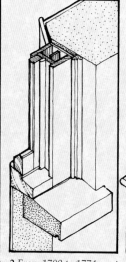
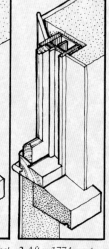

Fitting in a wooden wall
1 Soffit lining
2 Header or lintel
3 Sill
4 Subsill
5 Inner lining (architrave)
6 Outer lining

EIGHTEENTH-CENTURY BUILDING ACTS

Before 1709 sash-window frames were set practically flush with the façade of a house (1). The Building Act of that year stipulated that the frame should be set back by 100mm (4in) to reduce the risk of fire spreading (2). The act was strengthened in 1774, and from then on frames had to be recessed behind the brickwork (3). These regulations were only enforced in London, where the risk was greatest – and even there you can find later houses with the earlier types of window frames.

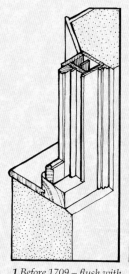

1 *Before 1709 – flush with brickwork* **2** *From 1709 to 1774 – set back 100mm (4in)* **3** *After 1774 – set back and recessed*

REPAIRING SASH WINDOWS

CONTRARY TO THE PROPAGANDA *put out by some manufacturers and installers of replacement windows, it is nearly always possible to repair wooden-sash windows. It is also very satisfying to preserve what are important features of a period house, especially when it proves to be much cheaper than replacing them. Some aspects of the work are quite time-consuming, but most of it is well within the capabilities of a reasonably competent woodworker.*

CORDS AND CHAINS

Waxed-cotton sash cords are made in a range of diameters numbered 6 to 12, but sizes 7 and 8 are the ones most commonly used for domestic windows. Don't be tempted to economize by fitting lightweight cords to a heavy window. You could find you have to replace them again in a matter of weeks.

Very heavy windows may be hung from chains. The cheaper chains are made with folded metal links. Better-quality ones are made with riveted links, like a bicycle chain.

Try not to smear paint onto cords or chains when redecorating. Paint clogs chain links and weakens cotton cord.

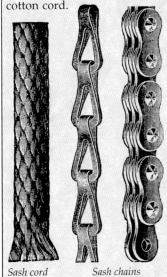

Sash cord   Sash chains

Broken sash cords

When one or both sash cords break, a sash window becomes difficult to open. A sash with weight on one side only may be out of balance; and if both cords are broken, the sash may be too heavy to lift. If you have to dismantle a sash window, it is worth taking the opportunity to replace both the cords before reinstalling it.

Drive a wide paint scraper between the stop bead and the jamb on one side of the window (1). Then, starting halfway up the window, use the same tool to begin prising the bead away from the frame. Once a few nails lose their grip, bend the bead by hand until you can free the mitre joint at each end. This will allow you to swing the lower sash out of the frame. Disconnect intact cords or chains and lower the sash weights to the bottom of the jambs.

To remove the upper sash, prise out the parting beads (2) and disconnect cords or chains as before.

Retrieve the weights by opening the pocket in the pulley stile on each side of the window (3). Pull the parting slips aside to reach the outer weights.

Using an old cord as a guide, mark off its length on the new replacement cord, but don't cut it to length at this stage. Tie a bent nail or a similar small weight to a length of string and pass it over the pulley into the hollow jamb (4). Lower the weight until it appears at the open pocket, then tape the other end of the string to the new cord. Pull on the string while feeding the cord over the pulley until you can retrieve it from the pocket.

Tie the cord to the ring on the end of the sash weight (5), or make a figure-of-eight knot to locate in the recess cast in some weights (6).

Pull the weight up to the pulley on the inside of the jamb, then lower it by about 100mm (4in). With the sash resting on the sill, nail the premarked cord into the groove in the sash stile, using three large blued tacks. Fix the lower 150mm (6in) only (7), then cut off excess cord with a sharp knife. Alternatively, fit a knotted cord in the sash stile – or screw a sash chain to the stile, instead.

Attach other weights and cords, then replace the sashes, checking that they run smoothly before nailing the parting beads and stop beads to the jamb.

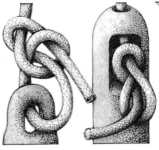

1 Break paint seal with a scraper

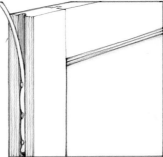

2 Prise out the parting beads

3 Take out the pocket piece

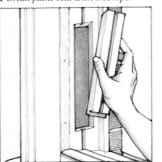

4 Pass weight over pulley wheel

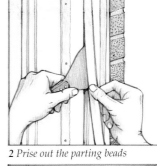

5 Tie cord to the sash weight   *6 Or tie a figure-of-eight knot*

7 Nail the sash cord in the groove

EASING A STICKING SASH

One of the most common and frustrating properties of sliding-sash windows is their refusal to budge or to open and close smoothly. Not only is a sticking sash window annoying to live with, but the strain imposed by forcing it to move puts additional load on joints that may be weak already. There are several reasons why a sash can stick, so it pays to try the simpler solutions first.

OVERPAINTING

Unless a freshly painted sash is moved regularly while the paint is drying, there is every possibility that the wet paint will act as an adhesive. When this happens, if the next painter does not bother to free the sash and simply paints it *in situ*, that makes matters even worse.

Take a sharp craft knife and carefully score around the sash, then work the blade of a wide paint scraper (or, better still, a flexible filling knife) between the sash and the surrounding beads. You may find that you also have to ease the sash from the outside.

Grasp the meeting rail and try shaking the sash from side to side in order to break the paint seal.

Misplaced beads

A sash may be difficult to move because a misplaced stop bead is virtually clamping it against the parting beads. Prise suspect beads from the frame and reposition them.

Seized pulley

If a pulley is not running freely, the friction will impede the movement of the sash cord. A drop of penetrating oil may be all that's needed to free the pulley – but you are more likely to find that it has been overpainted at some time, causing it to seize up. If so, disconnect the sash cord and remove the pulley, which is normally fixed to the stile with two woodscrews. Use paint stripper to dislodge the paint, then lightly oil the pulley before reassembly.

Swollen or distorted sash

During humid or damp weather, a wooden window can expand considerably, especially if it has been neglected and the paintwork is in poor condition. If you have a sliding sash that sticks intermittently, wait for dry weather then prepare and paint it to seal the wood.

A twisted or bowed sash probably sticks most of the time, and it will usually exhibit signs of wear or scuffing in areas that are rubbing against the frame. Take the distorted sash out of its frame (see BROKEN SASH CORDS) and shave the worn areas with a sharp block plane. Before you reinstall it, lubricate the sash by rubbing a candle along its running surfaces.

Trim a twisted sash with a plane

Loose sash joints

South-facing windows are particularly susceptible to the effects of weathering. With the alternate swelling and shrinking of the wood, glued joints begin to work loose, exhibiting wide gaps along their shoulders. An expanding sash may jam in its frame, but more serious problems can arise when rainwater and condensation penetrate the joint and rot the wood.

As a temporary measure, rake out loose material from the gap along each shoulder and close up the joint as best you can. Screw an L-shaped metal plate onto the outside of the sash to clamp the joint and prevent it deteriorating further. To make a more permanent repair, you should dismantle the sash and reglue the joints. Remove the sash and lay it flat on a convenient surface, so you can remove the glass without breaking it. Lay the glass aside, then clamp the frame to a bench.

Inspect the joints to see if there are any wedges or locking dowels that would prevent them coming apart. If necessary, chop wedges out with a small chisel. However, you may find they are loose or missing. Locking dowels can be drilled out.

Try tapping the joints apart with a hammer, using a softwood block to protect the sash (1). Work alternately, first at one end of the stile then the other, to avoid breaking a joint. If any of the joints are stuck fast, play steam from a kettle along the shoulder line to soften the glue – then tap again.

Using a sharp chisel, scrape old glue from the joints. Before proceeding to reassemble the sash, consider stripping the paint

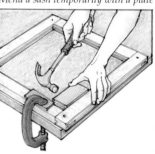

Mend a sash temporarily with a plate

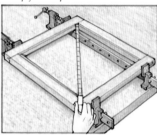

1 Tap joints apart with a hammer

2 Check the sash is square

and applying a liquid preservative to all surfaces, including the joints.

Use a waterproof synthetic-resin adhesive to glue the sash, and hire long sash cramps to pull the joints together. Measure from one corner to another (2) to check that the sash is square. Both diagonals should be identical. Replace wedges or dowels as required. When the glue has set, replace the glass and reinstall the sash.

CURING RATTLING SASHES

Our forebears used to stop sash windows rattling by driving small rubber wedges between the sashes and the beads. Another solution is to fit a fastener that has a cam action, which will pull the two meeting rails together.

REPLACING GLASS

I T IS DIFFICULT TO APPRECIATE *the quality old glass gives to a building until you see a façade with all its original glazing, each pane catching the light at a different angle and distorting reflections. It pays to preserve any antique glass you find intact and to replace it with a similar form of glazing when broken. The various types of glass described below were used for glazing domestic windows from the eighteenth century onwards.*

CROWN GLASS

Until about 1830 windows were glazed with handmade crown glass. This was produced by blowing a bubble of molten glass, which was then attached to a metal rod, called a pontil, directly opposite the glass-blower's pipe. Once the blowpipe was cut from the bubble, the glass was heated again and spun on the pontil until it formed a disc about 1.5m (4 to 5ft) in diameter. The disc was then cut into square, rectangular or diamond-shape panes for glazing windows. The centre of the disc, which had a scar left by the pontil, was either thrown back into the furnace or sold as cheap glazing for poorer houses or agricultural buildings. The popular belief that bull's-eye panes were fitted for decorative reasons is a modern idea. Crown glass is thin and brittle, and the spinning process left curved ridges or striations in the glass that distort the view through a window. It is these subtle flaws and imperfections, coupled with its highly fire-polished surface and variations in colour, that endow crown glass with its special character.

Spinning crown glass

CYLINDER GLASS

Cylinder, or 'broad glass', was the only real alternative to crown glass for windows until the middle of the nineteenth century. Although not of the same quality as crown glass, larger panes could be made from cylinder glass. A large sausage-shape bubble of glass some 1.5m (4 to 5ft) long and 250 to 300mm (10 to 12in) in diameter was blown over a pit, which provided room for the extending cylinder. The two ends of the cylinder were removed, then it was split lengthwise before being reheated and opened out to make a flat sheet about 900mm (3ft) wide. The top surface of the sheet was relatively flat, but the underside inevitably puckered as the cylinder was unrolled, creating a slightly wavy surface that breaks up reflections in a most attractive manner when cylinder glass is installed in a window.

Making cylinder glass in the traditional manner

Genuine crown or cylinder glass enlivens a façade

PLATE GLASS

As a result of mechanization, manufacturers were able to make larger and larger cylinders of glass. But there was clearly a need for a process that could produce large flat sheets.

Plate glass was invented as early as the seventeenth century, but its production was so labour-intensive that it was almost exclusively used for making mirrors for the wealthy.

Molten glass was poured onto a metal casting table. Then, after cooling, it was painstakingly ground and polished to make a sheet that was optically almost perfect.

During the second half of the nineteenth century improvements were made whereby the glass was rolled flat, but the texture left on both sides of the sheet by the rolling process still had to be laboriously ground out before polishing.

DRAWN-SHEET GLASS

Although rolled-plate glass was popular for shopfronts, it was too expensive to be at all widely used for houses. However, the development of drawn-sheet glass early in the twentieth century made it possible to manufacture large flat sheets much more economically.

A ribbon of molten glass was drawn vertically from the melting pot and allowed to cool. Since the thickness of the glass was determined by the speed at which it was drawn from the pot, it was impossible to guarantee a uniform thickness.

As a result, although early drawn-sheet glass lacked many of the imperfections of handmade glass, it still tended to distort reflections and so produce a distorted view through a window.

Early-Victorian plate-glass rolling mill

FLOAT GLASS

Float glass is a relatively modern development, having been pioneered in the 1950s. This optically superb glass has a highly polished surface, made by floating it on molten metal. Float glass tends to look a little too perfect when installed in an old house, especially if it can be compared with old glass in other windows.

CURVED GLASS

If you have to replace curved glass – in a bow window, for example – you will need to employ a specialist glazier. The making of curved glass demands considerable skill, as it cannot be cut to size once it has been shaped and must therefore be measured accurately beforehand. A flat sheet of glass is heated in a furnace and allowed to sag onto a curved metal mould. Making a new mould is costly, but an experienced glazier may be able to adapt existing stock. Measure the window sash carefully and make an accurate cardboard template of the required curve. Alternatively, take the sash itself to the glazier.

FINDING REPLACEMENT GLASS

You can buy genuine old glass from an architectural-salvage company, but it is expensive and you will find that it's quite difficult to cut antique glass without breaking it. If you use crown glass, it looks best with the convex side outwards.

Cylinder glass is made for restoration purposes, in the traditional manner, in sheets 3mm (⅛in) thick measuring up to 600 x 900mm (2 x 3ft). Although it is far more expensive than modern float glass, cylinder glass will integrate perfectly with original glazing and is often used for restoring coloured leaded lights.

A cheaper alternative for clear glazing is to use imported horticultural glass made for greenhouses. This is 3mm (⅛in) thick and is sold in sheets measuring 750 x 1425mm (2ft 6in x 4ft 9in). Being a second-quality glass, it exhibits some of the imperfections of Victorian drawn-sheet glass.

1 Remove the broken glass

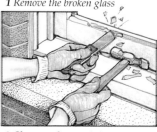

2 Chop out the remaining putty

REPLACING A BROKEN PANE

Wearing goggles and thick work gloves to protect your eyes and hands, remove the broken glass piece by piece, rocking it gently backwards and forwards to loosen the putty (1). Chop out what remains of the putty from the rebates with a glazier's hacking knife (2) or an old chisel. Using pincers, remove the sprigs or glazing points that hold the glass in place, then clean out the rebates with a stiff bristle brush. (Glass is held in rolled-steel windows with small spring clips.)

Apply primer to the rebates, to prevent oil being soaked out of the new putty; or use linseed oil diluted 50 per cent with turpentine.

Measure the height and width of the opening. If you don't want to cut the glass yourself (see opposite), you will need to order replacement glass 3mm (⅛in) smaller from top to bottom and from side to side.

Knead a fist-size ball of linseed-oil putty until it has an even consistency. Remove some of the oil from sticky

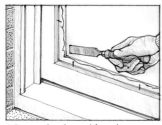
3 Secure the glass with sprigs

4 Smooth the putty with a knife

fresh putty by rolling it in newspaper. Conversely, soften stiff putty with a drop of linseed oil.

Shape the putty into a thin 'rope' and press it firmly into the rebates all round the opening. Set the new pane of glass into this bedding putty, pressing around the edges only to squeeze excess putty from the rebates. Secure the glass every 200mm (8in) or so with sprigs or glazing points, tapping them into the wood with the edge of a firmer chisel (3). Cut excess putty from the inside of the window with a putty knife.

Press more putty into the rebate to cover the fixings, smoothing it to form an even bevel with the point of a putty knife (4). Dip the knife in water from time to time to prevent it sticking to the putty. Clean putty smears from the glass with methylated spirits.

Leave the putty for a week or so to harden, then paint it (at least with an undercoat) within a month. To seal the edge of the putty, let the paint overlap very slightly onto the glass.

RENEWING OLD PUTTY

Old putty is often so loose you can pick it out with your fingers. Not only does loose putty admit water to rot the woodwork, it is also a security risk since it enables a pane of glass to be removed silently. Old putty is extremely hard; and if sections are still firmly attached to the sash, trying to chop it out in the conventional manner may crack the glass. Soften hard putty with a coat of chemical paint stripper. A paste stripper is best because it can be covered with strips of plastic sheeting to keep it moist and active, for up to 48 hours, until the putty is soft enough to scrape from the rebates. Prime the rebate, then apply new putty (see left).

Glaziers at work

CUTTING GLASS

If you have never cut glass before, practise on some spare glass before you start a job in earnest.

Lay a sheet of glass on a flat worktable covered with a blanket, then thoroughly clean the area to be cut with methylated spirits to remove traces of grease, which can cause a glass cutter to skid. An ordinary glass cutter has a steel wheel that scores the glass, but better-quality diamond-tipped cutters are also available. Use a wooden straightedge (preferably a T-square) to guide the cutter.

Lubricate the tip of a wheeled glass cutter by dipping it in light oil. Then, holding the tool between your index and middle fingers (1), draw it towards you with one continuous movement that scores the glass from edge to edge. A harsh grating sound means you are pressing too hard, sending shock waves through the glass that could cause the cut to wander; a light irregular sound may mean you are not scoring a continuous line.

Slide the glass towards you until it overhangs the edge of the worktable, then tap the glass directly under the scored line (2) to start the cut. Place a gloved hand on each side of the line (3) and snap the glass with a twist of the wrists.

Cutting shapes

To cut a shaped piece of glass, make a thick cardboard template that fits the window opening but is 1.5mm (1/16in) smaller all round (not forgetting to allow for the thickness of the glass cutter).

Hold the template on the glass with double-sided adhesive tape and score a cut line along each edge (4). Run each cut out to the edge of the glass (5) and cut the waste alongside a curved edge into segments.

Snap the glass, holding it as previously described, or use ordinary pliers padded with masking tape to grip awkward pieces (6).

1 Hold a cutter between your fingers

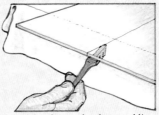
2 Tap the glass under the scored line

3 Grip glass on each side of the line

4 Score alongside a template

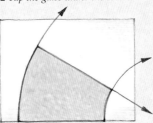
5 Run each cut out to an edge

6 Snap a strip with padded pliers

DEALING WITH ROTTED WINDOWS

D RY ROT BREAKS OUT *only in dark, unventilated enclosed spaces where moisture is present. It may start inside the hollow parts of a sash-window frame and then gradually invade neighbouring components. Alternatively, a window can be affected by dry rot creeping from some other source.*

In practice dry rot occurs comparatively rarely in window frames, but wooden windows do frequently suffer from the effects of wet rot. Wet rot most often occurs at points where moisture is able to penetrate the end grain of timber, such as the ends of the sill, the bottom of both jambs and the joints.

Neglected paintwork is one of the most common causes of wet rot, as are the breakdown of the mortar seal around the frame, bad pointing, loose putty and rising damp – in fact, anything that is responsible for the wood becoming saturated regularly.

Before attempting to treat the symptoms of rot, always locate and eradicate the source of the dampness that has caused the fungus to develop.

Neglected paintwork and missing putty lead to wet rot

Checking for wet rot
Peeling paint, where the wood has expanded beneath, is often the first sign of wet rot. Wood suffering from wet rot is spongy when wet, but becomes dry and crumbly as it dries out in warm weather. It is always relatively soft, and areas of rot can be pinpointed by probing with the point of a screwdriver.

Checking for dry rot
If you become aware of a strong musty smell when you are changing a sash cord or making some other repair to a wooden window, open the pocket and inspect the inside of the jamb with a torch and a small mirror. If you notice a dusting of red spores or any of the other signs of dry rot, have the window inspected and treated by a professional as soon as possible.

TREATING AREAS OF WET ROT
Gouge out decayed wood until you reach relatively sound material, then apply preservative and consolidate the affected area by painting a liquid wood hardener onto it. One coat of hardener is enough to reinforce weakened fibres and seal the wood against future penetration.

After six hours, fill holes, cracks and crevices with a flexible exterior wood filler.

Patching a deep hole
Having gouged out soft decayed wood to investigate the extent of the damage, chisel out a cavity that is slightly larger than the damaged area and, if possible, undercut the edges to lock the new patch in place (1).

Cut a patch from timber similar to that of the component, with the grain running in the same direction. Shape the patch to match any undercuts and leave it very slightly oversize, both in thickness and in width, for planing down after fitting (2). Paint the prepared area and the new timber with a chemical preservative before gluing the patch in place with a waterproof synthetic-resin adhesive.

When the glue has set, plane the patch flush then coat it with preservative again before filling any gaps with a flexible wood filler.

1 Chisel out a cavity with undercuts   *2 Plane the patch repair to fit*

REPLACING ROTTED TIMBER
If the extent of the wet rot has structurally weakened a component of a wooden window, cut out the damaged wood and repair it by inserting a new section or replace the entire component.

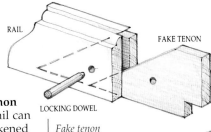

RAIL

FAKE TENON

LOCKING DOWEL

Repairing a broken sash-rail tenon

The tenon of a sash rail can become severely weakened by wet rot. Once you have dismantled the sash, you could replace the entire component, but that would involve having a matching moulding cut into the rail. However, provided serious damage goes no further than the tenon itself, the joint can be repaired relatively simply by installing a fake tenon. The same repair is also appropriate for the tongue of a meeting-rail bridle joint.

Set a mortise gauge to the width of the tenon and mark an angled housing for the fake tenon on the outer edge of the rail (1). Cut off the remnants of the tenon flush with the shoulder of the joint, then mark the housing on the end grain (2).

Saw down each side of the housing with a tenon saw (3), then pare out the waste with a mortise chisel. Use similar timber to make a fake tenon that fits the housing but is slightly wider than the sash rail (4).

Treat both components with preservative, then glue the tenon into the housing. When the glue has set, plane and shape the tenon.

Last of all, insert a glued locking dowel to reinforce the joint (5).

Making replacement components

An entire rail, stile or glazing bar can be copied from the original. Whether you do the work yourself or employ a professional joiner, it is important to reproduce the mouldings exactly. Some joiners use antique moulding planes for this type of work, but it is probably easier to have an electric-router cutter ground to match the profile.

Fake tenon

1 Mark out the housing

2 Mark out housing on end grain

3 Saw down each side of the housing

4 Make the tenon slightly oversize

5 Shape tenon and fit a dowel

PREVENTATIVE TREATMENT

Considering the expense and time involved in curing the effects of rot in wooden windows, it pays to take preventative measures whenever possible.

Chemical preservatives

Having stripped a window for repainting, you might take the opportunity to treat the bare timber with a chemical preservative. Two or three applications are ideal. You will need to leave it for between two and five days before painting, depending on drying conditions.

For replacements, either use pressure-treated timber or paint the wood with a preservative yourself.

Repairing a damaged weatherseal

If a window has a decayed weatherseal, rake out loose mortar to expose the joint between the window frame and the masonry surround. The traditional way to fill large gaps was to stuff them with wet newspaper before reinstating the mortar seal, but it's probably simpler and more efficient to inject an expanding polyurethane foam, provided there is no possibility of it impeding the movement of sash weights.

Finally, seal the joint with a gun-applied mastic (1) or press-in-place strip sealant (2). To preserve the original appearance, you can cover a mastic seal with mortar.

SAFETY WITH PRESERVATIVES

- Follow the preservative maker's instructions very carefully.
- Wear protective gloves to handle preservatives, and goggles when applying them. Use a face mask if you are working indoors.
- Make sure that there is adequate ventilation while preservatives are drying.

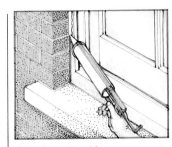

1 Apply mastic with a gun

2 Or use a press-in-place strip

REPLACING AN ENTIRE WINDOW

It is rarely necessary to replace an entire window, but if decay is so extensive that repairs are not practicable then replacement may be your only option. However, resist any temptation to install inappropriate modern-style windows in a period house. It isn't necessary, given that any competent joiner is capable of reproducing sliding-sash or casement windows, and there are several companies that specialize in making exact replicas of individual windows in treated softwoods or hardwoods (some types of window can even be supplied fully draughtproofed). If you have sufficient experience, you might want to install the windows yourself; or you can get the supplier to fit them for you.

CASEMENT WINDOWS

DESPITE THE POPULARITY *of the double-hung sash window, hinged casements have never really been out of fashion. They have remained in use in one form or another since medieval times, especially for smaller houses and workers' cottages. They are likely to comprise simple wooden frames divided by one or two glazing bars, constructed as individual windows or in pairs that close together with rebated stiles down the centre. Alternatively, there might be a single casement that opens within a group of fixed sashes. French windows are perhaps the most extreme example of twin casements, being in effect pairs of glazed doors opening onto a terrace, patio or balcony.*

Edwardian bay with leaded-light casement windows

THE REVIVAL OF THE CASEMENT WINDOW

The earliest casements had wrought-iron or wooden frames surrounding a tracery of cames (grooved lead strips) that held small diamond-shape or square glass panes. Similar forms of casement reappeared in Victorian times with the revival of Gothic and Queen Anne styles.

The same nostalgic sentiments were expressed in the fenestration of the late-Victorian and Edwardian 'Old English' styles and neo-Tudor interwar housing. Elegant mass-produced rolled-steel casement windows represented an opposing taste during the interwar decades, their uncluttered and severely practical lines being ideally suited to the avant-garde Art Deco architecture of the 1930s.

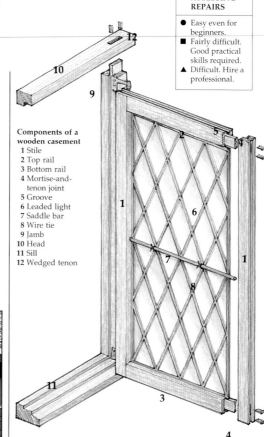

ASSESSING REPAIRS

- Easy even for beginners.
- ■ Fairly difficult. Good practical skills required.
- ▲ Difficult. Hire a professional.

Components of a wooden casement
1 Stile
2 Top rail
3 Bottom rail
4 Mortise-and-tenon joint
5 Groove
6 Leaded light
7 Saddle bar
8 Wire tie
9 Jamb
10 Head
11 Sill
12 Wedged tenon

Swollen casement
A wooden casement may swell and jam.
- Plane the frame (page 118).

Loose hinge
A loose or worn hinge allows the casement to drop and jam.
- Repair the hinge (page 118).

Rotted wood
Wet rot develops in poorly maintained wood components.
- Patch and repair minor areas of rot (page 114).
- ■ Replace rotted components (page 115).

Damaged weatherseal
Mortar falls out around frame.
- Reseal to prevent water seeping in (page 115).

Broken glass
- ■ Replace broken glass (page 112) or leaded lights (page 132).

Loose putty
Old putty no longer holds the glass or leaded lights securely in place.
- Replace the putty (page 113).

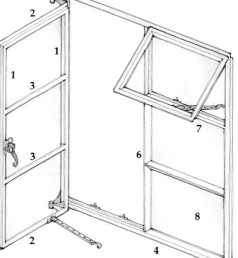

Glass held with putty

Components of a metal casement
1 Stile
2 Top and bottom rails
3 Glazing bar
4 Frame
5 Corner joint
6 Mullion
7 Transom
8 Fixed light

Corrosion
Some corrosion is present in all metal casements.
- Unless extremely advanced, it is fairly easy to treat (page 118).

Broken glass
- ■ Replacing broken panes in metal casements is quite straightforward (page 119).
- ■ Repairing a leaded light requires different skills (page 132).

Bent sections
Hinged casements are difficult to close if metal sections are bowed or distorted.
- ▲ Expert treatment may be required (page 119).

Damaged weatherseal
A deteriorating seal between the wall and window frame can cause serious corrosion.
- Seal with mastic (page 119).

HOW CASEMENTS WERE MADE

ALTHOUGH RELATIVELY SIMPLE *in construction, a wooden-casement window is similar to a sliding-sash window in that the various components are jointed together and, when necessary, can be dismantled for repair or replacement.*

A rolled-steel casement window, on the other hand, is made in complete sub-assemblies at the factory. The hinged casement itself can be removed, but it is impossible to replace individual components except by cutting and rewelding sections.

WOODEN-CASEMENT CONSTRUCTION

A hinged wooden casement comprises two vertical stiles **(1)** and horizontal top **(2)** and bottom rails **(3)** jointed at the corners with wedged through mortise-and-tenon joints **(4)**. The outer faces of the stiles and rails are rebated to accept the glass and are usually moulded decoratively on the inside A groove **(5)** around the outer edge stops water seeping in.

Although they may be divided by wooden glazing bars, casement windows are often glazed with leaded lights **(6)**. These consist of a lattice of lead 'cames' (grooved strips) holding square or diamond-shape panes of glass. To support this relatively weak lattice against wind pressure, 6mm (¼in) steel or iron saddle bars **(7)** are placed at strategic intervals. Each end of a saddle bar is located in a hole in the stile, and lengths of copper wire soldered to the lead cames **(8)** are twisted around the bar to tie the glazed panel securely in place.

Most casements are side-hung, like a door, being attached by hinges to a vertical stile. You sometimes find small wooden casements placed above larger ones, such as door-height French windows. They are usually hinged at the bottom and open inwards. When open, they are supported by metal stays or chains.

METAL-CASEMENT CONSTRUCTION

Early metal-casement windows were handmade from wrought iron, but late-nineteenth-century technology made it possible to mass-produce window casements and frames from rolled-steel sections. The stiles **(1)** and top and bottom rails **(2)** are made from identical Z-section pieces of metal. T-section glazing bars **(3)** divide the casement and support the glass panes, which are held in place with spring clips and a special putty formulated for use with metal.

Construction of the frame

The surrounding frame **(4)** is constructed from the same metal section used for the casement. The corner joints **(5)** are welded. Frames may be divided by T-section mullions **(6)** and transoms **(7)**, and often include fixed lights **(8)** as well as the hinged casement.

Wooden casement windows

Construction of the frame

A simple casement is hinged from a surrounding wooden frame comprising two vertical jambs **(9)**, a top rail or head **(10)**, and a sill **(11)** across the bottom. If the frame was to hold two or more casements, it was divided vertically by a mullion and, if need be, horizontally by a transom. A tenon on each end of the jamb passes right through the head and sill, and is secured with glue and wedges **(12)**. These joints are sometimes pinned with dowels in the manner of sliding-sash mortise-and-tenon joints. The frame is rebated externally to receive the casement.

Metal casement windows

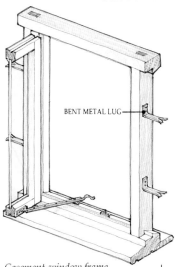

BENT METAL LUG

Casement-window frame

HOW WOODEN WINDOWS WERE FITTED

Wooden window frames were nailed directly to a timber-frame wall or to preservative-treated pallets (wooden strips), which were built into the mortar joints at 600mm (2ft) intervals as a masonry wall was being constructed. Another method was to nail into wooden plugs driven into holes cut in a finished masonry wall. Alternatively, bent metal lugs screwed to the frame at strategic points were bedded in mortar joints during the building of the opening. As well as being bedded in mortar, frames may also have been sealed with mastic.

HOW METAL WINDOWS WERE FITTED

Rolled-steel windows were either screwed to a wooden surround or to plugged masonry or, alternatively, bent metal lugs bolted to the metal frame were built into the mortar joints.

The window frames were bedded in mastic.

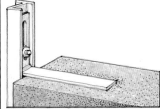

Fixing lug bolted to a metal frame

RESTORING CASEMENT WINDOWS

WOODEN-CASEMENT WINDOWS *generally suffer from problems very similar to those associated with sliding-sash windows, although leaded lights need special care and you may have to hire an expert to deal with extensive deterioration to the leadwork and the glass itself.*

REPAIRING WOODEN CASEMENTS
As with sash windows, rotted wood may have to be consolidated and either filled, patched or replaced, joints may need to be dismantled and reglued, loose putty replaced, and new panes of glass inserted. Joints around a frame can be resealed with mastic.

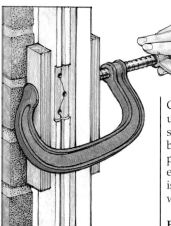

Glue a split frame and apply a cramp

CORRECTING A LOOSE HINGE
You may find that a hinged casement is binding against its frame because a loose hinge is allowing it to drop.

First of all, inspect the upper hinge to see if there are missing or loose screws; then lift the casement *in situ* to check whether the hinge knuckles are worn and have become slack. Swapping the top and bottom hinges may be enough to even out the wear and correct the fault.

Alternatively, the screws may have lost their grip as a result of the wooden frame splitting. The best solution in this case is to remove the casement, then work some waterproof glue into the split with a knife blade.

Close the split with a cramp until the glue has set. If the split will no longer close because the wood has expanded, fill it flush using an exterior wood filler that is tough enough to accept a woodscrew.

EASING A SWOLLEN CASEMENT
If a casement sticks or is difficult to open, inspect its edges for signs of abrasion where it is rubbing against the frame. Skim those areas with a finely set block plane until the window opens and closes smoothly. Take care not to remove too much wood, especially if the swelling could be due to humid conditions.

REPLACING A WOODEN CASEMENT
If a window has deteriorated beyond repair, have a joiner make an exact replica. Avoid the temptation to buy a cheaper ready-made casement window from a builders' merchant. The chances of it being a suitable style for an old house are very remote indeed.

Rolled-steel casements are often sadly neglected and needlessly replaced, largely due to a widely held view that metal windows are not worthy of conservation. But a rolled-steel window may be no less important to the integrity of a building than a Georgian sash window in a different context.

REPAIRING METAL CASEMENTS
Many people are under the impression that metal-casement windows are more difficult to restore than wooden ones, but with basic metalwork skills and equipment it is possible to do a great deal of repair work and restoration before it is necessary to replace a window.

DEALING WITH CORROSION
Corrosion, or rust, begins whenever moisture is able to penetrate the protective paint that coats a rolled-steel window. Neglected decoration is perhaps the most obvious cause of corrosion, but defective putty can lead to even worse symptoms, allowing corrosion to eat away at the metal section beneath. A faulty weatherseal around the perimeter of a metal frame is equally damaging, allowing rust to develop unnoticed until it eventually breaks through the paintwork.

Flaking or blistered paintwork is often the first sign of corrosion. Probing the affected area with a pointed tool will detect the degree and extent of the rust, which in turn determines the required treatment.

Light rust
If the metal is firm and flaking paint is due simply to a light accumulation of rust on the surface, rub it down with silicon-carbide paper dipped in white spirit to remove the rust, feathering the edges of sound paintwork surrounding it. Wipe away the dust with a cloth dampened in methylated spirits, then paint the

bare metal immediately with a rust-inhibiting primer. Repaint the window with two coats of paint that is compatible with the primer. It often pays to use a paint and primer made by the same manufacturer.

Medium rust
If the metal flakes when probed, wire-brush all corroded surfaces until you reach sound metal. For extensive corrosion, use a wire-brush attachment in a power drill. Wear goggles and a face mask, and protect adjacent masonry and glass. First neutralize the rust by applying an anti-corrosion acid-based gel, then fill pitted metal with an epoxy-based car-body filler. Prime and paint the window.

Heavy corrosion
If corrosion is ignored for a long time, it can weaken metal-window components to such an extent that your only recourse is to cut out damaged sections and weld new ones in their place. The casement or even the frame itself may have to be transferred to a workshop to be repaired by an expert. Replacing a rolled section of metal can be difficult unless you have an identical scrap window from which to plunder parts.

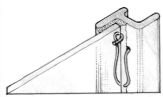
Glass held in place with a spring clip

REPLACING BROKEN GLASS

To reglaze a rolled-steel casement, follow the instructions for removing broken glass and installing new panes in a wooden window. However, the glass is held in place by spring clips, which you should remove and put aside for replacement. Use a special metal-window putty, available from a glazier or a builders' merchant.

STRAIGHTENING BENT COMPONENTS

Bent components can make it impossible to close a metal casement properly, perhaps leaving gaps that cannot be draughtproofed successfully. A badly distorted window will have to be repaired professionally, but you may be able to straighten a slightly bent component *in situ* yourself. After removing the glass, apply pressure to the bent component, using a stout wooden batten to spread the load evenly and prevent the metal kinking.

REPLACING A DECAYED WEATHERSEAL

Rake out any loose material from around the metal window frame, then seal the gap between the frame and the surrounding masonry with a gun-applied mastic.

REPLACING STEEL WINDOWS

Some manufacturers have continued to produce rolled-steel windows unchanged since their introduction in the 1920s and 1930s, which can be used as replacements for earlier versions. They are also available with superior galvanized or stoved finishes and can be ordered with draughtproofing and double glazing.

SHUTTERS

WINDOW SHUTTERS *have now largely fallen out of fashion, and sadly many have been rendered inoperable or ripped out. Yet it is hard to imagine why this should be so, considering that shutters are extremely practical, screening out harsh sunlight and noise, preventing draughts, and providing welcome additional security.*

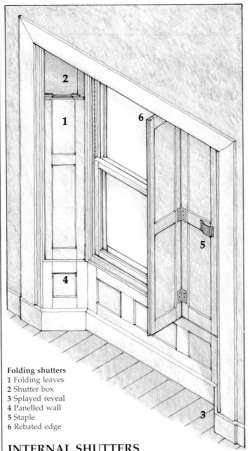

Folding shutters
1 Folding leaves
2 Shutter box
3 Splayed reveal
4 Panelled wall
5 Staple
6 Rebated edge

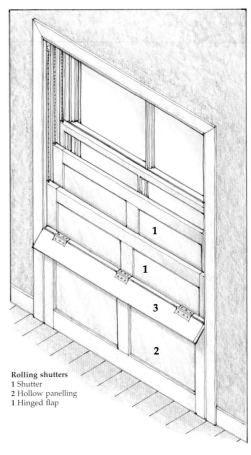

Rolling shutters
1 Shutter
2 Hollow panelling
1 Hinged flap

INTERNAL SHUTTERS

Folding or rolling shutters were a feature of many Georgian and Victorian interiors. Yet they were so ingeniously designed to be unobtrusive that sometimes householders are completely unaware of their presence.

Folding shutters

Panelled shutters, which generally comprise a pair of leaves on each side of the window (1), fold back into deep shutter boxes (2) in the reveals. The reveals may be square to the window, but often they are splayed (3) to admit more daylight. The wall below the shutter boxes (4) and the window is usually panelled to match the shutters themselves. Once folded out flat against the window, the shutters are secured by metal bars that engage strong staples (5) fixed to the back of the leaves. Leaf stiles are rebated (6) to make lightproof joints.

Rolling shutters

Rolling shutters are comparatively rare and are even more unobtrusive. They work on the same principle as a sliding-sash window, being counterbalanced by cords and weights.

The shutters (1) are housed behind panelling (2) constructed between the window and the floor, and are accessible by means of a hinged flap (3) that forms the internal window board.

REINSTATING INTERNAL SHUTTERS

If you have wood-panelled reveals or unusually deep window boards, it might be worth stripping a small section to see if there are shutters hidden beneath layers and layers of paint. There's every chance that the shutters themselves are in perfect condition, perhaps requiring a drop of oil on the hinges or a new set of cords.

If you decide to strip all the paint from panelled shutters, either do it yourself or make sure a professional stripper uses a cold-chemical dip – since a hot-caustic stripping solution can split the relatively thin panelling used for shutters.

EXTERNAL SHUTTERS

With outward-opening casements it is difficult, if not impossible, to reach exterior shutters from the upper floors of a house. This problem has been overcome in some houses by the use of an ingenious worm gear that controls the position of each shutter by cranking a handle on the inside.

Small houses and cottages are most likely to be fitted with shutters of frame-and-panel construction or simple ledged-and-braced boarded shutters with strap hinges that are either screwed to the wooden window frame or hung from hooked pins driven into the wall.

Routine maintenance is all that's required with these types of shutter, and even complete replacement is no problem to a reasonably competent joiner. Unless they are traditional in the area where you live, avoid having shutters made with cutouts – which can make an attractive cottage look unconvincingly twee.

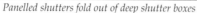

Panelled shutters fold out of deep shutter boxes

Adjustable louvred shutters control the light

LOUVRED SHUTTERS

Louvred shutters or blinds are to be found both internally and externally on Georgian and early-Victorian villas. Especially valuable are the ones with pivoting slats that are operated simultaneously by a vertical wooden rod, attached to the edge of each slat with staples.

Banks of small louvred shutters are sometimes mounted one above the other to provide a greater degree of flexibility when in use. The bottom half of a window, for example, can be screened for privacy while the top half is left partly open for light and ventilation.

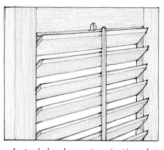

A stapled rod operates pivoting slats

Attractive external louvred shutters

Sturdy framed shutters with raised-and-fielded panels

FANLIGHTS

THE TERM FANLIGHT *was coined in the eighteenth century to describe a semi-circular fixed light or window with a radiating pattern of glazing bars. It was installed above a doorway to admit light to the hallway or passage beyond. In time, 'fanlight' became a general term for similar fixed lights of any pattern, including rectangular ones.*

FANLIGHT PATTERNS

A simple fan of wooden glazing bars was probably the earliest fanlight pattern. It was developed sometime during the first quarter of the eighteenth century. The techniques required to make this type of fanlight would have been familiar to a joiner used to constructing semi-circular-head or segmental-head sash windows.

Fanlights of similar design were made by fretting the pattern of glazing bars from a single piece of solid wood. However, fretted fanlights that break with tradition are often extremely decorative. Wooden fanlights were often embellished with 'compo' (a mixture of whiting and glue) and hand carving.

The introduction of metal fanlights in the 1770s made it possible to produce the delicately beautiful traceries that are a feature of classic Georgian design. There were countless variations on the original fan, and patterns such as the umbrella and the batswing and its derivative the teardrop were extremely popular, too.

Traditional patterns were frequently adapted to suit rectangular fanlights; and abstract patterns such as intersecting circles or Gothic arches were devised to make the most of the increasingly fashionable rectangular fanlight shape.

A relatively early fretted and carved fanlight

Variation on the fan motif in a wooden doorcase

Delicate umbrella-pattern fanlight

Gothic-style fanlight with simple wooden glazing bars

Simple rectangular fanlight

Classic metal fanlight above a Georgian door

Typical metal teardrop fanlight

Batswing with hinged ventilator

METHODS OF CONSTRUCTION

A wooden fanlight has a substantial outer frame **(1)** enclosing glazing bars **(2)** that accommodate the glass in the usual way. But, unlike most wooden windows, the moulded side of a fanlight faces the street.

A metal fanlight has brass or tinned wrought-iron ribs **(3)** fixed inside a wooden sash. Decorative lead-alloy strips **(4)** soldered to the leading edges of the ribs form the glazing rebates. Very often they incorporate rosettes or scrolls, or other ornamental motifs, that do not support the glass in any way. The metal framework is attached to the sash by means of thin strips of tin **(5)** nailed to the wood. The sash itself either locates in rebates cut in the doorframe or may be fixed directly to the masonry and plastered in.

REPLACING FANLIGHTS

There are relatively few professionals with the skill and knowledge required to repair, let alone reconstruct, authentic metal fanlights. As a result, the space above many a Georgian door is now filled with a blank sheet of glass or a cheap imitation of a period fanlight.

Look for a craftsperson who will remake corroded ribs, attach new tin fixing strips, and resolder cast-lead ornamentation. A first-class workshop will even cast new sections from existing fragments to reproduce missing ornamentation. A craftsperson with this type of experience will probably be able to make a copy of a neighbour's fanlight if your own has been discarded at some time in the past.

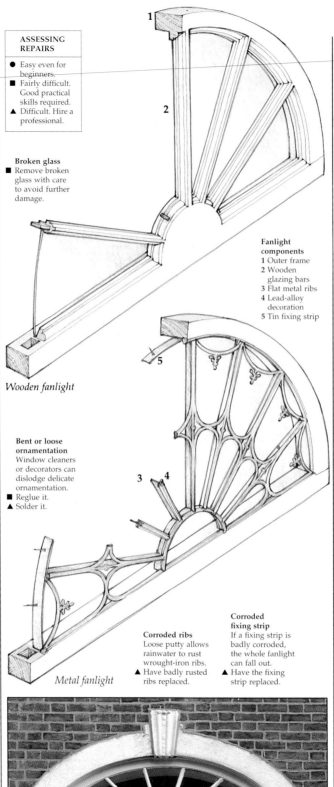

ASSESSING REPAIRS

- ● Easy even for beginners.
- ■ Fairly difficult. Good practical skills required.
- ▲ Difficult. Hire a professional.

Broken glass
- ■ Remove broken glass with care to avoid further damage.

Wooden fanlight

Bent or loose ornamentation
Window cleaners or decorators can dislodge delicate ornamentation.
- ■ Reglue it.
- ▲ Solder it.

Metal fanlight

Fanlight components
1 Outer frame
2 Wooden glazing bars
3 Flat metal ribs
4 Lead-alloy decoration
5 Tin fixing strip

Corroded ribs
Loose putty allows rainwater to rust wrought-iron ribs.
- ▲ Have badly rusted ribs replaced.

Corroded fixing strip
If a fixing strip is badly corroded, the whole fanlight can fall out.
- ▲ Have the fixing strip replaced.

Elliptical-head fanlight designed to fit above a wide doorcase

Some fanlights incorporate lanterns

REPAIRING FANLIGHTS

Restoring a wooden fanlight is no more difficult than working on any other similar window, except that if you need to remove the whole sash you will probably have to hack away some interior plasterwork. Look for signs of filler covering the sash-fixing nails, and drive them right through the outer frame with a punch.

Metal fanlights, especially ones that have reached an advanced stage of corrosion, can be extremely fragile; and clumsy attempts to repair them can make matters even worse. Inspect a fanlight closely before you start work to ascertain whether you need expert help or advice.

Avoiding damage to the glass

Old fanlights sometimes still contain the original crown glass, which should be preserved if at all possible. When you are removing glass, especially from a metal fanlight, soften the putty with paint stripper to avoid distorting the frame and cracking other panes.

Replacing loose cast-metal ornamentation

You frequently find cast-lead strips and ornamentation that are bent or peeling away from the metal glazing ribs behind them. Straighten the components, and refit them with an epoxy glue or get an expert to resolder them.

WINDOW FURNITURE

THE APPROPRIATE HARDWARE *or 'furniture' is important to the security and smooth operation of both casement and sliding-sash windows. It is preferable to restore antique hardware; but if you need to replace a broken or missing fitting, you can buy reproductions that are almost indistinguishable from original pieces. Whenever possible, it is best to remove fittings for cleaning, lubricating or stripping. So you can put back the fittings in their original positions, don't fill fixing holes when decorating. Brass screws should be used for attaching brass fittings.*

SASH FASTENERS

Antique fasteners made to secure double-hung sash windows provide minimal security and prevent sashes rattling in the wind. Some fasteners were designed in such a way that they could not be opened by a blade slipped between the meeting rails, but by themselves they do not conform to modern standards of home security. It is therefore recommended that you fit a lock or security bolt with a removable key to any accessible window, in addition to a traditional sash fastener.

Cam fastener

Cam fasteners have been fitted to sash windows since Georgian times. A lever on one half of the fitting engages a cam-shape lug on the other, pulling the meeting rails together. Cam fasteners, originally made in bronze or brass, are often very decorative, with brass or ceramic knobs fitted to the lever.

Screw the fitting to the tops of the meeting rails, as close to the centre of the window as possible. Fit the lever first (on the upper sash) and use it to position the lug, making allowance for the cam action.

Fitch fastener

A Fitch or crescent fastener is even better for windows with loose sashes. The rim of a helical metal cam engages a hook on the other half of the fitting. Turning the cam forces the sashes apart vertically while pulling the meeting rails together.

Screw the hook to the upper sash first, then use it to position the cam on the other meeting rail.

Always remember to turn the cam back completely before opening the window, or the fastener may gouge wood out of glazing bars in the upper sash.

Screw fastener

Like other sash fasteners, a screw fastener pulls the meeting rails together – this time by means of a knurled nut on the end of a pivoting lever. Unless the lever is raised properly when the window is opened, it will get caught under the meeting rail of the lower sash when you close the window.

Victorian sash screw

Sash screw

A sash screw passes right through one meeting rail into the other so that neither sash can be opened. Period brass sash screws are most attractive – however, unlike modern ones that can only be extracted with a key, security is compromised if a pane of glass is broken.

SASH LIFTS

Sash lifts are screwed to the bottom rails of heavy lower sashes to make them easier to open. They are fitted approximately 150mm (6in) from each end of the rail.

Hook lift

Simple brass lifts are still manufactured today, but antique hook lifts with cast decoration are even more attractive. On some lifts the hook forms a complete ring, but they offer little practical advantage over the simple hooked variety.

Flush lift

Flush lifts provide a more positive grip, but because a recess has to be cut in the wood in order to set them into the rail they are more difficult to fit.

SASH HANDLES

Upper sashes without horizontal glazing bars that form finger grips are difficult to open. One solution is to screw a pair of D-shaped handles to the underside of the meeting rail, close to the stiles. Sash handles can only be reached by raising the lower sash.

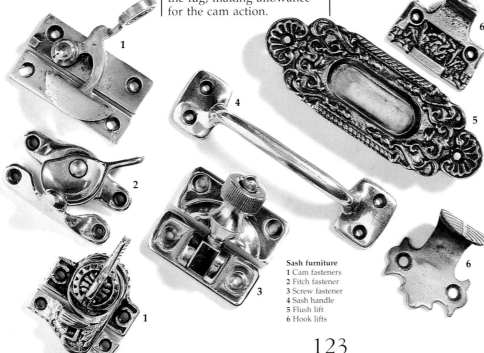

Sash furniture
1 Cam fasteners
2 Fitch fastener
3 Screw fastener
4 Sash handle
5 Flush lift
6 Hook lifts

CASEMENT FASTENERS

A hinged casement is held closed by a one-piece pivoting handle known as a cockspur fastener. The window is held open in a number of positions by means of a metal bar or stay.

Cockspur fastener

A cockspur fastener comprises a metal handle with a projecting spur that engages a slotted striker plate screwed to the frame or, alternatively, a hook screwed to the face of an adjacent fixed casement.

The traditional iron rat-tail fastener with its coiled handle looks well on a casement of any period up to the end of the nineteenth century. Twentieth-century casements are generally fitted with cast-metal cockspur fasteners, made from either sherardized iron, bronze, or aluminium alloy. Similar fasteners for rolled-steel casement windows are frequently of the 'two-point' or 'three-point' types with slotted spurs. The slots locate on the edge of the window muntin or stile, holding the casement ajar to provide ventilation.

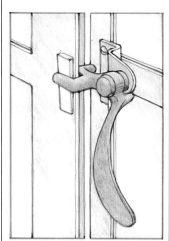

A two-point cockspur locates on the muntin to hold the window ajar

Casement stay

A casement or peg stay is a flat, rigid metal bar pivoting on a metal plate screwed to the bottom rail of a hinged casement. A short peg screwed to the sill engages one of a series of holes that run the length of the bar, holding the window open. When the window is closed, a second peg holds the bar parallel to the bottom rail. You can buy stays made to match the various styles of cockspur fasteners.

Sliding stays that are fixed permanently to rolled-steel casements are secured in an open or closed position by a thumbscrew or lever.

Sliding casement-window stay

CASEMENT HINGES

Standard butt hinges are fitted to many wooden-casement windows. However, special extension hinges are sometimes used to facilitate cleaning both sides of the glass, especially on windows situated on the upper floors of a house.

Extension hinge

When a window is open, extension hinges provide a clearance of about 100 to 125mm (4 to 5in) between the hinge stile and the frame, making it possible to clean the outside of the window from inside the room. Rolled-steel windows are invariably fitted with extension hinges.

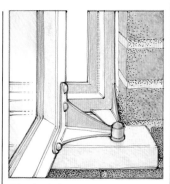

Metal-window extension hinge

ESPAGNOLETTE BOLTS

Victorian and Edwardian door-height French windows are frequently fitted with espagnolette bolts. Turning a centrally fitted door handle simultaneously closes two substantial bolts running parallel with the closing stile of the window. One bolt shoots into the window head, the other into the sill.

Casement furniture
1 Rat-tail cockspur fastener
2 Rat-tail stay
3 Iron peg stay
4 Simple cockspur fastener
5 Brass two-point fastener

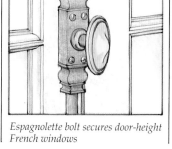

Espagnolette bolt secures door-height French windows

CHAPTER ELEVEN

ORNAMENTAL GLASS

WHETHER IT IS THE FEELING OF OPTIMISM conjured by the early-morning sunshine streaming through a colourful landing window or the welcoming sight of a back-lit stained-glass door on a winter's evening, ornamental glass can influence our emotional attachment to a house in a most direct and effective manner.

In fact, decorative glass is such a valuable asset, financially as well as aesthetically, that any householder would be well advised to preserve even the most modest items and to replace any that have been removed.

For a period of a hundred years or so, from the early nineteenth century onwards, grand and humble houses alike were enriched with all manner of decorative glass. But the beginnings of handcrafted glass are very much earlier. Stained glass, for example, has a pedigree stretching back to before medieval times. Nevertheless, crucial aspects of the technology had to be rediscovered by the Victorians before the craft could be exploited with a fresh momentum that would carry it beyond the ecclesiastical tradition into the wider domestic context.

The technical innovations of the Industrial Revolution introduced more and more possibilities for using glass cheaply as well as decoratively in practically every Victorian home. In particular, with the increased density of urban housing, various forms of acid-etched, sandblasted and machine-rolled glass were used instead of clear glazing to preserve Victorian and Edwardian sensitivities.

A spectacular Art Deco door panel

The welcoming sight of stained glass is most appealing

Typical Victorian landing light

Late-C19th hand-painted glass panel

PATTERNED GLASS

SO-CALLED PATTERNED GLASS *was made by passing it in a molten state between water-cooled rollers, one of which was embossed in order to press a texture on one side of the sheet. A notable feature of patterned glass is that it's impossible to see anything through it save for vague distorted images. Sometimes known as obscured glass, from Victorian times onwards it has been used in bathrooms, toilets and elsewhere to afford privacy.*

But it was not only its practical applications that appealed to the Victorians. They were also quick to recognize the aesthetic qualities of patterned glass. It was used extensively in door panels and fanlights; and in windows it was often employed in the form of marginal lights or as small decorative panes across the top of a sliding sash, thus providing a contrast to large panes of clear glass.

Even in the early twentieth century its popularity was such that literally hundreds of patterns were offered for sale. However, very few are stocked today, even by specialist glaziers, and the number of patterns available varies according to the whims of the market. The ones listed below are modern copies of original patterns that can be used as substitutes for old glass no longer produced.

Muffled and waterglass
Muffled glass, which closely resembles rippled water, was widely used in Victorian and Edwardian leaded lights. Fortunately, there is still a reasonable range of colours to choose from.

Waterglass is a modern glass similar to some old versions of muffled glass that are no longer manufactured. Several colours are available.

Cathedral
Cathedral, also known as 'German cathedral', is a subtly textured glass used for decorative leaded lights. 'Rolled cathedral' is a version that includes flecks and air bubbles.

You can buy a wide range of single-colour and 'streaky' (two-colour) cathedrals from specialist glass suppliers.

Muranese
A deep-textured machine-rolled glass, Muranese has a pattern resembling a crystal-line structure. The modern version is slightly smaller than its Victorian equivalent. As well as clear glass, you can buy a limited range of colours.

Reeded
Victorian and Edwardian glaziers employed the unremarkable texture of reeded glass to spectacular effect in leaded lights by arranging quarries (small panes of glass) in such a way that the flutes made a variety of linear patterns. However, it may be difficult to match using modern glass, which is generally made with comparatively wide flutes. It is only produced as clear glass.

Edwardian patterned-glass window

Rich combination of patterned glass

Muffled glass

Waterglass

Cathedral glass

Muranese glass

Reeded glass

Flemish glass

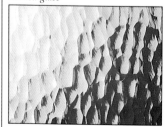
Hammered glass

Ice-crystal glass

LEADED LIGHTS

THE TERM STAINED GLASS *is commonly used for any coloured window – but unless the window includes painted glass, strictly speaking it is a leaded light. This does not imply that leaded lights are inferior. The 'palette' of glass available to Victorian and Edwardian artisans was such that many a house is enriched with coloured windows and door panels that do not contain a single pane of painted glass.*

Leaded lights were all constructed in a similar way, the only real difference being the way the lead was incorporated. The leadwork for clear-glass windows is invariably constructed from straight cames only. But coloured glass arrests the eye and focuses attention on the dark lines created by the leadwork – so artists and craftsmen tended to form the lead into sinuous shapes, almost as if they were drawing with it.

Clear-glass leaded lights

Detail from a 1930s door panel

Flemish
Another clear 'commercial' glass available from high-street glaziers. Our forebears could choose between 'big' and 'little' Flemish, but you will probably be offered only one size today.

Hammered
This Victorian textured glass is still available from good high-street glaziers. Its closely dimpled texture makes it look as if it has been struck repeatedly with a ball-peen hammer. Hammered glass is usually clear, but you may come across coloured versions.

Ice-crystal
Clear glass with a texture resembling crushed ice has been manufactured for decades under various names. The modern version has a relatively small-scale texture compared with some Victorian examples.

CUTTING AND FITTING PATTERNED GLASS
When cutting patterned glass, score the flat side (not the textured side).

For ease of cleaning, fit the glass with the textured surface facing the inside of the house.

A beautiful example of free-flowing linework and coloured glass

GLASS FOR LEADED LIGHTS

If you look closely at a decorative leaded light, you may be surprised to see just how many different types of glass have been used in a single window. Victorian stained-glass artists in particular had a vast range of both handmade and mass-produced glass to choose from. Although today the selection is much more limited, many of the original types of glass are still manufactured, so you stand a good chance of finding a similar pattern, colour or texture, if not an exact replica of the original glass.

Antique glass

Leaded lights were once commonly fashioned from handmade glass, either spun into a disc (crown glass) or formed into a large tube that was split lengthwise then opened to make a flat sheet (cylinder glass). Today, clear and coloured handmade 'antique' glass is still being produced, using precisely the same methods employed by our forebears. These traditional processes imbue the coloured varieties in particular with interesting characteristics not found in mass-produced glass.

Even clear glass can be bought as 'plain' (free from blemishes and of uniform thickness), 'reamy' (rippled due to variations in density) or 'seedy' (containing trapped air bubbles).

Coloured types (1) include 'pot colours' (strong even colour throughout), 'tints' (pale tones) and 'streaky' (two or more colours mixed in one sheet). Some colours, such as deep red or blue, are too dense to use as pot colours. Instead, they are applied as a thin layer over a sheet of clear or coloured glass. These are known as 'flashed' colours (2). Glass is flashed with pure gold to create dramatic pink or ruby hues. 'Opal' glass is made by flashing opaque white on clear glass. 'Opalescent' is opal glass mixed with at least one other colour to create a marbled appearance.

Rolled glass

As if the range of handmade glass was not sufficient, leaded-light artists availed themselves of the variety of patterns and textures created commercially in the form of machine-rolled glass.

Roundels

A roundel (3), or 'bullion', is a small disc of spun crown glass that includes the scar left at its centre by the glass blower's pontil. Roundels were, and still are, made specially for leaded lights.

Jewels

Jewels (4) are faceted square and circular pieces of glass that were set among flat quarries to catch and break up the light You can buy modern 'jewels' – but some professionals consider them to be inferior to nineteenth-century examples, which are sold at a premium whenever an old window is broken up for scrap.

A bold yet simple abstract design

Formalized fruit-bowl motif

Art Nouveau transom light incorporating a floral wreath and swags

Jewels and roundels

CAMES

Each piece of glass in a leaded window is surrounded by H-section strips of lead known as cames (5). These are made either with a convex surface (round lead) or with a flat one (flat lead). Flat lead is the earlier type.

Because lead is a very soft metal, the cames are practically unmanageable until they have been stretched. This both straightens and work-hardens the came. It is done by holding one end in a vice and pulling the other end sharply with pliers.

Towards the end of the nineteenth century a new technique for joining glass quarries was developed in America by Louis Tiffany. A strip of copper foil was wrapped round the edges of each quarry. With the foiled quarries butted together, a bead of solder was run along both sides of the window to make a neat continuous joint. It is an ideal method for joining small pieces of glass However, the cost of restoring or remaking a copper-foiled window is likely to be higher than for a conventional leaded light.

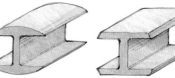

Round lead   *Flat lead*

Copper foil

Components of a leaded light
1 Coloured glass
2 Flashed glass
3 Roundel
4 Jewel
5 Cames
6 Soldered joint
7 Cement seal
8 Saddle bar

ASSESSING REPAIRS

- ● Easy even for beginners.
- ■ Fairly difficult. Good practical skills required.
- ▲ Difficult. Hire a professional.

Loose wire ties
The solder breaks from joints.
■ Replace the wire ties (page 131).

Cracked quarry
Slamming a door or window can crack the quarries.
■ Strap with lead (page 132).

Broken joint
Weak lead cracks near joint.
■ Resolder joint (page 132).
▲ Have lead replaced (page 133).

Corroded lead
Lead becomes brittle due to pollution.
▲ Have lead replaced (page 133).

Seriously damaged panel
Severe damage can be caused by a break-in.
▲ Have the panel professionally repaired (page 133).

Missing panel
Panel discarded or sold by a previous owner.
▲ Have replacement made (page 133).

Dirty glass and lead
Airborne pollution leaves deposits on leadwork and dirties the glass.
● Clean and polish (page 133).

Loose quarries
Brittle old cement falls out. Quarries rattle if you tap the window with your fingertips.
● Seal with fresh cement (page 131).

Broken quarry
A quarry may get broken as a result of an accident or vandalism.
■ Replace the quarry (page 132).

Buckled panel
A buckled window or door panel can be caused by slamming or wind pressure.
■ Straighten panel (page 131).
■ Install saddle bar (page 131).

SOLDER

The joints between lengths of came are secured with solder **(6)** made from 60 per cent lead and 40 per cent tin. Professionals tend to use gas soldering irons to melt the solder, but you may find a thermostatically controlled electric iron more convenient. Tallow, cast in stick form, is the flux favoured by professional stained-glass artists and restorers.

CEMENT

To create a weatherproof seal, a mixture of whiting (powdered chalk), linseed oil and turpentine known in the trade as 'cement' is packed into the gaps between the glass and lead **(7)**. Vegetable black or grate polish is included to colour the mixture.

You can buy ready-made cement, in the form of a special quick-setting putty, but for a single repair it is cheaper to use ordinary glazier's putty mixed with grate polish.

SADDLE BARS

Vulnerable leaded lights are supported on the inside by steel or iron rods, 6 to 9mm (¼ to ⅜in) in diameter, known as saddle bars **(8)**. Copper-wire ties soldered to strategic joints in the lead are twisted round each bar to secure the window.

If straight saddle bars would spoil the appearance of a leaded light, they can be shaped to follow the line of the leading. Alternatively, steel inserts, known as lead strengtheners, can be run inside the cames.

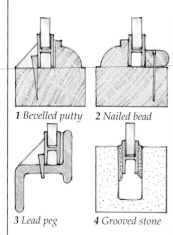

1 Bevelled putty **2** Nailed bead

3 Lead peg **4** Grooved stone

HOW LEADED LIGHTS WERE FITTED

Leaded lights were installed in the same way as ordinary window glass. The panel was bedded in linseed-oil putty and secured in the rebates with sprigs or tacks, then more putty was added and shaped to form a bevel all round **(1)**. When leaded lights were installed in sliding sashes, relatively large counterweights were required to counterbalance the weight of the lead.

Interior leaded lights were often secured with wooden beads screwed or nailed to the rebates **(2)**.

Lead pegs driven into holes in the frame held leaded lights in metal casements, and putty was used to fill the rebates **(3)**. If the leaded light has been repaired in the past, the pegs may have been cut off flush with the frame and the plugged lead used as fixing points for nails or tacks.

A leaded light fixed in a stone surround was located in grooves (or sometimes in rebates) cut in the masonry all round the opening **(4)**. Deep grooves allowed the panel to be slid into place then centralized. If the grooves were shallow, the lead flanges around the panel were bent back for fitting then straightened out into the grooves. Pointing with mortar made the joints surrounding the window waterproof.

REPAIRING LEADED LIGHTS

ALTHOUGH MINOR REPAIRS *to leaded lights can often be undertaken by a reasonably competent amateur, full-scale restoration requires the skills of a professional. Don't expect your high-street glazier to be able to restore stained glass. It is a craft that takes years of training and experience to perfect.*

Consequently, stained-glass artists are a relatively rare breed. When looking for a professional to work for you, it is therefore worth contacting associations such as the British Society of Master Glass Painters and the Guild of Master Craftsmen who can recommend experts practising in your part of the country.

You will find that most professionals have a portfolio of their work to show you. You should also ask to see an actual job in progress, in order to ascertain the quality of the detailing.

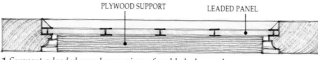
PLYWOOD SUPPORT   LEADED PANEL

1 *Support a leaded panel on a piece of padded plywood*

REMOVING A LEADED LIGHT

Try to disturb an old leaded light as little as possible. Careless repair work or clumsy handling may cause further damage, requiring expensive restoration.

Though some jobs can be done with the leaded light *in situ*, many repairs can only be tackled efficiently with the window laid flat on a bench.

If possible, take the whole casement or door off its hinges and lay it on a workbench with the leaded panel supported from below by a piece of plywood cut to fit the opening **(1)**. If necessary, use wads of newspaper to raise the support slightly.

If the leaded light is in a fixed frame or surround, or has to be dismantled to facilitate a repair, you have no alternative but to remove it from the opening. Cut wire ties with pliers, then remove wooden beads or use an old chisel to chop out the putty holding the leaded panel in place. If the putty is very hard, it is probably safer to soften it first with paint stripper (see RENEWING OLD PUTTY).

Remove any nail fixings, then run a blade all round the leaded panel to loosen it.

If necessary, use a sharpened paint scraper to gently lever out the panel, working from the other side of the window **(2)**. Insert the blade of the scraper as close as possible to joints in the lead, and work alternately on opposite sides of the frame.

Carry a leaded light on edge, keeping it as vertical as possible. If you cannot lay the panel flat on the bench immediately, rest it in an upright position against a wall and place a weight on the ground to prevent the bottom sliding outwards.

If a leaded light has to be removed for more than a day, as a security measure temporarily install ordinary glass in its place.

2 *Gently lever out the panel*

WORKING SAFELY WITH LEADED LIGHTS

- You have to work with lead for relatively long periods before the metal presents a serious threat to your health. Nevertheless, it pays to wear barrier cream and to wash your hands thoroughly after handling it. Do not eat or prepare food in the workshop, and always work in a well-ventilated environment.
- Wear protective gloves when handling glass, and protect your eyes with safety goggles when you are cutting it.
- Be careful not to exert too much pressure on a leaded light – if the lead suddenly buckles, you may thrust your hand or arm right through the window.

RECEMENTING LOOSE QUARRIES

If glass quarries are loose because of damaged cames, you will need to have the window releaded. However, you are more likely to find that the quarries are rattling because expansion and contraction of the lead has caused brittle old cement to fall out.

There's no need to spend money on special cement for just one or two quarries. Instead, you can knead a ball of ordinary linseed-oil putty to a fairly stiff consistency (if need be, removing some of the oil by pressing it between newspaper) and mix in black grate polish until the putty is dark grey.

Use your thumbs to push the putty under the edges of the cames surrounding the loose quarries **(1)**. You can do this with the window *in situ*, but don't forget to fill both sides.

Remove excess putty by running a pointed tool along the edges of the cames **(2)**, then consolidate the putty by brushing in all directions with a bristle brush.

1 Push putty under the cames *2 Scrape off excess putty*

FLATTENING A BUCKLED PANEL

The force generated by the repeated slamming of a door or window gradually bows the lead outwards, and even strong winds have been known to distort a large leaded light. If there are no other obvious signs of damage, it may be possible to straighten out a bowed or distorted panel – but consider first whether this is really desirable.

Slight buckling of the lead creates interesting reflections that add to the character of a window. Furthermore, it is not always possible to flatten a leaded light satisfactorily. If the lead has been buckled for some time, it may have become inflexible and brittle and will resist any attempt to straighten it out. This is often exacerbated by the sharp edges of the glass cutting into the inside of the cames as you attempt to move them.

Taking great care, try to push the cames back into position with the window in place. Wear thick protective gloves, and press very gently and evenly. If the glass does not flex, do not try to force it – remove the leaded light and leave it in the sun for a day with a weight such as a book carefully placed on the leadwork. Once the panel has been flattened, you may need to renew the cement.

Before reinstalling the panel, consider whether adding a saddle bar might prevent a recurrence of the bulging in future.

If the window already has a saddle bar, renew the wire ties (see right) before you put the panel back *in situ*.

INSTALLING A SADDLE BAR

Most movable windows and doors, and any fixed light that is over 600mm (2ft) in height, are likely to benefit from the addition of a saddle bar. It is therefore worth installing one when leaded lights are removed for repair. You may need to fit several bars if the panel is very large.

Select a position for the bar (or bars) that will not detract from the design of the window. Saddle bars usually look best running alongside a continuous horizontal came or a row of soldered joints. Mark the chosen position on the inside of the window frame.

The length of the saddle bar should be the width of the frame plus 12mm (½in) at each end **(1)**.

Drill holes for the bar **(2)** on both sides of the window. One hole should be 12mm (½in) deep; the other should be 25mm (1in). The deeper hole will allow you to slide the bar into place then adjust its position until it is located at both ends.

Cut 75mm (3in) lengths of copper wire to serve as ties, and solder their centres to conveniently placed joints that will align with the bar **(3)**. Space the ties as regularly as possible.

Install the leaded light and saddle bar, then wrap each tie around the bar and twist the ends of the wire together with pliers **(4)**.

Cut off excess wire and fold the twisted tail under the bar. Apply putty all round the window on the outside (see REPLACING A BROKEN PANE).

If beads are used on the inside to secure the panel, notch them so they fit over the saddle bar.

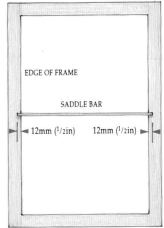

1 Allow extra on length of bar

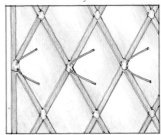

2 Drill holes in the frame

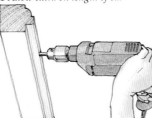

3 Solder wires to the joints

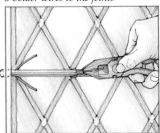

4 Twist wire ties with pliers

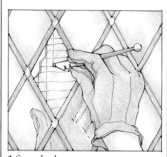

1 Score broken quarry

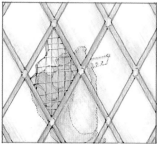

2 Tap the quarry to break the glass

3 Cut the joints with a knife

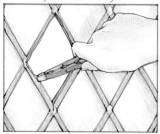

4 Bend back the lead flanges

5 Rub down the cames

REPLACING A BROKEN QUARRY

If only one or two quarries are broken, provided the lead is in good condition you can replace them *in situ.*

Make a tracing of the broken quarry by drawing along the inner edge of the surrounding cames. This tracing will serve as a template for cutting the replacement glass.

Support the back of the window and, using a glass cutter, score what remains of the quarry with a series of crisscross lines (1). Wearing protective gloves and safety goggles, tap the back of the glass in the middle of the quarry to break out most of the fragments (2). Use a penknife to loosen small pieces of glass trapped in the cames, then scrape out the residue of old cement with a small screwdriver.

Cut the corner joints, on the inside only, with a stout craft knife (3). Because you are cutting through solder, which is harder than lead, it is important to keep the knife blade at an angle that doesn't put sideways pressure on the leaded panel, making it buckle.

Use a small pair of pliers (ordinary engineer's pliers are too large), with the jaws padded with tape, to bend back the flanges all round (4). Don't bend the flanges too far or they will crease, making it impossible to close them up neatly.

Select a piece of glass that matches the broken quarry and cut it to size (see CUTTING GLASS). The new piece should be 2mm (¹⁄₁₆in) larger all round than the tracing you made from the original quarry.

Insert the new glass and close up the cames, using a home-made tool known as a lathykin or larrikin. This is a round-pointed stick made from a piece of wood about 6mm (¼in) thick and 40mm (1½in) wide. Rub down the cames all round (5), and make sure the corners are closed up neatly.

As this operation is performed on the inside of the window, it is not absolutely essential to resolder the joints. If you want to complete the job with solder, take the door or window off its hinges and lay it flat on the floor or workbench.

Seal the cames with cement (see RECEMENTING LOOSE QUARRIES). For at least the next week, close the door or window very gently.

STRAPPING A CRACKED QUARRY

Strapping entails soldering a flat piece of lead over cracked glass, in effect creating a false came. Although individual quarries can be replaced, it is sometimes desirable to strap cracked glass, especially if it is rare and expensive. Strapping a narrow strip of glass in a border, for example, is relatively simple and the repair is hardly noticeable.

Shorten the blade of an ordinary paint scraper and sharpen it to make a lead-cutting knife. Use this knife to make a strap by slicing off one flat side of a came (1).

Clean a section of came next to each end of the crack in the glass by scraping the lead with a blade. Lay the strap over the crack and solder one end to the edge of the came (2). Pull the strap taut and cut off the other end flush with the opposite came (3). Solder it, then repeat the process on the other side of the window and darken the lead with grate polish.

1 Slice a flat strap from a lead came

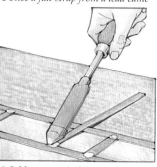

2 Solder one end of the strap

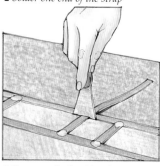

3 Cut strap flush with other came

REPAIRING A BROKEN LEAD JOINT

When a soldered joint in a leaded light cracks, it is not normally the joint itself that breaks but the piece of lead next to the solder.

You can repair the joint with solder; but if it breaks again, it's a sure sign that the lead is weak and you should consider having the window releaded.

REPLACING CORRODED CAMES

Decades of airborne pollution can seriously weaken leadwork. It becomes brittle, and pieces gradually break away until whole sections of glass are in danger of falling out. If you have a window in this state, get a professional to remove it and take it away for releading. He or she will make a rubbing of the window as an exact guide to the layout of the cames. A full-size drawing called a 'cutline' is made from the rubbing, each line representing the position of the central web or 'heart' of each piece of leading.

The leaded light is carefully dismantled and each piece of glass laid out in the correct pattern. The old cement is then scraped from around the edges of the glass with a lead-cutting knife. Any damaged quarries are replaced at this stage.

The full-size drawing is laid on the bench and two wooden battens are nailed through it, one aligning with the bottom of the drawing, the other with the left-hand side. Starting with the corner formed by the battens, new lead is cut and the old glass refitted, using the drawing as a guide. Horseshoe nails are used to clamp the loose cames in place as, piece by piece, the panel is rebuilt.

When it is complete, the joints are cleaned with a wire brush, and tallow flux is wiped across each joint before soldering. Then the panel is turned over and the joints are soldered on the other side.

Using a small scrubbing brush, cement is brushed in all directions on both sides of the panel until the lead is sealed. Dry whiting is then sprinkled onto the panel to absorb excess oil.

About two hours later a pointed tool is used to remove cement from around the edges of the cames, then the panel is scrubbed again with a clean soft-bristle brush. After another two hours the lead is darkened with grate polish.

Jewel about to fall from brittle lead

RE-CREATING A BADLY DAMAGED PANEL

A badly damaged leaded light, perhaps one that has been smashed by a burglar, can be re-created exactly by a professional stained-glass artist. He or she will take critical measurements, note the types of glass used and make a rubbing of what's left of the leaded light.

If you happen to have another identical window, the artist can use that as a pattern for restoring badly damaged sections. Otherwise, he or she will have to deduce what the window looked like from the remaining fragments.

If the original window has been completely destroyed, then your only recourse is to find a restorer able to design a replacement (see below).

REPLACING A MISSING PANEL

You often come across clear-glass door panels and fanlights where a previous owner was not prepared to pay for the repair of leaded lights. If you want to have a new window made to the original style, you need to find a stained-glass artist with creative skills equal to his or her craftsmanship. Together, you can research the subject and may be able to track down an example in your neighbourhood to serve as a model.

If you can't find a suitable authentic pattern or original to copy, you will need to discuss with the artist the style of design you want and the types of glass to be used. The artist will then prepare a coloured drawing for your approval and will submit an estimate for making and fitting the window.

Make sure the artist gives you a date for starting the work and an estimate of how long the job will take. Also, any savings in cost or alterations to the design must be clearly agreed at this stage.

Each job is different, but normally you can expect to pay one-third of the fee in advance.

ENLARGING OR REDUCING A PANEL

Salvaged leaded lights and stained-glass panels bought from a dealer are unlikely to fit your window opening without modification. However, a professional may be able to enlarge a panel by adding sympathetic borders.

Reducing the size tends to be more difficult – so if a panel is too large, it may be necessary to keep the best parts only and have the surround redesigned to fit.

PROTECTING FINISHED WINDOWS

Rare painted windows in churches and other public buildings are sometimes protected with a sheet of clear polycarbonate. If you are thinking of protecting your glass in a similar way, consult a professional about the technical problems of sandwiching a sheet of plastic in the existing rebates. You may also want to check whether your window is valuable enough to warrant the extra expense.

CLEANING LEADED LIGHTS

Even if leaded lights are cleaned regularly, dirt tends to collect around the edges of each quarry. In addition, pollution affects the lead, which develops a white powdery deposit. Not only does this make the cames unsightly; rainwater and condensation tend to wash it onto the glass, too.

Unless the glass is etched or sandblasted, clean the cames with a soap-filled pad or with a small brass-wire brush (such as a suede brush) dipped in moistened scouring powder. Wipe the lead with a rag, then wash the glass carefully with warm soapy water.

Darken the cleaned lead with a touch of grate polish on a shoe brush. Brush across the cames, not along them. Grate polish will not adhere to clean glass, even if it is painted. It also polishes the glass. If the glass is dirty, you may need to wipe the polish off, using a rag dampened with white spirit.

133

STAINED & PAINTED GLASS

GLASS PAINTING *is one of the foremost skills in a tradition of craftsmanship in glass that is centuries old – but in terms of its use in relatively ordinary houses the Victorian era must surely rank as its heyday. At that time, an artisan's labour was so cheap that even the aspiring middle classes could afford exquisitely painted windows and door panels for their villas. Floral motifs and animals and birds were particularly fashionable themes, but a client could choose any subject from landscape to portraiture. Although the demand for true stained glass has declined steadily since the First World War, skilled glass painters practising today can restore or reproduce even the best of their predecessors' work.*

Birds and flowers have always been popular subjects

Bright luminous colours with the minimum of modelling

An exceptionally detailed autumnal scene

A landscape is the centrepiece of this circular door panel

REPRODUCING PAINTED GLASS

Developing the necessary skills for restoring stained glass is out of the question for the average amateur, especially if you only have to repair one or two pieces. Furthermore, the cost of the specialized brushes and vitreous paints needed (let alone a kiln in which to fire the glass) would almost certainly be higher than an expert's fee for restoring the glass. Nevertheless, it pays to familiarize yourself with glass-painting techniques so you are able to discuss the various options with a professional.

A skilled glass painter can reproduce damaged portions of a window, using broken fragments or undamaged areas of glass as a guide. If you need to re-create an entire stained-glass window, the painter will either copy a suitable existing example or design a new window for you that is in character with your house.

Tracing

The glass painter's first task, known as tracing, is to paint outlines and other linework onto each piece of glass, using dark pigments (either brown, green, red or black) thinned with various media and mixed with a binder that makes the paint adhere to the glass.

After tracing, most artists fire the glass to fuse the paint to the surface of the

134

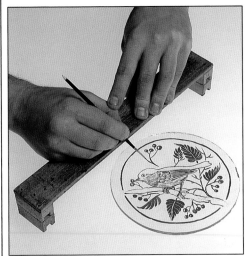

The linework is traced with a fine brush

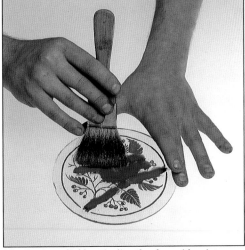

Matting is applied by stippling the glass with paint

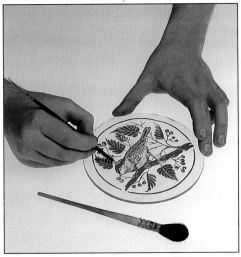

Scratching creates highlights and areas of light tone

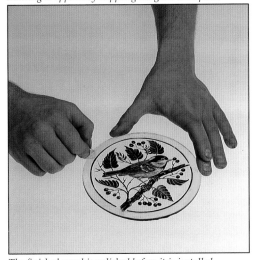

The finished panel is polished before it is installed

glass permanently. But some mix the pigments for subsequent layers of paint with a different medium that will not disturb the tracing, and delay firing till a later stage.

Matting
Areas of tone and modelling are applied to the painting using a process known as matting. An even layer of paint is brushed or stippled over the tracing. When it has dried, part of the paint is removed with a variety of brushes, pointed sticks and pens, creating areas of lighter tone and highlights. After firing, a second matt, possibly in another colour, can be applied over the first.

Colouring glass
Enamels are used to colour areas of glass and for painting details. These paints are opaque when applied, but become transparent when fired at a relatively low temperature. Considerable experience is required to determine the end result with any degree of certainty. Enamels are not as permanent as other vitreous paints.

Staining glass
A range of yellows, from pale lemon to a deep amber, can be achieved by staining glass with silver nitrate. Mixed with water, silver stain is milky in appearance when applied to the back of the glass. Firing causes the

stain to change colour and permeate the glass. Inexplicably, this single process has been responsible for the term 'stained glass' being used for the entire craft of making windows in coloured glass, despite the multiplicity of techniques involved.

Etching
Hydrofluoric acid is used to modify the colour of flashed glass. Depending on how long the glass is immersed in the acid, it is possible to grade tones or remove the coloured surface entirely. Hard edges are created by masking areas of colour, and acid can be painted on freehand in order to create a modelled effect.

AGEING THE APPEARANCE
Even though a stained-glass artist will attempt to match the glass, colours and style of a window exactly, a restored window may still look too 'new' when compared with an original. If the window is to be viewed from a distance, no one may ever notice the difference. But if it is to be fitted where it can be inspected closely (in a door, for example) then a stained-glass artist may decide to age its appearance artificially.

Metalling
Metalling is the term used by glass painters to describe the effect of overfiring silver stain – which acquires a darker, more opaque appearance as a result.

A painter normally strives to avoid metalling, but it may sometimes be the only way to match the colour of old stained glass.

Heavy matting
A heavy application of paint during the matting process can reproduce the mellow colours typical of ancient painted glass.

Etching the glass
Careful use of hydrofluoric acid dulls the glass slightly to mimic etching caused by long-term pollution.

Distressing the lead
If you want to simulate the distressed look of old leadwork, tap new cames here and there with the blade of a knife or screwdriver before colouring them with grate polish (see CLEANING LEADED LIGHTS).

ACID ETCHING & SANDBLASTING

ACID ETCHING (ALSO KNOWN AS EMBOSSING) imparts a matt-white 'frosted' texture to glass. By applying an acid-resistant mask to selected areas, it is possible to create patterns with alternating clear and textured glass. Very beautiful subtly toned etched images are made by repeating the process two or three times using different masks. Acid etching was developed towards the end of the eighteenth or early in the nineteenth century. But, apart from the types of mask or 'resist' used to protect the glass, the process remains virtually unchanged, and modern production methods can reproduce old embossed glass exactly.

Sandblasting, which was patented in 1870, is a comparatively new industrial process. Bombarding the surface of the glass with fine aluminium-oxide grit (sharp sand was used originally) leaves a texture similar in appearance to acid etching. Although it is possible to vary the texture by the depth of cut, sandblasting cannot reproduce the subtlety of two-tone or three-tone embossing. However, it is much cheaper, and only an expert eye can distinguish between sandblasting and single-tone etching.

Authentic Art Nouveau design

Overall patterns are still available

Triple-etched Victorian door panel

BUYING FROSTED GLASS FROM STOCK

Semi-obscured frosted glass was installed in Victorian and Edwardian bathroom windows, landing skylights, and doors of almost every conceivable kind.

Glazing with an overall repeat pattern, similar to wallpaper, was cheap and could be cut to fit any size or shape of window. Several original patterns are still made as stock sheet glass.

A frosted background provides maximum privacy, while a fine pattern etched on a clear background is the ideal form of glazing for conservatories and other areas where an unobscured view is required

You can buy antique-style frosted-glass transom lights and door panels from a good glazier. Only a limited range is available, but if you are fortunate you may be able to find an item that is an exact fit. Should that prove to be impossible, there are lights without borders designed to fit most locations.

INSTALLING FROSTED GLASS

Sandblasted and acid-etched textures attract dirt, which is why the textured face of a decorative window always faces inwards.

Mask the outer edges of the textured face to prevent linseed oil from fresh putty spreading and staining the frosted area. Brush washing-up liquid onto the outermost 50mm (2in) of the glass all round the panel (or rub a cake of soap onto it).

When the liquid becomes tacky, fit the panel in the normal way, taking care not to touch the textured face with oily fingertips. Leave the putty to dry for a couple of weeks before washing off the protective soap.

CLEANING FROSTED GLASS

A new replacement pane installed next to old frosted glass often looks too white by comparison. Clean the old glass with a soft-bristle brush dipped in undiluted household bleach. Rub the bleach into the texture with small circular brush strokes. After half an hour, repeat the process and then wash the window. You can remove specks of paint from frosted glass with chemical paint stripper, but don't touch the surface with an abrasive or a metal blade.

BRILLIANT-CUT GLASS

FINDING PROFESSIONALS

It isn't practicable for an amateur to reproduce an antique embossed or sandblasted window – not least because both processes are subject to strict health and safety regulations.

Sandblasting can only be performed inside a specially built enclosed cabinet, and hydrofluoric acid (the medium used by professional etchers) is so corrosive that it's never sold to the general public. A weaker acid paste is available in kit form for etching small items of glassware, but it is not really suitable for reproducing the majority of antique embossed windows.

Unless your local glazier is able to recommend a reliable firm, your best chance of finding professional acid etchers or sandblasters is to approach an association such as the Glass and Glazing Federation, the British Society of Master Glass Painters, or the Guild of Master Craftsmen. Alternatively, look through the advertisements in a good trade magazine.

REPLACING AN ACID-ETCHED WINDOW

If one of a pair of embossed door panels is broken, a professional acid etcher can make an exact reproduction of the surviving window. It may be possible to make a rubbing of the glass, but if the etching is too shallow a professional will have to trace the design, instead. At the same time, he or she will make a note of the different textures involved and measure the opening where the glass is to be installed.

Back at the workshop, the rubbing or tracing is converted into an accurate drawing before transferring the design to a sheet of glass. This is achieved by masking all areas that are to remain clear with a resist. Most professionals employ a form of screen printing to apply an acid-resistant coating, but simple shapes can be cut from self-adhesive film stuck to the glass. Areas to be etched are peeled off before the glass is immersed in acid. To create a second tone, acid-resistant paint is brushed over selected areas before the glass is returned to the acid. The etched glass is then washed thoroughly to remove the resist.

REPLACING A SANDBLASTED WINDOW

Sandblasted glass can be copied using methods similar to those employed for acid etching. However, sandblasted designs are hardly ever deep enough to be picked up as a rubbing, so it is usually necessary to make a tracing.

Provided the design is relatively simple, such as a numbered transom light, you can cut your own mechanical mask from the type of self-adhesive film used to cover kitchen shelves. As the textured surface always faces the inside of the house, remember to reverse your design so that it appears the right way round from outside. Having stuck the film to the glass, draw your design on it; then cut the film and peel it from areas you want to be textured. Rub down all the edges of the mask before taking the glass to be sandblasted.

If the window you want to reproduce has a very fine or complicated pattern, ask a professional to print a resist onto the glass and sandblast it for you.

BRILLIANT CUTTING, *a craft that was introduced to Britain from America in the middle of the nineteenth century, consists of grinding a pattern or motif into glass with a stone then polishing the cut until it sparkles. It is a highly skilled process that demands near-perfect hand and eye coordination, with little room for error. The effect is luxuriant, especially when deeply cut polished decoration is set off by matt-white acid etching.*

Brilliant cutting is often found in commercial premises such as banks, department stores and public houses. But, apart from the ubiquitous 'glory stars' that were set into the corners of thousands of doors and windows, it was seldom used in private homes except for those built on a relatively grand scale. In keeping with that type of house, brilliant cutting is frequently found in glazed doors leading from an entrance lobby into a hallway.

BEVELLED GLASS

Examples of bevelling (a poor relation of brilliant cutting) can be found in practically every home in the country. Until comparatively recently mirrors were almost always made with bevelled edges, the glass being ground to a shallow angle then polished since it was felt that they gave a mirror a 'finished' appearance. For the same reason, windows and leaded lights were invariably bevelled as part of the brilliant-cutting process.

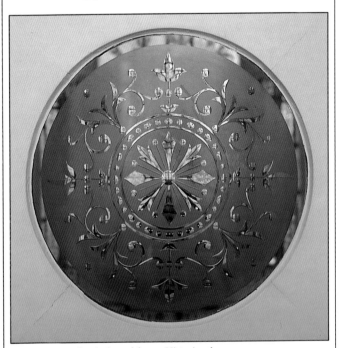

Brilliant-cut and etched panel from a Victorian door

Brilliant-cutting by hand in 1840

REPLACING BRILLIANT-CUT WINDOWS

Brilliant-cut glass is not as vulnerable as some other forms of ornamental glass. It is too tough to wear out and usually too thick to break easily; and if it's mounted indoors, it will not be affected by atmospheric pollution. However, if a brilliant-cut window does get broken, unless you can find a suitable reproduction, you have no choice but to find a professional able to make a replacement.

Brilliant cutting was always done by hand and, although modern computer-controlled machines can cut very intricate patterns, they can't reproduce hand-cut glass exactly. The furniture trade relies on cutters and bevellers to reproduce old mirrors and glazed doors for display cabinets, and a good antique-furniture dealer will almost certainly be able to recommend a small firm who can copy hand-cut glass. A high-street glazier may also have contacts, but the price is likely to be lower if you deal with a brilliant cutter direct.

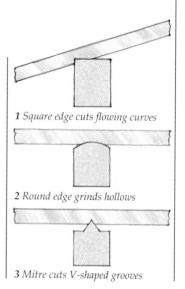

1 Square edge cuts flowing curves

2 Round edge grinds hollows

3 Mitre cuts V-shaped grooves

REPLACING GLORY STARS

Decorative marginal lights were often enhanced with corner panes of flashed ruby, blue or green glass featuring brilliant-cut star-shaped motifs. You can buy perfect reproductions inexpensively from most decorative-glass suppliers to replace missing or damaged originals.

Copying the design
Take the broken glass to the cutter, who will tape the fragments together and make a rubbing of the decoration. This rubbing is laid under a sheet of plate glass, and the outline traced onto the glass with a felt-tip pen.

Cutting the glass
The sheet of glass is pressed against the edge of a vertically mounted sandstone wheel that revolves slowly. Straight lines and flowing curves are cut on the corner of a square-edged wheel (**1**), while round-edged wheels are employed for grinding hollows (**2**) and 'mitre' wheels for incising V-shaped grooves (**3**). The brilliant cutter may use any of these wheels in combination in order to follow the pen lines traced from the original window onto the new sheet of glass.

Polishing the cut
Grindstones leave a striated grey finish that has to be polished out of the glass in two stages. Traditionally the first stage of polishing was done on willow or elm wheels, but nowadays many cutters use a synthetic-rubber wheel, with pumice powder mixed with water as a polishing agent. The result is very attractive, though it is still matt and parts of the design may be left untouched after this first stage of polishing. But for the true brilliant-cut finish, a cork wheel is used with cerium-oxide powder to buff the cut until it's gleaming and the glass is clear.

BEVELLING
Today straight edges, and even simple curves, are usually ground by machines with built-in diamond-grit wheels and felt polishers. However, bevellers in the antique-restoration trade can still employ traditional methods when called for.

Hand bevelling is similar in principle to brilliant cutting, but larger, horizontally mounted stone wheels are used and the glass is ground on the sides of the wheels, not on the edges. The glass is shaped initially on a silicon-carbide wheel lubricated with water, followed by a sandstone wheel that smooths the bevel. A thick wooden wheel coated with pumice is used for the first stage of polishing, then the job is completed on a hard-felt wheel dressed with rouge.

Modern reproduction glory stars

RESILVERING MIRRORS

Antique mirrors are often 'fogged' by damp that has penetrated the silvered backing. Resilvering an antique mirror may reduce its value; but if you want to restore a mirror so that it's usable, you can have the damaged silvering stripped and replaced. Glass bevellers frequently include resilvering as part of their service.

First, they strip off the old silver, using acid, and wash the glass thoroughly with distilled water. They then brush tinning solution onto the back of the mirror before spraying on silver nitrate. This is much faster than the traditional method of pouring it from a jug onto a sheet of glass supported on timber wedges. The wedges were then adjusted to control the flow of nitrate until it covered the back of the mirror.

The silver was once coated with varnish to protect it from damp, but nowadays it is sprayed with a copper solution then dried by being passed under a blower. Last of all paint is rolled onto the back of the mirror and any residue of silver washed from the face with acid.

CHAPTER TWELVE

PLASTERWORK

LINING THE INTERIOR WALLS *and especially the ceilings of a house with decorative plasterwork was a common practice even in ancient times, but in Britain it was not till the sixteenth or seventeenth century that plastering developed as the highly skilled craft we recognize today.*

The Georgian plasterwork of the eighteenth century was elegant, tasteful and, very often, classically inspired. All the features familiar today were employed, including the ceiling centrepiece, the moulded cornice masking the junction between wall and ceiling, the decorative frieze below the cornice, and strip mouldings delineating wall and ceiling panels.

In the Victorian period, especially after the introduction of mass-produced reinforced fibrous-plaster mouldings, plasterwork became ever more ornate. This new manufacturing process made it possible to prefabricate elaborate cornices, ceiling roses, overdoors and other mouldings that could be installed by general tradesmen, rather than calling for expensive specialist plasterers as in earlier times.

The First World War marked the end of decorative plasterwork in the average home. Fashionable taste dictated starker lines, the principal rooms of a house often being distinguished by nothing more than a simple cornice and, at most, a matching centrepiece.

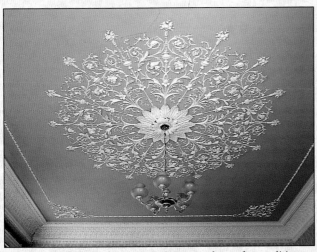

Delicate mid-Victorian plaster centrepiece restored to perfect condition

Expertly painted and gilded ceiling with grapevine enrichments

Overdoors enhance a landing

Elaborate frieze upgrades a cornice

Cornice with modillions and rosettes

Highly ornate plaster corbels

THE STRUCTURE
OF PLASTERWORK

THREE-COAT PLASTER *was trowelled directly onto
solid masonry walls or applied to laths (wooden
slats) nailed across wall studs or ceiling joists.
The first coat was squeezed through the spaces between
the laths so it spread out behind them to form keys that,
when set, held the plaster in place.*

*Prefabricated plasterboard became available towards
the end of the First World War but was rarely used in
houses until the late 1940s.*

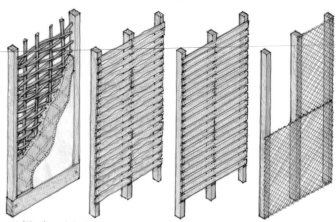

1 *Wattle and daub* 2 *Riven laths* 3 *Sawn laths* 4 *Metal lathing*

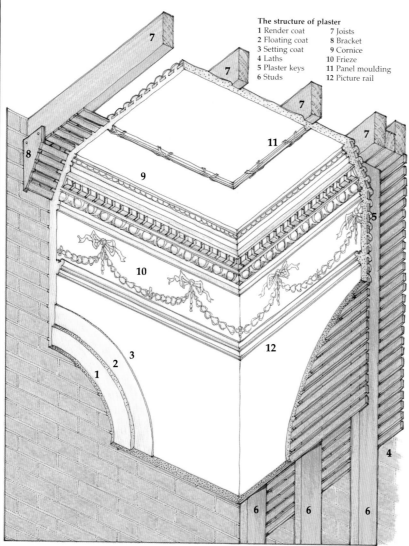

The structure of plaster
1 Render coat   7 Joists
2 Floating coat   8 Bracket
3 Setting coat   9 Cornice
4 Laths   10 Frieze
5 Plaster keys   11 Panel moulding
6 Studs   12 Picture rail

ASSESSING REPAIRS

● Easy even for beginners.
■ Fairly difficult. Good practical skills required.
▲ Difficult. Hire a professional.

Overpainted mouldings
Moulded plasterwork may become clogged with paint.
● Wash off distemper (page 142).
■ Remove paint with chemical stripper (page 142).

Damaged or missing mouldings
Mouldings may be damaged or missing due to neglect or modernization.
■ Run a new cornice (pages 146–8).
■ Cast and install new enrichments (page 148–9).
■ Fit new fibrous-plaster mouldings (pages 147, 149–50).

Sagging ceiling
Ceilings sag when nail fixings decay or plaster keys are damaged.
■ Screw back the detached laths (page 143).
■ Secure ceiling from above (page 143).

LATH-AND-PLASTER WALLS AND CEILINGS

Lath-and-plaster walls and ceilings are a development of wattle and daub (1), the age-old practice of infilling timber-frame walls by smearing a mixture of lime, sand, straw and dung onto a lattice of interwoven hazel twigs and upright oak or willow slats.

The earliest laths (2) were riven (split by hand) from baulks of timber, which produced strips 3 to 6mm (⅛ to ¼in) thick and 25 to 35mm (1 to 1½in) wide. These were nailed to the structural timbers, leaving 'keyway' slots approximately 10mm (⅜in) wide between the slats. In order to stop cracks developing as the plaster dried out, the laths were staggered and the butt joints between them positioned over the wall studs or the ceiling joists.

In the 1820s machine-sawn laths (3) were introduced and increasingly became the norm. These had similar dimensions to hand-riven laths but were more regular.

Wire-mesh lathing was patented as early as 1797. However, expanded metal (4) was not widely employed as a plastering support until the end of the nineteenth century – and even after that a great many plasterers continued using the traditional wooden laths for at least another 30 or 40 years.

Delaminated setting coat
The setting coat may flake due to damp or poor adhesion.
■ Seal and replaster (page 145).

Stains
Dampness and pollution stain plasterwork.
● Seal stains before you decorate (page 141).

Holes in plaster
Damp or vibration can make patches of plaster fall from walls and ceilings.
■ Fill holes with fresh plaster (page 144).

Cracked plaster
Shrinkage causes cracks, most of them harmless.
● Fill cracks before you decorate (page 143).

INGREDIENTS OF PLASTER

Early-C20th representation of a tradesman mixing plaster

Up to the 1930s the normal practice was to apply plaster to walls and ceilings in three flat coats or layers.

First a 'render' coat about 8mm (⅜in) thick was trowelled on in order to grip the wall or ceiling securely, then the surface of the render coat was scored to create a key for the second layer.

The second or 'floating' coat, which was about 6mm (¼in) thick, provided an even surface for the final layer. Like the render coat, the floating coat was keyed in order to achieve more effective adhesion.

The last layer, known as the 'setting' coat, was about 3mm (⅛in) thick and was trowelled perfectly smooth to provide a suitable surface for decoration.

Traditional three-coat plaster was composed of lime and sand mixed with water. Animal hair was mixed into the first two coats in order to bind the material together. Quicklime (crushed limestone heated to a high temperature) was mixed with water on site and then left to slake (hydrate) for a minimum of three weeks. Thoroughly slaked lime, which had the consistency of soft butter, was known in the trade as lime putty. To make 'coarse stuff' for the render and floating coats, 1 part lime putty was mixed with 3 parts sharp plasterer's sand.

Pure lime putty was sometimes used for the setting coat. Alternatively, 3 parts putty was mixed with 2 parts fine sand.

Lime plaster took about three weeks to dry between each coat. This considerably delayed the completion of any building. Consequently, towards the end of the nineteenth century the practice of 'gauging' lime plaster by adding gypsum or cement was introduced in order to speed up the setting time.

Patching plaster

When repairing plasterwork, there are two important issues to consider. First, how to eradicate the cause of the deterioration of the plaster; and then what material to use for making the repairs.

If the plaster in need of repair is lime-based, then it is often best to replace it with the same type of material, particularly if the plaster is to be applied to the inner face of an external wall, from which it needs to exude moisture.

Lime putty can be bought ready-mixed with various grades of sand for use as a top-coat render, or mixed with sand and hair as a base-coat render. Lime render is easy to apply to the irregular surfaces found in many old houses. Wear goggles and gloves when working with lime plasters.

If you decide on a gauged lime plaster for the first two coats, mix 1 part gypsum (Class B hemihydrate plaster) with 1 part lime putty and 6 parts sand. For the setting coat, mix equal parts of gypsum and lime putty. You don't have to add animal hair to the mixture when patching small areas of old plaster.

BASIC REPAIRS & RESTORATION

HOUSE RESTORERS *are often, understandably, reluctant to tackle traditional plastering. However, cleaning and stripping or minor repairs to plasterwork do not require specialized skills and are well within the capability of most people.*

DEALING WITH SURFACE STAINS

Plaster can become stained for a variety of reasons. Dampness is a major cause of staining. As the moisture spreads, it tends to draw impurities to the surface of the plaster, where they create permanent stains that are evident even when the plaster dries out. Damp conditions may also lead to black mould or efflorescence (white crystals), which spoil the appearance of plastered walls and ceilings. Nicotine and airborne dust both cause widespread staining, while wood preservative seeping from an attic leaves the most stubborn stains. Always seal stained plaster before redecorating, otherwise the stains are likely to bleed through the paint.

Damp and nicotine stains

Locate and cure the source of damp, then let the plaster dry out before applying an aluminium spirit-based sealer to the affected area. Use the same sealer to prime a yellow nicotine-stained ceiling before redecorating it.

Preservative stains

When treating an attic for rot or insect attack, avoid flooding the ceiling with preservative. If it does soak through the ceiling, wait till it is dry then paint the stain with an aluminium wood primer before redecorating.

Efflorescence

This is the result of mineral salts from building materials being drawn to the surface by dampness, which must be eradicated before treating the condition. These same crystals can form on fresh plaster as it dries out.

Brush the crystals from the plaster with sacking or a stiff bristle brush. If you try to wash them off, the salts will be reabsorbed by the plaster and re-emerge when it dries. Keep removing efflorescence until crystals stop forming; then if you are planning to redecorate with an oil-based paint, seal the plaster with an alkali-resistant primer.

Mould

Black specks of mould can appear on damp plaster anywhere, but they often occur on ceilings below an inadequately insulated loft as a result of water vapour condensing on cold plasterwork. When this happens, since the mould tends to grow less vigorously on the comparatively warm and dry plaster directly below the joists, it may create pale stripes between the areas blackened by the mould.

The remedy is to brush a sterilizing solution of one part household bleach mixed with 16 parts water onto the ceiling (use a 1:10 solution if the mould growth is very heavy). It is advisable to wear goggles to protect your eyes. Four hours later scrape off the mould, then wash the ceiling again with sterilizing solution. Allow the plaster to dry naturally.

To stop mould recurring, think about how you can improve your heating, ventilation and insulation (see SURVEYING YOUR HOUSE).

STRIPPING PAINT FROM PLASTERWORK

Before modern emulsion paints were available, distemper was the preferred finish for plastered walls and, especially, ceilings. The friable nature of distemper, combined with the fact that it is soluble in water, makes it a very poor base for redecorating with modern paints or wallcoverings. You can bind distemper to plasterwork by painting over it with a proprietary stabilizing solution. But if layers of distemper have been applied to decorative plasterwork, the fine detail of the original may be almost obliterated. So should you strip all the paint back to the plaster finish? Before embarking on this tedious and time-consuming task, consider whether it will result in the loss of historic paint that could give clues to the original decorative scheme. It any case, it's worth working on a trial area in order to establish what method is suitable for the type of plaster.

Late-Victorian cornice all but obliterated by layers of old paint

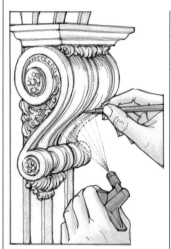

Pick out softened distemper

Removing distemper with water

You can sponge distemper from flat plasterwork with water containing a little proprietary wallpaper stripper. Cleaning decorative plaster takes greater care and effort.

Working on a small area at a time, moisten the distempered plaster with water from a plant spray and, as the paint softens, scrape it from the mouldings with an old toothbrush. You will have to pick thick distemper out of the deeper crevices with a sharpened stick. Finally, wash the plaster with clean water and apply a stabilizing solution to bind any traces of distemper.

Steam-cleaning plaster

Stripping a ceiling rose or an ornate cornice by hand with water is a laborious, back-breaking task. To save yourself several days of work on each room, you may be able to hire a specialist contractor to strip the distemper with steam. It is not easy to find professionals able to undertake this type of work safely and proficiently. Make sure they can protect the fabric of your house and collect the copious amounts of water generated by the process. A steam generator in unskilled or inexperienced hands can destroy irreplaceable plasterwork, so insist on references from recent customers.

Steam leaves plaster clean and crisp

1 Stipple stripper onto plasterwork

2 Peel away fibrous-tissue covering

Using a chemical stripper

Special ready-mixed paste strippers will remove any combination of distemper, emulsion and oil-based paints. Sheets of laminated plastic and fibrous tissue, supplied with the stripper, are used to cover the paste while it softens and absorbs the paint. If you can't face the prospect of stripping a ceiling yourself, there are specialists who will do the work for you.

When buying this type of stripper, check the details on the container to make sure it is suitable for use on plaster. Follow the manufacturer's safety recommendations carefully when handling these chemicals. Wear long plastic gloves taped to your sleeves and protect your eyes, face and hair from falling paint, dust and stripper.

Stipple the paste into the nooks and crannies of moulded plasterwork with an old paintbrush (1); then trowel it onto flat and convex surfaces, building up a layer of stripper 3 to 6mm (⅛ to ¼in) thick. Straightaway, lay the sheets (plastic side outward) over the pasted plaster and press each sheet into the stripper, rubbing the plastic gently in order to expel air bubbles.

Leave the sheets in place for 24 to 48 hours, during which time the stripper will emulsify the paint and draw it away from the plaster. Lift the edge of one of the sheets from time to time and, when all the layers of paint appear to have been absorbed into the fibrous tissue, peel away the sheets (2) and dispose of them carefully.

Wash the stripped plaster with water, using a scrubbing brush or sponge, then leave it to dry out for a few days.

1 Drag filler across crack

2 Then smooth it lengthwise

FILLING CRACKS

Hairline cracks in plaster are usually the result of shrinkage and require nothing more than filling followed by redecoration. However, wide cracks should be investigated to make sure that they are not a sign of serious structural movement.

With a masonry wall, probe the crack with a screwdriver or pencil to see if the damage extends farther than the depth of the plaster. If in doubt, chop out a small section of plaster on each side of the crack to determine whether the wall behind is affected. If you discover cracked masonry, get a surveyor to inspect it.

It is more difficult to tell with cracked plaster on a wooden loadbearing wall. If there are extensive cracks more than 3mm (⅛in) wide, have it inspected by a surveyor, unless the damage has an obvious cause such as a burst pipe.

REFIXING A SAGGING CEILING

When the lath fixings fail, a lath-and-plaster ceiling will sag under its own weight (1), although the laths themselves provide some measure of reinforcement. If the plaster keys become detached or are broken due to damp conditions or physical damage (2), the unsupported plaster hangs free and the ceiling is likely to be in imminent danger of collapse. Go into the loft or lift a few floorboards in the room above, as appropriate, in order to inspect the ceiling and ascertain the most suitable course of action.

Filling hairline cracks

Widen fine cracks by raking out loose material with the corner of a scraper. Moisten them with a paintbrush, then press plasterboard-joint filler or cellulose wall filler into the cracks. Drag the blade of a filling knife across the cracks (1), then smooth the filler by drawing the blade along them (2). When the filler has set, use medium-grade abrasive paper to sand it flush with the plaster.

Filling wider cracks

Use a bolster chisel to undercut the edges of a wide crack, then brush out loose debris. Thoroughly wet the crack, using a paintbrush, and fill with a proprietary wall filler, building it up gradually in layers until it is very slightly proud. Let the filler set hard, then sand it flush. Fill deep cracks almost completely with plaster of Paris, which sets quickly, then finish the repair with a sandable filler.

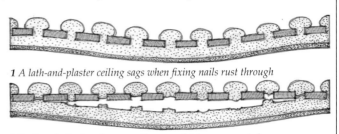

1 A lath-and-plaster ceiling sags when fixing nails rust through

2 Broken plaster keys leave a ceiling completely unsupported

Screwing back detached lath and plaster

Screw sagging lath and plaster to the joists with stainless-steel screws and washers. Vacuum debris from beneath the joists, then shore up the ceiling with several stout softwood props wedged between the ceiling and the floor below. Protect the plaster with plywood panels about 1m (3ft) square, placing a square of carpet underlay between the panels and the ceiling. Drill pilot holes through the lath and plaster into the joists, then twist a coin into the plaster to make depressions for the washers and screw heads. Insert the screws, remove the props and cover the screw heads with filler.

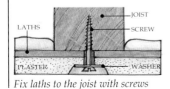

Fix laths to the joist with screws

Securing unsupported plaster

When the plaster has broken away from the laths, you can use lengths of stainless-steel wire and washers to support a sagging ceiling. This method merely holds the plaster in place, instead of pulling it up against the joists. It accommodates a certain amount of flexing, and so may prevent loss of plaster from a fragile or valuable ceiling.

Drill holes through the plaster on each side of the joists and make depressions for washers as described left. Cut lengths of wire and bend one end over to 90 degrees. Pass the other end through a washer and then up through one of the holes into the void above. Pull the washer up against the plaster, then bind the other end of the wire over a narrow strip of perforated metal laid across the joists and screwed to the wood.

Another method, which makes the ceiling rigid but at the cost of adding weight, is to secure the plaster from above with a bonding agent. This is perhaps more suitable for an ordinary flat-plastered ceiling. Support the ceiling on stout props (see far left), and then paint the upper surface of the lath and plaster with diluted PVA bonding agent. Spread a 12mm (½in) deep layer of retarded plaster of

Paris (see RUNNING A PLAIN CORNICE) between each pair of joists above the damaged ceiling. Bed strips of jute-scrim reinforcement into the wet plaster (the strips need to be wide enough to span the space between the joists and turn up the sides). Trap the jute with battens screwed to the joists, then add a second layer of plaster before the first has set. Don't remove the props until the plaster is hard.

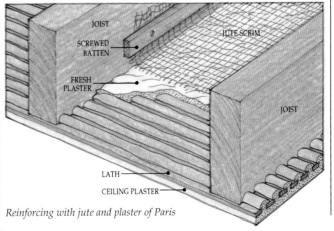

Reinforcing with jute and plaster of Paris

PATCHING HOLES IN GYPSUM PLASTER

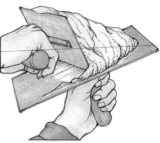

TO PLASTER A LARGE EXPANSE *of wall or ceiling successfully requires a skill that can only be developed with a great deal of experience. However, patching damaged plaster is not difficult, and satisfactory results are practically guaranteed with a modicum of practice.*

Before embarking on a repair, tap the wall or ceiling in the vicinity of the hole to check that the area of loose plaster does not extend too far. If it sounds 'hollow' over quite a wide area, get advice from a professional plasterer before you dislodge any more plaster.

The only specialized tools you need are a plasterer's steel trowel and a hawk – a small square sheet of wood or metal with a handle mounted beneath it, which is used for carrying the plaster to the wall or ceiling.

MIXING PLASTER

As a rough guide, you need to mix approximately equal proportions of clean water and dry powdered plaster.

Almost half-fill a plastic bucket with clean water and sprinkle plaster into it until the bucket is nearly full. Leave the plaster for a few minutes to absorb the water, then stir vigorously until it has a uniform creamy consistency. If you overstir the plaster, that will accelerate its setting time.

1 Scoop plaster onto a trowel

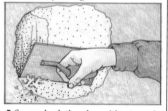
2 Sweep plaster onto the wall

3 Key the render coat by scoring it

PATCHING HOLES OVER MASONRY

If plaster has broken away down to a masonry background, chop the loose plaster from the perimeter of the hole with a bolster chisel until you reach sound material.

Exterior walls

Before you start to patch plaster on the inside of a brick or stone exterior wall, find out what has caused the plaster to deteriorate in the first place. If the wall has been damp, make sure the problem has been resolved and that moisture within the wall has had plenty of time to dry out. Salts may migrate to the surface of the wall during the process of drying out, and if you replaster too soon the salts can spoil the new plaster surface.

Pick up some fresh plaster on your hawk, then tip the hawk towards you slightly so you can scoop plaster onto your trowel (**1**). Holding the trowel at a slight angle to the wall, spread the plaster on the masonry with a sweeping upward action (**2**). Cover the masonry to an even depth of about 8mm (⅜in) and, as the plaster begins to get firm, score it with shallow scratches (**3**) to form a key for the next coat.

Let the render coat set for about two hours, then apply the floating coat in the same way – but this time there is no need to add a waterproofer to the plaster. Build the coat almost flush with the surrounding plaster, then scrape it level with a length of wooden architrave or some similar straightedge (**4**). You will find a zigzag action works best. Fill in any hollows with fresh plaster, then scrape again. Once the floating coat begins to get firm, use the trowel to scrape the outermost 150mm (6in) or so of the new plaster, so that it is about 3mm (⅛in) lower than the edge of the old plaster around it (**5**).

Hammer some panel pins through a piece of softwood so that the points of the pins are just protruding. Using this improvised tool, key the floating coat with circular strokes (**6**).

About two hours later trowel on a setting coat of renovating finish plaster. It is easier to achieve an even

Plasterer's trowel   Hawk

thickness if you make two applications of plaster. Spread the first quite firmly (almost like buttering toast) to fill any hollows, then immediately apply more plaster, leaving it as smooth as possible and flush with the old plasterwork. When this coat is firm but has not yet set hard, dampen the trowel and use it to 'polish' the plaster. Holding the face of the tool at a very shallow angle, sweep the trowel in all directions across the patch (**7**).

Interior walls

You can patch dry interior walls in the same way. But use a Class B hemihydrate hardwall undercoat plaster for the render and floating coats, and a similar general-purpose finish plaster or a universal one-coat plaster for the setting coat. Seal the wall with a bonding agent – there is no need to add a waterproofer to the plaster.

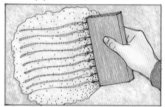
4 Level the floating coat

5 Scrape back the edge with a trowel

6 Lightly key the floating coat

7 Polish with circular strokes

CORNICE PATTERNS

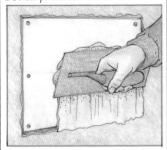

1 Screw plasterboard to studs

2 Finish with one-coat plaster

PATCHING HOLES IN LATH AND PLASTER

Chop away the plaster at the edge of the hole to reveal the nearest studs or joists at each side. Cut a plasterboard panel to fit the hole and fix it over the laths using plasterboard screws driven into the studs or joists **(1)**. Paint the edge of the surrounding plaster with diluted bonding agent, then trowel on universal one-coat plaster to form a smooth flush surface **(2)**.

REPAIRING DELAMINATED PLASTER

Areas of the setting can break away from a wall or ceiling even when the underlying plaster is perfectly sound. This may result from poor adhesion or from badly mixed plaster.

Provided that the plaster behind is sound and dry, scrape off any loose setting-coat plaster, then make sure the suction is consistent and stabilize the floating coat by painting on two coats of diluted PVA bonding agent.

While the second coat of bonding agent is still tacky, apply a fresh setting coat (see opposite page), using either a Class B hemihydrate gypsum finishing plaster or a universal one-coat plaster.

F ROM THE EIGHTEENTH CENTURY *until the First World War no principal room would have been considered complete without a decorative cornice running around the edge of the ceiling. As a result, cornices are among the most common plaster features that house restorers have to contend with.*

Cornices can be categorized into two main groups – plain run and enriched mouldings. Plain run cornices rely on a combination of concave flutes, convex beads and square corners for their visual appeal. They were fashioned by plasterers who either ran metal templates through plaster in situ or created cornices on a bench and then fixed them in place at a later stage.

Basically, enriched cornices were run mouldings that incorporated flat areas to which separately cast decoration was applied in the form of continuous strips or individual brackets, rosettes and other motifs. With the invention of fibrous plasterwork, it became possible to design an elaborate ornamental cornice that was cast as one long piece.

Plain-run Edwardian cornice

Mid-C19th enriched cornice

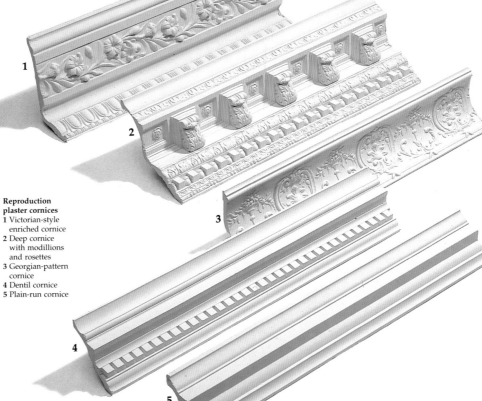

Reproduction plaster cornices
1 Victorian-style enriched cornice
2 Deep cornice with modillions and rosettes
3 Georgian-pattern cornice
4 Dentil cornice
5 Plain-run cornice

Anthemion

Swags or festoons

Leaf and dart

Acanthus leaves

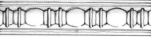

Greek-key design

Egg and dart

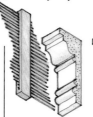

Bead and reel

Fluting

DECORATIVE MOTIFS

It is impossible to assign a specific date to motifs employed in decorative plasterwork, since many of them have been used in one form or another for centuries

However, Georgian enriched cornices were invariably based on classical orders. The Ionic dentil cornice, with its row of small square 'teeth', is a typical example; so are the decorative brackets known as modillions (often interspersed with paterae or rosettes) found on Corinthian cornices. Pictorial motifs such as the anthemion (stylized honeysuckle flower), elegant vases, human figures and festoons (better known as swags) were also favourite Georgian motifs. All these motifs are also found on Victorian cornices, along with deeply modelled fruit, flowers and foliage – but Victorian cornices are generally larger and more elaborate than the Georgian versions.

Other motifs commonly incorporated into cornices are egg and dart, leaf and dart, bead and reel, Greek key, fluting and acanthus leaves.

FRIEZES

Deep decorative panels or friezes were added on the wall below a cornice to make it more impressive. Similarly, narrow mouldings were often run or stuck on the ceiling to increase the visual width of a cornice.

Deeply modelled plaster frieze with Art Nouveau influence

RUNNING A PLAIN CORNICE

IF YOUR ORIGINAL CORNICE HAS BEEN REMOVED *and discarded, it is perhaps easiest to buy a suitable fibrous-plaster replacement. However if you have a badly damaged plain run cornice, or one with fairly simple enrichments, you can copy an intact fragment and make a reproduction of the original cornice.*

Only a skilled plasterer can run a cornice in situ, but an amateur who is prepared to accept a certain amount of trial and error before achieving satisfactory results should be capable of running a cornice on a bench for fixing in place once the plaster has set.

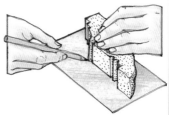

1 Profile gauge   2 Card template   3 Draw round a plaster template

DUPLICATING THE PROFILE

To match a cornice accurately it is necessary to copy its profile and reproduce the shape in the form of a metal template. Professional plasterers refer to the process of copying the profile as 'taking a squeeze'. You may be able to use a DIY profile gauge, pressing its retractable steel pins against the moulding **(1)** – but you are unlikely to find a profile gauge that is large enough to accommodate the majority of cornices.

If you can saw a shallow slot in the cornice, insert a piece of card and trace around the moulding with a pencil **(2)**.

Alternatively, coat a small section of cornice with a film of cooking oil, to act as a release agent, then coat it with a layer of plaster of Paris 50mm (2in) thick. When the plaster has set, ease it off the cornice and saw through it to produce a section that can be used for tracing the outline onto the template **(3)**.

MAKING A RUNNING MOULD

Cut the template from a zinc sheet with tinsnips and shape it with files. Burnish the cut edge with a nail to remove any burrs, which would create striations in the plaster. Cut a thick plywood backing board roughly to the shape of the template and cut back the edge to about 45 degrees **(1)**. Pin or screw the template to the board, then screw a baseboard onto the backing board and secure it with a triangular brace **(2)**.

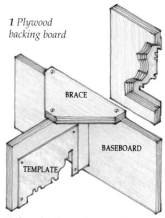

1 Plywood backing board

BRACE

BASEBOARD

TEMPLATE

2 Completed running mould

LINING THE BENCH

Make the running surface for your mould from a smooth melamine-faced board fixed to a workbench. The running surface must be kept flat, so a thick kitchen worktop is ideal. The baseboard needs to project sufficiently to run against the edge of your running surface (1). In order to reduce the weight of a wide cornice, build a melamine-faced backing board on your running surface and add a triangular wooden fillet (2), which should be coated with a film of cooking oil. Add to the mould a second triangular brace running along the top of the backing board.

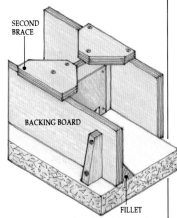

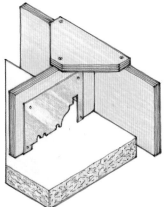

1 Baseboard runs against front edge

2 Running surface for wide cornice

RUNNING THE CORNICE

Sections of cornice approximately 3m (10ft) long are a convenient size to mould and install. You will find that plaster of Paris is the best material to use for running a cornice. Neat plaster is suitable for a smallish cornice, but since it sets in only a few minutes you may prefer to retard it slightly if you are moulding a cornice that is large or complex. One pinch of cream of tartar in half a bucket of plaster should give you plenty of time (though some plasterers prefer to add wallpaper size). After a little experimenting, you will discover how much retardant suits your particular speed of operation. Mix the plaster of Paris to the consistency of pourable cream.

It is best to have an assistant mix and pour the plaster, so that you can concentrate your attention on running the cornice and washing the template between passes.

To reinforce the cornice, place one or two laths on the running surface along the line of the moulding. Temporarily nail the laths at each end. Lay a strip of jute scrim dipped in plaster on top and rub it down so that it sticks to the laths.

Pour the first coat of plaster onto the running surface and make the first pass with the mould, keeping it firmly pressed against the front edge of the running surface (1). Straightaway, wash the remaining plaster from your mould in a bucket of water while your assistant pours another layer of plaster over the first. Then make another pass with the mould.

As the plaster begins to set, the shape of the casting starts to form rapidly. Continue adding more plaster to the hollows between passes until the cornice appears to be complete.

Once the plaster is firm, splash water along the cornice and make a pass without adding fresh plaster. This will skim the cornice as the plaster swells during the setting process. Repeat the process as often as necessary until the plaster is stable.

Remove minor blemishes from the set cornice with a scraper or chisel dipped in water. Fill any tiny holes or irregularities. After about 20 minutes, scrape off excess plaster left on the running surface on each side of the moulding (2) and remove the finished cornice.

1 Make a pass with running mould

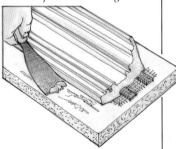

2 Scrape off excess plaster

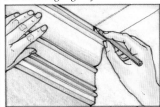

1 Trace along edges of cornice

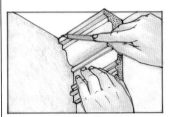

2 Transfer guideline to cornice

INSTALLING THE CORNICE

When installing lengths of plain run cornice to match an existing moulding that is still *in situ*, strip and clean what remains of the original and cut the ends square so you can butt the new cornice against them. (The procedure described here is also used when installing ready-made fibrous-plaster mouldings.) Before commencing work, you will need to erect a sturdy platform for you and an assistant to stand on.

Paint some PVA bonding agent, diluted following the manufacturer's instructions, along the junction between walls and ceiling to ensure that the suction is consistent. While it is drying, cut off a short section of cornice to use as a template for marking out guidelines.

Starting with the longest run of wall that is visible as you enter the room, hold the template in the corner so it fits snugly against the wall and the ceiling. Trace along the top and bottom of the cornice with a pencil (1), then repeat the procedure at the other end of the wall and join the marks by snapping a chalked string against the plaster. Continue in the same way around the room until you have marked every run, including the sides of any chimney breast or alcoves.

Using a tenon saw or a fine-tooth panel saw, cut the first length of cornice to fit between the two walls. With the help of your assistant, lift the moulding into position and transfer the ceiling guideline onto the front edge of the cornice at each end (2).

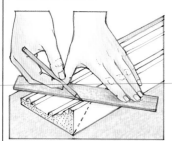

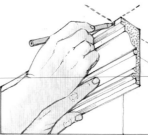

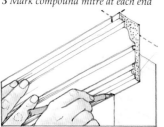
3 Mark compound mitre at each end

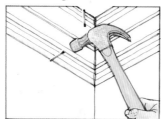
4 Mark ceiling line at a corner

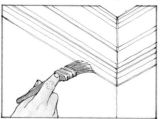
5 Then mark the corner itself

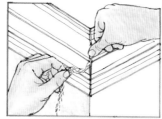
6 Support cornice on nails

7 Clean off excess filler with a brush

8 Fill wide gaps with jute scrim

Lay the cornice on its back and, using a straightedge, draw a line from the mark to the bottom corner (3). After doing this at both ends, cut along these lines to form a mitre joint. Irregularities can be filled after the cornice is installed. Repeat the whole procedure for the lengths of cornice on adjacent walls.

For external corners, cut the cornice a bit longer than required and mark on it the ceiling line (4) and corner of the wall (5). Join these marks across the face of the cornice and cut along this line.

On a very long wall, you will need to butt two lengths of cornice end to end.

Use diluted PVA bonding agent to seal the back of each section and plasterboard-joint filler to glue it in place. Spread the filler on the back of the first length of cornice, then lift it into position and press it against the wall and ceiling, squeezing out excess filler. The suction created will help to hold the cornice in place. Nevertheless, to keep it secure while the filler

is setting, it is best to drive galvanized nails or masonry pins through it at strategic points, carefully punching the nailheads below the surface of the plaster.

Alternatively, in order to avoid damaging a delicate moulding, drive nails into the wall and ceiling so they support the top and bottom edges of the cornice, then remove them once the filler has set (6). Very heavy cornices should be fixed with brass woodscrews driven into joists or wall studs.

Before the filler sets, use a damp brush to clean off any filler that has squeezed out around the edges (7); brushing the edges also helps fill any gaps between the cornice and the wall.

After fitting each length of cornice, fill any gaps and disguise all nailheads with joint filler. Fill wide gaps at corner joints with rolls of jute scrim dipped in joint filler (8). Use your finger to fill the joints flush, then smooth the filler with a damp cloth or paintbrush.

CASTING ENRICHMENTS

MUCH OF THE ORNAMENTATION *that is found on cornices consists of individual castings glued in place with plaster. Even what appears to be continuous moulded decoration is often made from short sections of cast plaster butted end to end. The same can be said of elaborate early ceiling roses, which were in fact constructed from dozens of individual castings glued together on the ceiling. Damaged or missing enrichments of this sort can be replaced by taking castings from specimens that are still intact.*

REMOVING AN ENRICHMENT

It is essential to strip paint from an enrichment in order to obtain a clean casting, so the newly made replicas will resemble the original enrichments still *in situ*.

Once all the paint has been removed, you should be able to insert the tip of a screwdriver or old chisel behind the selected enrichment and prise it carefully away from the plaster so you can make a mould on a bench.

MAKING A MOULD

Any number of individual enrichments can be cast from a custom-made flexible mould. Cold-cure silicone rubber is perhaps the easiest to use. Furthermore, if it is impossible to take down an enrichment without damaging it, you can buy a thixotropic additive that enables you to brush the silicone rubber onto the ceiling or wall. Admittedly, hot-melt mould-making compounds are cheaper, but they require very careful handling and you need a special melting pot in order to use them.

Construct a softwood box with a melamine-faced base to surround the enrichment, leaving a generous margin all round so that the mould will have strong walls. Stick the original to the base of the box with plaster and fill any

Cornice with applied enrichments

gaps to prevent moulding compound flowing beneath the casting. Spray the original with the sealer/release agent supplied as part of the moulding kit. Mix the cold-cure silicone rubber with its catalyst, following the manufacturer's instructions, then pour it slowly and steadily into the bottom of the box until the enrichment is covered completely. Leave the rubber to set overnight, then dismantle the box and peel off the flexible mould.

Make a softwood box with a base

1 Level the plaster with a spatula

2 Score the plaster when it has set

MAKING A CASTING

Lay the mould on a level bench and fill it to the brim with plaster of Paris. Tap the sides in order encourage air bubbles to rise to the surface. Draw a spatula across the mould to level up the plaster **(1)**. As soon as the plaster begins to get firm, score the surface to form a key **(2)**. After 10 minutes or so peel off the mould, which can be used immediately to cast further identical copies.

INSTALLING AN ENRICHMENT

Use a pencil to mark the positions of the individual enrichments on the plaster, then key the spots where they are to be installed by scoring them with a pointed tool. Paint the scored plaster and the backs of the enrichments with slightly thinned PVA bonding agent.

Spread plasterboard-joint filler onto the back of each enrichment and press it into position, sliding it back and forth slightly to squeeze out excess filler. The suction thus created will grip the enrichment – nevertheless, it's best to hold it in place while you remove excess filler with a scraper and clean up with a damp paintbrush.

FIBROUS PLASTER

I T IS NOT DIFFICULT TO IMAGINE *the enthusiasm with which fibrous plaster was greeted when it was patented in 1856. For the first time it became possible to mass-produce a large, complex and detailed moulding as a comparatively lightweight single piece that could be fitted on site without special skills.*

Fibrous plaster was also relatively cheap to produce, and the range of standard castings was extensive. As a result, it was not long before decorative plasterwork was common even in fairly humble homes.

Fibrous-plaster reproductions
1 Oval centrepiece
2 Corbels
3 Wall plaque
4 Overdoor
5 Fluted pilaster with Ionic capital

FIBROUS-PLASTER MOULDINGS

Fibrous-plaster mouldings, made from ordinary plaster but reinforced with scrim and strips of wood, are still manufactured in the traditional way and are sometimes cast from original moulds. If plasterwork in your home has been removed or damaged, you can therefore take comfort from the fact that there is an enormous variety of authentic-looking fibrous-plaster mouldings available – ranging from the simplest coves to richly embellished combinations that include deep friezes and decorative ceiling plates.

Ceiling roses, for example, from which to hang pendant light fittings or chandeliers, range from elaborate centre-pieces as much as 1350mm (4ft 6in) in diameter to plain discs a mere 200mm (8in) across. Most are circular, but it's possible to buy roses that are octagonal or elliptical. Unlike earlier ceiling roses, which were often made by plastering individual enrichments together on the ceiling, fibrous-plaster roses are manufactured in one piece and so are very much easier to install.

Strips of delicate plasterwork that can be combined with cast plaques and fancy corner mouldings are available for constructing wall or ceiling panels – which were considered vital for dividing up plain plaster surfaces into acceptable proportions.

In addition, there are more unusual items such as complete archway sections and ornate supporting brackets or corbels – and there is a huge selection of columns, pilasters and capitals, wall niches, overdoor mouldings, fire surrounds, and even classical urns and statues.

FITTING A CEILING ROSE

A central ceiling 'rose' made from plaster was a feature of practically every Victorian drawing room and parlour, from large country houses to modest terraced working-class cottages. The earliest ones were intended for use with gas lighting and provided a means of extracting unpleasant fumes: small holes that formed part of the moulded pattern led, via pipes, to an airbrick in an outside wall. However, the prime function of the ceiling rose was to act as a focal point or to enrich what would otherwise have been a plain ceiling. The procedure for fitting a ceiling rose involves the same methods as fitting any simple fibrous-plaster moulding.

Originally roses were often built up on the ceiling from separate enrichments

Accommodating an electrical fitting

Reproduction plaster centre-pieces are often designed to house a light fitting. Sometimes there is just a circular recess at the centre of the rose that accommodates a standard plastic backplate and a screw-on cover. However, the more elaborate ceiling roses are made with decorative plaster bosses mounted on the plastic cover, concealing the whole fitting except for the flex, which hangs from a hole in the centre of the boss.

Always make sure that an electrical fitting is screwed securely to a ceiling joist – not just into the plaster rose. Unless you have the knowledge and experience to fit it yourself, get an electrician to install and wire the light fitting. The electricity supply must be switched off at the mains while you are fitting the ceiling rose itself.

Preparing the ceiling

If necessary, strip paper and paint from the area where the rose is to be fitted. Hold the rose against the ceiling in the required position and draw a circle round it with a pencil (1). Score the plaster within the circle and seal it with diluted PVA bonding agent. Treat the back of the rose in the same way.

Probe the plaster with a pointed tool to locate at least one joist within the circle. Mark the position of the joist with a pencil (2).

Fixing the rose

Orientate the rose so you can bore two holes through it to align with the centre of the joist, preferably within an area of pattern that disguises their presence. These holes are for brass woodscrews, which will need to be long enough to reach through the rose and ceiling plaster into the joist itself.

Spread plasterboard-joint filler or ceramic-tile adhesive on the back of the rose. Press the rose against the ceiling, moving it slightly from side to side to squeeze out excess adhesive and to align the screw-fixing holes with the joist. Insert the screws (3) and clean off the excess adhesive with a damp sponge or paintbrush, then cover the screwheads with filler.

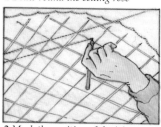

1 Draw round the ceiling rose

2 Mark the position of the joist

3 Screw through rose into joist

CHAPTER THIRTEEN

PAVING & WALL TILES

VIRTUALLY ALL THE EARLIEST FLOORS – *which were no more than rammed earth, frequently compounded with ashes and ox blood – have long been covered over with riven-flagstone paving, square quarry tiles or brick-shaped paviours. Many of these surfaces have survived unaltered for hundreds of years, except that generations of footsteps have endowed them with a subtle patina of colour and texture. The majority of them are utilitarian floors found in kitchens, workshops and cellars – but with increased affluence, ostentatious or aesthetically minded house owners chose to have entrance halls, vestibules and passageways laid with patterned floors constructed from coloured stone or marble slabs.*

Ceramic tiles were used initially for flooring, and at a later date as wallcoverings. Glazed wall tiles (both plain and decorative) were particularly popular with the hygiene-conscious Victorians, and they have remained the most practical surface finish for bathrooms ever since.

In the recent past, tiled surfaces were not infrequently carpeted over or obliterated with paint. Being hard-wearing and durable, many of them will have survived relatively undamaged, only waiting for someone to rediscover and restore them.

Colourful paving is an asset that should be preserved at all costs

Exceptionally well-preserved Edwardian wall tiling and mosaic floor

PAVED FLOORING

ORIGINALLY PAVED FLOORING *was a luxury only the wealthy could afford. But from the late seventeenth or early eighteenth century, with increased affluence and the availability of cheaper materials, it was adopted by all strata of society.*

Stone paving, one of the costliest forms of flooring to lay today, was most often used in humble dwellings or in the service areas of more prosperous households.

Man-made tiles were equally practical, and with improved industrial processes quite ordinary home owners found they were able to afford elaborate floors composed of decorative ceramic tiles.

Attractive unfinished random-flagstone floor

Slate floors are often found in period kitchens

Quarry-tile floor in a Norfolk farmhouse

STONE PAVING

Sedimentary rocks that split easily along the planes of natural bedding or cleavage were ideal for making flag-stones, which could be anything from 25 to 100mm (1 to 4in) thick. Before the days of damp-proof courses, flagstones were laid over an earth floor on a bed of ash or coarse sand. As a result, porous limestone or sand-stone floors were invariably subject to rising damp in all but the driest conditions.

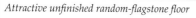

Slate, on the other hand, being impervious to water, was ideally suited to paving, and houses with slate floors were always comparatively dry. Originally it was only used for domestic paving in areas where there were slate quarries within easy reach. But in the nineteenth century, thanks to vastly improved transportation, slate became readily available to Victorian builders in all parts of the country. As a result, many of them used it for paving base-ments and cellars in larger houses, where it is still to be found in perfect condition.

Marble, whether imported or one of the native varieties, was used for effect in the more public areas of a house.

Marble slabs were laid with tight-fitting joints and set out with precision. Often they ran diagonally across a room or hallway, with contrasting colours employed to make a chequerboard pattern.

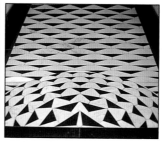

Early-C20th mixed-marble hallway

QUARRY TILES

Where stone was not a local commodity, our forebears tended to use quarry tiles when a hard-wearing floor was required. Traditionally made from yellow or brick-red kiln-fired clay, quarry tiles were normally unglazed and laid to a grid pattern.

Old quarry tiles were not as standardized as modern mass-produced ones. They were mostly larger, being up to 300mm (1ft) square and some 38mm (1½in) thick; but smaller square, octagonal and hexagonal tiles, which tended to be thinner, were also produced.

Manufacturer's floor-tile pattern

Medieval-style encaustic tile of 1845

Fully glazed Victorian encaustic tile

Interlocking patent mosaic tile

ENCAUSTIC TILES

The medieval practice of making inlaid clay floor tiles was lost with the dissolution of the monasteries in the sixteenth century. Hundreds of years later it was revived by Victorian tile makers inspired by the Gothic-revival movement, who developed mechanical methods for reproducing the designs that Cistercian monks had once made by hand.

A tile body, usually of soft red clay, was pressed into a mould that left an indented pattern. Once fired, the indentations were filled flush with slip (liquid clay) of different colours, then the tile was fired a second time.

Initially these unglazed tiles were manufactured for Victorian churches built in the fashionable neo-Gothic style and for paving other large-scale public buildings. But they were so striking and attractive in appearance that encaustic tiling was enthusiastically adopted for late-Victorian and Edwardian domestic use. As a result, there are still a great many houses that have encaustic paving in the entrance hall and corridors, frequently extending to conservatories and exterior pathways and patios. True encaustic tiles were sometimes mixed with simpler plain-coloured tiles of different sizes and shapes known as 'geometrics'. Laid with consummate skill and patience, these paved areas are one of the most delightful legacies from the Victorian era.

This encaustic-tile floor has retained its fresh colours since it was laid in 1869

An intricate late-Victorian pattern of geometrics and small encaustic tiles

MOSAICS

Mosaics composed of tiny coloured ceramic tesserae are also to be found on the floors of Victorian buildings, but are much less common in domestic interiors. They were painstakingly pieced together in factories where female workers pasted the tesserae one at a time onto a full-size drawing to build up the required design. When complete, the mosaic was cut into convenient pieces and transported to the house, or other building, for laying.

Typical of Victorian ingenuity were the 'patent mosaic tiles'. These were relatively large coloured floor tiles manufactured with deeply incised grooves. Once a complete area of tiling had been laid, the grooves were filled with cement to create the impression of genuine mosaic paving.

Patent mosaics pass for real tesserae

PRESERVING FLAGSTONE FLOORS

FLAGSTONES *are fairly large slabs of stone used to provide a hard-wearing floor. Most old stone floors have a mellow, rustic quality well worth preserving. They are an important period feature, and minor problems such as an irregular surface or a somewhat cold feel are a small price to pay for preserving such an attractive form of flooring.*

DEALING WITH WORN FLAGSTONES

Worn flags are an intrinsic feature of an old stone floor and, unless they are dangerous, should be accepted as part of the character of a house. If a stone has sunk unevenly, it may be sensible to lift and re-lay it. Similarly, a badly worn slab can be lifted, turned over and reset in mortar. When lifting out a slab, take care not to damage it or the surrounding stones with the levering tools.

CLEANING STONE FLOORS

Stone floors generally need nothing more than regular sweeping to keep them in good order. However, some stones are more porous than others and, particularly in work areas, may become heavily soiled.

Wash a lightly soiled stone floor with a bucket of water containing two tablespoons of washing soda. For a dirty waxed floor, use a cupful of soda and detergent to a bucket of water. Coat the whole floor first, then work back over it with a scrubbing brush before rinsing.

A tablespoon of caustic soda to 4.5 litres (8 pints) of water removes deep grease stains and heavy soiling. Rinse the floor thoroughly after scrubbing the surface. Protect your eyes and skin.

Treat organic growths such as mildew with dilute household bleach or a biocide.

For removing stains from marble, see FIREPLACES.

FINISHING STONE FLOORS

In most cases it is unnecessary to apply a surface finish or sealant to flagstones. In fact, some authorities advise against it on the grounds that it can create a dangerously slippery surface on impervious stones, and trap moisture in more porous ones, leading to structural breakdown.

However, polishes and sealants are available for finishing stone. These need to be applied to a dry, dust-free surface. Generally two even coats of sealant are recommended, applied with a radiator paint roller. Always follow the manufacturer's instructions carefully. To maintain the slight sheen produced by a sealant, you can apply wax polish from time to time. All finishes will darken and enrich the natural colour.

To bring out the colour of slate, apply a 1:4 mixture of linseed oil and white spirit, then wipe dry.

SAFETY

Handling stone flooring is hard and heavy work.
- Always wear gloves when handling stone slabs.
- Bend your knees and keep your back straight when lifting flagstones.
- Wear goggles and a mask when cutting stone, using a hammer and chisel or an angle grinder fitted with a stone-cutting disc.

New flagstones can coexist with old weathered paving

DEALING WITH DAMP

If a stone floor is damp, try to establish the underlying cause and determine whether other parts of the building have been affected. It may be that external ground levels are too high, or rainwater pipes may be leaking and soaking the ground.

Old stone floors were often laid directly upon bare earth, but with adequate ventilation any moisture that rose through the floor evaporated naturally. However, impervious floor-coverings can prevent evaporation, so try removing them and see whether the stone dries out – this may take some time. Similarly, modern impervious floor finishes and sealers can prevent natural evaporation.

Dampness in kitchens and laundries may be the result of condensation – in which case, better ventilation and heating may go some way towards solving the problem.

Lifting and re-laying an old stone floor with a new sub-floor that incorporates a damp-proof membrane (DPM) is not something to tackle yourself unless you have the relevant building experience. It is hard time-consuming work, and there is always a risk of driving the damp into the walls. Also, replacing old stone slabs may destroy historical evidence in the process.

CERAMIC FLOOR TILES

W HEN REPAIRING A TILED FLOOR, *take the damaged tile, or tile fragments, to the supplier so that you can buy a close match in size, colour and pattern.*

QUARRY TILES
Since quarry tiles are usually laid in a regular grid pattern, any replacement has to be an exact fit. However, old quarry tiles were made in a range of sizes and could be anything from 12 to 38mm (½ to 1½in) thick. Modern quarry tiles, on the other hand, are generally 12mm (½in) thick.

Should you need to make patch repairs to an old quarry-tile floor, you may find you have to pack out replacement tiles that are too thin with bedding mortar, or even cut back the sub-floor to accommodate ones that are too thick.

Reproduction encaustic tiles and small geometrics

ENCAUSTIC AND GEOMETRIC TILES
Encaustic tiles are still made by hand. Each tile is based on a moulded body, to which different coloured clays are painstakingly added to build up a polychromatic decorative pattern. After firing for 24 hours, the tiles are measured for accuracy then cut on a diamond wheel to precise dimensions.

Encaustic and geometric tiles are made to special order for restoration work. The reinstatement of a traditional floor takes great skill and is a job for a flooring specialist.

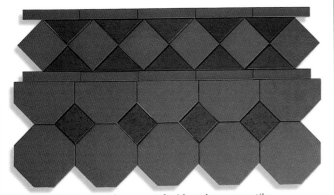

Victorian-style floors can be re-created with modern quarry tiles

Special-purpose border tiles

Fixing the pieces
Carefully prise out loose pieces from the floor, using either the blade of a knife or a narrow scraper. If the paving is indoors, glue them back in place with a PVA bonding agent.

For an exterior repair or if a large patch has become detached, make a reference drawing of the pattern before you lift the loose pieces. Chisel away the old mortar to a depth of about 6mm (¼in). Vacuum the surface and dampen it with water. Apply a bed of cement-based flooring adhesive, then replace the tiles, tamping them down level with the surrounding surface. Once the adhesive has set, apply grouting to the patch if necessary.

Cutting quarry tiles
The thickness and hardness of quarry tiles makes them difficult to cut. You can score the surface and edges of a single tile with a tile cutter and give the back a sharp tap with a cross-peen hammer, but if you have to cut a number of tiles it is easier to hire a heavy-duty commercial tile-cutting jig.

CLEANING TILES
Quarry tiles in good condition require practically no maintenance. To keep them clean, simply sweep the floor then wash the tiles with warm water and household detergent. After washing, rinse the surface of the floor with clean water and a sponge mop.

For ingrained heavy soiling, apply a proprietary tile cleaner, using plastic scouring pads or a hired scrubbing machine. Always follow the manufacturer's instructions and wear protective clothing when using these products.

Encaustic and geometric tiles have similar properties to unglazed quarry tiles, and so can be maintained in a similar way.

Making repairs
Although very hard-wearing, both encaustic and geometric tiles frequently work loose. Fancy floors are particularly likely to have loose or missing tiles, since the small shaped tiles that make up the pattern do not bond so well. The close fit of the tiles helps keep them in place, but this should not be relied on since in time dirt and grit will build up under them. The edges exposed then get damaged, and small pieces may become dislodged and get lost.

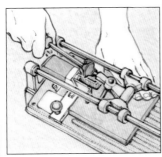

Using a tile-cutting jig

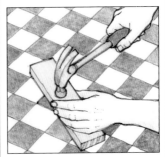

Tamp tiles level with the surface

CERAMIC WALL TILES

Hand-painted Victorian porch tiles

DECORATED CERAMIC TILES, *especially those made in Victorian times and earlier, are highly prized by collectors, and considerable sums change hands even for individual examples. If this is a measure of their value, one can appreciate how important it is to preserve areas of tiling that are still intact. Happily, unless damaged by acts of deliberate vandalism or as a result of woeful ignorance, ceramic wall tiles are practically indestructible, and they also require very little maintenance.*

Dutch delftware overlaid with an English tile of 1750

Seventeenth-century Dutch polychrome delftware

DELFTWARE

Holland and Flanders had a thriving ceramic industry in the seventeenth century that exported tin-glazed earthenware, including handmade blue-and-white tiles, to all parts of Europe. At around that time, Dutch and Flemish potters set up workshops in England in order to manufacture these tiles, which became known as delftware after the most celebrated production centre of the day. Before long, English potters began to compete with the immigrant tile makers, copying typical Dutch designs depicting figures, animals, landscapes and birds. By the middle of the eighteenth century, English tile makers had cultivated a substantial market for their own wares and were confidently designing tiles that were much less dependent on the traditional Dutch themes.

Delftware tiles were made by cutting squares from clay that had been rolled flat like pastry. These blanks were fired in a kiln, then coated with a liquid glaze that dried leaving a powdery surface on the face of each tile. The design was freely painted onto the absorbent surface, then the tile was fired for a second time, which fused the colour into what became a hard, opaque white glaze. Blue or sometimes purple were the colours most often painted onto delftware, but yellow, green or orange were also used occasionally.

In England the success of delftware was short-lived, as the increasing popularity of other types of ceramic began to force a decline in the manufacture of tin-glazed pottery and tiles. By the turn of the century, not one delftware manufacturer was still in business in this country.

VICTORIAN WALL TILES

In the first quarter of the nineteenth century, tile production in Britain was virtually nonexistent. Initially Victorian manufacturers built their businesses on the production of encaustic floor tiles, and it was not until the 1860s and 1870s that they started to make decorated glazed wall tiles in earnest. However, towards the end of of the century the demand for tiles of every description was simply enormous, and the larger manufacturers exported their wares all over the world, including parts of Asia and America.

Glazed tiles were especially practical in kitchens and bathrooms, where washable surfaces were essential. Decorative tiles would often be used to form borders or to break up areas of cheaper white or plain-coloured tiles. It was not regarded as necessary, particularly in a bathroom, to tile entire walls. Very often ceramic tiling was restricted to the lower part of a wall, forming a dado, or was simply used to create splashbacks behind the bathtub and washbasin.

Tiled dadoes were a fairly common feature in blocks of flats, as well as public buildings, and exterior porches were often flanked with tiled panels that were sometimes decorated with painted landscapes or floral themes.

Sets of tiles that formed a design were also made for inserting in cast-iron fire grates (see TILED FIREPLACES) and were incorporated in washstands, coat racks, and other items of furniture.

New methods of production were required to meet the demand. Experiments in printing onto tiles had been fairly successful as early as 1756, when John Sadler

Transfer-printed tiles of c.1780

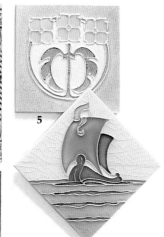

1 Block-printed tile
made in 1880
2 Transfer-printed
hand-coloured tile
3 Multicoloured
block-printed tile
4 Art Nouveau
embossed tile
5 Glazed wall tiles
manufactured
between 1930
and 1935

developed the process of transfer printing. An image incised into a wood block or engraved on a copper plate was transferred to the face of a tile by means of a soft-paper tissue. The printing on early tiles was vulnerable to wear, but the images on Victorian tiles were protected by a coat of transparent glaze. The basic design was normally printed in one colour, usually black or dark brown, and areas of colour were often added by hand.

An alternative method for mass-producing tiles was block printing, whereby simple areas of colour were transferred from a metal plate on which the image had been created in relief. Each colour used in a block-printed pattern required a separate plate.

Dust-pressing, invented in 1840, was yet another significant breakthrough in tile production. Slightly moist powdered clay was compressed between two metal dies, creating beautifully smooth, even tiles. It was a method ideally suited to the manufacture of embossed tiles, a shaped die being employed to create the same low-relief image on the face of each tile. Once fired, an embossed tile was either coated with a single glossy translucent glaze or parts of the image were picked out with different colours.

Fully tiled bathroom originating from the late 1930s

TWENTIETH-CENTURY WALL TILES

From the turn of the century, tile production continued unabated until the First World War. During that time the Art Nouveau movement had a notable effect on the tile-making industry, and many of the tiles, especially embossed ones, exhibit Art Nouveau influences.

In the 1920s and 1930s taste changed dramatically. Tiling became more austere, often comprising nothing more than a field of plain white tiles with a border of slim red, blue or black tiles. Fireplaces were still tiled, but gone were the ornamental side panels – instead, the whole surround was usually faced with mottled tiles in subdued colours. The last spark of the decorative tradition was kept alive by devotees of the Art Deco movement who designed colourful tiles, some of them embossed, that incorporated bold geometric shapes.

PRESERVING CERAMIC WALL TILES

WALL TILES, *like ceramic floor tiles, are very hard-wearing and need little maintenance. Although generally the same standard size as most floor tiles, they can be recognized by their thinner body and glazed finish. Tile glazes vary in thickness, and cleaning methods should take the thickness of the glaze into account. If the surface is crazed or you are unsure how thick the glazing is, seek expert advice before cleaning with strong chemicals.*

Victorian embossed tiles languishing beneath a coat of red paint

CLEANING WALL TILES

The glasslike surface of glazed wall tiles not only enhances their decorative effect but also makes them easy to clean. However, the ceramic body of wall tiles is not as impervious as that of most floor tiles. Care must therefore be taken, particularly if the glaze is crazed, that dirt is not absorbed into the tile during the cleaning process. It is best not to bleach tiles *in situ*, in case the stains are absorbed. But if you have unfixed tiles that need cleaning, you can soak them in water (preferably distilled) then apply dilute household bleach since presoaking the tiles will prevent dirt or stains being drawn into the ceramic body.

Tiled walls need to be cleaned regularly in order to maintain their surface finish. All that's usually needed is to wipe the surface with a damp cloth or sponge. If dirt has been allowed to build up, wash it off with a household washing-up liquid, or use a teaspoonful of washing soda in a bucket of warm water. Rinse the surface and wipe dry as you go.

For heavy soiling, use a proprietary tile cleaner and rinse the surface thoroughly. Tile cleaners are caustic and must be used with care, as they can cause some Victorian ruby lustre glazes or gold finishes to fade. When working with them,

wear rubber gloves and protect your eyes. Always try out cleaning agents on an inconspicuous area of tiling before you proceed with cleaning. Use a fibre scouring pad to remove stubborn deposits of dirt. In some cases a pad of very fine wire wool can be used on thick-glazed tiles, but generally it is advisable not to use abrasive materials and cleaners at all on glazed ceramic tiles. If you use wire wool, all traces of metal particles must be removed so rust staining doesn't occur.

Cleaning grout

Grout is a cementitious material that is used to fill and seal the joints between tiles. The appearance of a field of light-coloured tiles can be spoilt by old dirty grout. To refresh sound grout, apply a tile cleaner or household cream cleaner with a stiff nylon toothbrush, working along the joint lines. Rinse down thoroughly as you go. Mould growth can be treated with a solution of household bleach and hot water.

If grout is in a poor state, remove it and regrout the joints. Use a dental pick or suitable pointed tool. Control the tool carefully, so as not to damage the surface. Leave any part of the grouting that is in good condition intact. Brush and vacuum out all loose material, and then apply new matching grout.

Gently scrape off paint with scalpel

Removing paint

You may find that ceramic wall tiles have been splashed with paint, or even painted over entirely in an attempt to alter the character or colour scheme of the interior.

As a general rule, it's safer to use mechanical methods to remove paint rather than resort to chemical strippers. For example, it is possible to gently remove splashes of paint with a sharp scalpel.

However, if a sizeable area of tiling has been painted over, you have little choice but to use a water-washable stripper. Apply it following the maker's instructions and remove the softened paint with a wooden or plastic scraper. Wash off the residue with water, working a bristle brush into crevices, and then wipe the surface dry.

REPLACING DAMAGED TILES

Having first removed the surrounding grout, carefully chisel out a cracked or broken tile with a narrow cold chisel and a club hammer, working from the centre. Chisel a recess into the background, then vacuum away all loose material.

Apply a wall-tile adhesive to the back of the replacement and press it into place. Allow the adhesive to set, then finish with matching grout.

DRILLING TILED WALLS

When appliances or fixtures need to be fixed to a wall, try to avoid drilling into the face of old tiles – especially ones that are decorative or rare. If you do have to drill the wall, position the hole or holes on a joint line or corner whenever possible.

To prevent a masonry drill bit skidding on the face of a tile, before drilling mark the centre of the hole on the tile with a felt-tip pen and then stick a patch of clear adhesive tape over the mark. Run the drill at a slow speed and apply light pressure. Drill the hole to match the length of a suitably sized wall plug plus the thickness of the tile. Insert the plug into the hole fully, so when the screw is tightened the expansion of the plug will not fracture the glazed surface of the tile.

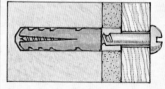
Insert the plug fully

CHAPTER FOURTEEN

WALL PANELLING

WOODEN WALL PANELLING, sometimes known as wainscoting, was usually made from painted softwood when used for finishing the walls of the entrance hall and principal rooms in many of the better-class eighteenth-century houses. It was classical in style, influenced by the pattern books of the Renaissance architects, and used sophisticated frame-and-panel joinery.

The use of wood panelling as an attractive and practical wall lining was not new, having been employed both for this purpose and as partitioning in much earlier times. This early panelling consisted of hand-wrought vertical planks that were either nailed in place or slotted into grooved studs or muntins and held by a sill and a head member. By the end of the fifteenth century a refinement in joinery techniques led to the development of Tudor frame-and-panel wainscoting. Although the style had declined by the close of the seventeenth century, it enjoyed something of a revival in the mid-Victorian period, when it was widely imitated.

Tongue-and-groove matchboarding was also used in the eighteenth century. It was simpler to make and install, and was more refined than earlier boarding of this type. It usually featured a bead moulding, and was most commonly found in provincial houses.

Elegant painted C18th wall panelling

Late-C19th Tudor-style oak panelling in an Arts and Crafts interior

TYPES OF PANELLING

THE EARLY FRAME-AND-PANEL WAINSCOTING *was made from oak, using small plain panels set in a simple pegged mortise-and-tenon framework. The frame consisted of a top rail and bottom rail and a number of intermediate rails, all jointed into vertical stiles. Muntins (short vertical members) were jointed into the rails, usually spaced at equal intervals across the width of the frame. The inner edges of all the frame members were grooved to hold the panels without use of glue, so they were able to expand and contract freely without splitting.*

Traditionally the edges of the frame that surrounded and held the panels were shaped with a simple stuck moulding, which was cut by hand into the edge of the

wood, using a scratch stock. Where the moulding of the muntins met the edge of the rails, mitred corners had to be carved in the rails after the fashion of a mason's mitre joint.

The top edges of the intermediate rails were often finished with a stopped-chamfer detail. This detail was almost certainly influenced by masons' work too, as it recalls the sloping top face of a stone sill. Some panels were decorated with low-relief carving, the linenfold pattern being a typical design.

Tudor-style panelling has been widely copied. However, although later versions sometimes have handmade joints and mouldings, more often the mouldings are machined and the shoulders of the joints are scribed.

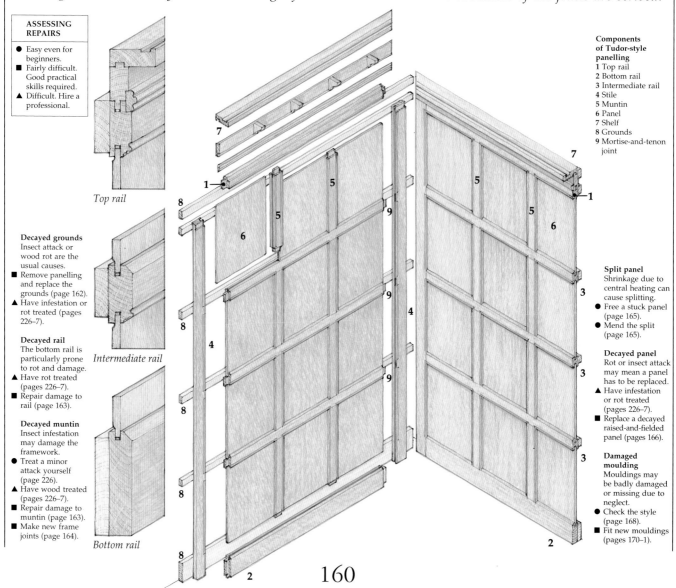

ASSESSING REPAIRS

● Easy even for beginners.
■ Fairly difficult. Good practical skills required.
▲ Difficult. Hire a professional.

Top rail

Decayed grounds
Insect attack or wood rot are the usual causes.
■ Remove panelling and replace the grounds (page 162).
▲ Have infestation or rot treated (pages 226–7).

Decayed rail
The bottom rail is particularly prone to rot and damage.
▲ Have rot treated (pages 226–7).
■ Repair damage to rail (page 163).

Intermediate rail

Decayed muntin
Insect infestation may damage the framework.
● Treat a minor attack yourself (page 226).
▲ Have wood treated (pages 226–7).
■ Repair damage to muntin (page 163).
■ Make new frame joints (page 164).

Bottom rail

Components of Tudor-style panelling
1 Top rail
2 Bottom rail
3 Intermediate rail
4 Stile
5 Muntin
6 Panel
7 Shelf
8 Grounds
9 Mortise-and-tenon joint

Split panel
Shrinkage due to central heating can cause splitting.
● Free a stuck panel (page 165).
● Mend the split (page 165).

Decayed panel
Rot or insect attack may mean a panel has to be replaced.
▲ Have infestation or rot treated (pages 226–7).
■ Replace a decayed raised-and-fielded panel (pages 166).

Damaged moulding
Mouldings may be badly damaged or missing due to neglect.
● Check the style (page 168).
■ Fit new mouldings (pages 170–1).

160

CLASSICAL INFLUENCES

By the late seventeenth century wider panels (known as wide-board panelling in America) had become fashionable, and their vertical dimensions reflected the proportions of the classical orders of architecture.

Solid oak was still in use, but increasingly pine was used for large and painted panelling. The panels were either plain or raised-and-fielded. The framing was worked with stuck moulding, or the joins between the panels and the frame might be finished with a planted or a bolection moulding.

Pilasters in the classical style were often used to add relief to a run of panelling or to serve as an architrave that hid the join between the stiles of meeting sets of panels.

This style of solid-wood panelling remained fashionable until the nineteenth century. However, only the owners of relatively grandiose houses could afford it, and painted plaster and wallpapers became more commonly used.

Classical orders influenced styles

THE PANELLING REVIVAL

Wall panelling was revived by members of the Arts and Crafts movement, whose influence continued into the early twentieth century.

Started by William Morris in England, the ideas of the movement were taken up with enthusiasm by Gustav Stickley and the Greene brothers, among others, in America.

The movement embraced artists, designers and architects whose aim was to return to the simple 'honest' styles of earlier times as a reaction against the excesses of mass-produced ornamentation. Well-executed, functional designs employing traditional methods and materials were the principles on which they based their work.

Natural oak was widely used both for panelling and furniture. The designs were deliberately plain, with only restrained decoration to complement the natural features of the wood. Arts and Crafts wall panelling tended to stop round about door or head height, often terminating with a shelf, the upper part of the wall being finished with painted plaster. This design was not adopted for purely aesthetic reasons: it also gave light to interiors that would otherwise have been gloomy in view of the dark wood and small windows favoured by architects working in the new style.

Although the aim of the Arts and Crafts movement was to keep the old craft skills alive, it did not halt the progress of mechanization. By the early twentieth century traditional panelling had become rare and machine-made plywood panels had taken over from solid wood.

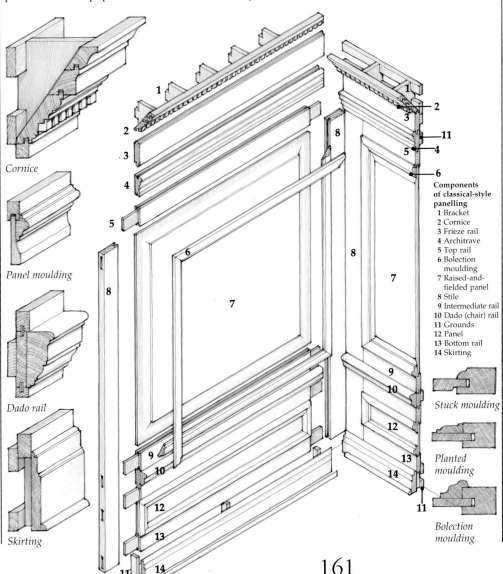

Cornice

Panel moulding

Dado rail

Skirting

Components of classical-style panelling
1 Bracket
2 Cornice
3 Frieze rail
4 Architrave
5 Top rail
6 Bolection moulding
7 Raised-and-fielded panel
8 Stile
9 Intermediate rail
10 Dado (chair) rail
11 Grounds
12 Panel
13 Bottom rail
14 Skirting

Stuck moulding

Planted moulding

Bolection moulding

DADOES

By Victorian times wainscoting generally only extended up to the chair-rail moulding, forming a dado. The moulding and dado protected the walls from being damaged by chair backs and general traffic. It also provided a visual division of the wall following classical principles. Dadoes were constructed using frame-and-panel methods or, in some cases, tongue-and-groove boarding.

By the mid nineteenth century the dado rail began to go out of fashion for main rooms, but it continued to be used as a finishing detail for embossed-paper dadoes in stairways and entrance halls. The last vestiges of the classical panelled wall were the picture rail and the skirting. Picture rails were a common feature of 1930s interiors, and skirting boards are still in use today.

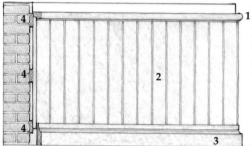
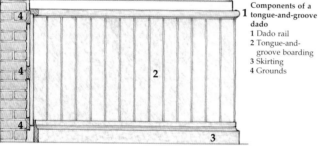

Components of a frame-and-panel dado
1 Dado rail
2 Top rail
3 Stile
4 Muntin
5 Bottom rail
6 Panel
7 Skirting
8 Grounds

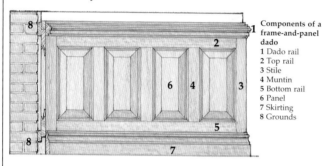

Components of a tongue-and-groove dado
1 Dado rail
2 Tongue-and-groove boarding
3 Skirting
4 Grounds

Oak raised-and-fielded panelled dado on a late-nineteenth-century staircase

HOW PANELLING IS FIXED

Wooden battens or 'grounds' are used for fixing panelling to brick or stone walls. The battens are levelled and nailed or screwed to plugs set in the wall. The fixings used to hold the panelling to the grounds are either discreetly placed or hidden by wooden pellets cut to match the grain of the wood, or they may be disguised with a coloured filler.

REMOVING PANELLING

It's worth making strenuous efforts to preserve original panelling – but only remove it from the wall for repair when absolutely necessary.

If you have to remove panelling to make a repair and your house is recorded as a listed building, you will first need to obtain consent from the relevant authority. If you think your house may be a listed building but are not certain, contact the Conservation Officer in your local planning office.

Seek out fixing points and remove them carefully. If you have to prise the frame from the wall, place the lever close to the fixing. Even if you exercise great care, you may find that the grounds to which the panelling is fixed pull away from the wall and need to be refixed.

The procedure for removing panelling should be the reverse of the way it was installed. Remove skirtings, dado rails and cornice mouldings first. These are usually nailed in place, but take care when dismantling them since some components may be fixed together with tongue-and-groove joints. Always try to make minor repairs *in situ*, since removing panels can create further damage.

PANELLED CEILINGS

The earliest ceilings were little more than the underside of the roof covering or the floorboards of the rooms above. Plaster was sometimes used to finish the underside of the boards, leaving the beams exposed – a common feature of many cottages over the centuries.

In the Tudor period the structural beams were decoratively carved, and wooden panels and mouldings were often used to fill the spaces between them. Eventually this developed into similar plaster forms. Tongue-and-groove boarding was also used as an infilling between the beams, and sometimes plain boards were fixed over the joists to provide a flat ceiling that could be painted. Frame-and-panel ceilings, made and fitted in a similar way to wall panelling, were employed for some interiors but were not as common.

By the late sixteenth century plaster had become the standard material for ceilings, although timber panelling saw a revival during the Victorian era and timber-boxed beams and strapwork (a grid of flat strips of wood) were used by architects of the Arts and Crafts movement.

Late interpretation of beamed ceiling

MAKING REPAIRS TO THE FRAME

SPLITS, CHIPPED EDGES AND GENERAL BRUISING and discoloration are normally regarded as part of the character of old panelling. However, where wood rot or insect attack has seriously weakened the framework, you may have no option but to remove the panelling and replace the infected timber.

Try to retain as much of the original panelling as possible. Before you begin work on repairs, take reference photographs of the panelling and make measured drawings of the components. Use a profile gauge to record the shape of the mouldings, and transfer it to your drawing in the form of full-size sections. Cut out the affected timber and make a new section to replace it. Make the new components from the same species of wood, with grain that closely matches the original.

The new wood will not, of course, be the correct colour – but you can tone it down with wood stain or bleach it, as appropriate. This is less important when dealing with painted panelling. Some argue that new work should not be disguised in any way. However, if the colour blends with the original, that helps maintain the harmony of the panelling as a whole, instead of drawing attention to the repair. Distressing the wood in order to age it is perhaps less justifiable.

Repairing a bottom rail

Support the panelling on a bench or trestles, depending on its size. Use lengths of wood spanning the trestles for extra support. The repair described here is for damage around the bottom rail, which is the most vulnerable area, but the method can be used for other parts of the panelling, too.

Carefully saw or router across the rail to remove the infected area back to sound wood (1). If there is a muntin tenoned into the part to be removed, carefully drive out or drill out any pegs holding the joint together. You can then knock the joint apart, using a hammer and a scrap of wood to take the blows. Should the joint be glued, soften the glue with steam from a kettle. A jet of steam from a flexible neoprene tube attached to the spout gives greater control. Wear protective gloves and take care not to scald yourself when working with steam.

Lap-joint the new wood into the old. First, cut the shoulder of the lap in the ends of the old wood at 45 degrees to the face of the rail (2). Cut the shoulder lines not less than 50mm (2in) from the ends, and stop at the groove. Then pare off the waste to this level.

Cut the new wood to size. Plane a groove in the top edge to match the old one. Chamfer or cut a matching moulding in the front edge. Shape the moulding with a scratch stock, multi-plane or power router, as appropriate. Cut away the back of the rail at each end to match the lap in the old material. Bevel the ends of the new lap to fit the angled shoulder already cut (3). If necessary, mark out and cut a mortise for a muntin tenon (4).

Try the new work for fit. If all is well, glue the lap joints and the mortise and tenon. Take care to keep the glue away from the panel, which must be free to move. If need be, remake or reuse the peg for the joint, drill a new hole for it and glue it in place.

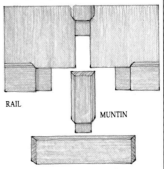

1 Cut out infected wood

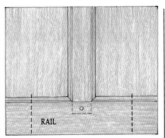

2 Cut shoulder to 45 degrees

3 Bevel the ends of the laps

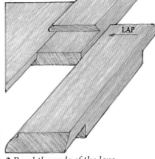

4 Cut a mortise if necessary

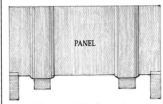

5 Repair muntin as for rail

Muntin repair

If the muntin members are damaged, proceed as for repairing the bottom rail (see left) then cut away the muntin and repair it with new wood lap-jointed into place (5).

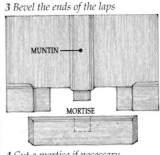

Cut rail on outside of muntins

Panel repair

In order to take out a panel for repair, cut the bottom rail outside the muntins on each side, then remove the rail and slide out the panel. For how to make a replacement for a damaged raised-and-fielded panel that is beyond repair, see MAKING A RAISED-AND-FIELDED PANEL.

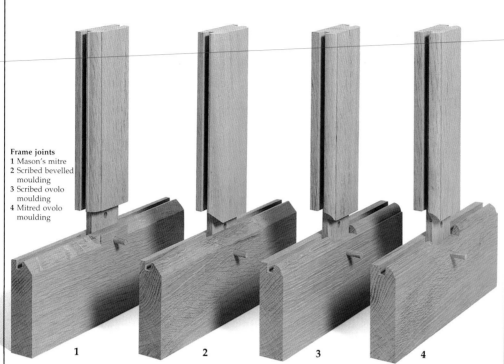

Frame joints
1 Mason's mitre
2 Scribed bevelled moulding
3 Scribed ovolo moulding
4 Mitred ovolo moulding

1   2   3   4

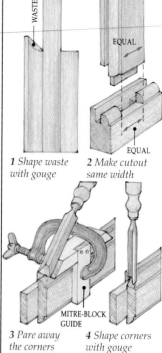

1 Shape waste with gouge   *2 Make cutout same width*

WASTE   EQUAL   EQUAL

MITRE-BLOCK GUIDE

3 Pare away the corners   *4 Shape corners with gouge*

FRAME JOINTS

Traditionally the framework for panelling was constructed with hand-cut mortise-and-tenon joints – the top, bottom and intermediate rails being tenoned into the stiles, while the muntins are tenoned into the rails.

Although the basic principles of making the joint apply to all periods, the techniques for dealing with the mouldings vary. Early examples had the moulding stopped or run out, or were given the appearance of a mitred corner by the use of a mason's mitre.

Various methods for treating the moulding are shown, using a muntin-to-rail joint as an example.

MASON'S MITRE JOINT

This was a technique used by masons for carving a mitre in stone blocks where two mouldings met at an internal angle. Early joiners adopted the method, using a scratch stock and moulding planes and chisels.

To make this type of joint, run the moulding the length of the tenon member. On the mortise member you can't run the moulding through, so work the moulding with the scratch stock and stop close to the mortise. Using small chisels and carving gouges, carve the remaining 'corner' in the form of a mitre to meet the shape of the other member when the joint is assembled.

SCRIBED JOINTS

Joiners ran the moulding plane through on the edges of both workpieces, then scribed the shoulder of the tenon member to the reverse contour of the mortise member. This method gave the appearance of a mitred joint when two matching moulded edges, such as a bevel or an ovolo, met. It had the advantage over true mitred joints in that cross-grain shrinkage was less apparent.

The technique is still used today for moulded joinery, since the edges of the parts and the end-grain shoulders of the tenons can quickly and accurately be shaped by machine.

Bevelled moulding

To make this joint by hand, you have to cut a tenon member with one long and one short shoulder. The difference between the two shoulders is determined by the size of the moulding. A simple bevelled edge is shown above.

Plane the groove, cut the mortise, and form the bevel on the front edge of the mortise member. Groove the edges of the tenon member, then mark and cut the long-and-short shouldered tenon as required. Make the saw-cuts the same length **(1)**. Saw out the waste to match the bevel on the mating rail **(2)**.

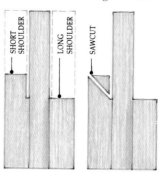

SHORT SHOULDER   LONG SHOULDER   SAWCUT

1 Tenon for bevelled-edge joint   *2 Saw out waste on short shoulder*

Ovolo moulding

This joint can be made in a similar fashion to a bevelled moulding, but you have to shape the bevelled shoulder of the tenon further, using an in-cannel gouge **(1)**.

However, an alternative method for making a moulding such as an ovolo is to cut away part of the moulding from the mortise member.

Make the width of the cutout the same width as the face of the tenon member **(2)**. Now, instead of shaping the full width of the short tenon shoulder, it only remains to pare away the corners of the moulding carefully.

To produce the required contour, first mitre the end of the moulding with the aid of a simple home-made mitre-block guide. Clamp the guide block to the work level with the long shoulder. Pare away the corner with a chisel to form a mitre **(3)**. Remove the guide block and, making vertical cuts with an in-cannel gouge, carefully pare away the wood in order to shape the corners, finishing on the line created by the mitre cut **(4)**.

164

REPAIRING PANELLING

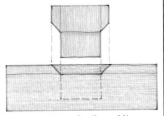

Mitre muntin and rail moulding

MITRED JOINTS

You can use mitred joints for mouldings with any kind of profile – including under-cut mouldings, for which a scribed joint cannot be used.

First, cut a long-and-short shouldered tenon. Then cut away the moulding on the mortise member to the width of the face of the tenon piece. Using the mitre block as a guide, pare away the corners of the moulding on the tenon member. Clamp the guide to the mortise member, and mitre the moulding in the same way.

MITRING APPLIED MOULDINGS

When mitred corners are to be used, make sure applied mouldings have a stable moisture content. If the wood should shrink after the mitres are made, they will open up on the inside of the corner (1); if it takes up moisture and expands, they open up on the outside (2).

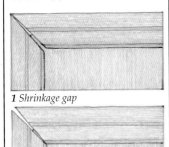

1 Shrinkage gap

2 Expansion gap

WOOD EXPANDS AND CONTRACTS *because of changing moisture conditions, the greatest movement taking place across the grain. The grain of the panels nearly always runs vertically; so, to allow for movement, more clearance is usually allowed in the side grooves of the frame than at the top and bottom. In order to keep the framework relatively light, it was necessary for the panels to be thin. This was not at all easy to achieve, since early panels were cut by hand and the edges had to be thinned down considerably to fit into the grooves in the framework. The thinning of the edges may be worked on the back, as with flat or sunken panels, or featured on the front to form a fielded panel.*

SPLIT PANELS

To allow for movement, solid-wood panels should never be fixed in their grooves. Nevertheless, distortion in the frame members or applied finishes can cause them to stick. Should a stuck panel shrink due to excessive drying out, it is likely to split. The decision then has to be made as to whether a split should be repaired or left as part of the panel's ageing character. Also, any repair must take account of the need for the wood to move. But, first of all, you need to try to free the panel in the groove.

Freeing a panel

Should a panel be held fast by a distorted frame, there is not much you can do to free it short of removing the entire assembly – a remedy that is hardly justified by the problem. However, usually the problem only arises if the wood shrinks drastically due to dry conditions, as caused by central heating.

If the panel is stuck with paint or varnish, carefully tap around the edge to try to free it. Don't strike the panel itself, but place a batten along the edge to protect the wood. Otherwise, try sliding a thin knife blade between the panel and the frame.

Dealing with splits

Splits in naturally finished show-wood panels can look quite acceptable. The split is likely to follow a weakness in the wood that relates to the grain (1). If the split runs in from one edge and tapers off, it would be difficult to close up, anyway, and filling with a coloured stopper would not be acceptable.

In the case of a wide painted panel where a butt joint between two narrow boards has opened up, it may be visually desirable to close the 'split'. If the panel is free to move, clean the joint by scraping it with a narrow blade and work woodworking glue into the joint. Push the parts together with the palms of your hands (2), wearing rubber gloves to increase friction. Tape the joint while it sets.

Alternatively, use two narrow chisels to lever one part up to the other (3), protecting the frame with card. Wipe away any excess glue and, when it has set, fill the indentations in the wood before repainting.

Flat or sunken panelling

Raised-and-fielded panelling

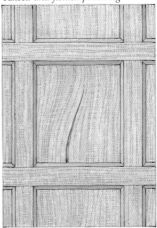

1 Split is likely to follow the grain

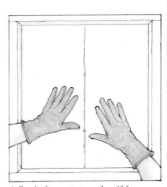

2 Push the parts together if free

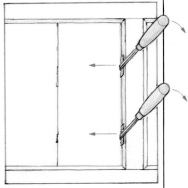

3 Carefully lever panel with chisels

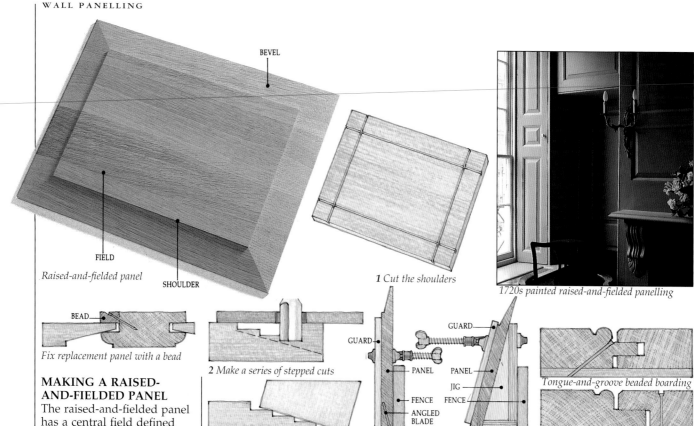

BEVEL

FIELD

SHOULDER

Raised-and-fielded panel

1 Cut the shoulders

1720s painted raised-and-fielded panelling

BEAD

Fix replacement panel with a bead

2 Make a series of stepped cuts

3 Use rebate plane to finish surface

GUARD

GUARD

PANEL

PANEL

JIG

FENCE

FENCE

ANGLED
BLADE

*4 Always guard
the saw blade*

*5 Use a jig on a
non-tilting saw*

Tongue-and-groove beaded boarding

Rebated beaded boarding

MAKING A RAISED-AND-FIELDED PANEL

The raised-and-fielded panel has a central field defined by a shallow raised shoulder combined with a bevelled border. If you have a panel of this type that is beyond repair (due to insect attack, for example), make a replacement to match the original.

The panelling will need to be removed and the frame dismantled to make replacement possible. Alternatively, particularly in the case of a middle panel, free the damaged panel by routing out the back of the groove in the frame. You can then drop the new panel into the resulting rebate and pin a bead behind the panel to secure it.

Preparing the wood

If possible, use the old panel as a pattern; if not, take the dimensions from adjacent panels. Select new wood that closely matches the original (take the old panel or a piece of it with you to your timber supplier) and have it machined to thickness. If you are unable to find wood that is wide enough, you can butt-joint pieces together. Leave the panel to acclimatize for several weeks in the room where it is to be fitted. Hire a moisture meter to check the moisture content of the new wood against that of the old panelling.

Cut the panel to width and length. Then use a marking gauge to mark the width of the fielded border on the face of the panel and to mark the depth of the bevel all round the edge.

Cutting the bevel

Originally raised-and-fielded panels were shaped with purpose-made panel-raising planes. These wooden planes had the sole shaped to the contour of the border, with the blade set at a skew so that they cut cleanly across the grain at the ends of the panel. Although some craftsmen still use these planes, it is possible to shape the edge with a rebate plane, power router or table saw, or to use a combination of these.

First, cut the shoulders using a table saw or a power router (**1**). You can continue to remove much of the waste in this way by resetting the depth of cut and making a series of steps (**2**). Use a rebate plane to finish the stepped surface (**3**). In order to save all the resetting, use the rebate plane by itself to shape the bevel

If you decide to cut the bevel on a table saw, use a stiff tungsten-carbide-tipped blade; if your table saw has a tilting facility, set it to the required angle and depth of cut. Clamp a piece of board to the face of the panel to act as a guard when cutting the bevel (**4**). If your saw table is non-tilting, make a jig to hold the work at the desired angle (**5**). Plane the sawn surface to finish it.

Finishing the panel

Sand all the faces with fine abrasive paper, then apply the finish to both sides. This will help to keep the panel stable. When it is thoroughly dry, install the panel in the framework.

BEADED WAINSCOTING

Beaded wainscoting is a form of panelling that uses either tongue-and-groove or rebated boarding. The boards are nailed into place along one edge, the beaded side being held by the fixed edge of the adjacent board. In this way each board is free to move. The moulded bead forms a definite visual break that helps mask the variable gaps at the joints.

Replacing a damaged board

Beaded wainscoting is still a popular wall finish and is available from most timber suppliers. However, you can't be sure that a modern pattern will match an old one exactly. If you need to replace a few boards, you can have them made to order or make them yourself.

Have new boards machined to the required size by your supplier. Use a power router or combination plane to tongue and groove the edges. Cut the bead moulding with a scratch stock.

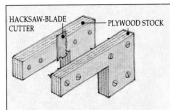

HACKSAW-BLADE CUTTER — PLYWOOD STOCK

HOW TO MAKE A SCRATCH STOCK

This is a simple home-made tool used for shaping small mouldings or parts of larger mouldings.

Make the stock of the tool from two L-shaped pieces cut from 150 x 75 x 18mm (6 x 3 x ¾in) plywood. Fix them together with 32mm (1¼in) countersunk screws. Fashion the cutter from a piece of old hacksaw blade. This is made of very hard steel and can be snapped to length. File the reverse shape of the bead profile in the end of the cutter blade. Clamp the cutter between the stock pieces at the desired setting.

To shape the moulding, hold the shoulder of the scratch stock firmly against the edge and push the tool away from you, working the tool with even strokes.

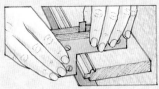

Work the tool with even strokes

MAINTAINING A WOODEN CEILING

Little maintenance is needed for sound wooden ceilings other than general cleaning, preservative treatment and, if appropriate, repainting. Exposed oak beams should not be stained black, as there is no historical precedent for this. Painted woodwork that would originally have been a natural colour should be chemically stripped (see STRIPPING DOORS) and either left unfinished or waxed.

FINISHING THE REPAIR

Unless you plan to strip the entire wall of its finish, you will need to use a compatible finish for your repair so as to preserve the original patina.

Oil-based resin varnishes were introduced early in the sixteenth century and are to be found on panelling of the period, although they may have been applied at a later date.

By the early nineteenth century spirit-based shellac polishes were available, but by this time paint (which was in effect a pigmented varnish) had become the fashionable finish for wood panelling. If you are lucky enough to discover panelling finished with early casein (milk-based) paint, it should be preserved.

Testing the finish

To determine which finish to use, test a small unobtrusive area of panelling. Clean dirt and wax polish from the surface, using a cotton cloth dampened with a solution of 4 parts spirit to 1 part linseed oil. Next, wipe the surface with a cloth damp-ened with methylated spirit, which is the solvent of shellac. If the finish softens and can be wiped off, then it is spirit-based shellac. Oil-based varnishes and paints will not react to meths in this way – and white spirit, which is their solvent, won't redissolve them.

If you are aiming for total authenticity, have a slice of the finish analysed by an expert to establish its type and date. A national or local conservation organization will tell you who to contact for this specialist service.

Preparing the new wood

To prepare the new wood for a natural finish, you will

Wax polish gives natural-wood panelling a subtle sheen

need to stain it to tone down its colour.

Water-based stains are simple to apply, and wipe off easily if the colour proves to be too strong; however, they may raise the grain. Spirit-based stains do not raise the grain; but they dry rapidly, so they are difficult to apply evenly. Oil-based stains are thinned with white spirit. They are easy to apply and will not affect the grain, but they may bleed into an oil-based varnish.

You can buy stains in a variety of common wood shades. To test the colour of a stain, apply it to offcuts of the wood used for the repair. Dilute the stain if necessary; or for darker shades apply extra coats. Different colours can be obtained by mixing stains of the same type. When dry, apply a wax or varnish finish to evaluate the darkening effect it has on the colour. Modify the stain accordingly.

When you have achieved a match with the original material, proceed to colour and finish the repair. Make sure the stain is dry before applying the finish.

Wax finish

For a wax finish, prepare the newly stained wood with a

coat of clear sanding sealer. This prevents the first coat of polish sinking in excessively. A range of ready-prepared traditional wax polishes is available. Apply two or three coats of polish, using a pad of fine wire wool or a cloth. Allow each coat to dry, then buff with a soft cloth.

Varnish finish

Newly applied varnish can never match the worn patina of an old finish, nor will it have the subtle character of a wax finish. However, if you are trying to match an old varnish finish, use a compat-ible oil-based varnish (never a modern polyurethane one).

Apply an oil varnish with a brush, laying the finish on evenly in thin coats. Let each coat dry, and rub down with fine silicon-carbide paper between coats.

After varnishing, apply a wax polish on a pad of fine wire wool.

Paint finish

Colour matching is never easy, and matching old paint can be particularly difficult. If you think your interior finish is original, discuss the work with a specialist or an adviser from a historical society before embarking on any repairs.

ARCHITECTURAL MOULDINGS

MOULDED SKIRTINGS, *dado rails, picture rails and cornices play an important part in creating the attractive character of an old house, and deserve to be preserved or reinstated if they have been removed. Although their use may have been primarily functional, they were also employed to give balance and enrichment to the wall surface to which they were applied.*

Traditional wooden moulding planes

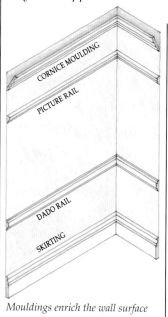

Mouldings enrich the wall surface

Stuck moulding

Applied moulding

Wooden interior mouldings

1 Victorian-style skirting
2 Torus skirting
3 Cornice mouldings
4 Straight-run dado rail
5 Carved-type dado rails
6 Small straight-run dado rail
7 Small carved-type dado rail
8 Astragal panel moulding
9 Picture rail

Wooden interior mouldings

Mouldings are produced by making a series of shaped parallel cuts that combine to give a contoured form to the edge or face of a workpiece. There are two types: either the moulding is worked directly into the component, in which case it is known as a stuck moulding, or it can take the form of an applied moulding (a moulded length of wood that has to be fixed to the background).

Most wooden mouldings are intended to be painted and are therefore made from an inexpensive softwood. Nevertheless, good-quality selected timber is used, in order to avoid knots that are difficult to cut. Before the woodworking trade became mechanized, all mouldings were laboriously fashioned by hand using moulding planes. Each one needed an individual size or shape of plane, and some required the use of several special planes.

Early interior mouldings were relatively simple and were worked in vernacular styles by local craftsmen. But from the early seventeenth century mouldings began to be influenced by classical styles, and by the eighteenth century wooden mouldings inspired by Roman and Greek architecture were the standard forms.

The Roman versions were rather heavier in style than the Greek ones – the former being based on segments of a circle, while the latter were based on elliptical curves.

Skirtings

Skirtings or baseboards are used to line, or 'skirt', the base of interior walls. They help conceal the junction between the wall and floor and protect the surface of the wall from impact damage.

The size and complexity of the moulding and the materials from which it is made are dependent on the quality of the house. Most old skirtings are made from single softwood boards up to 200mm (8in) in height and shaped with a simple classical moulding. Some Victorian skirtings, however, can be up to 350mm (14in) in height and made from two or three elaborately moulded softwood or hardwood sections. The shoulders of the tongue-and-groove edges fall on a line of the moulding to disguise the joint.

Main rooms and hallways were fitted with impressive decorative skirtings, while bedrooms were mostly fitted with a simpler style. Attic and basement rooms were normally fitted with plain square-edged boards.

Standard mouldings are generally available, but you may need to have elaborate skirtings purpose-made by a specialist joinery company. Give them a sample of the moulding or a dimensioned sketch to serve as a guide.

1   2   3   3   4   5

Dado rails

Dado rails, sometimes called chair rails, are a legacy from classical panelling and the wainscot or dado panelling of Victorian times. The cap moulding of dado panelling served as a rubbing strip that protected the wall finish from wear and tear by chair backs. The dado rail, which was usually set about 1 to 1.2m (3 to 4ft) from the floor, continued this tradition after the use of wood panelling had declined. Dado rails did not feature in rooms beyond the nineteenth century, but they were still widely used as a trim for the fashionable embossed wallcoverings that lined the dadoes of so many halls and stairways in late-Victorian and Edwardian times. Dadoes had ceased to be a common architectural feature by the mid 1920s.

Straight-run and carved mouldings in hardwoods and softwoods are available from specialist sources.

Picture rails

Like the dado moulding, the picture rail is an echo of the earlier panelled walls. The position of the rail varied according to the height of the room, but it was usually positioned 300 to 500mm (1ft to 1ft 8in) below the ceiling cornice to form a frieze. For this reason, it is sometimes known as a frieze moulding. The true picture rail had a quirk (narrow groove) in the top edge, into which picture hangers fitted.

The picture rail figured widely in Victorian interiors and is a common feature in many houses well beyond the 1930s. The later versions tend to be smaller and less fussy than the Victorian ones. Traditional mouldings are available from specialist suppliers in softwoods and a limited range of hardwoods.

Cornice mouldings

Wooden cornice mouldings were used to finish the top of panelling that terminated below ceiling level. For full-height panelling, they were fitted up to the ceiling. The moulding formed an integral part of the panelling.

They were also sometimes fitted in place of the more widely used plaster cornice at the junction between un-adorned plastered walls and the ceiling. Wooden cornices are generally smaller than the plaster versions.

Suppliers who specialize in reproduction mouldings stock a range of ornamental hardwood cornices.

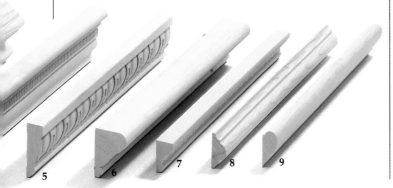

5 6 7 8 9

RESTORING MOULDINGS

I F THE ORIGINAL STYLE *of the interior of your house is not known, you will need to find references to serve as a guide for repair work. The chances are that your house will be one of a number in your street built in the same style. Not all of the houses will have been altered in the same way, and with luck you may find original mouldings to copy.*

Decorative mouldings used to perfection in a late-Victorian sitting room

DETECTING MISSING MOULDINGS

Unless your walls have been replastered, you will be able to detect the use and original position of missing mouldings when the wallpaper has been stripped. Parallel streaks of varnish or paint on the plaster of the wall will indicate the exact location of a dado or picture rail. You can also use the patches of plaster covering the original fixing points as a guide. If the walls have been painted over, you may find that you can detect the patches by shining a light obliquely across the surface to show up irregularities.

DADO AND PICTURE-RAIL FIXINGS

Picture rails and dado rails were fixed with cut nails, either driven directly into the masonry or into wooden plugs set in the vertical joints of the plastered brick-work. Timber-frame walls had the rails nailed directly to the studs. The plugs are unlikely to have survived – so when fitting new rails to masonry, either use cut nails or modern masonry nails or drill and plug the walls for screw fixings. Use oval nails for timber-frame walls.

The dado rail defines the panel below

Fitting a new rail

Using a long straight batten and a spirit level, mark a horizontal fixing line at the required height. If you have no original marks to go by, position a dado rail about 1 to 1.2m (3 to 4ft) from the floor. For a rail following the slope of a staircase, use a length of chalked string to snap a straight line onto the wall. Hold each end of the string at a point where vertical lines level with the end of the skirting of the hall and landing meet the line of the horizontal dado at the top and bottom of the staircase.

The position of the picture rail depends on the period of the house. Houses at the turn of the century had high ceilings, and the rail was generally positioned about 300 to 500mm (1ft to 1ft 8in) below the cornice moulding.

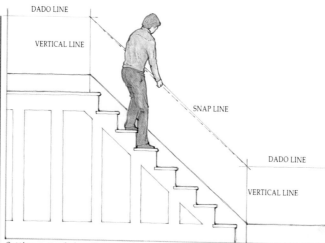

DADO LINE
VERTICAL LINE
SNAP LINE
DADO LINE
VERTICAL LINE

Setting out a dado rail on a stair

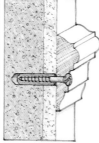
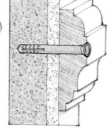
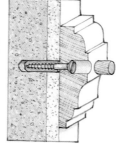

Plug and screw fixing   *Nailable plug fixing*   *Counterbored and plugged screw fixing*

Later interiors usually had lower ceilings, so the picture rail was fitted at door height.

Cut the rails to length as you work round the room, and mitre or scribe the ends where they meet. With the aid of an assistant, hold the rail on the marked line and nail it in place. Sink the nail-heads below the surface with a nail punch.

For a screw fixing, first drill countersunk or counter-bored clearance holes in the rail, at 600mm (2ft) intervals, for No8 50mm (2in) screws. Temporarily fix the rail in place by partly driving in a few nails. Mark the position of the holes on the wall and remove the rail. Drill the plug holes, then insert the wall plugs and screw the rail in place.

For a larger rail, you can use nailable plugs. Drill the wood and plug hole together, and drive the fixing through the face of the rail.

Fill the fixing holes with a fine plaster filler and, when it is set, sand it smooth ready for painting. Alternatively, use a coloured wood filler for a natural wood finish.

For a superior finish, you can use counterbored screw fixings and make matching wooden plugs to fill the holes. Cut the plugs from offcuts of the wood, using a plug-cutting bit and a power drill set up in a drill stand. Alternatively, turn the plugs on a lathe, with the grain running across the width of the plug. Glue the plugs into the holes, ensuring that the grain aligns with that of the rail. When the glue has set, carefully pare off the waste.

Joining lengths of moulding

Try to buy the mouldings in lengths that will cut up economically – but always allow extra for waste, particularly if you are having the mouldings specially made.

For a long wall, you will no doubt have to join lengths together. Cut the meeting ends to form a mitred butt joint, as this is neater and more effective than a plain butt joint. Mark the top back edges of both pieces of moulding where they will join. Cut the angles accurately, with the moulding held vertically in a mitre box.

For wide mouldings such as skirtings a mitre box is impractical, so use a circular saw or power jigsaw with the blade set to 45 degrees. Mark the required length on the bottom edge of each piece. Mark off the angle with a mitre square, and square the line across the face. Pin a wooden strip to the surface to guide the sole plate of the saw. Set it the required distance from the cut line (1). Make sure you cut on the waste side of the line on each piece (2).

1 Pin guide strip to surface

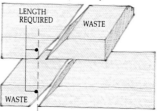

LENGTH REQUIRED
WASTE
WASTE

2 Cut on waste side of each piece

SKIRTING REPAIRS

Whereas seemingly redundant dado and picture rails may have been stripped out by fashion-conscious home owners, the skirting boards are likely to remain as they still perform a necessary function. However, you may find that an attractive period skirting has been ripped out and replaced by a plain modern version.

Most original skirtings suffer some form of damage, such as dents, or from overpainting. A certain amount of denting is acceptable; but if the skirting boards are badly dented, repair them with a fine plaster filler prior to repainting. When the filler has set, wrap abrasive paper around shaped blocks and sand the filler to the contour of the moulding.

Blurring of the moulding's detail due to overpainting or poorly applied paint (often incorporating dust from the floor) can be remedied by stripping the paint back to bare wood then repainting. Use a hot-air gun (but not on old lead paint) or a chemical stripper to soften the paint, then scrape it off carefully. Remove the paint from fine decorative moulding with a pad of wire wool dipped in chemical stripper. Most strippers are hazardous, so protect your eyes and skin and ventilate the room when working with them.

Skirting fixings

The method used for fixing skirting boards will usually depend on the quality of the building. Cut nails may be used to fix the boards directly to a plastered masonry wall or driven into wooden plugs set into the wall to receive them. In better-class houses softwood grounds are fixed to the wall and the plaster is worked up to them. The grounds consist of horizontal battens, one of them set close to the top of the skirting, and vertical blocks known as 'soldiers' set 600 to 900mm (2 to 3ft) apart. In Victorian houses that have elaborate built-up skirtings, stepped soldiers may be used.

If the grounds pull away from the wall when you are removing a skirting board, they can be refixed with masonry nails or screws and wall plugs. Make sure the grounds are level and true. Replace any that are rotten or badly infested with woodworm. Treat the wood with an insecticide before fitting.

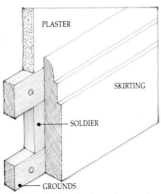

Skirting fixed to horizontal grounds

PLASTER
SKIRTING
SOLDIER
GROUNDS

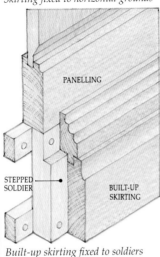

Built-up skirting fixed to soldiers

PANELLING
STEPPED SOLDIER
BUILT-UP SKIRTING

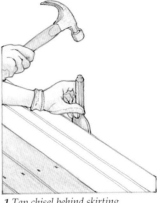

1 Tap chisel behind skirting

2 Protect the plaster with plywood

Removing skirting

You may be forced to remove more of the skirting than you want to if the damaged section is trapped behind an adjacent scribed board.

Starting at an end or at an external corner, tap a bolster chisel between the top of the skirting and the plaster **(1)**. Level the skirting away from the wall, taking care not to split short lengths. Wedge it with a thin strip of wood, and work along the edge to the next fixing point. Use a crowbar if better leverage is required. Place a piece of 6mm (¼in) plywood behind the crowbar to protect the plaster **(2)**. Expect some bruising and scuffing of the plaster at the edge where it meets the skirting, but try to minimize the damage. Continue in this way until the skirting pulls free.

If you are going to reuse the skirting board, pull the old nails out through the back with pincers. If you try to knock them out from behind, you risk splitting the face of the board.

Fitting skirting boards

When replacing a damaged piece of skirting, you can use the old piece as a template. This is particularly helpful if the end is scribed. It is best to check that the old skirting was a good fit, as gaps may have opened up if the building structure has moved due to settlement. In any event, you will need to measure the relevant length of wall.

Mark and cut the board to length. Scribe or mitre the end, if required. Mark the position of soldiers, if fitted, on the face. Level the board, and nail it in place with oval nails. If you are replacing all the skirting boards, follow the sequence shown below. Scribe internal corners and mitre external ones.

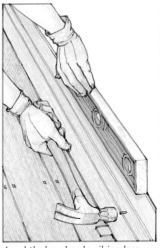

Level the board and nail in place

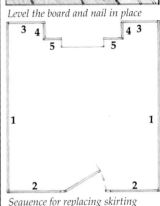

Sequence for replacing skirting

EMBOSSED WALLCOVERINGS

DECORATED PAPER *began to be used as a cheaper alternative to canvas and leather hangings or wood panelling during the sixteenth century. It was handmade and by the eighteenth century it had become a fashionable wall finish, although only found in the grandest houses.*

However, this was to change when in 1841 Potters of Darwin, in Lancashire, manufactured the first continuous machine-made wallpaper, thus making printed wallcoverings widely available at an affordable price.

Then in 1877 Frederick Walton invented Lincrusta, a high-relief wallcovering that quickly became popular because of its durability and washability (both selling points attractive to Victorian householders) as well as its decorative appeal. Some 10 years later Anaglypta, a lighter-weight embossed paper, appeared. Both were intended for painting and were widely used for dadoes and friezes and as general wallcoverings.

Should you strip a wall, particularly in a hallway or beside a staircase, and discover a dado-height band of different plaster or numerous patches, you can be sure that an embossed wallcovering has been removed. In which case, using a Lincrusta or period Anaglypta wallcovering will restore the original decorative style.

LINCRUSTA

Frederick Walton had been involved with the manufacture of linoleum for some years, and Lincrusta was a dense and moderately stiff material based on a similar formula to linoleum. A mixture of oxidized linseed oil, resin, paraffin wax, fibre and whiting was applied to a canvas backing (this was later changed to waterproof paper) then passed through rollers under high pressure. One roller was decoratively engraved, leaving a continuous impression in the soft compound. The material was then left to dry in a heated environment for two weeks.

When, in 1883, Lincrusta was manufactured under licence in America, it quickly established itself as a very popular wallcovering and a variety of new patterns were introduced specifically for the US market. Lincrusta went out of fashion in the second quarter of the twentieth century and ceased to be produced – until recently, when British manufacturers reintroduced a limited range of panels, rolls and borders featuring original patterns.

The late-Victorian patterns were inspired by classical decorative themes (one was called 'Italian Renaissance'). Several of the later patterns had Art Nouveau motifs.

A Lincrusta frieze provides an attractive border to the upper part of a wall

Classically inspired embossed dado

Painted Anaglypta stairway dado

ANAGLYPTA

At the time when Lincrusta was finding a ready market in America the launching of its rival, Anaglypta, was being proposed in Britain. It was Thomas Palmer, one of Walton's employees, who suggested making a cheaper, lighter and more flexible embossed wallcovering from cotton and paper pulp. When Walton rejected the idea, Palmer patented the process, left the company (in 1886) and together with the Storey brothers developed the material, which became available for sale by 1888.

Like Lincrusta, Anaglypta was intended for painting and was washable; however, it was not so durable. Being relatively easy to hang, it was particularly suitable for friezes and ceilings. It very soon became widely used in place of Lincrusta and has continued to be available, in modern as well as traditional designs, to this day.

You can detect whether an old embossed wallcovering is Lincrusta or Anaglypta by pressing the raised surface. If it is compressible, then it is Anaglypta, which is hollow.

As with Lincrusta, the embossed patterns reflected current fashions, and Palmer employed leading artists and architects to devise fine Art Nouveau and floral designs.

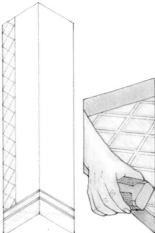

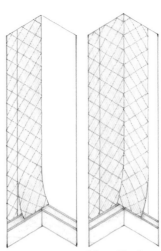

1 Wet the back of each piece

2 Trim off waste with craft knife

3 Measure the width

4 Bevel the cut edge

5 Hang first piece, followed by the offcut set on a plumbed line

HANGING LINCRUSTA

Although it is relatively stiff and heavy and requires careful handling, Lincrusta is not a particularly difficult material to hang. As with other decorating techniques, thorough preparation of the surface and careful setting out is necessary.

Since it is a fairly expensive wallcovering, calculate your requirements accurately. Most patterns are a straight match, but some have offset or random designs – in which case, you will need to make sufficient allowance for waste.

Papered walls

Remove traces of old wallpaper and paste, and inspect the bare plaster surface for holes or loose patches. Make good where necessary with plaster filler. When it is dry, apply a wallpaper size.

Painted walls

Scrape off powdery, flaking or blistered emulsion paint, and bind the surface with a clear stabilizing primer.

Wash off most of a waterbased distemper-type finish from the wall before you apply a stabilizing primer.

Key the surface of sound oil-based paintwork with abrasive paper, then wash it down with sugar soap.

Lining the walls

If the wall plaster has been unevenly patched, lining paper will help to even out suction and create a smooth surface for the wallcovering.

Cross-line the walls with a good-quality lining paper. Use a heavy-duty wallpaper paste containing a fungicide.

Applying the covering

Measure and cut individual lengths from a roll, taking note of any pattern-matching required and allowing about 50mm (2in) for waste on each length. Trim the selvage from the rolled material with a straightedge and sharp craft knife. Hold the knife at a slight angle to undercut the edge of the material.

Using a plumb line, mark a vertical line on the wall. Hold the edge of the first piece of wallcovering on the line and check the fit of the top end against the ceiling, cornice moulding or picture rail. If need be, mark and cut the edge to fit any irregularities. Trim the other pieces to match, if required.

Sponge the back of each piece with warm water and leave it to soak for up to 30 minutes (1). This allows the material to soften and fully expand, so that it doesn't blister when you are hanging it. Wipe off any surplus water before applying the special Lincrusta glue. Stir the glue thoroughly and apply it evenly with a wide paintbrush or paint roller, depending on the length of the piece. Ensure the edges are well covered with glue.

Apply the first piece to the wall level with the vertical line and butting the top edge. Press it into place with a cloth pad or rubber roller. Mark the line of the skirting on each edge of the piece, then peel it back just far enough to place a piece of hardboard under it on which to cut the end. Trim off the waste with the craft knife and straightedge (2), then press the edge down and clean off surplus glue with a damp sponge. Continue in this way, butting subsequent pieces together.

Dealing with corners

At the end of a run you will meet an internal or external corner. You can work the material round a curved corner without cutting it, but not round an angled one. The cut edges will need to be mitred, and an allowance made on the width for the thickness of the material.

If the wallcovering is to continue onto the adjacent surface of an angled corner, first measure the distance between the edge of the last piece and the corner. Take measurements from the top, middle and bottom (3). Mark the widths at corresponding heights on a length of the wallcovering (for an external corner, adding the thickness of the material). Cut it to size with a craft knife, holding a straightedge on the marks.

Control the knife carefully, as it will have a tendency to follow the pattern. Make the cut with a series of knife strokes. Bevel the edge with a sanding block (4). Hold the length flush with the edge of your worktable to provide good support. Hold the material face down when shaping an external-corner piece (the thinner parts are brittle and likely to crumble, so handle with care).

Hang the prepared piece of wallcovering in the usual way. The remaining offcut is now used to turn the corner. The pattern will then follow through, but there will be a slight mismatch because of the cut edges. The corner may not be quite vertical, so mark a plumbed line on the adjacent wall on which to set the straight edge of the offcut (5). Trim and level the cut edge as required.

After hanging this piece, continue to hang the covering as before. Fill the joints with plaster filler, and make good any broken edges.

173

DADO PANELS

Lincrusta dado panels come ready trimmed to width and length (you can also buy a moulded border). Applying them to a plain wall is therefore quite straightforward. However, if the wall has a dado rail, you may need to trim the height of the panels or even reposition the rail.

The panel designs form a complete pattern, so avoid reducing the height if you can. If you have to trim the panels, remove the surplus from the bottom edge only. Before hanging the panels, prepare the wall as required and cross-line it.

In order to hang Lincrusta dado panels on a plain wall, mark a horizontal guideline at panel height (1) then set out and apply the covering as already described. If there is to be a border, after hanging the panels cut the border to length and glue it in place to finish the top edge (2).

1 Mark horizontal guideline

2 Finish top edge with border strip

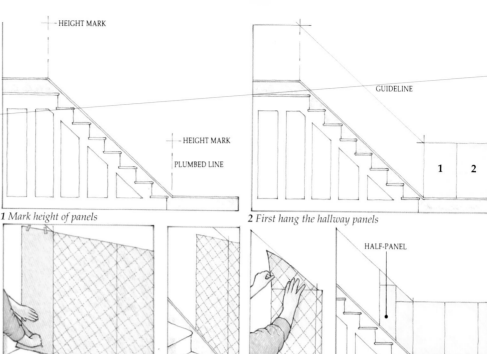

HEIGHT MARK

HEIGHT MARK

PLUMBED LINE

GUIDELINE

1   2

1 Mark height of panels

2 First hang the hallway panels

HALF-PANEL

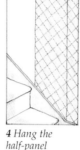

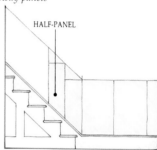

3 Crease the paper into the angle

4 Hang the half-panel

5 Hang the corner piece

6 Cut and hang other half-panel

DEALING WITH STAIRWAYS

To set out dado panels for a stairway wall, first mark a plumbed line at the foot and top of the stairs where the stringboard meets the skirting. Mark the height of the panels on the vertical lines measured up from the skirting (1). On a long stair, set out intermediate marks in the same way, then join them up with a straightedge – or snap a line, using a chalked taut length of cord or twine.

Hanging the panels

Hang the panels in the hall first, working away from the vertical line at the foot of the stairs (2). The panels that follow the slope of the stairs must be cut to the required angle before hanging. Cut the first panel vertically into equal halves. Make the cut dead straight, guiding the knife with a straightedge.

Cut a sheet of paper to the exact size of one of the half-panels in order to make a pattern (lining paper is handy for this). Temporarily tape the paper to the wall, with the long edge against the vertical line and level with the top of the dado at the foot of the staircase. Crease the paper into the angle of the stringboard (3). Remove the paper, and fold the end along the crease line. Trim off the triangular end along the line.

Lay the paper pattern over the half-panel, with the top and side edges flush. Mark the panel where the slope of the pattern meets its edge. Place a straightedge from the corner to the edge mark, and cut off the corner. Take care to make a clean cut and not to damage the triangular offcut, as it will be needed.

Prepare the panel and offcut for gluing, as already described. Hang the half-panel, with the angled cut edge butted up to the stringboard (4). Then add the triangular piece to the top of the half-panel level with the guideline and the long edge of the panel (5). Cut and hang the other half-panel in the same way (6). Follow this method up to the vertical line at the top of the staircase (you may have to make the last piece a narrower infill panel), then continue with full panels on the landing. You can finish the top edge with a border strip, mitring the ends of the strip at the top and bottom of the stair.

REPAINTING LINCRUSTA

Avoid stripping paint from Lincrusta unless absolutely necessary. Should you have to strip paint from the wall-covering, don't use a strong chemical stripper (which could dissolve the material). Before proceeding, test an inconspicuous corner of the wallcovering to make sure that the paint stripper is not too strong. Never remove old paint with a hot-air gun – Lincrusta is flammable and will soften with heat.

HANGING ANAGLYPTA

Anaglypta is hung on walls and ceilings in the same way as a conventional wallpaper.

After cutting the lengths to size, apply heavy-duty wallpaper paste and leave it to soak for about 10 minutes. Fold the paper on itself, then carry it to the wall or ceiling and apply it to the surface with a paperhanger's brush. Avoid using excessive pressure, so you don't flatten the embossing. Cut off the waste with scissors.

Let the paper dry out for a few days before finishing. Use an eggshell oil paint for walls, and an emulsion paint for a ceiling.

CHAPTER FIFTEEN

DECORATIVE WOODWORK

WOOD IS BOTH A VERSATILE MATERIAL and one that is relatively easy to work. These properties, coupled with the desire of craftsmen over the centuries to decorate their work, have resulted in all manner of shaped, carved and fretted woodwork. In the past, decoration was regarded as a sign of wealth, and elaborate carved work was frequently commissioned for both interior and exterior joinery in the stylish houses of the rich.

In Victorian times, speculative builders, encouraged by increasing prosperity and the new manufacturing methods brought about by industrialization, often indulged in widespread use of flamboyant decorative woodwork to embellish even fairly modest homes.

Most household joinery is made from the cheaper softwoods, which suffer from weathering if not adequately maintained. In addition, later house owners viewed Victorian styles as grotesquely old-fashioned. As a result, many fine examples of decorative woodwork have been reduced to a shadow of their original glory or ripped out and replaced by modern substitutes. However, with a fairly modest outlay it is possible to re-create period woodwork in appropriate style – restoring an important part of a house's character.

Carved solid-oak bargeboard

Pierced canopy with dogtooth edges

Porch made from painted laths

A delightful combination of balusters and fretted porch brackets

Unusual layered bargeboard

Carved console supporting a jetty

Superb detail in good condition

BARGEBOARDS

BARGEBOARDS *(also known as vergeboards) are used to finish and protect the verge of a gabled roof, porch or dormer. They provide a striking exterior feature and were first used to full effect in the medieval period, when important houses had decorative carved oak bargeboards.*

Simple modern versions are little more than wide plain boards, but elaborately fretted and carved bargeboards were fashionable during the Gothic revival of the nineteenth century. Indeed, the bargeboard's original function was sometimes almost forgotten in the enthusiasm for decorative extravagance.

A simple but striking design cut into the edge of a bargeboard

Carved-oak Tudor-style bargeboard

Sturdy white-painted bargeboard

TYPES OF BARGEBOARD

Bargeboards can be fitted close to the wall, or may project forward – in which case they are known as oversailing gables. Usually, these are supported by shaped brackets and the underside is finished with a soffit board. Turned or shaped wooden finials or fretted panels may be fitted at the apex to complete the decorative effect. Extensive use of cutouts produced highly ornate tracery designs. These were often structurally weak, so were sometimes applied to a backing board – a style known as appliqué.

GABLE CONSTRUCTION

A simple gable roof consists of ordinary rafters notched over wooden wall plates, which are supported by the load-bearing side walls. The top ends of the rafters are nailed to a ridge board, while the bottom ends are tied together by the ceiling joist, forming a rigid triangular structure. A horizontal timber support, called a purlin, may be used to brace the rafters if they are likely to bend under the weight of the roof covering.

At a gable end of a brick-built house the ridge board and wall plates, and possibly the purlins as well, extend through the brickwork to provide fixing points for the bargeboard.

For an oversailing gable, rafters are usually fixed outside the wall on extended wall plates and ridge board.

Intermediate supports may be fitted between the inner and outer rafters, and a soffit board added to finish the underside (**1**). The shaped bargeboard is nailed to the outside rafters to cover the ends of the battens used for fixing the tiles or slates, and is set slightly proud of the top face of the battens in order to tilt the roof covering at the edge. This is to direct water away from the face of the board. A fascia moulding is usually applied at the top of the board under the overhanging edge of the roof covering.

In some timber-frame houses the bargeboard may be nailed directly to the side wall in order to cover roof sheathing boards (**2**); or to extended boarding, in order to form an oversailing or boxed gable (**3**).

Components of a gable roof	
1 Common rafter	6 Bargeboard
2 Wall plate	7 Intermediate support
3 Ridge board	8 Fascia moulding
4 Ceiling joist	9 Finial
5 Purlin	10 Soffit

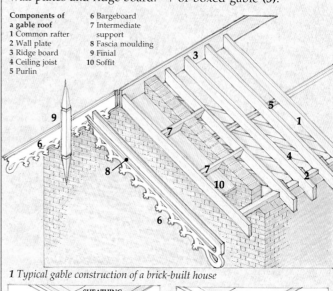

1 *Typical gable construction of a brick-built house*

2 *Bargeboard nailed to sheathing*

3 *Bargeboard forming boxed gable*

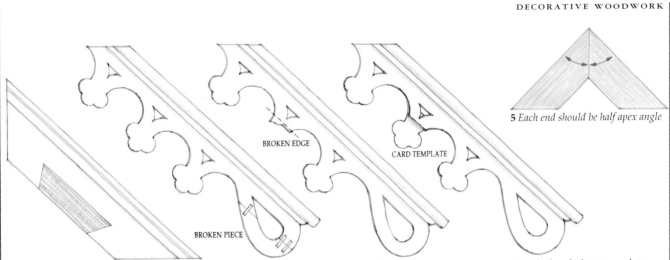

5 *Each end should be half apex angle*

BROKEN EDGE

CARD TEMPLATE

BROKEN PIECE

1 *Undercut the ends of the patch*　　**2** *Reinforce joint with dowels*　　**3** *Plane broken edge square*　　**4** *Mark planed edge on template*

REPAIRING A BARGEBOARD

Victorian and Edwardian bargeboards were made from soft-wood and finished with paint. Repainting the bargeboards is not infrequently omitted from general redecoration because of their height from the ground. Nevertheless, it is important to maintain the paintwork regularly, as the boards are in an exposed position and can weather badly.

If you have a decorative bargeboard that has decayed, it's worth making the effort to repair it in preference to fitting a cheaper, plain replacement. Try to make repairs *in situ* – but if the wood is beyond repair, remove it and make a new bargeboard to the old pattern.

Removing a bargeboard

Unless you have a single-storey house, working on a bargeboard is a tricky operation because of the height. Most bargeboards are large and awkward to handle, so it generally takes two people to remove them.

Always work from a safe platform, such as a scaffold tower, and make sure it is stable and well secured. If you are not confident when working at heights, call in a professional.

Nails are normally used to fix the joinery together, although screws may be used where short-grained wood is present. Locate the fixing points. Then if the bargeboard is fitted with a fascia moulding, remove it using a bolster chisel. Tap the chisel between the moulding and the board, and lever it off close to the fixings. Further fixings may now be revealed, in which case you will need to prise the bargeboard free from the roof timbers.

Fitting a plain patch

If you find a minor patch of rot, rake out the infected wood and treat it with a preservative, a proprietary hardener and a wood filler. Where the rot has occurred along a plain edge, cut it away back to sound wood. Undercut the ends to give improved holding. Make a patch of matching wood to fit your cutout **(1)**. Fix the patch in place with an exterior woodworking glue. When it is set, treat the new wood with a preservative in readiness for painting.

Repairing a shaped edge

The projecting details of a decorative sawn edge some-times break away because of weak short grain. If that has happened, you may be able to make the repair *in situ*, assuming you still have the piece that has broken away.

Hold the piece in place and mark one or two lines at right angles across the break line. Square the lines across the broken edges of the two parts. Set a marking gauge to half the thickness of the wood and mark a centre line on each part. Drill 10mm (⅜in) dowel holes where the lines cross. Finally, glue the broken piece in place, inserting wooden dowels to reinforce the joint **(2)**.

Replacing missing parts

Bargeboards are often decorated with a repeat pattern. If part of the pattern has rotted or broken off and is lost, you can replace the missing part.

Take a rubbing of part of the decoration that is still intact, using a wax crayon and plain paper. Tape the paper onto the bargeboard for easier handling. Cut out a card template, following the outline of the rubbing.

Plane the broken edge of the bargeboard square **(3)**. Holding the card template behind the bargeboard at the point where the section is missing, draw the position of the planed edge on it **(4)**.

Mark the shape of the new section on a suitably sized board and cut it out with a power jigsaw or a coping saw. If the pattern includes pierced details, drill a hole in the waste so you can insert the saw blade. Smooth the sawn edges. Dowel and glue the new piece in position, and treat it with a timber preservative before priming and finishing with paint.

MAKING A REPLACEMENT

Neglected bargeboards in an exposed position can decay beyond reasonable repair, making replacement necessary. Remove the old one as carefully as possible, to keep it in one piece. If it looks too weak to survive removal intact, first record its size and shape with full-size drawings and photographs. Buy new boards of knot-free straight-grained wood. Give your supplier the finished dimensions and have the timber machined to size.

Lay the original barge-boards or your drawing of them on the new boards and mark out the shape. Check the angle of the mitred ends with a sliding bevel. Each end should be half the angle of the apex **(5)**.

Cut the board to shape with a power jigsaw or a coping saw, including cut-outs. If the boards are bevelled and carved, use chisels and gouges to shape them (see CARVED WOODWORK).

Bring all the surfaces to a smooth finish, then treat them with a wood preservative, following the maker's instructions. When the preservative is dry, finish all the surfaces with a good paint system and nail the finished boards in place. Sink the nailheads, fill the recesses, and paint to match. Refit the original fascia moulding or, if need be, replace it.

BRACKETS

FINIALS

The apex of a gabled roof is often fitted with a turned or square-sided wooden post called a finial that protrudes above the roof line. Sometimes the bottom end of the post extends downwards and is detailed in a similar way (the part that projects downwards is known as a pendant). The post may also be embellished with decorative wrought ironwork.

Reinstating a finial

Finials and pendants can be cut from flat board or from square-sectioned wood. They may either be nailed to the bargeboard or fixed to structural roof members with the bargeboards butted up to them.

If your roof has a not very interesting stub of wood at its apex, it is probably the remains of a finial that has been sawn off due to decay. If the remaining wood is sound, you can purchase a ready-made turned finial from a specialist supplier or have one made to order. Either dowel and glue the new component or use a screw dowel to fix it to the end of the old wood (1).

You can make square-sectioned finials with sawn decorative profiles yourself, using either a band saw or a powered fret saw. Mark the profile, based on a suitable pattern, on two adjacent sides of the wood. Cut along the guide lines on one face. Tape the waste in place, then turn the wood over to present the other marked face and cut the second pair of sides (2). Fix the new finial in place, using the same type of fixing used for the original. Last of all, treat the finial with a timber preservative and apply a good paint system.

Finial with pendant fitted at apex

WOODEN DOWEL

SCREW DOWEL

1 Dowel and glue or use screw dowel

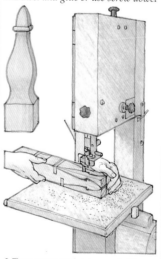

2 Tape waste and cut second sides

BRACKETS *are normally fitted to provide support between horizontal and vertical members, but fretted brackets are often used for decorative rather than functional purposes – to add richness and texture to gables, porches or door openings.*

Shaped with a saw, fretted brackets are relatively easy to make. Interior examples are generally made of thinner wood than exterior ones. You can have fancy brackets made to order or buy them ready-made from specialist suppliers. Choose a style that suits your house – don't be tempted by a design that is readily available but out of character.

MAKING A BRACKET

Make a pattern by tracing the shape of an existing bracket onto stiff paper. If you don't have a suitable bracket available, draw one to your own design, basing it on a pictorial reference from a library source or catalogue. You may perhaps be able to determine the size of the missing original by looking at fixing marks left on the adjacent woodwork. If you need to produce a number of brackets, make a template. Transfer the shape of the pattern onto hardboard, and cut it to shape with a jigsaw or coping saw. Smooth the edge with abrasive paper.

Prepare straight-grained knot-free wood to the size and thickness required. If need be, glue several boards together to make up the thickness, using interior or exterior woodworking glue as appropriate. Mark out the shape of the bracket on the wood, positioning the pattern so that it follows the direction of the grain (1). This avoids short weak grain that can break easily (2).

Cut the bracket to shape, using a power jigsaw or a band saw. Finish the cut edges with a spokeshave, plane or files, as appropriate. Use screws to fix brackets – in preference to nails, which

1 Position pattern to follow grain

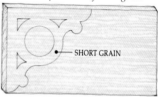

SHORT GRAIN

2 Short weak grain can break easily

may split the ends. Drill counterbored clearance holes for suitably sized screws.

Fitting a bracket

Hold the bracket in position, and mark the position of the screw holes with an awl. Drill appropriately sized pilot holes in the adjoining woodwork. If the holes are set at an angle, use the bracket as a guide for the drill. Apply mastic sealant to the joining faces of the bracket, then fix it in place with zinc-coated screws. Fill the counterbored holes with glued wooden plugs. When set, trim the plugs to the contour of the bracket and apply a primer. Finish the new work with paint, making sure the end grain is well covered.

Fretted brackets help support the porch roof

**Decorative
wooden brackets**
1 Fretted porch
bracket with
spindles
2 Fretted porch
brackets
3 Moulded exterior
consoles
4 Carved console

CONSOLES

Consoles are fretted or carved solid-wood brackets. They were commonly used as an exterior feature under soffits in imitation of the stone corbels used in Italianate architecture.

Wooden consoles were also often used as interior features, and may be found under mantel shelves and in door openings or supporting beams.

A range of designs for replacing missing consoles is available, in both softwoods and hardwoods, from specialist suppliers.

Maintaining consoles

Both interior and exterior consoles are likely to suffer from overpainting, which obliterates the crisp edges and details of the carved decoration. Where this has occurred, use a chemical stripper to soften and clean off the build-up of paint. When clean and dry, repaint the wood.

Making a console

Wet rot can cause deterioration of exterior consoles exposed to the weather. If the damage cannot be successfully treated with a preservative and repaired with wood filler, make a new one.

Make a pattern for the profile, based on another console. Fretted consoles sometimes comprise a central section of thicker wood sandwiched between decorative scrolls or pierced side pieces, made of thinner wood. If the central section is to stand proud of the side pieces, or the side pieces are to protrude beyond the central section, make a second pattern from the first, increasing or reducing the size as required.

Wooden consoles decorating a soffit

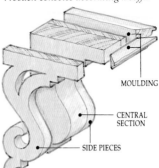

MOULDING

CENTRAL
SECTION

SIDE PIECES

Fretted-console construction

Mark out the profiles on wood prepared to the correct thickness and cut them to shape. Smooth the edges. Pin and glue the side pieces to the centre piece, with the back and top edges flush. Cut a suitable decorative moulding to size with the meeting ends mitred. Pin and glue the moulding around the front and side edges of the top part of the console.

Exterior wooden consoles are usually painted; interior ones may either be painted or stained and varnished. Apply a timber preservative and the finish to an exterior console before fitting it; an interior console can be finished after fitting.

Fix the bracket securely with counterbored nonferrous screws. Then plug the holes with wooden pellets and trim them to shape. If the console is already painted, finish the pellets to match.

179

BALUSTRADES

WOODEN PORCHES, *verandas and balconies are a delightful feature most commonly found in coastal and colonial-style houses. They were also frequently used, largely for decorative effect, by the architects of Victorian and Edwardian suburban 'villas'. Designed to provide shade or shelter from inclement weather, and as a vantage point in seaside houses, with their turned or slatted balusters they add charm and character to a building.*

Turned posts and balusters create a most attractive veranda

Ornate fretted softwood balusters

Balustrade with turned balusters

BALUSTERS

Slats and balusters – which simultaneously give a sense of security and allow air to flow – are often used decoratively, having shaped edges that in turn make shapes of the gaps between them. Sometimes cutouts within the width of the balusters add to the decorative effect.

Normally the top ends of the balusters are nailed to the underside of the handrail, which may be grooved to receive them, and are either fixed or jointed to a horizontal rail at the bottom.

If a flat baluster is broken or missing, it is usually a straightforward matter to make a replacement. Simply make a pattern from a sound identical baluster and cut a new one to match. Treat the new wood with a timber preservative, ensuring that the porous end grain is well covered. Paint the surfaces with primer and, when it is dry, nail the new baluster in place. Fill the nail holes and apply a paint finish. For repairs to turned balusters, see WOODEN STAIR REPAIRS.

CARVED WOODWORK

CARVING IS A METHOD *of shaping and decorating wood with special chisels and gouges. The techniques are centuries old and have been applied to wooden artifacts and furniture as well as being used to embellish internal and external features of houses. Stylistically, woodcarving can range from abstract or naturalistic low-relief work to more sculpted high-relief or fully three-dimensional features.*

The techniques for carving low-relief decorative motifs are relatively easy to master, but carving in the round and high-relief work call for a keen eye and a well-developed sense of form. All early carved work was hand cut, and repeat patterns often display subtle differences in shape. It is this human touch that makes early work more interesting and valuable than the machine-cut versions of recent times.

With practice you can undertake woodcarving yourself – but if the features are particularly ornate or important, it's best to have the work carried out by a professional. You may also be able to use ready-made carved woodwork available from specialist suppliers.

Decorative beam with relief-carved mythical beasts and painted motifs

A porch made of oak and decorated with low-relief carving

Shapes of blade
1 Straight chisel
2 Straight gouge
3 Curved gouge
4 Spoon-bent gouge
5 Back-bent gouge
6 Fishtail chisel
7 Parting tool

CARVING TOOLS

Woodcarving is so versatile that generations of craftsmen have developed hundreds of different tools to meet their needs. The blades are made in a variety of length shapes, cross-section profiles and cutting-edge widths. There are five basic length shapes: straight, curved, spoon-bent (also known as front-bent), back-bent, and fishtail (or spade) tools. Eighteen cross-section profiles are available, most of them in a range of sizes from 2mm ($\frac{1}{16}$in) to 50mm (2in).

The principal categories of carving tools are chisels, gouges and parting tools.

Chisels are ground with a square or skewed cutting edge and are used for general shaping, cutting straight lines, detailing and finishing.

Gouges are the main tools for shaping. They constitute the largest group of carving tools, having a comprehensive range of shallow to deep sweeps (curved profiles). All the sweeps are true radius curves except for the veiner type, which has straighter sides. The larger gouges are used for taking the wood off quickly, the medium-size and smaller ones for general and fine shaping.

Parting tools are V-shaped in section and are made in three profiles. They are used for outlining, lettering and detail work.

A basic set of carving tools might comprise a range of gouges, one or two straight chisels, a skew chisel, a parting tool and possibly a veining tool for fine work. You will need a round-headed carver's mallet, which is heavier and more versatile than a carpenter's mallet. A selection of flat, round and half-round rasps and files is desirable for shaping and finishing sculptural work. Rotary rasps held in a flexible drive or in the chuck of a power drill are handy for shaping. Punches are used for adding texture to the surface of the wood and for refining detail, but are not essential for most work.

Carved and painted Phoenix motif

Using the tools

Carving tools can be driven by hand pressure or with a mallet. When using hand pressure for lighter work, grip the handle with one hand and steady the blade and the thrust of the tool with the other (**1**). Use the mallet for difficult woods or larger cuts. Hold the carving tool low down the handle, with the mallet in your driving hand (**2**).

Carving tools have fine cutting edges and are prone to damage if driven into cross-grain hardwood. When a vertical cut on a line is required (known as setting in), use a small deep gouge or parting tool to carve a groove adjacent to the line. The remaining waste will then cut away cleanly with little effort (**3**).

The tools will readily cut across the grain. In fact, cross-grain cutting is generally preferred for roughing in the shape – since there is less chance of the grain tearing ahead of the tool or of the blade wandering off, which can easily happen when cutting with the grain.

Follow the grain for fine finishing cuts. When cutting at a tangent to the grain (if you are carving a groove around a circular motif, for example), work in the direction that will give a smooth cut on the motif side (**4**).

Use curved gouges to work the bottom of hollows where a straight tool would tend to dig into the wood (**5**). Spoon-bent tools are used for similar but more detailed work (**6**).

HOLDING THE WORK

Unless the wood is being cut *in situ* (when making a patch repair, for example), the work has to be held securely. Specialized vices, pivoting clamps and a screw-in holding device known as a carver's screw are helpful. However, they are by no means essential, as you can use most woodworking and metalworking vices and cramps quite effectively.

1 Steady the blade and thrust of the tool

2 Hold the tool low down the handle if using a mallet

3 Cut waste

WASTE

4 Cut in the right direction

WASTE

5 Use a bent gouge for hollows

6 Use a spoon-bent gouge for details

CARVING IN THE ROUND

CARVINGS IN THE ROUND *are pieces that are fully three-dimensional and intended to be seen from all sides. They are not as common as relief carvings in most houses but may be used for finials, pendants, stair newel posts, brackets, or overmantel ornamentation. Some may be turned shapes that are then carved and decorated with floral motifs. The subject matter for sculptural carvings can be inspired by either naturalistic or fanciful forms.*

If original carved work has been stripped out in an attempt to modernize the interior, you may want to re-create the missing details. Take note of the style of ornamentation appropriate for the period, and seek out references on which to base your design from libraries and from houses of a similar type. You can then either commission a professional carver or, if the work is not too demanding, attempt it yourself.

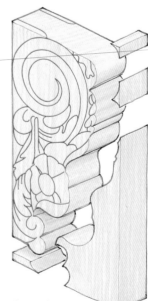

Carved doorhood console

1 Cut profile with a saw

2 Rough in the shape   *3 Shape the contours*   *4 Refine the shape*

CHOOSING THE WOOD

Virtually any wood can be carved, but some species are more difficult to carve than others. The best woods are those with a fine even grain. Lime, a favourite of the master carver Grinling Gibbons, is a light-coloured hardwood that carves and finishes extremely well. Softwoods such as ponderosa pine, yellow pine and sitka spruce carve well, too.

If the work has to match an existing feature, then the choice is made for you. However, many tropical hardwoods are now classified as endangered species – so if a tropical hardwood such as mahogany was used for the original feature, make sure the new wood comes from a sustainable source.

If you cannot find a single piece of wood large enough for a particular carving, one solution is to glue sections of timber together. Gluing sections together also helps reduce the risk of shrinkage problems, such as splitting, which are often encountered with large or thick balks of partially seasoned timber.

Though it's possible to carve 'green' (unseasoned) wood, there's a much greater risk of splitting. Reducing the bulk of the timber and hollowing out the centre helps to promote even drying out – but it is best to use seasoned wood whenever possible.

SETTING OUT

A good eye for form and well-developed drawing and craft skills are required for carving in the round. It is essential to have a clear idea of the shape to be cut, and preparatory sketches and elevation drawings will help you to achieve satisfactory results. Some carvers also find that it is helpful to make a maquette, so they can see the shape and take scaled measurements from it.

Make full-scale drawings of the form, showing the front and side elevations and possibly the back and plan views too. You can either use printed grid paper or draw a grid with 25mm (1in) squares over your design. Use carbon paper to transfer the design to the faces of a prepared block of wood.

BASIC SHAPING

Although you can use a gouge, it is usually quicker to do the rough shaping with a band saw or a powered fret saw. Saw round the profiles marked on the faces of the block. With some shapes, only one profile may be cut in this way **(1)**.

When two faces are cut, the waste from the first is likely to carry the profile for the other. Temporarily tape the waste offcuts back in position, then cut the second profile with the saw.

After sawing, remove the waste and draw in the outlines of the shapes that fall within the shaped block as a guide for carving.

CARVING THE SHAPE

Begin to rough in the shape using a straight medium-sweep gouge and a mallet **(2)**. As the work progresses, use suitably shaped smaller and flatter gouges to shape the contoured planes and hollows **(3)**. Keep viewing the work from all sides. Refine the modelling and add textures and small details, using small gouges, chisels, parting tools, punches and files **(4)**. You may want to retain the tool marks to create an interesting texture. Otherwise, take the surface to a smooth finish with progressively finer abrasive paper, folding the paper to finish fine inside details.

CHAPTER SIXTEEN

WOOD FLOORING

EARLY WOODEN FLOORS *used random-sized hand-cut boards of oak, elm, pine or fir. The boards were usually wide and of varying thickness. It is not uncommon to find thinner ones resting on packing over a joist, or the underside of thicker ones trimmed with an adze to make the floor level. By the eighteenth century the size of floorboards had become more regular. Boards about 100mm (4in) wide were used in better-quality houses to avoid shrinkage and distortion problems, while houses of lesser quality had boards 200 to 250mm (8 to 10in) wide. However, it was not until the earlier part of the nineteenth century that the introduction of mechanized production methods made consistent floorboard sizes generally available.*

Georgian houses often had tongue-and-groove pine floorboards, but their light colour was not looked on with favour so they were usually painted to resemble more expensive hardwoods. Other materials were imitated, too, including marble, stone and slate set out in geometric patterns. Sometimes the boards were simply finished with a plain matt colour. Floor coverings of carpet, painted cloth or matting were also used. These were often fitted wall to wall, unless laid over a quality hardwood floor, in which case the boards would usually be exposed to form a border. As a cheaper alternative to carpeting, sometimes floors were painted overall and then decorated with attractive free-hand or stencilled designs.

Parquet, a flooring made from strips or blocks of wood laid in a geometrical pattern, appealed to the Victorians because of its decorative nature. Since it was fairly expensive to lay, as it still is today, initially its use was largely confined to better-quality houses. Nevertheless, parquet became increasingly fashionable and it retained its popularity throughout the Edwardian period and the 1920s and 1930s.

The pale-coloured walls harmonize well with the unfinished pine boards

The dark stained and polished floorboards suit this cottage interior

TYPES OF FLOORING

A WOOD FLOOR, *like other features and materials in a period house, derives its character from the patina of age. Provided the material has been well maintained, the inevitable scrapes, wear, light stains and all-over mellow tone combine to give an acceptable – indeed, often desirable – appearance that is worth preserving. Well-worn boards in high-traffic areas such as halls and doorways tell a story, and so long as they are not structurally weak they don't need to be replaced.*

Nevertheless, age and neglect can take their toll, and there are times when the introduction of 'new' wood is unavoidable in order to preserve the floor.

MATCHING OLD WOOD

Always try to obtain the appropriate species of wood when making a patch repair or replacing part of an old floor. This may not always be easy, but flooring specialists stock many of the species used traditionally and often keep reclaimed wood for repairs of this kind. It is also worth trying timber suppliers, who stock a wide range of woods from which boards can be cut.

New and even resawn old wood will not have the mellow colour of the original, so you may find that the replacement has to be toned down with a wood stain, or needs bleaching if a lighter colour is required.

TYPES OF WOOD

The majority of floors are constructed from softwoods, such as yellow-heart pine, Columbian pine, pitch pine, spruce and fir. However, a number of hardwoods are used too, particularly for the types of parquet that are laid on a sub-floor. Hardwood species used for flooring range from blond and dark-brown woods – including maple, ash, beech, elm, oak, walnut and teak – to redder woods such as cherry, mahogany, utile and jarrah.

Wood usually changes colour as it ages, which can make identification difficult. If you are not sure of the species used for your floor, take a sample to a timber supplier, who should be able to identify it for you. If the underside of a board does not show the original colour, plane off a shaving to reveal the true colour beneath.

Handsome wide elm boards

Herringbone-pattern parquet floor

Square-edged board

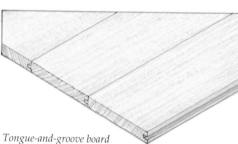

Tongue-and-groove board

Tongue-and-groove strip flooring

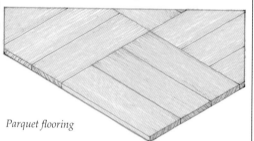

Parquet flooring

TYPES OF BOARD

You can buy wood flooring in the form of boards, strips and parquet. Boards come in long lengths and are planed to a finished thickness of about 18mm (¾in) or more. Their width can vary from 100 to 300mm (4 to 12in), and the edges may either be planed square (plain-edged) or tongued and grooved.

Strip flooring is normally made from hardwoods in narrow tongue-and-groove widths of about 75mm (3in). Strips for laying directly onto joists have a nominal thickness of 25mm (1in). Thinner versions are made for laying on a sub-floor.

Parquet is made in various forms. The thicker versions are sometimes referred to as woodblock flooring. These have plain-edged or tongue-and-groove blocks approximately 75mm (3in) wide and 225 to 300mm (9 to 12in) long, with a nominal thickness of 18mm (¾in). The thinner versions of parquet are made from strips about 25 to 50mm (1 to 2in) wide and 225 to 300mm (9 to 12in) long. You can also buy parquet panels, with short strips of wood bonded to a backing sheet. These are produced in various configurations and are laid like tiles.

SELECTING BOARDS

Because it is a porous material, wood expands and contracts as it reacts to changes in its moisture content. The amount of 'movement' also depends on the species of the wood and how the wood is cut from the log. The latter is a particularly important consideration for flooring.

Most logs, for reasons of economy, are flat-sawn (1). This produces wide boards with an attractive sweeping figure. However, they are prone to warping, splitting and uneven wear. When boards are cut in this way, the annual growth rings run more or less across the width of the board or from edge to edge. Because wood shrinks more in the direction of the growth rings than across them, this leads to a greater reduction on the width of a board than on the thickness. Also, shrinkage is uneven, since the 'longer' growth rings shrink more than those on the heart side (the side nearest to the centre of the tree), which causes the board to distort or cup (2). The movement of the wood can cause nails to loosen; if the board is securely held, the movement may make it split.

Using boards that have been converted by the

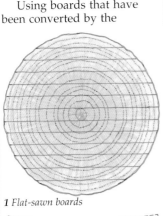

quarter-sawn or rift sawn method overcomes these problems. The log is cut more or less radially (3). This produces boards known as edge-grain timber with short even-length growth rings that appear as lines on the face sides. Since shrinkage is minimal across the growth rings, the effect on the width of the board is negligible.

Quarter-sawn boards are more expensive than flat-sawn ones, since the method of milling is more wasteful, but their greater stability and resistance to wear far outweighs the extra cost.

To check the cut of your old boards, look at the end grain (4). Always choose quarter-sawn boards for repairs, unless you are matching the figure of old flat-sawn floorboards.

Traditional log cutting Saw

1 *Flat-sawn boards*

2 *Shrinkage causes boards to cup*

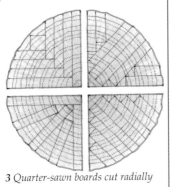

3 *Quarter-sawn boards cut radially*

4 *Look at end grain to check cut*

FIXING METHODS

WOODEN FLOORING IS USUALLY FIXED *with nails or glue, or both. The method will depend on the type, quality and profile of the flooring. The profile can be plain-edged, rebated (shiplapped) or tongued and grooved. Where nails are used as a feature, try to match their type and spacing when making repairs.*

PLAIN-EDGED AND REBATED BOARDS

The most common method for fixing plain-edged and rebated boards is to nail them through the face, using cut floorboard nails. These are rectangular in section and are driven in with the wider face parallel to the grain. The square-cut tip is designed to sever the fibres as it punches through the wood – instead of parting the fibres, causing the wood to split, as can happen with pointed round wire nails.

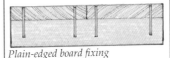

Plain-edged board fixing

Rebated board fixing

TONGUE-AND-GROOVE FLOORBOARDS

Tongue-and-groove boards are secret-nailed through the tongue. The grooved edge is held by the tongue of the previous board. Lost-head finishing nails are driven in at an angle of about 45 degrees. A nail punch must be used to sink the nails, as it is easy to mar the edges with a hammer. Nowadays professional floorlayers use a powered nail gun, which drives the nails in quickly and neatly at a set angle.

Tongue-and-groove board fixing

PARQUET FLOORING

Traditionally, the thicker type of parquet flooring was laid using hot bitumen. After the pieces of wood had been cut to shape, each piece was dipped in a shallow tray filled with the hot adhesive and laid in place. Once the bitumen had set, the surface of the wood was planed and scraped level ready for finishing. Nowadays a cold-set flooring adhesive is used for parquet flooring. The adhesive is spread over the sub-floor with a serrated-edge trowel, then the wood blocks are set in it.

Thinner parquet flooring is usually pinned or glued. If individual parquet strips need to be replaced, apply a flooring adhesive and fix with 20mm (¾in) panel pins through the face. Sink the nailheads and fill them with a coloured filler. In order to avoid splitting close-grained hardwoods, drill holes for the nails before fixing. The backing fabric of parquet panels provides a generous surface area for gluing, so they do not require pinning.

FLOATING FLOORS

Modern woodstrip 'floating floors' are constructed from thin tongued and grooved hardwood boards. These are not secured to the sub-floor in any way, but are usually glued together edge to edge.

Although it isn't a traditional type of wood flooring, the style and quality of a floating floor can make it acceptable in a period house.

REPAIRING WOODEN FLOORS

WOODEN FLOORS *are subjected to considerable daily wear and tear, which may ultimately necessitate repairs. However, the patina of wood improves with age and a floor only looks old if it bears visible signs of its past. So, before undertaking repairs, consider whether there is a case for preserving the floor in its present state, especially if it contributes significantly to the character of the house.*

Gaps between boards, surface damage, splits and insect infestation are the most frequently encountered problems that mar old floors. Not all of these will need attention if you are planning to cover the floor, but they can look unattractive if exposed.

DEALING WITH GAPS

As well as being unsightly, gaps between plain-edged floorboards admit draughts. Gaps are the result of shrinkage, usually caused by the introduction of a modern heating system. Provided that the wood has stabilized, they can be filled.

From the point of view of appearance, the most satisfactory solution is to lift all the boards and re-lay them so they fit snugly together, filling the space remaining at the end of the operation with an additional board or two. However, lifting and re-laying the boards demands considerable effort and can cause further damage to the floor – so it's best to have the work done by a tradesman unless you have some experience yourself, and only to have an old wood floor re-laid if absolutely necessary.

To fill wide gaps without lifting the boards, use strips of matching wood cut with a slight taper **(1)** on a table saw or with a circular saw. Not all the gaps will be the same size, and they may not all be parallel throughout the length of the floor. So you will need to make the strips slightly wider than the gaps and plane them down to fit.

Before cutting the strips, scrape the edges of the floorboards to clean them. You can make an ideal scraper tool with an angled end from a strip of steel. The angled end should be ground to a 1-in-20 taper **(2)**; the taper that you cut on the wooden strips needs to be the same.

Apply some woodworking glue to the angled face of the wooden strip and tap the strip into place. Wipe off the surplus glue and, when set, plane the top edge flush with the surface of the floor. If need be, apply wood stain.

For narrow gaps, use a flexible wood filler. Clean the gaps with an old saw blade and vacuum out loose material. Press the filler into place with a filling knife. To keep filler off the surface of the boards, lay strips of masking tape on each side of the gaps. When set, sand the filler to a smooth finish.

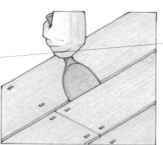

1 Lever up the end of the board

2 Cut the tongues to release board

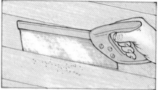

3 Saw at a shallow angle

4 Set depth of cut to board thickness

5 Cut board level with the joist

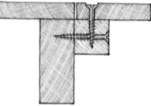

6 Screw wooden block to side of joist

LIFTING FLOORBOARDS

To lift plain-edged boards, insert a wide-bladed bolster chisel into the gap between the boards, close to the end. Start to lever up one edge of the board, trying to avoid crushing the edge of the one next to it **(1)**. Change sides, and repeat the operation in order to ease the end free. Move to the next fixing point along the board, and do the same again. Place a batten under the loose end to help the board pull free as you continue working along it.

To lift a damaged tongued and grooved board it is necessary to cut through the tongue on one or both sides of the board to be removed **(2)**. You can use a tenon saw or circular saw. If you use a tenon saw, the gap between the boards can serve as a guideline or you can tack a straight batten along the cut line to guide the saw. Make the cut at a shallow angle **(3)**. If using a circular saw, fit it with a carbide-tipped blade and fix a guide batten to the floor against which to run the baseplate. Position the batten so that the sawcut will

be just clear of the adjacent board. Set the depth of cut to the thickness of the board **(4)**. Prise out the cut board with a wide chisel. If you need to lift the neighbouring floorboards, they can now be levered up from below.

Before inserting a replacement, you will need to plane off the tongue to allow the board to drop into place. Fix the new board in position with finishing nails driven through the face.

When a section of board needs to be replaced, it is often simplest to remove the whole board and saw off the damaged part. However, if the board is continuous and is trapped at each end, you may have no alternative but to cut it to length *in situ*. To locate the joist nearest to the proposed cutting point, insert a knife blade between the boards. Drill a hole next to the side of the joist, insert a padsaw or power jigsaw and cut the board level with the joist **(5)**. Screw a wooden block to the side of the joist to provide support for the new floorboard **(6)**.

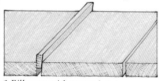

1 Fill gaps with tapered strips

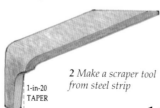

2 Make a scraper tool from steel strip

1-in-20 TAPER

DEALING WITH SPLITS

Splits occur where the fibres of the wood have parted, either at the end of a board or within the face, depending on the grain structure. They are usually caused by shrinkage, but sometimes occur where nails have been driven in. Unless they are disfiguring or likely to cause splinters, they don't necessarily require attention

If the boards do need to be repaired, glue the parts that have split (if need be, applying pressure by inserting wooden wedges between the boards); or use wood filler if the wood is stable and not liable to splinter.

Square brick pattern

Diagonal brick pattern

Herringbone pattern

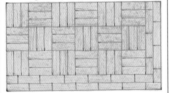

Square basket pattern

Diagonal basket pattern

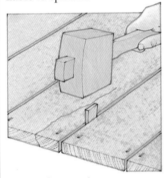

Use a wedge to apply pressure

CURING SQUEAKING BOARDS

Over a period of time, the flexing of the floor or expansion and contraction of the timber may loosen the floorboard nails. It is the resulting movement of the wood against the nails or against the neighbouring boards that produces the typical irritating squeak.

The simplest cure is to drive the floorboard nails in deeper with a nail punch, which allows the tapered edges of the nails to grip the wood more securely. However, this may not be a lasting solution. If the problem persists, use either larger or ring-shank nails. The latter are designed to give a better grip, but are not traditional and require clearance holes drilled through the boards. Fill any redundant holes with a matching wood filler.

If the boards can't be renailed satisfactorily (for example, because of twisting or bowing), use countersunk stainless-steel woodscrews. Bury the heads of the screws deep enough to cover them with filler or with matching wooden plugs. Dampening the wood thoroughly before fixing will help it to 'give' as the boards are screwed down.

PARQUET FLOORS

Parquet flooring is usually made from quality materials and, unless neglected, does not require major repairs. However, sections of a thick parquet floor laid on a concrete base can lift due to expansion of the wood. This may be caused by deterioration of the damp-proof membrane (DPM) beneath the floor, or by water that has been allowed to soak into the wood from leaking plumbing.

Eliminating the water leak and letting the wood dry out while pressed down flat with a weighted board may effect a satisfactory solution, but the area that has lifted may have to be refixed and will no doubt need to be refinished.

If the source of moisture is from below, consult a surveyor or specialist contractor. It is possible that the entire floor will have to be taken up and a new bituminous or epoxy damp-proof membrane applied before the blocks can be re-laid. If you re-lay the floor yourself, number the blocks in sequence with chalk or a wax crayon before taking them up.

Patch repairs

If individual blocks get damaged, they can be replaced with blocks of matching wood cut to fit. First drill out most of the old wood, using a large drill bit, then trim out the remainder of the waste with a chisel. If the blocks are tongued and grooved, you will need to remove the tongues so the new blocks can be dropped into place. Spread flooring adhesive into the recesses, and tap the blocks down with a mallet and a block of scrap wood.

A neglected thin parquet floor generally has a number of loose, warped or missing strips. If it is laid on a wood sub-floor, refix loose strips with woodworking glue and fine nails, which must be punched below the surface.

It may be possible to fix a slightly warped strip in the same way. If it is too badly distorted to respond to this treatment, prise the strip out and dampen it with water, then press it flat between two pieces of particle board held in a vice. Let the strip dry out completely before you fix it back in place.

Missing strips should be replaced with timber of the same species, bought from a flooring specialist or timber merchant. Unless you have machine tools for planing it, have the wood cut to size with the dimensions slightly larger all round than those of the finished piece. Leave the wood to acclimatize in the room for several weeks.

Make a paper pattern of the recess and transfer the dimensions to the wood. Trim it to size with a tenon saw and plane. Use a mitre box for sawing the 45-degree angle needed on end pieces for parquet floors that have a diagonal pattern. Glue and nail the new strips in place. Then plane them flush with the surrounding wood, taking care not to mar the surface. Finish the new strips to match the rest of the floor.

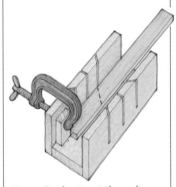

Use a mitre box to cut the angle

FINISHING FLOORS

IT IS ALWAYS POSSIBLE THAT *originally an exposed wooden floor in an old house, particularly if made of softwood, may not have been treated with a finish of any sort. Over the years the bare boards would have acquired a patina produced by the effect of light on the colour absorption of dirt plus burnishing from use and the 'natural' finish imparted by regular scrubbing.*

Nevertheless, you are unlikely to find a wood floor that has remained untreated to the present day – since, with changes in fashion and ownership, virtually all uncarpeted floors have now been treated with a stain, oil, wax, varnish or paint.

Which is the 'right' finish to adopt now is debatable, so let the floor itself be your guide. If you have an old floor that's in good condition, use a traditional finish. But if the wood has been replaced or low maintenance is important, you may prefer to use a modern finish.

Reproduction of a decorative boarded floor made for a Georgian house

SANDING FLOORS

Think carefully before sanding an old floor – the room may lose some of its character as a result. Although wood changes colour with age, it doesn't do so all the way through. So, unless the wood is very deeply stained, removing the surface by sanding will reveal the original colour beneath, which will look more like a new floor than an old one. Also, if the floor has had woodworm, their tunnels may be exposed by sanding.

The only efficient way to sand a wooden floor is to hire a commercial drum sander and, for the edges, a rotary floor-sanding machine.

Preparing for work
Make sure all the boards are fixed down securely, and use a nail punch to drive the nail heads below the surface of the boards. Clear the room and seal the gaps around the door. Always work with the windows open and wear a face mask.

Operating a drum sander
Fit an appropriate abrasive paper to the drum of the sanding machine, following the supplier's instructions. To operate the machine, tilt it backwards and switch on. Gently lower the drum until it comes into contact with the floor. Don't push the machine, but keep it under control, so it moves forward at an even pace. Don't stop with the drum in contact with the floor, or it will cut a hollow that is difficult to remove. Each 'band' of sanding should overlap the previous one.

If the boards are very uneven, start by working across the room diagonally, using a coarse abrasive paper (1). Then sand the floor diagonally with coarse paper again, working across your first sanding (2). Change the paper and sand along the boards, using first a medium grade and then a fine grade to smooth the wood (3). Vacuum the dust from the floor between each sanding.

Cleaning up
Using the rotary sander, sand the borders missed by the drum sander. Finally, use a long-handled scraper to finish the corners. A sanded surface marks easily, so it is advisable to wear soft shoes throughout the entire sanding operation.

Once sanding is complete, vacuum the entire floor area thoroughly and wipe the surface with white spirit in readiness for finishing. If you are unable to proceed with finishing straightaway, cover the floor with clean paper. Rolls of wall-lining paper provide a handy way of protecting a large area.

An alternative to sanding
To avoid sanding altogether, remove surface dirt and old finishes with a plastic scouring pad dipped in a proprietary agent used for cleaning antique furniture. This leaves the floor almost intact, retaining the scars and patina that the wood has acquired over a long period.

1 Work diagonally across the room

2 Then sand the other way

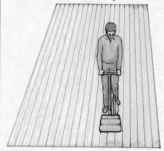

3 Follow the boards to finish

TYPES OF FINISH

Floor finishes can be divided into two main groups: those that penetrate the wood and those that form a protective film on the surface.

Oil finishes such as linseed oil, tung oil, Danish oil and teak oil are all penetrating finishes. Both traditional and modern lacquers and varnishes are surface finishes, as are paints – which are, in fact, pigmented varnishes. A wax finish can be either. It can be employed as a penetrating finish on bare wood, but it is more often used on surfaces that have already been sealed with one of the other types of finish.

Oil finishes

Oil is a traditional finish for wood, especially for woods that are naturally oily, such as teak and afrormosia. Suitable both for hardwoods and softwoods, an oil finish gives wood a natural-looking and pleasingly mellow quality. It is ideal for most board and parquet floors.

Commercially prepared oil finishes such as Danish oil and teak oil are fairly quick-drying and simple to apply. Like all oil finishes, they are easy to maintain.

Varnishes and lacquers

Traditional varnishes were based on natural oils and resins, whereas modern ones are based on synthetic resins. Most varnishes use white spirit as a solvent – but they are not solvent-reversible and need a chemical stripper to remove them.

Polyurethane is a modern hard-wearing, heat-resistant and waterproof synthetic-resin finish available in gloss and matt versions. It is best suited to new dirt-free floors, as careful preparation of the surface is required in order

Mellow early-C19th sealed and waxed pine board floor

to ensure good adhesion. Its hard-wearing properties are useful in high-traffic areas, such as hallways or kitchens.

Catalysed lacquers give an extremely hard-wearing surface that is resistant to heat, solvents and scratches. They are a modern invention, and cure by chemical action. Precatalysed lacquers include a hardener and set on exposure to air; two-part lacquers cure when a separate hardener is added.

All 'clear' varnishes darken the wood to some degree, and some are pretinted. Oil-based ones mellow with age.

Paint

When painting a bare wood floor with a traditional paint system, a primer has to be applied first, followed by an undercoat and top coat; on previously painted floors, the primer can be omitted. Some paints are now formulated in one-coat versions.

Old decoratively painted floors are now quite rare and should be preserved. If you have one that needs restoration, ask a specialist from a historical society for advice.

Wood stains

Stains are used to change the colour of wood but do not act as a finish. You can buy ready-made water-based, spirit-based and oil-based stains in a variety of shades.

Wax

A traditional finish for floors that protects and enhances the qualities of the wood, wax can be used either on bare wood or as a finish for sealed floors. It is available both as a paste and in liquid form. Liquid waxes are less laborious to apply, so most people prefer them for polishing floors.

CLEANING FLOORS

Whichever finish you decide on, you will need to clean the surface thoroughly as a preparatory measure. In fact, you may find that cleaning is all that is required and that the original finish is still in good condition.

Unfinished wood floors

Vacuum an unfinished floor to remove loose dust and grit, then wash it with warm water and detergent. To treat

light soiling, use a sponge and the minimum amount of water. To remove ingrained dirt, scrub the floor with a bristle brush, using scouring powder for bad patches. Rinse the surface as you go, then mop up the water quickly with a sponge and leave the floor to dry.

Waxed floors

Remove dust regularly with a soft brush, vacuum cleaner or dry mop. When necessary, use a liquid cleaning wax to improve the appearance of a floor that is lightly scratched or soiled but otherwise in good condition. Apply the wax with a clean soft cloth, working a small area at a time. The cleaning wax contains solvents that soften the finish sufficiently for the dirt to be absorbed by the cloth and leaves a film of polish on the floor. Let the finish dry, then buff to a soft sheen. An application of floor wax can follow if required.

To remove a wax finish, use white spirit and wire wool, working in the direction of the grain. Wipe up any residue of wet wax with a clean cloth and white spirit.

Oiled floors

Remove dust with a vacuum cleaner or soft brush. Wipe the surface with a lightly oiled cloth to give the finish new life. If necessary, wash the floor with soap suds, using a well-wrung mop and working a small area at a time. Rinse with clean water, in the same way, then dry the floor with a clean cloth. Allow the surface to dry thoroughly before applying a fresh coat of oil.

Varnished floors

Varnished floors should not be washed unless absolutely necessary, as there is always

Pine floor decorated with attractive stencilled design in muted colours

a chance that the water will penetrate under the finish and cause staining. Instead, use a solvent cleaner made of 4 parts white spirit to 1 part linseed oil. Apply the cleaner with a cloth, or fine wire wool for stubborn dirt, then wipe the surface dry with a clean cloth. If a varnished floor has been heavily coated with a wax polish, clean it like a waxed floor (see previous page).

Painted floors

Wash painted floors with a solution of warm soapy water or with a commercial paint cleaner. Working only a small area at a time, apply the solution or paint cleaner sparingly with a cloth or sponge mop, then wipe dry.

If a floor is to be repainted, rub the surface down, using fine silicon-carbide paper, and wipe clean with a tack rag before painting.

Clean decoratively painted floors with great care. After cleaning, apply a coating of wax floor polish to preserve the surface.

SAFETY

- Fumes from varnishes, paints and cleaners can be harmful when inhaled and should not be allowed to build up in a room. When using these materials, work with the windows open and wear a mask.
- Spirit-based finishes and finishes that have an oil or resin base are highly flammable. Extinguish all naked flames before working with them; and clean or destroy all used rags or cloths, especially ones that have been used to apply linseed oil, since they are liable to catch fire due to spontaneous combustion.

APPLYING A FINISH

Before finishing a wood floor, all new work or repairs must be completed, the surface needs to be smoothed or cleaned, and colour applied if not in the finish itself. When applying finishes, always follow the manufacturer's instructions.

Oil

When using a proprietary oil finish, apply a generous coat with a cloth or paintbrush. Allow it to soak in for a few minutes, then wipe off the excess. Let the wood dry for up to eight hours, depending on drying conditions, before applying a second and third coat in the same way. When dry, buff to a soft sheen.

Wax

On a bare wood floor, apply two coats of sealer, using either thinned varnish or a proprietary sanding sealer. Sand down the surface with very fine silicon-carbide paper. The sealer stops the wax sinking in too deeply, which would draw dirt into the wood.

Brush on a liberal coat of liquid wax and leave it to soak in. About an hour later, work over the surface with an electric floor polisher. Apply further thin coats with a cloth pad charged with wax and buff each in turn. Leave the surface to harden, then burnish with the polisher next day.

Paste waxes need to be applied sparingly, using a cloth pad and building up the wax in layers until you have obtained a satisfactory finish. Never apply thick coats of paste in an attempt to achieve quick results – it will remain soft, hold the dirt and look dull. Between coats, burnish the wood with an electric floor polisher.

Varnish

New wood should first be sealed with a thinned coat of varnish, containing about 30 per cent solvent. Brush it in well, working with the grain. On a previously finished surface, use the varnish full strength for the first coat.

When it has set, apply two or three coats of unthinned varnish, allowing each to set before applying the next one. Work first across the grain, to spread the varnish evenly, then finish by brushing with the grain. Between each coat, rub down the surface with fine silicon-carbide paper.

If you can't complete the job in a single session, finish on a joint between boards. Don't work back over varnish that's partly set, as it will pick up brush marks.

Catalysed lacquers

Mix a two-part catalysed lacquer carefully, using the proportions recommended by the manufacturer. Apply an even coat of lacquer with a well-loaded brush, working with the grain. Do not brush the lacquer too much; allow it to flow freely from the brush so that it forms a smooth surface. Work quickly – to maintain a wet edge, so you can blend in each brushload without leaving brush marks. The coating should set in two hours.

Apply a second and third coat at two-hourly intervals. Rub down the surface with fine silicon-carbide paper before applying the last coat.

Paint and wood stains

Apply paint in even coats, using a brush 75mm (3in) wide and laying off with the grain. Allow the paint to set, and rub down between coats as required. Semi-matt paints are best for floors, as their texture makes them easier to work. Always work towards a door if you are painting the whole floor, so you will have a means of exit without treading on the newly painted surface. Let the paint dry thoroughly before walking on it.

To create a decorative pattern, prepare the floor then set out the design, painting it freehand or using stencils purchased from a specialist supplier. For the decorative elements, use a fast-drying acrylic paint to speed up the work, particularly if the pattern is multi-coloured. Use a stippling technique for the smaller details; for the larger elements, brush away from the edges of the stencil.

You can apply wood stains with a stencil, too, using a cloth pad and the minimum amount of colour so the stain doesn't bleed into the wood and blur the pattern.

Protect newly painted floors with a polyurethane varnish. Stained floors can be varnished or waxed.

CHAPTER SEVENTEEN

DECORATIVE METALWORK

IRON – which had previously been employed primarily for functional purposes – began to be used for decorative architectural work around the beginning of the eighteenth century. Up to that time iron had been smelted in relatively limited quantities, its production relying on charcoal-fuelled furnaces that required a ready supply of timber. This restricted the development of the material until in 1709 the iron founder Abraham Darby pioneered the use of coke for smelting iron ore.

Beautifully crafted wrought-iron gates and railings were produced by master craftsmen patronized by the wealthy. The work of migrant black-smiths such as Jean Tijou was to have a profound influence on English wrought iron during the first quarter of the eighteenth century, and by the end of the century the production of iron for both wrought and cast work was well established. Without it, industrial development would have been impossible.

Although wrought iron was still employed for railings, porches and balconies until the mid nineteenth century, by this time cast iron had become the preferred material for decorative purposes. It was regarded not as a substitute for wrought iron, although designs were copied, but as a more substantial-looking material offering better value. Iron founders were now able to produce ornate castings cheaply in any number of identical pieces. This meant that architects could choose decorative ironwork from pattern books, instead of relying on the relatively expensive work of blacksmiths. It also gave them the freedom to create their own designs.

A C19th decorative balcony with cast-iron balustrade

Beautifully preserved 1830s wrought-iron hollow-urn newel post

TYPES OF METAL

METALS USED FOR TRADITIONAL BUILDINGS *can be divided into two main groups: ferrous metals (metals that contain iron, including wrought iron, cast iron and steel in its various forms) and non-ferrous metals (including copper, lead and brass). Non-ferrous metals generally resist corrosion better than ferrous metals do.*

Wrought iron
Being handmade by craftsmen, authentic wrought iron is no longer widely available. Its fibrous structure gives it good tensile strength and bending properties. A malleable iron, it is easily worked by forging and can be worked hot or cold. It can also be readily welded with modern welding methods.

Because wrought iron is a relatively corrosion-resistant metal, its traditional uses ranged from nails, locks, hinges and strapwork to fine examples of gates, railings, brackets and balustrades.

Cast iron
A heavy and relatively corrosion-resistant metal, cast iron is strong in compression but does not have good tensile strength. Cast-iron components are not easily worked, but can be machined and welded to make a repair.

Cast iron has been used for a wide variety of household fitments, including weights and pulleys for sash windows, door fittings, fireplaces and stoves, staircases, decorative brackets, railings, gates, balustrades, porches, roof crestings, and rainwater pipes and gutters.

Steel
Steel is a refined form of iron. It is a hard, tough and malleable metal. Although steel is very much a modern material, traditional 'carbon steel' was produced in the eighteenth century.

The most common type of steel today is mild steel. A general-purpose steel that can be worked hot or cold, it bends readily when heated and is available in various sections as well as in sheet form. In addition to its many other uses, it is now used as a substitute for traditional wrought iron.

Mild steel machines well and can be welded, but it is more difficult to forge-weld than traditional wrought iron. It does not have good corrosion resistance.

Copper
Copper was one of the first metals used by Man. In fact, there is evidence that it was being annealed and worked as early as 4,000 B.C. A soft metal that can be welded, brazed or soldered, it is both strong and malleable. Copper has excellent thermal and electrical conductivity and resistance to corrosion.

Brass
Brass is a yellow-coloured alloy of copper and zinc. Available in strip, bar, rod and sheet form, it is a common material for cast architectural fittings.

Lead
Lead is a heavy, malleable metal that is a bright silver colour when cut, but quickly oxidizes to a matt grey. It has excellent resistance to corrosion and is used for sheet roofing, flashings, pipes and gutters, as well as for decorative cast work.

IDENTIFYING THE METAL

IT IS NOT NECESSARY TO UNDERSTAND *the technical properties of metals, but it is useful to be able to identify the type of material used so that you can maintain it in an appropriate manner. Most examples of decorative metalwork, such as railings, balconies and brackets, are made of iron. However, since they are invariably thickly painted, it is not always easy to tell whether the metal is wrought iron or cast iron. Also, some of the decorative details may be made of other metals (for example, brass rosettes or finials cast in lead).*

Built-up construction and tapered scrolls are typical of wrought iron

Finely crafted wrought iron with delightful scrolls and repoussé work

Complex shapes and moulded surfaces are readily reproduced in cast iron

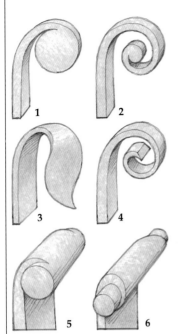

Wrought-iron scroll-work shapes
1 Halfpenny snub end
2 Solid snub end
3 Blow-over leaf
4 Ribbon end
5 Bolt end
6 Fishtail snub end

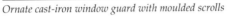

Ornate cast-iron window guard with moulded scrolls

1930's Art Deco decorative wrought-iron panel

Wrought and cast iron

To distinguish wrought iron from cast iron, first look at the style of the metalwork and the proportions of the elements that make up the design. Wrought iron is mostly based on standard square and rectangular sections of iron bar that are worked into decorative scrolls, twists and motifs. The ends of the bars are usually tapered or flattened and worked into snub ends or scrolls, each being individually shaped and subtly different from its neighbour. The overall appearance is crisp and elegant.

In contrast to wrought iron, each part of cast ironwork is precisely reproduced. Components tend to be thicker, incorporating a variety of sections and shapes, including turned forms. Look for 'flash lines' – the seams that run down the sides of a casting at the join between the moulds. The presence of flash lines provides conclusive evidence that a piece of ironwork is cast, not wrought, though on better-quality work these lines are filed away.

Typically the components of wrought ironwork are joined with rivets and collars, and incorporate joints familiar to woodworkers, such as mortise-and-tenon and cross halving joints. Forge or fire welding is also used to blend one part into another. Cast iron is joined by lead-caulked sockets or nuts and bolts fixed through cast lugs.

The surface texture also differs. Wrought iron tends to be smooth, albeit with some roller or hammer marks, whereas cast iron has a more granular feel.

Cracked or broken ironwork indicates the use of cast iron. If you examine the break, you will see the brittle crystalline nature of the material. Wrought iron, on the other hand, is malleable, so impact damage takes the form of bent rather than broken components.

Mild steel

Introduced in the latter part of the nineteenth century, mild steel is now commonly used for 'wrought' ironwork. Sections tend to be slimmer than traditional wrought iron. Also, if gas or electric-arc welding has been used for the joints, then that indicates that the metal is mild steel.

Copper

Polished copper has a rich pinkish-red colour, which oxidizes to a matt brown. With long exposure to the atmosphere, copper forms a green protective patina. Its main use in old buildings is as a sheet roof covering and for guttering, but it was also used for decorative details in Victorian interiors.

Weather vanes use various metals

Decoratively worked lead cladding

Brass

When stripped, the yellow colour of brass clearly distinguishes it from iron and lead, which are grey. When decorative brass details are found, it can be assumed that they were intended as additional ornamentation to contrast with painted ironwork. These should be cleaned carefully and protected from the elements with a clear lacquer.

Lead

Cast lead details can cause problems when stripping paint from old metalwork, since the softness of lead means that they are easily damaged. You may be able to detect the presence of lead under the paint by testing the metal with a sharp spike, to find out whether it is hard or soft, or by scraping the surface of the metal to reveal the bright silver colour beneath.

In order to preserve lead components, when stripping them don't try to burn off the paint or use abrasive stripping methods. Soften the paint with a chemical stripper, then wash it off with a bristle brush. Protect your eyes and hands when using paint strippers.

DECORATIVE IRONWORK

WELL-PRODUCED CHEAP CAST IRONWORK *was a boon to speculative builders, and from the early eighteenth century many town houses boasted a display of prefabricated decorative ironwork.*

Handmade wrought ironwork was revived by Arts and Crafts designers, who abhorred Victorian taste and machine-made products and valued traditional craftsmanship. The vogue only lasted until the 1920s, but their influence continues to this day.

ASSESSING REPAIRS

- Easy even for beginners.
- ■ Fairly difficult. Good practical skills required.
- ▲ Difficult. Hire a professional.

Damaged paintwork
Exposed iron-work is prone to corrosion.
- ■ Identifying the metal (pages 192–3).
- ● Wire-brush loose rust (page 194).
- ▲ Have metal abrasive-cleaned (page 194) or flame-cleaned (page 195).
- ● Chemically strip paint (page 195).
- ● Apply fresh paint system (page 195).
- ● Fill pitted metal (page 199).

Exterior ironwork
1 Balcony balustrade
2 Area railings
3 Gate
4 Window guards
5 Boot scraper

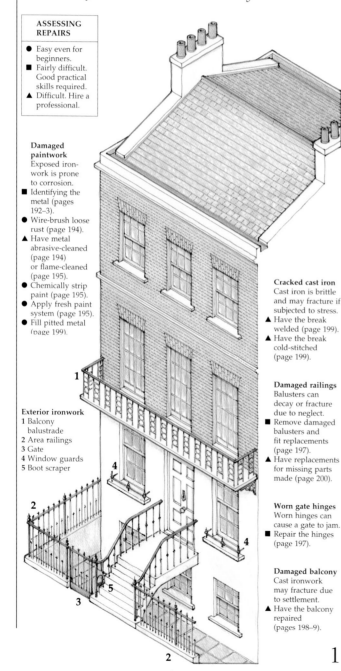

Cracked cast iron
Cast iron is brittle and may fracture if subjected to stress.
- ▲ Have the break welded (page 199).
- ▲ Have the break cold-stitched (page 199).

Damaged railings
Balusters can decay or fracture due to neglect.
- ■ Remove damaged balusters and fit replacements (page 197).
- ▲ Have replacements for missing parts made (page 200).

Worn gate hinges
Worn hinges can cause a gate to jam.
- ■ Repair the hinges (page 197).

Damaged balcony
Cast ironwork may fracture due to settlement.
- ▲ Have the balcony repaired (pages 198–9).

PAINTING METAL

UNLIKE METALS *that form a protective oxide film, iron requires regular painting to protect it from corrosion. Good adhesion of the paint system is essential, and it is vital that the surface is thoroughly cleaned and prepared.*

A conventional paint system comprises a primer, an undercoat and a top coat, although you can now buy some paints for metal that form a protective barrier in a single coat.

Preparing painted surfaces
The only preparation necessary for previously painted surfaces is to clean them before repainting. Wash the surfaces with a sugar-soap solution to remove all traces of dirt and grease. If there is a high-gloss finish, wash the paintwork then key it by rubbing down with fine wet-and-dry paper. Rinse and dry well before repainting.

Damaged paintwork
If the paintwork is damaged and localized corrosion has set in, causing blisters or flaking, remove the loose material with a scraper. Scrape away paint around the damaged area to expose all traces of rust. Clean the rusted areas to a bright finish, either by hand with a wire brush or using a brush attachment fitted into the chuck of a power drill (**1**). Feather the edges of the old paint with abrasive paper.

If the metal is pitted, it is very difficult to eradicate all traces of rust. To overcome the problem, apply a rust inhibitor (available from car accessory shops), which will convert the rust into an inert form of iron phosphate (**2**).

1 Wire-brush the rust

2 Apply a rust inhibitor

Abrasive cleaning
Dry abrasive cleaning (grit or shot blasting) offers an efficient and effective way to clean rusted metal. If you have a large area to clean, it could be worth employing a contractor.

The process creates a lot of dust, and if the work is being carried out *in situ* the contractor should provide some form of protective barrier around the work area. Old lead-based paints are poisonous and it is harmful to inhale the dust, so keep away from the area until the job is completed.

Thoroughly cleaned iron rerusts quickly, so the work should be prepared in stages and it is essential to apply a primer as soon as possible after cleaning.

Flame cleaning

Use an oxypropane torch to help remove loose rust and scale from wrought iron and steel (but not cast iron, since it suffers from intense localized heating). Wire-brush the metal immediately after heating and remove fine dust prior to priming.

Thin metal sections may distort with this method, and fumes from burning lead-painted surfaces can be a health hazard.

Chemical stripping

Over a long period normal routine maintenance causes a considerable build-up of paint that can mask the fine detail of decorative pieces. Where this has occurred or the paint has been damaged or neglected, causing corrosion to set in, it may be better to strip the paintwork and repaint completely.

You can apply a paste or gel stripper to interior and exterior ironwork *in situ* or, if the item is portable, send it to an industrial stripping company.

Apply strippers according to the maker's instructions. It's usually best to brush stripper onto fancy shaped work, so you can work the paste or gel into the crevices. Take care not to brush it on too thinly. Leave the stripper to soften the paint fully before scraping it off. You will find a stiff-bristle brush is best for cleaning paint from decorative details.

Most stripping agents are toxic. They therefore need to be handled with care during application, and materials contaminated by them must be disposed of according to local regulations. Wear eye protection, a face mask, vinyl gloves and, possibly, rubber boots when working with these materials.

APPLYING PAINT

Brush-applied oil-based paints provide a good serviceable treatment for most interior and exterior decorative metalwork. Treat derusted iron and steel with a rust-neutralizing inhibitor (some inhibitors require rinsing after treatment, others are self-priming). Then apply one or two even coats of zinc-phosphate primer. Always treat welded repairs with an additional coat. When the primer has set, brush on two layers of undercoat followed by one or two top coats.

Choosing a colour

Black has now become the standard colour for painted ironwork. However, in the Georgian period railings, balustrades and decorative metalwork were often painted dull green, a colour inspired by the patinated bronzes of antiquity. Other colours, including blue, brown and dark red, have also been used in the past.

If you plan to change the colour of decorative metalwork that is in a conservation area or part of a listed building, you may need to obtain consent from the appropriate authority.

Gloss paints give better weather protection than matt paints for exterior work.

Finishing non-ferrous metals

Brass and copper take on a mellow natural patina that can look attractive without treatment. However, where the atmosphere or degree of exposure is likely to cause corrosion, the metal should be protected with a clear varnish.

Clean the surface with a metal polish, then wash with a mild liquid detergent in warm water and rinse well. Dry the metal with a soft cloth, then apply a clear varnish or acrylic lacquer with a soft brush.

Lead develops an attractive coating of grey oxide that protects the metal, so does not need painting. However, new leadwork can discolour unevenly and stain adjacent materials, so a patination oil is used in order to provide a protective film while the natural patina is forming.

Although galvanization is a relatively modern process, you may find zinc-plated (galvanized) iron and steel have been introduced into an old building. When new, the surface provides a poor key for most paints, though it will improve if allowed to weather for at least six months. However, if you apply a calcium-plumbate primer, the surface can be painted in the normal way. Check that the finishing paints you plan to use are compatible with the primer.

Blue paint used as an alternative to the usual black

Late-C19th gilded wrought-iron railing

RAILINGS

R AILINGS ARE THE MOST COMMON FORM *of traditional decorative wrought and cast iron-work in city and urban areas. If you walk down a street lined with Georgian or Victorian houses that have basements, you are likely to find wrought-iron or cast-iron railings designed to prevent pedestrians falling into the basement 'area'. Iron railings were also used to flank gateways of town houses or country estates, to fence in small domestic gardens and enclose communal gardens in city squares. Sadly, many of the latter have disappeared from the streets of Britain, having been requisitioned by the government during 1941–2 to provide metal for munitions. However, the stubs of these railings often still remain in the coping stones of the low supporting walls from which they were removed.*

Wrought-iron and cast-iron railings can be made to original patterns by blacksmiths or iron foundries that specialize in supplying traditional cast ironwork. A varied selection of ready-made cast-iron railings is available, too. Nowadays some manufacturers use cast aluminium, which can be cheaper for small runs of elaborate designs.

Traditional wrought-iron railing heads

Reproduction cast-iron railing heads and finials

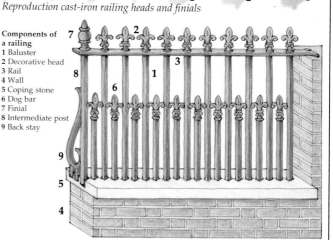

Components of a railing
1 Baluster
2 Decorative head
3 Rail
4 Wall
5 Coping stone
6 Dog bar
7 Finial
8 Intermediate post
9 Back stay

Handsome C19th cast-iron panelled area railing

The popular anthemion motif, used here for cast-iron railing heads

Construction

A typical iron railing has a run of uprights, or balusters, topped with decorative heads. The uprights are joined together just below the heads by a horizontal rail, through which they pass. The tops of wrought-iron balusters would be forged into decorative shapes, or cast-iron decorative heads applied. The heads of cast-iron balusters were either cast as part of the baluster itself or made separately and screwed on.

The bottom end of the railing was usually supported by a low wall capped with a coping stone, but sometimes a stone plinth was used instead of a wall. The traditional method for joining the metal balusters to the stone was to set them in lead poured into drilled holes. The soft lead allows the metal a certain amount of thermal movement without damage to the stone and provides protection against corrosion. In some cases, lead was also run into the joints between the rail and balusters. The ends of the rail were fixed to metal posts or to brick or stone piers.

An elaborate railing may have short uprights (known as dog bars) between the main balusters, as well as additional rails and decorative details.

Railings that had balusters fixed into a supporting wall or plinth were assembled on site. However, railings were also often made as panels, with rails near the top and the bottom for fixing to a post. Where there was a long span between end posts or piers, a lighter intermediate post or a decorative panel fitted with a back stay was used to give extra support.

GATES

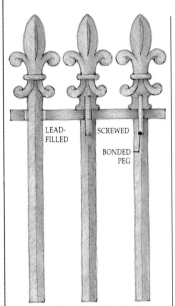

Fixing methods for railing heads

Replacing a baluster

Corrosion can set in where the base of a baluster is set into the stonework or around the joint with the top rail. If the baluster is badly corroded, you may be able to find a matching replacement from an architectural-salvage company or reproduction manufacturer. Otherwise, you can have a new baluster made to order.

Chisel out the lead from the stonework socket. Use an old (but sharp) narrow wood chisel for this operation.

If there is a detachable head, detach it and remove the baluster. Some detachable heads unscrew; but if the head is fixed to a peg, you will have to cut the peg in order to free the baluster.

If the head is an integral part of the baluster, remove the lead from the top joint (either melt it, using a blow torch, or trim it out with a chisel) then pull the baluster through the rail.

Fit the new baluster into place, and either set it in lead or use a two-part epoxy adhesive. If there is a detachable head, screw it in; or if it fits onto a peg, drill out the remains of the old peg and bond the head to a new one with the epoxy adhesive.

I N ADDITION TO PROVIDING SECURITY, *gates present the first impression of a property. Consequently, magnificent examples have been made in wrought and cast iron for grand country houses. These were often very large and topped with a decorative arch spanning the gateway, known as an overthrow. But for most domestic architecture, the gates were no more than waist or head height.*

Traditional iron gates are usually hung on cast-iron posts or brick piers. They are normally fitted with a wrap-round hinge at the top and a ground pivot at the base. Because iron gates are heavy, the pivots tend to suffer from wear.

Bold cast-iron railing panels make up this impressive pair of gates

Maintenance and repair

Keep the paintwork in good condition and grease the pivot points regularly in order to reduce wear and stop annoying squeaks.

Should the hinges be seriously worn, they may need to be replaced. The 'strap' of the top hinge, which wraps around a turned section of the gate-frame member, is usually bolted in place. Remove the bolts to inspect the condition of the parts. You may have to drill them out or cut them free with a hacksaw, in which case replace with a similar fitting.

Some assemblies include a bronze bush. If the strap or bush is badly worn and you are unable to do the work yourself, you can have a new one made by a blacksmith or foundry – or maybe by a local garage. Give the repairer the old part and, if possible, a dimensioned drawing of the assembly.

The bottom of the gate pivots in a metal collar or in a cup set in the ground, which should be kept free from dirt. If a cast-iron cup is broken, have a replacement cast by a specialist.

If an iron gate is missing, you can have a replacement made in the traditional manner by a blacksmith or foundry, either to an old design or to a new design in keeping with the character of the building.

Grand pair of iron entrance gates

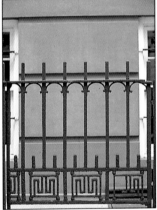

Area gate with Greek-key motif

Components of an iron gate
1 Strap hinge
2 Fixing bolt
3 Gate frame
4 Post
5 Pivot cup
6 Lock

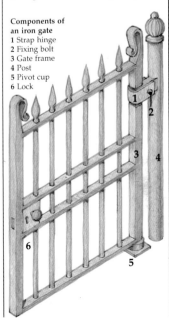

BALCONIES

Components of a balcony
1 Baluster
2 Handrail
3 Fishtail fixing
4 Cast-iron platform grid
5 Decorative bracket

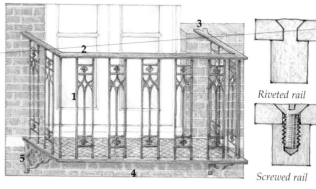

Riveted rail

Screwed rail

RENAISSANCE ARCHITECTURE *was the inspiration for the balconies that became such a popular feature of Georgian and Victorian town houses. At first-floor level, they provided a projecting terrace that enabled the occupants to step outside to enjoy the open air or view the scene below. Some balconies ran the entire width of the building, forming a continuous design with those of neighbouring houses, while others were only one window wide.*

Although stone was often used for the grander houses, most balconies were constructed of wrought iron or cast ironwork. These elegant and attractive structures were cantilevered from the façade, some having a projecting stone base surmounted by an iron balustrade while others were made entirely of iron. The latter type were usually constructed of panels of decorative cast iron. The heavier balconies were often supported by ornamental brackets, and sometimes by elegant cast-iron columns. Columns or traceried panel supports were also sometimes used when a balcony was surmounted by a roof or canopy.

Balcony construction

The stone bases of some balconies were built into the wall as the house was erected and formed an extension to the string course. The mass of the upper brickwork was used to counter the weight of the projecting stone, while brackets of stone or iron gave additional support. The supports for the iron balustrade panels were set into the slab and secured with lead. The ends of the handrail were fixed into a stone wall in the same way but would be built into a brick wall. In the latter case, the ends were split to form a 'fishtail' fork in order to provide a stronger grip in the mortar.

Balconies constructed entirely of iron were usually supported by the string course or window sill and fixed by the handrail at the top and by embedded lugs at the base. Cantilevered arms built into the wall or decorative brackets held by lead-packed lugs or bolts provided extra support for heavier versions.

Elegant iron balconettes complement the tall first-floor windows

BALCONETTES AND WINDOW GUARDS

The small bow or flat-fronted balconies, or balconettes, that grace a single window are often little more than window guards, their real function being to provide a barrier for the tall first-floor sash windows that almost touched the floor.

Window guards are lighter in construction than balconies and normally are not supported by brackets. Some have a platform consisting of a metal grille or open bars. They may be little more than a flat panel across a window opening or a decorative rail fitted to a deep stone window sill.

A lead-covered canopy provides shelter for this attractive balcony

Cast-iron anthemion balconette

Lattice-pattern window guard

REPAIRING & REPLACING IRON

Elegant cast-iron balconies, providing an ideal support for wisteria

METAL IS A TOUGH AND DURABLE *material, but if neglected it decays. Regular maintenance is therefore needed to keep it in good order and avoid expensive repairs. Although it is not particularly easy to work, you can carry out certain repairs yourself – and fortunately there are specialists who are able to deal with most problems and remake parts that are missing or beyond repair.*

Maintaining a balcony

A decorative iron balcony adds considerable character to a house. However, if it isn't maintained properly its prominent position can make it a distinct liability. Chipped or worn paint may result in rusting, which can stain the walls of the house and, if untreated, lead to structural failure. Broken or missing rails create an aura of neglect, and weak fixings may cause structural problems that are costly to repair.

Keep paintwork in sound condition and repaint regularly. Replace missing or seriously decayed elements, using matching parts bought from specialist suppliers or made to order.

From time to time, check the joints where a stone base meets the wall. The slab should slope away from the wall slightly in order to shed rainwater. If water is lying against the wall, it is likely to create penetrating damp. Have a surveyor inspect the structure, as settlement may be causing the problem and require the attention of a builder.

Stresses caused by settlement can crack brittle cast iron. If balusters or decorative iron panels are cracked, have them welded *in situ*. Continuous balconies with large panels of ironwork need to expand and contract to some degree. It is therefore important that welding repairs should not restrict thermal movement, otherwise the ironwork may suffer from further fractures. Large platform grids in need of repair may require strapping with bolted stainless steel plates rather than welding.

If a balcony is beyond repair or has been removed by a previous owner, consult a specialist supplier able to reproduce and install a new balcony for you. If the house is listed or in a conservation area, you will need approval for the replacement balcony.

Cold repairs to cast iron

Large hollow-sectioned porch or veranda columns, cast-iron newel posts and heavy-gauge brackets (for example, in a conservatory) can crack when subjected to subsidence stresses or impact damage. In order to avoid having to heat a large mass of metal, cracks in cast iron that is not less than 6mm (¼in) thick can be repaired by a specialist contractor using a technique known as cold stitching **(1)**.

If a non-structural part, such as a decorative detail, has broken off a cast-iron component, you can repair it with a two-part epoxy adhesive. For small pieces, simply mix the adhesive according to the maker's instructions, apply it to the broken surfaces and fix in place. For larger pieces, drill holes in each part and fit pegs cut from stainless-steel rod to reinforce the joint.

Pitting in rusted cast iron can be filled with an epoxy car-body filler. Clean the metal thoroughly and apply a rust inhibitor. Mix the filler and apply it with a plastic spatula so it is just proud of the surface **(2)**. When it has set, shape the filler with a file and rub it down with abrasive paper to follow the contour of the metal, as required. Prime and paint the repair to match the finish of the work.

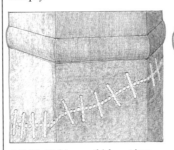

1 Cold stitching on thick cast iron

2 Apply filler proud of the surface

Welding broken cast iron

Cast iron is brittle and may fracture when struck sharply or weakened by rust. If the break is simple, provided the metal is still in reasonable condition, you can normally have it arc-welded *in situ* either by a blacksmith or a welding service that undertakes cast-iron repairs.

In order to avoid setting up stresses in the metal, cast iron has to be heated as part of the welding process. The edges of the crack are ground into a 'V', which is filled with weld metal. The weld should be continuous, without holes (which can encourage corrosion), ground flat, and thoroughly primed ready for painting.

IRONWORK MADE TO ORDER

If ironwork is missing or beyond repair, you can have a replacement made by a specialist. A number of blacksmiths and specialist foundries still exist, but sadly not as many as when ironwork was in its heyday.

Ordering wrought ironwork

Wrought ironwork is made by artist blacksmiths, using traditional craft skills. Now a rare breed, they fashion plain lengths of iron into beautiful forms by heating the metal and beating it on the anvil and on a variety of shaped stakes. This type of work has always been fairly expensive compared with mass-produced cast ironwork, but for one-off items it may be competitive. You can ask the blacksmith to reproduce an old pattern or to create a new design in a traditional style.

Ordering cast ironwork

Because cast iron is made in a mould, any number of identical pieces can be cast from the same pattern.

If you use an existing component as a pattern, you need to bear in mind that cast iron shrinks by about 1 per cent on cooling. For small items, the difference is insignificant. However, if a baluster or other item is 1m (3ft) long, the reproduction would be 10mm (⅜in) or so shorter than the original.

When a single baluster needs replacing, you may prefer to make up the difference with packing rather than spend money on having a special pattern made. If, on the other hand, you have a number of balusters that need to be replaced, you may consider it is worth getting the blacksmith or foundry to make a new pattern for you.

The patterns are normally machined and carved from wood, but clay and resins are used too. To make the casting, a special type of sand is packed all round the pattern in a two-part mould. Various channels are formed in the sand and the pattern is removed, leaving a hollow into which the molten iron is poured.

When the iron has set, the sand is cleaned away, leaving the casting and attached sprues (the iron solidified in the channels). These are cut away and the casting is fettled (filed) to remove the mould marks. Threads may then be 'tapped' (cut) into the component, depending on the method of fixing.

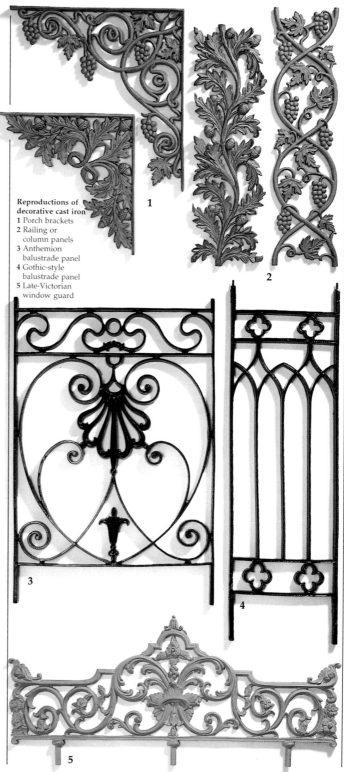

Reproductions of decorative cast iron
1 Porch brackets
2 Railing or column panels
3 Anthemion balustrade panel
4 Gothic-style balustrade panel
5 Late-Victorian window guard

CHAPTER EIGHTEEN

STAIRCASES

EARLY HOUSES RARELY HAD STAIRS, simple ladders being used to gain access to upper levels such as lofts. However, important medieval buildings often had internal or external stairs, most of them constructed from masonry, although some had wooden treads built into the walls.

Wooden framed staircases had generally replaced stone stairs by the late sixteenth century. At first these were robustly constructed from heavy sections of timber and featured rudimentary decoration, although handsomely carved staircases are found in Elizabethan and Jacobean mansions. The position of interior staircases varied, but as often as not they were tucked away in a corner or else advantage would be taken of a convenient alcove or chimney breast.

By the eighteenth century staircase building was highly developed, employing sophisticated building and joinery techniques. Main staircases were now generally made of wood, although stone stairs with iron balustrades were used in the grandest Georgian and Victorian houses. Since the foot of the main staircase was normally situated in the entrance hall, designers and makers took the opportunity to demonstrate their skills by constructing eye-catching straight or curving staircases. Some were relatively simple in style, while others featured ornate balustrades and finely carved decorative details.

Stairs leading to a basement were frequently made of wood or of stone and metal, and some were entirely constructed from metal. These were usually plainer than the main stairs, but cast-iron types were invariably produced in decorative designs. Cellar stairs were of the simplest kind, mostly being open-tread straight flights made of thick sections of wood.

The staircase is an important feature of this C18th entrance hall

A fine early-C18th mahogany balustrade with moulded handrail

TYPES OF STAIR

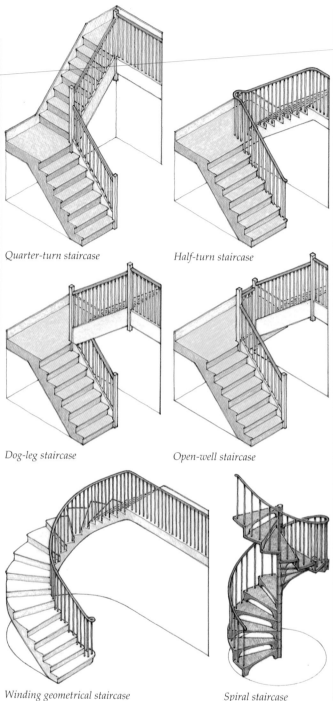

THE SIMPLEST TYPE OF STAIRWAY *comprises a single straight flight of stairs. However, short flights linked by landings are quite common. This type of stairway may be known as a quarter-turn or half-turn stair, depending on whether the turn is made through 90 or 180 degrees. Some staircases have tapered steps, known as winders, instead of landings.*

Dog-leg and open-well stairs are types of half-turn stair. The former, which began to be used in small houses around the late seventeenth century, gets its name from its elevational shape. It is used where the width of the stairway is restricted, and has the upper balustrade in the same plane as the lower one. The open-well stair has a space between the balustrades, providing a more satisfactory arrangement for the layout of the handrail.

Quarter-turn staircase

Half-turn staircase

Dog-leg staircase

Open-well staircase

Winding geometrical staircase

Spiral staircase

NEWEL STAIRS

The majority of staircases are constructed of wood, using a system of structural posts called newels or newel posts.

These are positioned at the ends of each flight in order to transfer the weight of the stair to the floor and support the balustrades, which are jointed into the newel posts at each turn. An open-well stair therefore has two posts at landing level, whereas the simpler dog-leg type needs only one landing post.

Late-C19th newel staircase

GEOMETRICAL STAIRS

Geometrical staircases are designed and constructed in such a way that supporting posts are unnecessary. The balustrade and inner string of this type of open-well stair form a continuous curving structure In grandiose late-Georgian and Regency houses they were sometimes made of stone. Wide sweeping geometrical staircases with radiating tapered steps are known as winding stairs. Elliptical stairs are of similar construction.

Spiral stairs are simply a form of geometrical stair with radiating tapered steps. Most are metal and have a central supporting column. Spiral stairs that are made on the open-well principle are called helical stairs.

WOODEN STAIRS

THE INTERIOR STAIRCASES *of the mid eighteenth century were mostly constructed of softwood, such as pine, though oak (which had generally been used earlier) continued to be used in the larger houses. Mahogany, at that time regarded as an exotic timber, began to be used for handrails and newel posts in better-quality houses, in combination with painted softwood balusters and framing.*

By the Victorian period mahogany had become much more commonplace. Most staircases were now fitted with mahogany handrails, and in some cases the entire balustrade was made of the wood. Oak was popular too thanks to the Arts and Crafts movement, which used it to revive styles of earlier times.

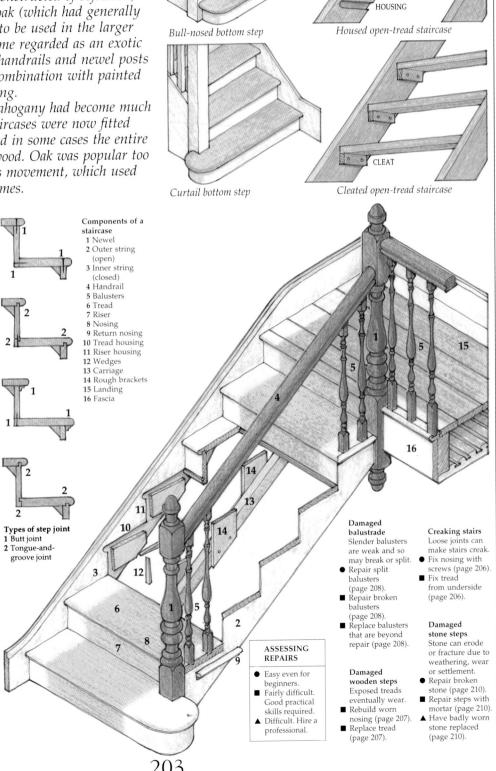

Bull-nosed bottom step

Housed open-tread staircase

HOUSING

Curtail bottom step

Cleated open-tread staircase

CLEAT

Steps

The steps of most wooden staircases are made in two parts, each step consisting of a horizontal tread board and a vertical riser. The risers are fitted between consecutive treads and are usually fixed to the treads with nail-fixed butt joints or with tongue-and-groove joints. Variations on these types of joint are also sometimes used for step assemblies.

The riser, which is about 18mm (¾in) in thickness, provides a closed back to the step. This allows the tread to be relatively lightweight, so the board is normally only 28mm (1⅛in) or so thick. The front edge of the tread, which is called the nosing, projects beyond the riser and is often rounded over.

The bottom step is usually made as a separate part that is added to the main flight. As it isn't fitted between the strings, it often has a shaped outer end. Bull-nosed and curtail steps are examples that are commonly found.

The steps of a traditional open-tread staircase are of very simple construction, merely having a thick tread that is either housed into both stringboards or fixed to them with cleats.

Types of step joint
1 Butt joint
2 Tongue-and-groove joint

Components of a staircase
1 Newel
2 Outer string (open)
3 Inner string (closed)
4 Handrail
5 Balusters
6 Tread
7 Riser
8 Nosing
9 Return nosing
10 Tread housing
11 Riser housing
12 Wedges
13 Carriage
14 Rough brackets
15 Landing
16 Fascia

Damaged balustrade
Slender balusters are weak and so may break or split.
● Repair split balusters (page 208).
■ Repair broken balusters (page 208).
■ Replace balusters that are beyond repair (page 208).

Damaged wooden steps
Exposed treads eventually wear.
■ Rebuild worn nosing (page 207).
■ Replace tread (page 207).

Creaking stairs
Loose joints can make stairs creak.
● Fix nosing with screws (page 206).
■ Fix tread from underside (page 206).

Damaged stone steps
Stone can erode or fracture due to weathering, wear or settlement.
● Repair broken stone (page 210).
■ Repair steps with mortar (page 210).
▲ Have badly worn stone replaced (page 210).

ASSESSING REPAIRS
● Easy even for beginners.
■ Fairly difficult. Good practical skills required.
▲ Difficult. Hire a professional.

Strings

The ends of the treads and risers are jointed into thick inclined boards known as strings (also as stringboards or stringers). These are the structural members that run up each side of the stairs. Two types are commonly used. The closed string has straight parallel edges with the inner face housed to take the ends of the treads and risers. The open or 'cut' string, introduced in the late seventeenth century, has a straight lower edge but is notched to the step shape along its upper edge to bear the treads and risers.

The stringboard fitted to the wall is of the closed type and is usually referred to as the inner or wall string. The other one, which carries the balusters, is usually called the outer string and may be either closed or open.

On some staircases an intermediate string, called a carriage, is fitted under the centre to give support. This is necessary for a stair more than 1m (3ft) wide. The carriage may be a thick notched board, but more often it is a bearer with rough brackets nailed to it. These brackets, which are short lengths of board, support the treads and are fixed to alternate sides of the carriage in order to distribute the load evenly.

On stairs that have a lath-and-plaster soffit, carriage bearers placed on one or both sides and at the centre provide support for the laths, which are nailed across them. Sometimes the laths run vertically, following the slope of the stair, and are nailed only to the underside edge of the steps.

Closed strings have the treads and risers housed into them. The housings are cut some 12mm (½in) deep, with a tapering bottom edge. Glued hardwood wedges are driven into the housings from the back to secure the treads and risers tightly. Triangular softwood 'glue blocks', measuring about 100 x 38mm (4 x 1½in), are rub-jointed into the angles between the tread boards and risers for extra support.

On open-string stairs, the joints between the outer string and the treads and risers are different from those of the closed wall string – the treads being simply glued and nailed to the horizontal edge of the stepped outer string. A 'return' nosing is nailed onto the end of the tread board to cover the end grain and the baluster joints. A fretted bracket is sometimes fitted under the nosing for decorative purposes. To conceal the end grain of the riser, a mitred butt joint is made between the outer end of the riser and the vertical edge of the string.

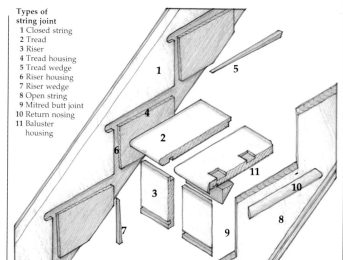

Types of string joint
1 Closed string
2 Tread
3 Riser
4 Tread housing
5 Tread wedge
6 Riser housing
7 Riser wedge
8 Open string
9 Mitred butt joint
10 Return nosing
11 Baluster housing

Late-C19th decorative string

C18th carved string brackets

C18th baluster-type newel made from mahogany

Mid-C19th staircase with solid newel post

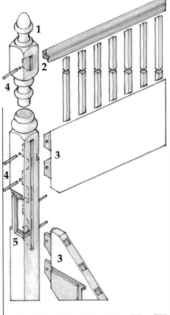

Construction details of a newel post
1 Intermediate newel
2 Mortise-and-tenoned handrail
3 Mortise-and-tenoned strings
4 Dowels
5 Tread and riser housings

Newel posts

Newels were included in the construction of the earliest framed staircases. Placed at the foot and the head or turn of the stair, they support the staircase and balustrade. They are usually cut from solid wood, though panelled versions are also found.

The newel at the foot is a prominent feature of most newel staircases by virtue of its material and its form or surface decoration, as well as its size. However, instead of ending with a large post, eighteenth-century staircases frequently culminated in a cluster of balusters, which often included a fine newel.

Bulbous solid-hardwood newels, often turned and richly carved, were fashionable in the grand houses of the early nineteenth century. These inspired the vogue for turned newels, found even in modest houses until the beginning of the twentieth century. Eventually, simpler square-sectioned newels, in the manner of the earlier seventeenth-century style, were to supersede the turned forms. Some, however, were capped with a turned knob.

The newel at the bottom of the stair and usually the first intermediate post, too, are fixed to the floor. Often they are nailed to floorboards, but fixing to a joist gives greater rigidity. Hollow newels are sometimes fixed with a long threaded rod inside. The top newels of a dog-leg or open-well stair are fixed to the top floor and cut short, forming a decorative drop detail.

The newels are housed to receive the steps, and if the post is panelled the outer string as well. The string is tenoned into a solid newel and pegged for security. The handrail is housed or tenoned into the post.

Typical patterns for round and square-turned balusters

Balustrades

The type of balustrade used for staircases from the seventeenth century until modern times consisted of a series of vertical balusters fixed to the top edge of the outer string or stair treads and to the underside of a handrail. On a newel stair the run of the balustrade is punctuated at every turn by the newel posts, while on a geometrical staircase the balustrade is uninterrupted.

The curving style of the geometrical stair became popular around the second quarter of the eighteenth century and continued into the Victorian era. The handrails are moulded or oval in section and relatively lightweight. At the foot of the stair, the rails often terminate with a volute supported by a group of balusters set on a curtail step.

Early-nineteenth-century balustrades have a handrail that terminates in a turned bun-shape cap attached to a slim newel post. Where the stairway changes direction or meets a landing, shaped handrail sections – called turns, ramps or swan necks, as appropriate – are used to cope with the change of level and direction. The various parts of the handrail are usually fixed together with dowel pegs or special bolts.

The balusters for newel and geometrical staircases may be decoratively turned (with a column-and-vase or twist pattern, for example) or they may simply be plain square sticks.

On well-constructed stairs the balusters are housed into the underside of the handrail and into the top edge of the closed string. Otherwise, they are simply butt-jointed and nailed in place.

Open-string stairs may have either two or three balusters fitted to a tread. These are normally secured with housing or dovetail joints, which are concealed by a return nosing fitted to the side of each step.

Painted mid-C18th Chinese Chippendale balustrade

C18th twist-pattern balustrade

WOODEN STAIR REPAIRS

MOST STAIRCASES ARE WELL CONSTRUCTED *and only require light repairs that can be carried out as part of your routine painting and decorating programme. However, structural repairs may become necessary as a result of infestation or rough treatment. Loose or weak parts should be repaired or replaced as soon as they are discovered.*

FIXING CREAKING STAIRS

Creaking stairs can be irritating and give the impression that a house is not properly maintained. The source is likely to be loose or flexing components rubbing together at their joints because of shrinkage or wear and tear. The most satisfactory repairs are achieved by working from the back of the step – however, if the stair has a plastered soffit it is much simpler to work from the front.

To identify the source of the creaking, remove the stair covering and walk up the stairs. Tread on and off each step, applying your weight to different parts to find out where the loose joints are situated.

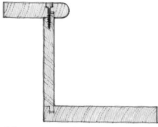

1 Screw the tread to the riser

Working from the front

One likely cause of creaking is a weak joint between the tread nosing and the riser. This is usually a tongue-and-groove joint, or a butt joint with a scotia moulding set into the angle between the riser and the tread. In either case, the easiest solution is to drill and counterbore the tread to take two or three 38mm (1½in) screws set directly above the centre line of the riser **(1)**. Inject woodworking adhesive into the holes and flex the board to help it penetrate the joint as far as possible. Insert the screws, which will pull the joint tightly together, and fit matching wooden plugs to cover the heads.

If the stair has featured hardwood treads, try not to use screws. Prise the joint apart a little and work glue into it with a brush. If this fails to get rid of the creaking, you will need to work from the underside.

Working from the back

If the underside of the staircase has a lath-and-plaster soffit, it will be necessary to cut into it to gain access to the problem area. To reduce the damage, locate the weak steps and note the position in relation to the underside. Chop away the plaster with a bolster chisel, then saw through or pull out the laths **(2)**. You will have to make good the plaster after completing the repair.

In many period houses the underside of the staircase leading up from the ground floor is enclosed with a partition between the outer string and the floor called a spandrel. This may be a lath-and-plaster stud wall or a wood-panelled frame. A door provides access to the cellar stairs or a cupboard space below the staircase. The underside of the stair is usually unfinished.

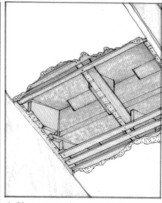

2 Clear away plaster and laths

3 Inject glue into the opened joint

4 Rub-joint blocks into place

5 Glue and screw back joint

Fixing the tread

Glue blocks are normally fitted into the angle between the tread and the riser. If old glue has failed, knock the blocks off and clean the glue from the surfaces.

Use a chisel to prise apart the joint between the front of the tread board and the riser. Inject woodworking glue **(3)** and rub-joint the blocks in place **(4)**. To strengthen the joint, make and fit additional glue blocks.

Similarly, prise apart the joint between the back of the tread and the riser. Inject glue into the joint and insert screws to pull it tight **(5)**.

Do not use the stairs until the glue has set.

6 Fit new riser and tread wedges

Fixing the housing joint

If the ends of the tread or riser are loose in their housings, prise out the wedges that help to hold the boards securely in position.

Use a narrow chisel to chip or pare out any hardened glue or splintered fragments of the old wedges that may remain in the housings.

Make new wedges from hardwood; apply woodworking glue and drive them into place. Fit the vertical wedge for the riser first and cut it to length, then fit the horizontal wedge for the tread **(6)**.

REPAIRING DAMAGED STEPS

The treads of a wooden stair eventually wear at the nosing, especially if they are unprotected and made of softwood. Badly worn treads are dangerous and should be repaired or replaced without delay.

Treads are difficult to replace, since they may be held with tongue-and-groove joints across their width and the treads of closed-string stairs can only be removed from the back. Unless you have the necessary experience, it is therefore best to employ a builder or a carpenter – particularly if the staircase has carriage bearers, which makes replacement an even trickier operation.

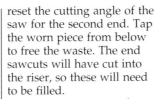

1 Guide the saw with a pinned batten

2 Saw in from front edge of tread

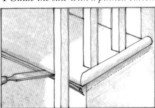

3 Prise off the nosing moulding

4 Cut the riser tongue with a saw

Rebuilding the nosing

Mark cutting lines around the worn area. Hold a drill at 60 degrees to the surface, and at one end of the section that needs replacing drill four 3mm (⅛in) holes close together to form a slot. Set a power jigsaw to 60 degrees and make a sawcut along the line. To help make a straight cut, pin a guide batten to the tread (1).

At each end of the marked section, saw in from the front edge of the nosing to meet the first cut at right angles (2). You will need to reset the cutting angle of the saw for the second end. Tap the worn piece from below to free the waste. The end sawcuts will have cut into the riser, so these will need to be filled.

Cut a new section of wood to fit the cutout. If the riser board has a tongue, work a groove into the underside of the new section to receive it. Shape the front edge of the nosing, then check the fit and glue the new section in place. When the glue has set, plane the surfaces flush.

Replacing a tread

Tread and riser assemblies may either be tongued and grooved or butt-jointed and nailed. In either case, the parts will probably need to be cut to free the tread.

Remove the glue blocks from under the tread and if there is a scotia moulding under the nosing prise it free with a wide wood chisel (3). Also, remove any screws or nails. Try to pull out nail fixings – however, if the tread has a butt joint, you can cut through nails by sliding a hacksaw blade into the joint.

To free a tongue-and-groove joint, drill a continuous row of 3mm (⅛in) holes along the shoulder of the nosing joint to form a slot. Cut the tongue either by hand, using first a padsaw and then a panel saw, or by inserting a powered sabre saw or jigsaw into the slot (4). If it is an open-string stair, cut the rear tongue from the underside in a similar way.

How you remove the tread will depend on whether the staircase is a closed-string or open-string type (see below).

Closed-string stair

Remove the wedges from under each end of the tread. Using a hammer and a block of wood, give the tread a sharp tap from above to free the back joint and housing joints (5). The tread should now be clear of the riser tongue at the rear, so you can drive it out of its housings from the front (6).

Make a new tread, but do not cut a groove on the underside. Build up the cut edge of the front riser with glued veneer or a thin strip of wood cut from a board with a machine saw. Apply glue, then insert the tread from the back and secure it with new hardwood wedges glued into place. Fit glue blocks inside the nosing. If needed, refit a scotia moulding under the front edge.

5 Strike the tread to free it

6 Drive out the tread from the front

Open-string stair

Prise off the return nosing carefully (7). Free and remove the balusters from the tread and handrail. Chisel out the wedge from under the tread housed in the wall string. Tap the open-string end of the tread from the rear to free it, then extract the board from the front (8).

Make a new tread of well-seasoned wood to match the shape of the old one and cut the joints for the balusters. Build up the cut edges of the risers with glued strips of wood. Glue and screw the tread to the risers and wedge the housing joint in the wall string. Fit the balusters, then fix the return nosing with a dab of glue and a nail at the mitred front end and a nail at the other.

7 Prise off the return nosing

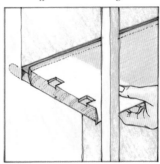

8 Pull the tread out from the front

REPAIRING BALUSTRADES

Much of the character of a staircase is provided by the balustrade. The repetition of the balusters, whether ornately turned or merely plain sticks, gives a pleasing decorative effect. If one or two balusters are damaged or missing, or have been replaced by non-matching ones, the symmetry is disturbed and the appearance spoilt.

Broken balusters are potentially dangerous, so should be repaired or replaced without delay. Try to preserve original turned ones. If they are beyond repair, either make replacements on a lathe yourself or have new ones made to order.

Baluster fixings

On well-constructed stairs the balusters are housed into the underside of the handrail and the top edge of a closed string (1). However, you often come across staircases where the balusters are simply butt-jointed and nailed in place (2).

Open-string stairs may have two or three balusters to a tread. Usually, housing or dovetail joints are used to secure them and the joints are covered with a return nosing (3).

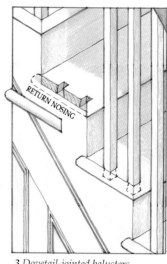
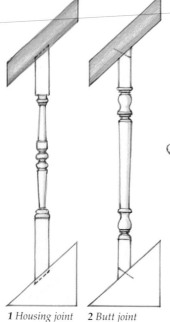

1 Housing joint 2 Butt joint 3 Dovetail-jointed balusters

Repairing a split baluster

Turned or slender wooden balusters tend to be fairly weak, and may break if they are struck from the side. A split baluster that has a long tapering break is simple to repair and there is normally no need to remove it from the balustrade.

Apply an even coating of woodworking glue to the surfaces of the break, then pull them together tightly with self-adhesive tape (4). Wipe off surplus glue with a damp cloth before binding up the repair. When the glue has set, peel off the tape. Clean up with a scraper and abrasive paper, then finish to match the other balusters.

Repairing a broken baluster

If a break – at a narrow section of a turned baluster (5), for example – is short due to a weakness in the structure of the grain, gluing alone may not make a sufficiently strong repair. It is therefore better to remove the baluster and reinforce the repair with a wooden dowel.

To enable you to drill a stopped hole that will accurately align in both parts, first drill a 9mm (⅜in) diameter hole about 50mm (2in) deep down the centre of one of the parts (6). Make sure that the part you choose has beads and coves or similar details close to the end.

Saw off the broken end with a fine dovetail saw. Make the cut on a shoulder line of the turned decoration (7), having made a pencil mark across the shoulder so you can align the parts when reassembling the baluster. Then glue the broken ends together carefully.

When the glue is set, drill down the other part of the baluster (8), using the glued-on piece as a guide – and again making the hole about 50mm (2in) deep. If need be, glue a piece of veneer to the end to make up the sawcut waste. Trim out the centre to reopen the hole.

Cut a length of 9mm (⅜in) dowel, then chamfer the ends and cut a groove along its length. Apply glue to the parts and assemble the dowelled joint, using the pencil mark to help you realign the parts correctly (9) Wipe away surplus glue with a damp cloth.

4 Bind break with tape 5 Weak section of baluster

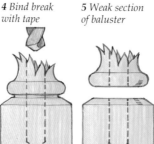

6 Drill a hole down one part 7 Saw off end on a shoulder line

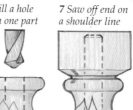

8 Drill the other part of baluster 9 Glue and dowel the parts

Replacing a baluster

If a baluster is beyond repair or missing, you will need to replace it. Select matching wood unless the baluster is to be painted. Plain square-sectioned sticks can easily be planed to size if they are not a standard timber section.

Making decorative turned balusters involves the use of a lathe. If you have access to one and have the necessary woodturning experience, either make a card template of the baluster's profile or take out a sound baluster to act as a guide. You can construct the template profile with drawing instruments, or use a profile gauge to take an impression of the shape.

If you lack the facilities to make a replacement yourself, take a sample baluster to a specialist woodturner and have a reproduction of it made. Some woodturning companies have copy lathes that reproduce the shape of an original automatically.

Whether you make a replacement yourself or have one made to order, the new baluster should be made overlength for cutting to size before fitting and finishing.

STONE STAIRS

STONE IS PRIMARILY *an exterior building material and is not commonly employed indoors. However, it can be used to provide attractive interior features. Grand stone geometrical staircases are occasionally found in large late-eighteenth-century and nineteenth-century houses, as well as secondary stone stairs leading to the basement. Decorative wrought-iron or cast-iron balustrades were generally used to complement the solidity of stone staircases.*

Many houses of this period have a basement or semi-basement. To enable a large window and a doorway to be built at the front, an open 'area' was created between the footpath and the front of the basement wall. Usually stone steps and a stone platform bridged the gap between the path and the front door, while a decorative iron or stone balustrade guarded the open area. The basement itself was reached by descending a stone or metal stairway that led down into the area.

1860s stone staircase with sweeping spandrel steps and cast-iron balustrade

STONE STAIR CONSTRUCTION

The design of stone steps can range from thick rectangular blocks **(1)** or thinner slabs forming treads and risers **(2)** to the more sophisticated carved wedge-shaped sections of spandrel steps **(3)**.

Spandrel steps are used in the construction of interior open-well geometrical stairs. The inner ends of these steps are left square and built into the wall for support. Each step sits on the back edge of the one below and is located by a mortared splayed rebate cut in the lower front edge.

The shaping of the nosing usually follows the conventional rounded form used on wooden stairs, including the return nosing detail at the side and sometimes a scotia moulding at the front.

Landings are made from slabs of stone built into the wall. To make installation easier they are constructed from pieces of a manageable size, which are locked together with 'joggle joints' (a kind of stopped tongue-and-groove joint).

1 Rectangular-block stone steps

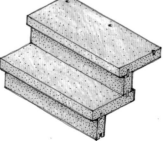

2 Stone slabs form treads and risers

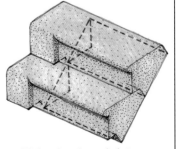

3 Wedge-shaped spandrel steps

Balustrades

Decorative iron balustrades are commonly used with stone stairs. The balusters are set in dovetail-shaped holes cut in the treads and secured by pouring molten lead into each hole. The solidified lead is then caulked and a stone-coloured mortar used to fill and finish the recess **(4)**.

Sometimes, where the stairs are narrow or simply for visual effect, the balusters are made to oversail the ends of the steps **(5)**. These are fixed into the side face of the step with caulked lead in a similar way.

The handrail of an iron balustrade may be made of iron, in which case it is attached to the top ends of the balusters with countersunk machine screws **(6)**. Alternatively, an interior stone staircase may have an elegantly moulded handrail made of a hardwood such as mahogany. A wooden handrail is secured with woodscrews through an iron strip that is fixed to the balusters with machine screws **(7)**.

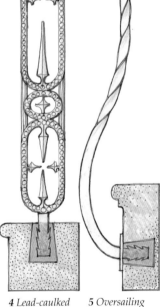

4 Lead-caulked metal baluster

5 Oversailing metal baluster

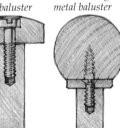

6 Metal handrail fixing

7 Wooden handrail fixing

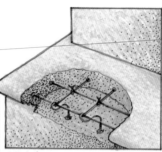

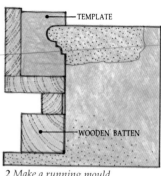

1 *Reinforce repair with metal rod*　　**2** *Make a running mould*

REPAIRING STONE STAIRS

Even indoors stone eventually wears; and if settlement takes place in the supporting material, it may crack. Interior open-well stairs showing signs of distortion should be checked by a surveyor. If it is not possible to cut out and reset or replace individual steps, a specialist builder may be able to build a framework of steel beams to reinforce the structure and box it in discreetly with a plaster soffit.

Worn exterior steps, especially when covered with ice, are dangerous and should be repaired or replaced. An outdoor metal balustrade needs regular maintenance if it is to remain a safe and attractive feature (see DECORATIVE METALWORK).

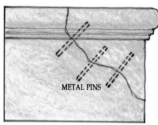

Reinforce the joint with metal pins

Repairing a damaged step

Working stone is a special-ized skill and for any major repairs you need to employ an experienced craftsman, but it is possible to under-take simple repairs yourself.

To refix a small piece of broken stone, mix a two-part epoxy adhesive and apply a very thin coat to both faces. Press the broken piece into place and, if need be, secure it with adhesive tape until the glue has set. Many glues will only set at a specified temperature, so do the work on a warm, dry day.

If there is still a gap along the break line, mix some crushed-stone dust with a little adhesive to make a filler. Apply it to the crack with a knife, taking care not to spread it on the surface.

A larger broken piece can be replaced in a similar way, but needs reinforcing with non-ferrous metal pegs. Use a power drill fitted with a masonry bit to bore two or three 3mm (⅛in) stopped holes about 12mm (½in) deep in each part. Rock the

drill to open up the inside of the holes slightly. Drill the holes in the broken piece first. Position it and give it a tap to deposit some residual stone dust from the holes onto the other half. Remove the piece carefully and mark around the spot of dust, then drill matching holes on the marked positions.

Cut short lengths of 3mm (⅛in) stainless-steel or brass rod for the pegs. Apply resin adhesive to the holes and to the broken faces of the stone. Insert the pegs and position the piece, then tape or clamp until the adhesive has set.

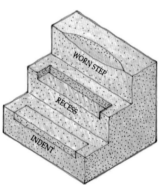

Indenting makes an effective repair

Fitting new stone

Indenting is an effective method for repairing steps that are badly worn. The damaged area is cut away to form a recess, then a stone 'indent' is fitted and resin-bonded into it. This is a job for an experienced builder or a flooring specialist.

Mortar repair

Patching the stone with mor-tar (commonly known as a 'plastic' repair) is a possible method for repairing worn or damaged steps. However, very careful preparation of the old surface is necessary. In addition, it is important that the mortar is capable of standing up to the physical demands put upon it, and it has to be compatible with the original stone.

Mixing a suitable mortar is the most difficult part of the operation, requiring a good deal of trial and error. Most mortars are mixes of lime, cement and sand or stone dust (see REPAIRING DEFECTIVE STONE). A local stonemason should be able to supply small quantities of dust from common types of stone.

Mix small portions of the materials to test the strength, colour and texture. Make up a number of mixes, varying the ingredients slightly and keeping a careful note of each. Leave them to mature and weather for some weeks (the longer, the better). Test their hardness by scraping the surface; also, judge their appearance against the natural stone. The strength of the mortar should always be weaker than the material being filled. To match a rough surface, use a coarser aggregate. To give a more weathered appearance, dry brush the surface lightly before the mortar sets.

Using masonry chisels and a club hammer, cut back the worn area to sound stone to form a level recess. Undercut the edges to provide a key

and a well-defined cutout, as mortar laid to finish with a feathered edge is likely to break away.

For recesses that are larger than 38mm (1½in), metal reinforcement is necessary, particularly at the edges of steps. Use non-ferrous metal, such as brass rod and wire bent to shape, and set in epoxy-resin-filled holes **(1)**. The reinforcement should be not less than 18mm (¾in) from the finished surface.

To help form steps with a shaped nosing, make a tem-plate from thin steel plate. Take the shape from a sound section of the step, using a profile gauge. Transfer the outline onto the metal and cut it to shape. Mount the plate in a running mould **(2)** (see PLASTERWORK). Square-edged steps can be shaped with a trowel.

Apply the mortar in layers or 'coats' to prevent shrink-age and cracking. Dampen the stone, and then apply the first coat. Build up the full thickness with coats no more than 9mm (⅜in) thick. Key the surface of each and allow it to set hard. Dampen the previous coat before applying the next one.

Apply the last coat of a moulded step so it finishes proud of the surface. Set up a straight wooden batten on which to run the mould. Shape the mortar to the finished profile. In order to stop the mortar drying out too rapidly, cover the repair with plastic sheeting or dampen it occasionally with a light spray of water.

CHAPTER NINETEEN

FIREPLACES

W ITH THE INTRODUCTION *of gas and electric appliances and central heating systems in the late nineteenth century, the open fire gradually ceased to be the focus of family activity. For centuries the solid-fuel fire had provided warmth, energy for cooking, and in some cases light. Early open-hearth fireplaces were literally at the centre of the household, but as buildings and chimney systems developed the fireplace took up its now familiar place against the wall.*

In medieval times logs were burned on the hearth within large fireplace openings, and this style continued to be popular in country houses for generations. But as timber became scarcer and coal fires more common the size of the opening was gradually reduced. Nevertheless, the architectural importance of the fire-place did not diminish. With the coming of the Industrial Revolution designers and manufacturers devised all kinds of patent grates and stoves, and these helped to ensure that the fireplace remained the focus of attention in the room until its decline in recent times.

Some fireplaces are grandiose and ornate, others elegantly stylish or plainly functional. All have character and add a certain charm to the home. As a result, many period fireplaces, stripped out to make way for central heating or modernized décor, are now being reinstated to bring back the original character of the interior.

A restored late-C18th open fireplace with moulded surround

Late-Victorian fireplace with classically styled mantelpiece

MANTELPIECES

T HE MANTELPIECE *forms a decorative 'fireplace surround' – a term frequently used today – that frames the fireplace opening. Traditionally the surround was made from stone (often marble or slate) or from wood or cast iron.*

Early rural fireplaces were simply large functional openings, without any surround. The inglenook type, with its massive timber lintel supported by exposed or plastered brickwork, provided a wide enclosure for heating and cooking and sometimes for seating, too. In more formal interiors, the fireplace was shaped in the current architectural style and had simple mouldings carved into the stone that formed the opening.

Inigo Jones-style chimneypiece

MANTELPIECE STYLES

In England, ornamental mantelpieces began with the Renaissance-style chimneypieces found in important houses of the late sixteenth century. The classical detailing served as an inspiration for architects such as Inigo Jones and Robert Adam in the following centuries and had a lasting influence on the style of the mantelpiece.

Inigo Jones established the fireplace as an architectural feature with his grandiose chimneypieces. The jambs were treated as columns, pilasters or volutes supporting a lintel or frieze in the style of an entablature. This was surmounted by an overmantel that continued the decorative detail to form a pedimented frame, which was sometimes filled with a painting or later a mirror.

In less grand houses, the treatment was simpler but followed classical forms. Late-seventeenth-century and early-eighteenth-century fireplaces had simple wood or stone surrounds with bold bolection mouldings. This type of mantelpiece did not always provide a shelf.

The eighteenth century

By the mid eighteenth century the use of decorative columns, pilasters and consoles to support a mantelshelf had become common. Elaborate rococo decoration featuring naturalistic forms came into vogue for a short time. Mirror glass, which had formerly been a luxury that only the very rich could afford, was now available in large sheets from France and was used to make richly decorative overmantels that reflected light into the room.

Mirrored overmantels and other mantelpieces inspired by Robert Adam were less ornate, being embellished with sophisticated low-relief classical decoration.

Victorian mantelpieces

The Victorian mantelpiece reflected a number of styles, including bolder interpretations of the classical forms. Marble surrounds were shaped to accommodate the cast-iron arched grate introduced around 1850. Mirrored overmantels also adopted an arched top. White and coloured marble continued to be used widely and, to cater for the fashionable black colour, slate was introduced too. This was sometimes artfully painted to simulate black marble, and gilding was often added to highlight incised mouldings. Frequently, softwood mantels were painted to simulate marble or hardwoods.

Elaborate cast-iron mantelpieces also appeared. Some were made entirely of iron, while others had wooden shelves. Ornate overmantels that had mirrored panels and fancy display shelves became fashionable in the late-Victorian period.

The twentieth century

The influence of the Arts and Crafts movement was reflected in the designs of the early twentieth century. Natural materials such as oak, stone and brick were now once again used for mantelpieces. The wooden mantels of the period were often ornamented with Art Nouveau fretted brackets and panels. Art Nouveau decoration was also applied to brass and copper hoods and to tiles used in cast-iron grates. But by the 1930s taste had changed, and marble, brick or plainly tiled mantelpieces had become the rage.

Impressive Edwardian painted-wood chimneypiece

Elegantly carved C18th stone mantelpiece

Grand stone mantelpiece with carved frieze and caryatid jambs

COMPONENTS OF A MANTELPIECE

The basic components of a mantelpiece are the jambs (**1**), which support the frieze or lintel (**2**), which in turn carries the mantelshelf (**3**). The jambs may be in the form of columns, pilasters, carved caryatid figures or simple architectural mouldings. The frieze or lintel may be a matching architrave moulding or a plain or decorated panel. The degree of ornamentation is dependent on the grandeur and style of the mantel. The shelf may be plain-edged or moulded.

Most marble mantelpieces are supplied as separate elements for assembly on site. The jambs and frieze are usually constructed from marble panels or slips (narrow strips), which are held together with plaster of Paris and reinforced with plaster-bonded spacer blocks fitted inside. Wooden fireplace surrounds are made up of boards glued together and assembled for fitting as a single piece. Cast-iron surrounds are made in one piece, except for the separate bolt-on shelf.

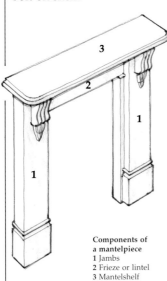

Components of a mantelpiece
1 Jambs
2 Frieze or lintel
3 Mantelshelf

HOW A MANTELPIECE IS FIXED

Marble mantelpieces are attached to the wall with steel-wire ties or hooks fixed into the back edge of the parts. These are set in plaster or tied with wire to screws or nail hooks set in the wall.

Wooden mantels are held in place with screws or nails fitted through metal plates attached to the jambs.

Cast-iron mantelpieces have cast lugs at the top and foot of the jambs for screw fixing. If there is a shelf, it is bolted to the top of the casting before the mantelpiece is positioned against the wall.

With all types, plaster is applied around the mantelpiece to conceal the fixings and help hold it firm.

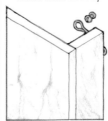
Marble fixing

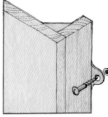
Wood fixing

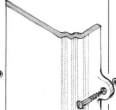
Cast-iron fixing

CLEANING MARBLE

Marble's variety of subtle colours and markings and ease of working have made it a favourite material for mantelpieces for centuries. However, it is a porous stone that can easily become dowdy or stained – which is why you sometimes come across marble mantelpieces that have been painted over. With care, marble can be stripped and cleaned to bring it back to its original finish.

General soiling

Use a soft brush and cloth to remove loose dust from the surface and crevices. Wash off surface dirt with warm soapy distilled water, working up from the bottom to avoid leaving streaks. Use a bristle brush to clean mouldings, and a toothbrush for fine detail. Rinse with clean water, then dry with a cloth.

For more persistent dirt, a commercial marble cleaner is often effective. Alternatively, use a solution of household ammonia, or try hydrogen peroxide (100 volume) in a solution of 1 part peroxide to 3 parts water (a few drops of ammonia can be added to it). Wear rubber gloves, a mask and eye protection when working with any of these substances. Wet the surface before applying the solution to prevent dirt being drawn into the marble. Don't use household bleach, as it can etch the marble. Also, don't mix bleach with ammonia, as toxic fumes are produced.

Removing stains

To remove deep stains, you need to apply a poultice. Commercial poultice materials are available, or you can make your own. A poultice consists of an absorbent substance (such as fuller's earth, powdered chalk or talc, or pulped white blotting paper or paper tissues) to which a stain solvent is added. Use baking powder mixed with distilled water as the solvent for soot stains; white spirit or acetone for oily stains; and ammonia or hydrogen peroxide for organic stains.

Mix the absorbent and solvent to make a paste and apply a layer, not less than 6mm (¼in) thick, over the stain. Tape plastic film over the poultice to stop it drying too rapidly. Leave for a day or two before removing the plastic covering. The solvent will be absorbed into the marble to activate the stain; then as the poultice dries, the stain substance is drawn out with the solvent. When the poultice is completely dry, scrape it off. You may have to repeat the process and change the solvent several times if more than one type of stain substance is present.

Finishing marble

Apply a thin film of marble polish or a fine white-wax polish and buff to a natural sheen. Maintain the surface by periodically washing with a mild soap solution then applying a little polish.

FIRE GRATES

Until the early eighteenth century *wood was the fuel most commonly used for open fires. Although it will readily burn on the hearth, large logs were usually supported on a pair of andirons or firedogs.*

When timber became scarce in and around towns and cities, it was more economical to burn coal. Coal burns at a higher temperature than wood and needs a good flow of air. Wrought-iron fire baskets were therefore produced to contain the fuel and concentrate the heat. They also kept the coals clear of the floor, improving air flow and combustion while allowing ash to fall away. Although it is often possible to date a fireplace by the type of grate, this can be misleading since many old fireplaces have been modified over the years.

FIREBACKS

The early wood-burning open fires were simply laid in stone or brick-built fireplaces. In order to protect the masonry at the back of the fire, cast-iron firebacks were introduced. Produced in various sizes, with ornamental tops and decorated with allegorical subjects, they were very widely used. As a result, a great many eighteenth-century firebacks have survived to the present day. Excellent replicas are also readily available, taken from original patterns.

FROM A SMOKY LIFE
AND A SCOULDINGE WIFE
ALL MEN THAT DOE ME SE
TAKE PETIE AND DELIVER ME
Inscription on C17th fireback

DOG GRATES

Dog grates (also known as basket or stove grates) were introduced in the early part of the eighteenth century and were used to burn coal. A freestanding fire basket, which incorporated a fireback and had iron or steel bars in front, was supported on legs similar in style to firedogs – hence the name.

By the middle of the eighteenth century these grates had been transformed into refined examples of metalwork, with polished steel bars at the front and decorative steel or brass legs, which were joined by a handsome pierced-metal apron. Late-eighteenth-century designs intended for quality houses followed neo-classical styles and sometimes included Adam motifs. Today this type of grate can be found in period-style houses that have a large brick-built open fireplace, although the modern interpretation is likely to be a gas-fuelled coal-effect or log-effect fire.

FITTED GRATES

The decline in the use of wood as a domestic fuel, coupled with a better understanding of fireplace technology and the development of mass-produced cast iron, led to a proliferation of novel designs for more efficient fitted grates in the late eighteenth century.

Hob grates

During this period the hob grate, which was fitted into the lower half of the fireplace opening, became popular. This type of grate featured wide decorative cast-iron front panels, fitted on each side of a high fire basket, and hob plates that provided a useful surface for keeping pots and kettles hot.

Register grates

The register grate was a further development. This had a front frame or plate that fitted the opening. The early examples had cast-iron back and side panels, which lined the upper part of the fireplace. Above, a closure plate sealed off the chimney opening except for an aperture controlled by an adjustable

Hob-style register grate in a Georgian house

Attractive reproduction cast-iron grate

Stylish 1930s marble-faced fireplace

plate known as a register. However, the name 'register grate' eventually came to mean any grate with a front plate that fitted the fireplace opening, regardless of whether a register was fitted. Today, this type is often referred to as an insert grate.

Late-eighteenth-century register grates in polished steel sometimes had wide baskets with small side hobs, under which ran a pierced decorative apron.

Although the register plate offered some control of heat loss up the chimney and slowed the rate of burning by restricting the air flow, it didn't solve all the problems – especially since the basket was still set high.

Arched grates
Until the mid nineteenth century, fire grates were generally either square or rectangular and most were still made entirely of cast iron. The second half of the century saw the introduction of the arched grate. This had a smaller fire basket set at a lower level and lined with firebricks, while the register became a semi-circular flap or damper that was opened once the fire was alight. The style remained popular until the end of the century.

Splay-sided fireplaces
Around 1870 a new style emerged that had a narrow rectangular opening with splayed sides decorated with tiled panels. The fire basket was now set very low, and the front bars lifted out as a single unit. An ash pan, fitted underneath, helped control the flow of air.

One-piece units
By the 1930s cast-iron grates had been ousted by plainer one-piece units, combining fireplace and mantelpiece as a single entity. Some of these were made of cast concrete and faced with marble or plain tiles, while others were constructed from brick.

MAINTAINING A GRATE
When open fires were in constant use, it was considered necessary that the grate was polished daily with black lead. Grate polish is still available, although modern heat-proof paints can now be used to reduce regular maintenance.

Blacking the grate
If you need to brighten up your grate, use a traditional-style graphite grate polish. This imparts an attractive silver-black finish that is ideal for highlighting decorative details. Apply it evenly with a brush, then polish with a soft cloth.

If a cast-iron grate shows signs of rusting, remove the rust with a wire brush – then either use grate polish or, for a stronger finish, apply stove paint. The latter is specially designed to withstand high temperatures and produces a matt black finish.

Polishing metal
Dull or lightly rusted polished steel can be revived with fine wire wool dipped in thin oil. Wear rubber gloves to protect your hands. Rub the surface to a bright finish, always working in the same direction, then use a cloth to wipe it dry. Alternatively, apply a proprietary abrasive liquid cleaner with a cloth.

Polish dull brass or copper with a suitable metal polish, following the maker's directions. If need be, use a heat-resistant transparent lacquer in order to protect the newly polished surface.

SOLID-FUEL STOVES

Wood-burning stoves are efficient space heaters that have been a popular means for heating homes in country areas of Europe and America since the eighteenth century. Made of cast iron or steel plate, and in some cases incorporating heat-retentive soapstone, they have been manufactured in a great variety of sizes and styles. Restored originals and reproductions of old designs are available from specialist suppliers.

The basic stove
Solid-fuel stoves are mostly designed to be freestanding, although you do sometimes see one fitted into a fireplace opening. Essentially, a stove is an enclosed chamber that is provided with a regulator for controlling the air flow. The fuel burns slowly and completely, the heat being absorbed by the casing then radiated out into the room. A stovepipe fitted into the top or rear carries away the smoke and also helps to radiate the heat. A hinged door, which may be glazed, or a removable top plate gives access for loading the fuel. Some stoves have a decorative top, while others provide a flat surface that can serve as a hotplate.

The general trend towards the use of cleaner fuels and central heating systems in the early twentieth century meant that old fireplaces and stoves became redundant in many homes. However, there is now a resurgence of interest in traditional heating methods and many disused fireplaces are being opened up or fitted with stoves.

Old stoves
It's easy to be tempted by an attractive antique stove – but make sure when buying one that it has been restored properly or is in genuinely good order. If you purchase an antique stove and intend to use it, establish that it is safe to use and that it meets

your heating requirements. Consult a stove specialist should you have any doubts.

A modern reproduction that can burn a variety of fuels may be a better option if you are planning to use a stove as your main source of heating, since most antique stoves are not airtight and are therefore much less efficient producers of heat.

Installation
In theory it is possible to fit a freestanding solid-fuel stove yourself. Nevertheless, it is advisable to employ or fully consult a specialist installer, as the relevant installation standards and regulations are constantly changing.

Most stove suppliers offer advice, plus an installation service designed to suit their customers' needs.

TILED FIREPLACES

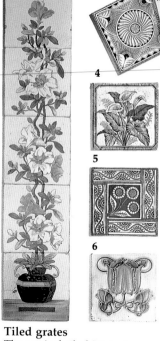

THE IMPORTANCE OF FIREPLACES *to interior design is evident from the degree of decoration applied to them throughout history. Mantelpieces of stone, wood and, later, cast iron – which relied as much on the colour and texture of the material as on carved embellishment for their effect – provided an ornamental frame around plain functional fireplace openings or sombre cast-iron grates. However, this was to change during the first half of the nineteenth century, as the use of coloured glazed tiles for grates and mantelpieces became increasingly popular.*

Fireplace tiles

The production of tin-glazed tiles had been developed in Holland during the sixteenth century. The Dutch designs and techniques inspired and influenced the English tile industry, which became established in the eighteenth century. The fire-resistant properties of clay tiles, as well as their tough easy-to-clean surface and decorative qualities, made them ideally suited for fireplace use.

As well as plain tiles and tiles in the Dutch 'Delft blue' style, decoratively moulded tiles were produced and a variety of fine tiles depicting domestic scenes, ancient and modern stories, animals and plants. Tile-manufacturing techniques newly introduced as a result of industrialization, combined with the mass production of cast-iron grates, meant that tiled grates could be produced fairly cheaply. They were soon to feature in the parlours of even modest homes. By the 1930s, fancy tiled cast-iron grates had finally given way to plainer types of fireplace.

Tiled grates

The typical tiled Victorian grate had splayed side panels with five 150mm (6in) square picture tiles fitted one above the other, although sometimes these were separated by plain or patterned half-tiles or quarter-tiles. It was also possible to buy sets of decorative tiles that, when assembled, made up a complete panel. The tiles were fixed with plaster into a pair of metal backing frames.

REPAIRING TILES

In order to extract a cracked tile for repair, it is necessary to remove the entire fireplace. Consequently, unless the break is particularly unsightly (if, for example, the tile is smashed and the parts have become dislodged), you may be better advised to live with the cracked tile.

If, on the other hand, you have bought a damaged grate from an architectural-salvage company or have to take out a fireplace temporarily for any reason, then it is clearly worth repairing any broken tiles.

Removing tiles

Remove any rust from the threaded fixing studs on the back of the grate with a wire brush. Apply penetrating oil to the threads to help free the nuts fitted on the studs. Remove the metal backing frame and prise out the tiles very carefully.

Cleaning tiles

Scrape off the old plaster from the backs of the tiles. These tiles are not grouted, so very little plaster will need to be cleaned from the edges. Wash them with a solution of detergent and distilled water. If tarry soot deposits have marked the surfaces, apply a coating of water-washable paint stripper. This will, of course, also remove paint if the tiles have been painted over.

Soak the tiles in distilled water before applying the stripper. This prevents the dirt being absorbed into the ceramic body. Remove the residue of the stripper from smooth-surfaced tiles with a plastic or wooden scraper, or with a bristle brush from textured ones. Wash the tiles in clean water and leave them to dry.

The grate is enhanced by the tile-panelled overmantel

Floral tiles decorate the sides and hood of the grate

Gluing the break

Dry-assemble the fragments to check the fit. If the tile is broken into several pieces, it may only be possible to re-assemble it in a certain order.

PVA is a good choice of adhesive for bonding a clean break in thick earthenware, and will dry clear. Wet the broken edges, then apply the glue to them evenly. Wipe squeezed-out glue from the surface of the tile with a damp cloth. Hold the pieces together with strips of sticky tape till the glue has set (1).

A two-part epoxy-resin adhesive mixed with a little titanium dioxide (available from pharmacists) will give a strong joint and is suitable for coloured tiles with a white ceramic body. Heat the tubes on a radiator to make the glue flow better, then mix the two components together and add the white titanium-dioxide powder. Apply the glue and assemble the pieces on a flat worktop covered with polyethylene sheeting. Wipe any glue from the surface of the tile with a cloth dampened with methylated spirits. Tape the join until the glue has set. If a white line remains, you can touch in the colour with enamel paint available from model shops (2).

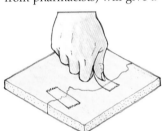
1 Hold the parts together with tape

Patching chipped edges

If the coloured glaze has been chipped at the edge as a result of the break, add some talcum powder to the epoxy adhesive to make a filler. Using a knife, apply the filler so it is just proud of the surface. When it has set, scrape it flush with a sharp knife blade. Paint the patch with enamel to match the colour of the tile.

Fitting the tiles

Set out the repaired tiles on the two backing frames and bolt them to the rear of the grate's side frames. Pack out the back of the tiles with small pieces of wood so that they butt snugly against the front (1). Apply plaster of Paris over the back of the tiles to fix them in place (2).

2 Touch in colours with paint

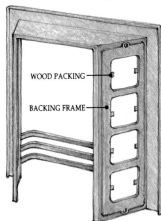
WOOD PACKING
BACKING FRAME
1 Pack out the back of the tiles

2 Fix the tiles with plaster

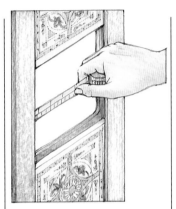
1 Measure the depth of the groove

REPLACING TILES

When you need to replace a tile but removing the entire fireplace is impractical, it is sometimes possible to work from the front. The replacement has to be cut down in width slightly – so if the tile is a rare one this may not be an appropriate repair.

Protecting your eyes, chip out the broken tile with a cold chisel; then clean out the grooves in each side of the iron frame. Measure the depth of the grooves (you will need to measure the deepest one if they are different) to determine how much to cut from the new tile (1). Reduce the width of the tile by half the depth of the groove, taking the material off both side edges, so that the design remains symmetrical (2). Wearing a mask and eye protection, remove the waste with a power grinder or with coarse abrasive paper.

Remove just enough to allow the tile to be fitted into the hole when one edge is pushed fully into the side groove. Apply a strip of self-adhesive tape to the face of the tile to form a tab, so you can hold the tile (3). Apply plaster of Paris to both side grooves and the back of the tile. Insert the tile fully into the side groove, then slide it back halfway into the other. Hold the tile until the plaster has set. Before it hardens, clean away the surplus from the face of the tile.

2 Ensure the design is symmetrical

3 Apply an adhesive-tape holding tab

HEARTH TILES

Cracked hearth tiles are common, as they tend to get broken by falling objects, such as fire irons. Loose ones also frequently occur, due to failure of the original cement adhesive. Old hearth tiles are not normally grouted. As a result, it is often possible to lift out loose tiles cleanly for replacement or repair.

Use a chisel and hammer to chip out some of the old cement to make sufficient room for fresh ceramic-tile adhesive, taking care not to damage the edges of the tiles still *in situ*.

Apply a thin bed of adhesive and press the new or repaired tiles into place. Use a straight batten to check that they are flush with the surrounding ones. If the old bedding cement is hard and difficult to remove, bond them in place by brushing on PVA adhesive.

ANATOMY OF A FIREPLACE

MANTELPIECE AND GRATE STYLES *have varied according to fashion, but the basic structural elements of a fireplace have not changed radically over the centuries. The early combination of a large stone or brick opening with a chimney built over it evolved from the obvious fact that smoke rises, rather than from a scientific understanding of how a well-devised flue system functions.*

Open wood and, later, coal-burning fires were very inefficient and it was not until Benjamin Thompson, known as Count Rumford, produced his thesis on the principles of fireplace design in 1799 that smaller grates and improvements in the internal shape of the opening were introduced.

ELEMENTS OF A FIREPLACE

A brick or stone enclosure **(1)** forms the basis of the fireplace. Variously known as the fireplace opening or recess or builder's opening, it may be set flush with the wall itself or built out into the room, forming a chimney breast **(2)**. A chimney breast rises through the height of the house, emerging through the roof to form a chimney stack. The gather **(3)** and flue **(4)** carry the smoke up the chimney. If the chimney is shared by several fireplaces on different floors, it may contain more than one flue.

The masonry over the fireplace opening is supported by a lintel or a brick arch **(5)**. Old inglenook fireplaces used massive oak beams, whereas a sturdy iron strap usually supports an early brick arch. Later fireplaces may have a straight arch supported by angle iron (an L-shaped iron bar), and early-twentieth-century ones often have a cast-concrete lintel. On no account should these structural beams and lintels be cut into or taken out without expert advice.

Constructed from non-combustible materials such as stone or tile-faced concrete, the hearth projects out into the room to protect the floor from falling embers **(6)**. In most old houses the hearth was set flush with the floor, although sometimes a superimposed hearth was used to raise the level. The area within the fireplace opening, which is known as the back hearth **(7)**, is usually level with the hearth itself.

A dog grate **(8)**, for burning wood or coal, may be placed on the back hearth. However, by the mid nineteenth century the cast-iron register grate, which filled in the opening, had become the fashion (SEE FIRE GRATES).

To complete the assembly, a mantelpiece – or fireplace surround, as it is often called today – is fitted to frame the grate or fireplace opening **(9)**. The mantelpiece itself may be constructed from stone, slate, marble, wood or cast iron. The walls around it may be finished with wood panelling, or more commonly with plaster, and in some instances the mantelpiece extends upwards to form an impressive chimneypiece. Mirrored overmantels were introduced in the late eighteenth century, and these became a common feature of Victorian sitting rooms.

Fireplaces
Poor design or lack of maintenance can cause smoke.
■ Modify fireplace opening (page 219).

Mantelpieces
The mantelpiece may be missing or in poor condition.
● Clean a soiled or stained marble mantel (page 213).
● Strip a painted mantelpiece, if appropriate (page 220).
■ Glue a cracked cast-iron surround (page 221).
▲ Or have it welded (pages 220, 221).
■ Replace a missing mantelpiece (page 222).

Grates
The grate may be damaged or missing.
● Maintain a grate regularly in order to preserve it (page 215).
■ Repair a damaged grate (page 220).
■ Replace missing or badly damaged decorative tiles (page 217).
■ Replace cracked or loose hearth tiles (pages 217, 221).
■ Choose and fit a replacement grate (pages 221, 222).

ASSESSING REPAIRS
● Easy even for beginners.
■ Fairly difficult. Good practical skills required.
▲ Difficult. Hire a professional.

Components of a fireplace
1 Fireplace opening
2 Chimney breast
3 Gather
4 Flue
5 Brick arch
6 Hearth
7 Back hearth
8 Dog grate
9 Mantelpiece

Flues
Blocked or decayed flues are unable to function properly.
▲ Have the chimney swept (page 219).
▲ Check that the flue is clear (page 72).
▲ Have the flue lined (page 74).
▲ Have the chimney repaired or rebuilt (pages 72, 73).

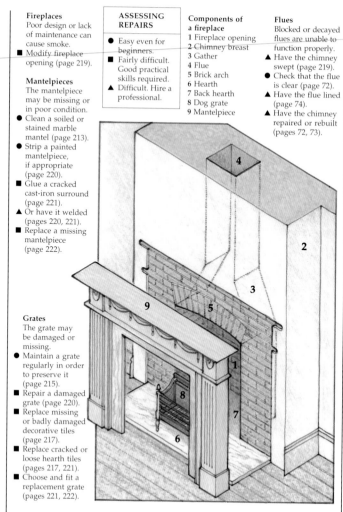

SOLID-FUEL OPEN FIRES

An open fire burning wood or coal is a cheerful sight, but if it is your only source of heat, as it was for centuries, the romantic image can soon fade – especially if the fire does not burn properly. Getting a fire started and keeping it alight then becomes a challenge, if not a chore.

How the system works

For wood and coal fires to burn well a good supply of air is needed under the grate **(1)**, as well as a means of escape for the hot gases and smoke **(2)**. The fireplace opening **(3)** safely contains the fuel, which is laid on an iron grate **(4)**. The barred grate holds the fuel clear of the hearth and allows air to circulate through it. As the fuel is consumed, waste ash drops through the grate so the fire isn't stifled. If the chimney is inadequate or the flow of air restricted, the fire will not function effectively.

How the system works
1 Air supply
2 Hot gases
3 Fireplace opening
4 Iron grate

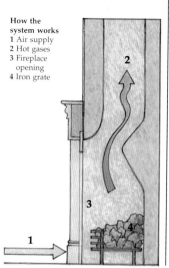

SMOKING FIREPLACES

The efficiency of an open fire depends not only on the supply of air but also on the size of the flue compared with the size of the fireplace opening. Count Rumford (see right) recommended that the cross-sectional area of the flue should be about a tenth of the size of the opening. However, fireplaces tended to be smaller after the mid nineteenth century. Modern flue-liner manufacturers favour a ratio of one to seven, and there are sizing charts published that give details of current standards.

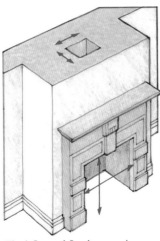

Check flue and fireplace opening dimensions (flue area/opening area ratio should be about 1:7 or 1:10).

Improving ventilation

If your fire smokes or won't burn properly, see if opening a window improves matters. If it does, you need better ventilation in the room.

One solution is to install a window vent, although this may cause an uncomfortable cross draught. A much more efficient form of ventilation is either a single ducted vent set into the floor in front of the fireplace or twin ducted vents set into the floor or external walls on each side of the chimney breast.

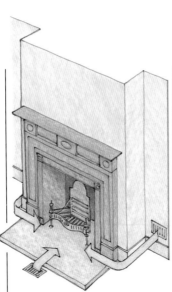

Alternative positions for air vents

Improving air flow

When wood and coal are burned, flammable gases, tarry substances, acids and dust are given off. However, because domestic fires are relatively inefficient not all of these substances are consumed. Instead, they rise up the chimney and some of them condense on the inside of the flue. Unburned carbon combines with these tars and acids, creating soot – which builds up over a period of time and effectively reduces the size of the flue.

Have chimneys that are regularly used swept at least twice a year – ideally before, during and at the end of the heating season. A soot-laden flue is a fire hazard, since the unburned elements of the soot can ignite, causing a chimney fire which may reach high temperatures and damage the chimney.

Modifying the flue

If a flue is too large, it can be reduced by fitting a flue liner. A variety of methods and materials are used (see FLUE LINERS), including liners made of flexible stainless steel, ceramic, lightweight concrete sections, or concrete cast *in situ*.

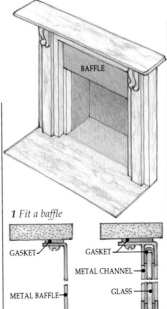

1 Fit a baffle

GASKET — METAL BAFFLE

GASKET — METAL CHANNEL — GLASS

2 Mount with discreet screw fixings

Modifying the fireplace opening

One way to reduce the size of the fireplace opening is to raise the hearth, though this may look out of character with the fireplace. In fact, it is probably both easier and more acceptable to install a baffle. This is fitted across the width of the opening **(1)** and can be made of steel, copper or heatproof glass.

In order to establish the size of the baffle panel, with the fire alight, temporarily tape a metal or thoroughly dampened plywood sheet across the top of the fireplace opening – and then adjust it up and down to determine the most effective position.

Make or commission a panel of the required size in a style and material that will harmonize with the mantelpiece. Mount the panel with discreet screw fixings and fit a fibreglass tape around the joint to act as a gasket **(2)**.

Fitting a hood or canopy

If a baffle is unsuitable or installing one is problematic, it may be worth asking a fireplace specialist whether fitting a metal smoke hood or canopy in the opening is the best solution.

RUMFORD'S REFORMS

Count Rumford in his essays on fireplaces proposed that the flue should be a specified proportion of the fireplace opening and that the area immediately above the fire should be narrowed down to form a throat. The throat causes the rising air to speed up as it passes through the constriction, thus improving the draught up the chimney.

To improve the efficiency of the fire further, he argued that the fireplace itself ought to be smaller and it should be lined with firebrick. The sides, he suggested, should be splayed to reflect the heat into the room, and the fireback made one-third the width of the opening. Also, the upper part of the fireback was to slope forward to reflect the heat. A smoke shelf formed at the throat by the sloping back helped prevent rainwater falling into the fire and was also thought to improve the air circulation within the flue.

Some large fireplaces in houses built before the late eighteenth century were modified in accordance with Rumford's principles. Some of these have splayed sides with marble or tiled panels around the fireplace opening, the original opening having been reduced.

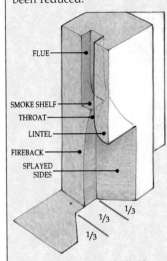

FLUE

SMOKE SHELF
THROAT
LINTEL
FIREBACK
SPLAYED SIDES

1/3   1/3   1/3

Diagram showing Rumford's ideas

RESTORING FIREPLACES

Chemical stripping, as shown on this partly stripped fireplace, will remove thick old paint to reveal the fine detail of the cast iron

ALTHOUGH FIREPLACES *contribute significantly to the character of a house, years of neglect can reduce a fine example to a poor state. Fortunately, however, the damage is often superficial.*

STRIPPING A MANTELPIECE

The efficiency of commercial chemical stripping processes and DIY stripping products has created a fashion for stripping painted fireplaces and mantelpieces. However, stripping them is not always appropriate, as some mantelpieces were intended to be painted. Stripping paint from a marble mantelpiece would seem to be an obvious improvement – but beware, a marbled paint finish on wood or slate can look like the real thing. It was also a common practice to treat softwood mantelpieces with wood grain effects imitating the appearance of the more expensive hardwoods.

Before proceeding to strip the paint, always try to detect which materials have been used in the construction of a mantelpiece. A wooden surround will feel warmer to the touch than one made of stone or cast iron. See if it feels as warm as the skirting.

The decorative mouldings applied to an Adam-style mantel were often made of plaster or gesso, and they can quite easily be damaged by stripping tools. If you discover a marbling paint finish that has been painted over, it is best either to seek the services of a specialist or to leave well alone.

Adam-style details made of gesso

Stripping methods

Cast-iron mantelpieces that have been removed can be efficiently stripped by an industrial stripping company, but it is better to strip all other materials by hand.

Modern chemical strippers can be used to remove paint from marble, wood and cast-iron mantelpieces. Use a gel or paste stripper, applying it according to the manufacturer's instructions. Try out the stripper on a small unobtrusive area first – and even if the test proves satisfactory, proceed carefully. Scrape off the softened paint (using a wooden or plastic spatula for marble) and clean out mouldings and carved detail with a bristle brush.

Apply fresh stripper in order to remove any residual film of paint, particularly from open-grained timber such as oak, then wash the wood down and wipe dry.

REPAIRING A GRATE

Cast iron is brittle and prone to cracking if struck sharply. As a result, the lift-off bars of grates are frequently missing, having been damaged and then discarded. Fortunately, however, missing or broken parts can be repaired or remade.

Grate bars

Cast iron can be welded. So if you have a grate that has broken bars, a blacksmith or a garage repair shop or fireplace specialist may well be able to repair them for you.

If the bars are missing, measure the size of the grate and prepare a dimensioned drawing to enable a fireplace specialist to supply or reproduce a replacement.

Architectural-salvage companies may also be of help. They sometimes keep useful parts from old grates that are no longer serviceable.

Measure the width and height between the locating holes, and the height above the floor or grate

Chipped edges

On a decoratively moulded grate a chipped edge may not show sufficiently to be a problem, but on a plain grate the defect may be obvious.

Providing the chip is not likely to be exposed to high temperatures, fill it with an epoxy metal filler. Overfill the defect slightly and, when the filler has set, rub down flush with the surface. Apply stove paint and grate polish to disguise the repair.

STRIPPING A GRATE

You sometimes come across grates no longer in use that have been painted to blend in with the décor. If you wish to restore the original finish, remove the paint with a chemical stripper. Hot-air stripper guns aren't suitable for this purpose, as the mass of metal dissipates the heat.

Cover the area around the fireplace with polyethylene sheeting and apply a gel or paste stripper, following the manufacturer's instructions. Remove the softened paint from flat surfaces with a scraper, and from moulded ones with a bristle brush. Wipe down and then apply grate polish or stove paint.

A grate that has been removed can be taken away for dipping in a chemical stripping tank – or for a bright finish you can have it sandblasted and polished. Remove any decorative tiles from a grate before you send it for sandblasting – and if vulnerable, for stripping, too.

Fill the crack with fire cement

BROKEN FIREBRICKS

Firebricks can be repaired *in situ*, but seriously decayed bricks need to be replaced.

Rake out a crack with the tip of a pointed trowel after wire-brushing to remove soot. Dampen the brick with clean water and fill the crack with fire cement or mould-able firebrick compound specially designed for this purpose. Press the cement in well with the trowel, and then smooth it flush with the surface. Do not use the fire for several days.

It is sometimes possible to repair a decayed brick in a similar way – but if it needs to be replaced, you will need to remove the grate in order to make the replacement. You may be able to purchase a matching firebrick from a fireplace specialist or from an architectural-salvage company. If not, cast one yourself using fire cement.

REPAIRING CAST IRON

If you lever out a cast-iron fireplace surround without removing the fixings from the lugs cast in the vertical edge of the jambs, that may cause the metal to fracture.

Have cracks in cast iron welded – or if the damaged part will not be subjected to high temperatures, repair it with a two-part epoxy glue.

Before gluing them, clean the surfaces with methylated spirits. Arrange the broken parts so gravity will hold them together or so they can be cramped properly.

Apply the adhesive to the broken edges and assemble the parts, making sure they are well seated. Cramp the parts or bind them with adhesive tape. Wipe off excess glue with methylated spirits.

FITTING A FIREPLACE

WITH THE DECLINE OF OPEN FIRES *in favour of more efficient or convenient methods – such as gas and electric appliances or central-heating systems – many old fireplaces were removed and the opening was filled in. Sometimes the fireplace was left in place and panelled over, making restoration a relatively straightforward job. Fortunately, there is a ready supply of original and reproduction grates and mantelpieces, so replacing a fireplace that has been taken out is not too difficult either, provided that the flue is in good order.*

REINSTATING AN OLD FIREPLACE

Before reinstating a fireplace, it is advisable to check that the fireplace opening, hearth and chimney are all in good condition, and that proposed alterations will comply with the Building Regulations.

These stipulate minimum requirements for the size and thickness of the hearth; the proximity to the chimney breast of combustible mater-ials, such as joinery, joists and floorboards; the thickness of the brickwork; height of chimney stacks, air supply, and type of flue lining. A certain amount of flexibility may be allowed in special circumstances, so it is worth seeking professional advice.

Clearing the opening

It is safer to leave chimney repairs to a professional, but you can prepare the opening and fit a fireplace yourself.

Demolition work always creates a lot of dust, so cover the floor and any furniture that cannot be removed from the room. Chop away the plaster with a club hammer and bolster chisel to expose the brickwork. Note the out-line of the original opening where it contrasts with the brick or blockwork infill. Cut out the infill material, taking care not to chip the original brickwork, especially the lintel. Remove all traces of

old rubble, leaving a clear opening. If the opening has been sealed with plaster-board over a timber frame, you will need to strip it out with a crow bar.

Selecting a fireplace

When choosing a grate or mantelpiece, keep in mind the type and size of room as well as the date of the house. Original examples can be bought from architectural-salvage companies, either fully restored or in need of some work. The price will reflect their condition and rarity. Alternatively, you could buy one of the many excellent reproductions that are available.

A register grate will need to be the right size – that is slightly larger than the mantelpiece opening. If this proves difficult, you could fill the space with marble, slate or tiled slips (narrow panels) plaster-bonded to the wall around the grate.

With luck, the overall size of the mantel can be deter-mined by the outline left in the old plaster where the original was removed.

Preparing the wall

Chop away plaster around the fireplace opening back to the brickwork, to leave a clearance of about 50mm (2in) all round the new mantelpiece when it is fitted.

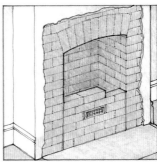

Remove the infill material

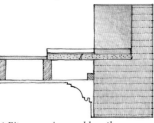

1 *Fit a superimposed hearth*

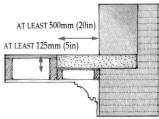

AT LEAST 500mm (20in)

AT LEAST 125mm (5in)

2 *A new hearth must be correct size*

Preparing the hearth

An inadequate hearth con-stitutes a fire risk. Cracked stone hearths should either be replaced or covered with a superimposed hearth **(1)**. To make one, have a slab of marble cut to size and set it level on a bed composed of 1 part cement, 1 part lime and 6 parts sand mortar. Build up the back hearth flush with the surface of the slab, using 1 part cement and 4 parts sand mortar.

If you are using tiles for the hearth and plan to have an open recess with a dog grate, lay the front and back hearth together on a 1:4 mix.

If alterations to the fire-place constitute new work, the constructional hearth **(2)** must be made to project at least 500mm (20in) in front of the fireplace opening and 150mm (6in) on each side. It must be at least 125mm (5in) thick, as stipulated in the Building Regulations.

FITTING A REGISTER GRATE

Before installing a register grate, make sure that the size of the flue is appropriate for the grate opening, and that there is a proper gather and throated lintel to divert the smoke into the flue.

Position the grate on the hearth, placing it centrally in the fireplace opening (or the chimney breast if they differ) and setting it against the wall. Check that it is plumb and square. If the opening is larger than the front plate, fill in the space at the sides with mortared brick. Should the top fall short, add a concrete lintel supported by the side brickwork (1).

Temporarily position the mantelpiece to see whether it fits snugly against the grate. If need be, pull the grate forward to butt up to the back edge of the mantel opening. Remove the mantelpiece, and then seal and secure the front plate to the wall with fire cement (2).

FITTING A MANTELPIECE

The method for fitting the mantelpiece will depend on its construction. Wooden and cast-iron types are relatively straightforward. Offer the mantel up to the grate and centralize it. Check that it is plumb and level. Mark the position of the screw holes through the fixing plates or lugs fitted to the side jambs (1). Remove the mantelpiece, then drill and plug the wall. Replace and fix the mantel with brass screws.

Backfill the area behind the grate with a lightweight concrete mixture of 6 parts perlite or vermiculite aggregate to 1 part cement. Fill the space through the damper aperture, and trowel the top surface so it slopes towards the opening (2).

1 Reduce the opening if required

2 Seal the front plate with cement

1 Mark the fixing holes

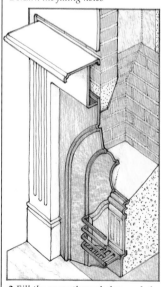

2 Fill the space through damper hole

Marble mantelpieces

Installing a marble mantelpiece requires a different technique, since the jambs, frieze and mantelshelf are usually separate pieces. If corbels located on wooden dowels or metal pins are to be fitted, bond them in place with fine casting plaster. Fit the jambs first. These have to be set the right distance apart. Also, check that they are plumb – at the same level at the top and in the same plane across the front (1).

Before fixing the mantelpiece in place, drill and plug the wall and fit fixing screws to fall inside the jambs close to the wire ties or hooks in the back edge. If no fixings are provided in the marble, use strips of expanded metal bonded with plaster.

First apply fine casting plaster on the hearth inside the base of each jamb. This sets quickly, so work fast. Bind the jambs with copper wire to the screws in the wall. Set them up accurately and apply a generous dab of plaster over the fixings. Apply generous fillets of the plaster adhesive inside the jambs, positioning them where you can reach to hold them securely.

Spread a fairly thin bed of plaster on the top meeting surfaces and place the frieze member across the jambs (2). Set the mantelshelf in place on a thin bed of plaster and bond it to the wall (3). Prop the shelf, if necessary, and check that it is level before the plaster sets.

Clean away excess plaster from the joints before it sets hard, using a wooden tool or a damp cloth if the plaster is still wet. Finally, make good the plasterwork around the mantelpiece with gypsum plaster before proceeding to redecorate the wall.

1 Check jambs are set true

2 Place frieze member across jambs

3 Set mantelshelf in place

REFERENCE

ENERGY CONSERVATION

G OVERNMENT AND PRESSURE GROUPS *are tireless in their attempts to persuade society to reduce carbon-dioxide emissions by limiting the use of fossil fuels through improvements to the energy efficiency of buildings.*

If you own a period house, you should consider how you can make improvements to assist in the effort to conserve energy – but at the same time you should ensure that any measures you take are not detrimental to the character of the house, and you also need to avoid the possibility of long-term deterioration to the fabric of the building. Architects, surveyors and local-authority Conservation Officers are able to offer specialist advice to assist you in your deliberations.

Shutters in good working order prevent draughts and reduce heat loss

BUILDING REGULATIONS

Energy efficiency comes within the scope of the Building Regulations (see LEGAL PROTECTION FOR OLD HOUSES), which are divided into various parts, each designated by a letter. Energy conservation is referred to as Part L, Conservation of Fuel and Power. The regulations apply to existing buildings when they are altered, extended or subjected to a new use. However, Part L makes it clear that the special characteristics of a historic building must be recognized. The aim of this revised part of the Building Regulations is to improve energy efficiency where it is practical to do so.

For existing buildings, Part L (2002) generally requires energy-conservation upgrading only for elements that are to be 'substantially replaced' as part of the work. The requirements do not apply to general repairs or to elements that do not need replacing.

Where proposed alterations or replacements could trigger Part L of the Building Regulations, care must be exercised in deciding whether or not such work will affect the building's character. If your house is listed, listed-building consent may be required. In some instances, a historic building may be in an almost totally original state and like-for-like replacement will be the only appropriate solution. In many cases, however, some thermal upgrading may be practicable – for example, between the joists within roof spaces and under suspended floors – provided it doesn't pose technical problems such as inhibiting ventilation. It may even be reasonable for this insulation to exceed the recommendations in Part L, in order to help make up for shortcomings elsewhere.

In terms of ventilation and moisture control, old houses can have quite different requirements from newer buildings. Houses built with solid walls without a damp-proof course and from permeable materials function differently from buildings constructed using modern standards and practices. As a result, these older buildings may require comparatively more ventilation to ensure their wellbeing. Nevertheless, a new extension to an old house will normally be expected to have a higher degree of thermal performance than the original building to which it is attached.

SAVING ENERGY

There are two ways to save energy. You can change the way you live – for example, by maintaining lower room temperatures and taking fewer baths or showers – although that is unlikely to be a popular choice. Or you can find ways to prevent heat escaping and also install more energy-efficient heating and lighting, then use these services more effectively. When weighing up the options for a period house, however, there are other important issues to bear in mind, too:

- Don't make unnecessary alterations to the building.
- Avoid making changes that could increase the risk of damage to other parts of the structure.
- Don't destroy important architectural features or spoil their appearance.

There are various measures open to you, ranging from inexpensive draughtproofing to efficient roof insulation, but each must be evaluated in the context of preserving the building's architectural style while saving energy.

Windows

Windows contribute greatly to the appearance of a house, and you should avoid taking any measures that would alter their proportions or details. Even the depth of the window opening and the position of the frame within it can be important historical features that need to be respected.

Double glazing is often cited as a desirable cost-saving improvement, but most systems on the market are unsuited to a period house. Double-glazed plastic (PVCu) windows can greatly detract from the appearance of an old house. And sealed double-glazed units are often made with thick glazing bars that are poorly proportioned compared with those of the original window. Worse still are poor facsimiles of glazing bars glued to the face of the glass.

Draughtproofing is cheap and effective

There is little point in replacing a venerable old window with a modern double-glazed unit if it's possible to repair and draughtproof the original. Draughtproofing and weatherstripping can be effective in reducing heating bills and noise levels and keeping dust out of the house.

Secondary glazing, fitted on the inside of the window, has similar advantages and, if the glazing is carefully designed, it can be relatively unobtrusive.

Shutters are charming and practical features that should never be discarded. Close-boarded or panelled shutters help to minimize heat loss at night and, when rooms are not in use, they can reduce or exclude harsh sunlight during the day. Internal shutters can also be draughtproofed. Hanging good-quality lined curtains is another effective way to reduce heat loss.

Doors
Original doors, especially those of historical value, should always be preserved and kept in good condition. Solid doors, in particular, have fairly good insulating properties, but a lot of heat may be wasted through gaps around the perimeter. Draughtproofing greatly improves matters.

Provided its design is in keeping with the interior, a draughtproof lobby might be a possibility, whereas the addition of a new external porch tends to look out of place on the majority of old houses.

Walls
Opportunities to improve the thermal performance of walls with external insulation is limited – it inevitably spoils the appearance of most period houses. Even insulating internally is likely to be a problem, as dimensional changes around window and door openings make the proposition unacceptable. The detailing around original features such as dadoes and cornices may be another difficulty.

Floors
The floors are often a distinctive feature of an old house, and so it is only when they have to be lifted – to install new services, for example – that there is a realistic opportunity to improve insulation.

Suspended floors constructed from floorboards can be insulated with comparative ease, either by installing sheet insulating material between the joists or by suspending blanket insulation on netting fixed to the underside of the joists. However, it's important to ensure that underfloor ventilation is not compromised as a result.

Solid floors can't be insulated successfully without first excavating beneath them, which is best avoided unless it becomes necessary in order to remedy some serious defect.

Roofs
Proposals to improve the thermal performance of the roof space have to be considered in relation to the use and performance of the rest of the building. Modern living tends to introduce more moisture into a house, especially the roof space, so effective measures may be required to ensure that the additional water vapour is able to escape harmlessly before it damages the fabric of the building (see ROOF VENTILATION).

There are a great many economical solutions to insulating roofs, and it is one of the most effective ways to reduce domestic fuel bills.

BUILDING SERVICES
People's expectations of comfort and convenience are higher now than in the past, and we all require central heating, electric lighting and power to run our modern appliances. When you live in an older property, it all requires careful planning to ensure the proposed work will be beneficial without compromising the essential character of your house.

The past few years have seen significant advances in efficient heating boilers and controls – so much so that the expense of replacing old worn-out equipment can often be recouped quickly in fuel savings. Long-life lamps (bulbs and strips) may be relatively expensive to buy, but they too save money in the long term.

Most hot-water storage cylinders are now supplied preinsulated, having a layer of foam sprayed on the outside. However, a lot of houses are still plumbed with older uninsulated copper cylinders that waste considerable amounts of heat. Wrapping a proprietary insulating jacket around the cylinder will start to have an effect on your heating bills within just a few months. Similarly, wrapping exposed hot-water pipes in foamed-plastic tubing is another energy-saving measure. Look especially for pipes running through unheated areas of the house, such as the cellar and roof space.

Preserving period fittings
In the rush to improve our plumbing and electrics, it is sometimes forgotten that period fixings and fittings are themselves of historic interest. You may have attractive cast-iron radiators, authentic period bathroom appliances, or antique light fittings and switches. Such appliances and fittings are all worthy of preservation.

There are various options to consider:

● Continue to use the fittings in their original state. However, this will probably not be possible in the case of electrical fittings – which are unlikely to comply with modern safety standards.
● It may be possible to have such fittings refurbished and brought up to standard.
● You could have unsafe or inefficient period fittings disconnected but left in place for their aesthetic appeal, and supplement the lighting or heating with other means.
● As a last resort, you could have fittings or appliances removed and put them into storage.

Avoiding unnecessary damage
When plumbing or rewiring older properties, take precautions to avoid damaging the fabric of the building.

Electrical wiring should be concealed whenever possible, but the cutting of the necessary holes and chases in plaster and woodwork must be done with care to keep damage to a minimum. Never cut through mouldings – and if possible, route the wires through existing voids in the walls and under suspended floors.

Plumbing can be even more destructive, but there are microbore and flexible pipes that are much easier to install in confined spaces.

It is also important to ensure there is no direct or indirect damage to period features resulting from the close proximity of services that emit heat or light.

ROT & INFESTATION

HOUSE TIMBERS *subjected to damp conditions with little or no ventilation are susceptible to decay. Prevention being better than cure, the best policy is to keep the house as watertight as possible and to undertake regular inspection and maintenance.*

Most period houses are likely to have had some form of insect infestation in their lifetime, so don't be overly alarmed if you see evidence of woodboring insects in your own home – there's a possibility that remedial treatment has been carried out already. Similarly, an outbreak of rot may have been rendered inactive by eradicating the damp conditions.

CHECKING FOR WOODWORM ATTACK

Insect attack manifests itself as flight holes produced by the emerging adult insects and possibly as a telltale layer of 'frass' – light-coloured droppings from woodboring beetle larvae. The wood can be unsound even when the flight holes are not extensive, since its interior may have been seriously weakened by a honeycomb of tunnels. Test the strength of the wood by probing it with the blade of a penknife. If in doubt about the seriousness of the problem, call in a specialist. It is usually possible to treat the wood with a preservative that will eradicate the woodworm and provide long-term protection against further outbreaks.

Treating a minor attack

If the outbreak is minor, you can use a fluid woodworm-treatment insecticide available from DIY stores. Brush a liberal coating onto the bare wood (painted or varnished surfaces have to be stripped first). Also, inject the fluid into flight holes, using an aerosol applicator or a can with a pointed spout.

Follow the manufacturer's instructions carefully, as these chemicals are hazardous. Most wood-preservative fluids are flammable, so avoid naked lights and don't smoke while working with them. Wear protective gloves, goggles and a respirator. Make sure the room is well ventilated.

Professional treatment

If the outbreak is extensive, your best bet is to call in an independent expert who has no vested interest in possible remedial work; or you can

contact a specialist treatment company, but make sure the company is a member of the British Wood Preserving and Damp Proofing Association. In either case, someone will inspect the property and give you an initial report. When the job is finished, you should expect to receive a guarantee for the work. Specialist operatives will clean then pressure-spray the infested wood. Where it is desirable to preserve a surface (if it has an original finish, for example), it is sometimes possible to have the preservative injected.

Completing the work

After treatment, consolidate any friable wood by applying a wood hardener to strengthen the fibres. There's no need to disguise the holes in old bare wood, but you can fill painted woodwork with cellulose filler when you redecorate.

WOODBORING INSECTS

Although most woodboring insects are beetles, they are generally known as woodworm, since it is usually the larvae that do the damage. The most common woodboring insects are the common furniture beetle, the deathwatch beetle, the house longhorn beetle and the powder-post beetle.

Seasoned but untreated house timbers – both softwoods and the sapwood of various hardwoods – are prone to infestation. Old plywood is also susceptible to attack, because the beetle larvae are partial to the glue that was used during the manufacturing process.

COMMON FURNITURE BEETLE

This small brown beetle, only about 3mm (⅛in) long, attacks joinery and the sapwood of structural timbers. It spends up to three years as a larva burrowing destructively through the wood, then emerges as an adult, leaving a flight hole about 1.5mm (¹⁄₁₆in) in diameter. If it is not treated, the infected wood can suffer from serious attack by generations of beetle larvae.

ACTUAL SIZE

DEATHWATCH BEETLE

The deathwatch beetle mainly attacks old decaying hardwoods such as oak. Its life cycle varies from five to twelve years, and the beetle emerges between April and June. It is brown in colour and about 6mm (¼in) in length. It produces a round flight hole approximately 3mm (⅛in) across.

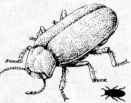

ACTUAL SIZE

HOUSE LONGHORN BEETLE

The house longhorn beetle is the largest of the woodboring insects. About 12mm (½in) long, it tends to attack the sapwood of modern softwoods. The beetle emerges in mid to late summer. It produces an oval hole measuring about 9 x 5mm (⅜ x ³⁄₁₆in). Its life cycle is from three to eleven years.

ACTUAL SIZE

POWDER-POST BEETLE

The powder-post beetle is approximately 6mm (¼in) long and leaves a small flight hole about 1.5mm (¹⁄₁₆in) in diameter. It only attacks the sapwood of hardwoods. The beetle emerges during the summer and has a life cycle of about ten months.

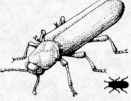

ACTUAL SIZE

WOODBORING WEEVIL

The woodboring weevil is no more than 3mm (⅛in) long and produces a small elongated hole. It thrives on decaying wood in damp conditions. Unlike other woodboring insects, the adults as well as the larvae infest the wood. The weevil is active throughout the year and has a life cycle of seven to nine months.

ACTUAL SIZE

WOOD ROT

Wood that's kept dry will not rot. All wood-rotting fungi, including dry rot, require a continuous supply of moisture in order to develop. Provided the source of water is removed, the fungus will die once the wood dries out. Wet rot and dry rot are the two main types of fungus that attack building timbers. The terms wet and dry can be misleading. For example, some people are under the false impression that building timbers are susceptible to dry rot as they dry out – and it is quite wrong to believe that the fungus can produce enough water to sustain itself after the original source of moisture has been removed. Dry rot is potentially the more serious, but only under specific conditions in a poorly maintained building. Get expert advice on the cause of the rot (usually rising or penetrating damp, but sometimes leaking plumbing) and have it rectified.

Wet-rot fungus under floorcovering

Wet rot

Many fungi will attack damp building timbers, but none is specially adapted to do so. All are basically woodland fungi and, to them, wet joists and skirting boards are no different to a pile of logs in the forest. Any type of decay other than dry rot is classed as wet rot, which frequently infects exposed and unprotected wood, such as window and door frames. It can also break out in damp cellars and where plumbing is leaking. Wet rot makes wood become soft and spongy, often exhibiting horizontal and cross-grain cracks. The fungus itself may take the form of grey-brown or black threadlike strands and, as the fungus grows, flat fruiting bodies may develop.

Depriving the fungus of moisture inhibits its further growth and stops continued deterioration of the wood.

appears as light-grey to black strands fanning out across infected surfaces.

The mature fungus develops a brown pancake-shaped fruiting body with a rough surface and a smooth white outer margin When the spores are released, they tend to cover surrounding surfaces with a layer of fine rust-red dust.

The fungus can grow rapidly – as much as 150mm (6in) in a month.

DEALING WITH WET ROT

First eradicate the cause of the damp – wet-rot fungus will only continue growing if the area stays wet.

If necessary, cut away structurally weakened wood and replace it with new preservative-treated timber, possibly sandwiching a strip of damp-proof membrane between the wood and any adjacent masonry.

Alternatively, treat the new sections of wood yourself after you have installed them. Brush on three generous coats of fungicidal wood preservative. Cover all wood in any surrounding area where moisture has been present. Wear, protective gloves, goggles and a respirator when handling preservatives.

Pressure injection of timber

For the treatment of larger sections of timber *in situ*, such as structural timbers, it is possible to have the wood impregnated, using a high-pressure injection system. This is undertaken by specialists, using one-way-valve plastic injectors that are inserted into holes drilled in the vulnerable areas. A special gun is connected that injects the fluid until it fully permeates the cells of the wood.

Dry rot

Outbreaks of dry rot occur on damp wood in dark unventilated conditions. Unlike wet rot, it cannot survive in well-ventilated areas.

Once established, dry rot spreads over timber and other materials as a network of fine tubular strands. These can spread very widely – even passing through cracks in building materials, such as plaster, stone, brick and concrete.

You may be able to detect an outbreak of dry rot by the pungent smell of the fungus. Painted wood may exhibit signs of buckling, and the surface may collapse due to decomposition of the wood.

The infected wood turns dark brown and, as it shrinks and splits, deep cracks form both with and across the grain, breaking the timber up into fine cubelike pieces. Dry rot

Mature fruiting body of dry rot

DEALING WITH DRY ROT

If you notice signs of dry rot, call in an independent expert who can identify the source of the damp, evaluate the extent of the damage, and tell you what needs to be done. This sometimes involves having to remove much of the surrounding material, and you should seek advice from your local Conservation Officer before allowing anyone to do that kind of work in a protected building.

Once the source of the moisture has been eliminated, the usual treatment recommended by many contractors involves stripping and replacing infected wood and plastered surfaces up to 1m (3ft) beyond the last sign of fungal attack, and applying a fungicidal solution to sterilize all woodwork, masonry and associated materials in the infected area. You may have little choice but to accept such drastic measures if a treatment guarantee is required. However, once the damp is eradicated and possibly extra ventilation provided, dry-rot growth will cease and chemical treatment may not be required – but be sure to get expert advice.

PAINT FOR PERIOD HOUSES

PAINT HAS TWO PURPOSES – *to protect and decorate. All paints are made up of three components: pigments, which provide colour; binder, which holds the pigments together and bonds them to the surface; and solvents, which act as a thinner for the mixture of pigment and binder.*

The protective properties of paint became more important in the seventeenth century as the use of imported softwoods, rather than more durable hardwoods, became more common. By the late nineteenth century making paint had become an industrial process, and the emerging chemical industry developed a wide range of synthetic pigments and media that were used in the manufacture of ready-made paints.

Period houses usually retain evidence of successive decorative schemes applied over the course of time, which reflect the changing fashions in interior decoration and the tastes of the occupants. If your house is of particular historic or architectural interest or has not undergone modernization in the recent past, you may wish to conserve old finishes and decorative schemes that have survived. If you find rare or historically interesting paint finishes or wallpapers, consider preserving them under modern lining paper, rather than stripping them or obliterating them with paint. Your local Conservation Officer will be able to give advice on how these finishes might be protected or conserved.

Period houses sometimes retain evidence of successive decorative schemes

PAINT BEFORE INDUSTRIALIZATION

Until the early twentieth century, house paints were traditionally either limewash, distempers or lead-based oil paints. All these paints are characterized by their water-permeable elastic qualities, which make them highly suitable for many older buildings.

Limewash

Limewash was applied as a decorative finish to a wide variety of different materials: stone, brickwork and timber framing. A cheap material, it provided protection, inside and outside, and was also an effective means of cleansing and disinfecting. The basic ingredients, still used today, were water and lime putty made from burnt limestone (calcium hydroxide). Often, coloured pigments were added.

Limewash is highly permeable – water vapour can escape easily, allowing the substrate to 'breathe'. Limewash can also be applied as a shelter coat to vulnerable materials, such as decayed stonework or old timber framing, where it acts as a 'sacrificial layer' and affords protection to the surface underneath.

Unlike modern masonry paints, limewash has a soft, subtle texture and varies in tone, which makes it a particularly attractive finish for many older buildings. It also weathers differently from modern paints, which tend to crack and blister in extremes, and can trap water in damp masonry. In contrast, limewash simply erodes gradually until a new coating is required.

Limewash has a subtlety of texture and tone that suits old buildings

But it can be as colourful as modern masonry paints

Making limewash
Limewash is a mixture of water and non-hydraulic lime putty. The lime putty can be purchased in tubs ready prepared. Generally, 1 part lime putty mixed with 2 parts water is sufficient, but you may need to adjust the mix to suit the porosity of the surface. You may also wish to add a coloured pigment, such as red or yellow ochre. A pigment should never be more than 10 per cent of the mix.

Before brushing on limewash, the surface needs to be wetted well, so that the surface will not absorb water from the limewash too quickly. It is important to wear goggles and gloves when mixing and applying limewash, as lime is a caustic substance.

Depending on the weather, it can take several hours, or even days, for limewash to dry.

Wear goggles and gloves

Distemper
A mixture of chalk and glue, 'soft' distemper – usually called simply 'distemper' – can be tinted with pigments and is very permeable. Because it can be brushed onto freshly applied plaster, distemper was commonly used as 'a builder's finish' – the temporary decoration applied to a house while the plaster carbonated and before the application of oil paints. It is an inexpensive finish, but having been mixed has to be applied within a few days. Distemper is not washable and takes marks easily, but it is perfectly suitable as a finish for ceilings and cornices.

Mixing distemper with materials such as casein – a binder of milk solids – produces what is sometimes referred to as 'milk paint'. Mixing it with linseed oil makes 'oil-bound distemper'. Being relatively hard, oil-bound distemper was the first washable permeable paint. It is still available from specialist paint manufacturers. These modified distempers, the forerunners of modern emulsions, are not as permeable as soft distemper.

Oil paints
Until the 1950s the basic ingredients of most oil paints were lead white and linseed oil. Oil paints were applied to a wide range of materials – wood, metal, stone and plaster – both internally and externally. Lead-based oil paint is an extremely durable and attractive finish, which weathers better than many modern gloss paints. Lead is no longer added to paint, and since 1992 its use is prohibited except for approved applications on Grade I and II* listed buildings (Grade A in Scotland).

MODERN PAINTS
Today, paints contain non-toxic pigments such as zinc and titanium instead of lead; and fast-drying alkyd resins have replaced traditional linseed oil. Vinyl emulsions provide a washable and more durable alternative to distemper.

Silicate (mineral) paints
Modern silicate paints are porous and soak into the substrate, where they bond with minerals within the underlying structure. As a result, they will last for at least 15 years.

HISTORICALLY ACCURATE SCHEMES
If you want to reinstate a historically accurate paint scheme or would just like to know the kind of colours likely to have been used during the history of your house, you could try to identify the dates when major alterations were carried out, as they may furnish clues to the styles fashionable at the time. To get a feel for a particular era, it is worth consulting books of contemporary paintings that illustrate decorative schemes popular during the relevant periods.

However, a more accurate record may exist in the accumulated layers of paint within the house itself, although teasing out the information can only be done by a skilled professional. After reviewing the historical and structural evidence, a specialist architectural-paint researcher will remove small sections of paint and substrate. These fragments are then examined under high magnification to determine the sequence of paints applied. This reveals the full story of how your house was decorated. The practice of taking 'paint scrapes' is now considered to be an old-fashioned method of paint analysis, and one that can be highly inaccurate.

Armed with your detailed analysis, you may be able to conserve or re-create one of the original colour schemes. Whether you decide to do this or prefer to decorate rooms in colours that reflect your own taste, there is now a wide range of historically matched colours and wallpapers available, some of them from specialist suppliers.

Whatever you decide to do, it is recommended that whenever possible you leave existing paint layers and any traces of old wallcoverings in place, as they constitute valuable evidence of what was done in the past. Areas of flaking paint and damaged woodwork have to be refurbished, but there is usually no need to strip well-bonded paint. Furthermore, old lead-based oil paint can be a health hazard should it ever become necessary to remove it. When rubbing down old paintwork, it is therefore best to assume it is lead-based. Use wet-and-dry paper dipped in water and wear a face mask. Burning off old lead paint creates toxic fumes.

The detail of decorative cornices and mouldings may be obscured by layers of soft distemper, which can be removed safely with water and a scrubbing brush.

Sympathetic modern colour scheme

History trapped in layers of paint

Changing colours and finishes
Unless your house is a Grade I or Grade II* listed building, changing the interior colour scheme is unlikely to require consent. But if you live in a listed building or in a conservation area, or if your house forms part of a significant group, it is advisable to consult a Conservation Officer before you make major changes to exterior colours or introduce new finishes.

PROFESSIONAL HELP

THERE ARE A NUMBER OF KEY PROFESSIONALS who can help you plan and carry out work on an old house. It is tempting to dispense with professional services in order to save money, but that often proves to be a false economy. You need people who are experienced in dealing with older properties, and who understand what you want to do and why you want to do it. Regrettably, many building professionals are trained and experienced in modern construction methods but are unable to handle the complexities and special requirements of repairing or modifying a period house.

FINDING THE RIGHT PROFESSIONAL
Depending on the size, complexity and nature of your building project, you may need to consult or employ one or more of the following.

Architect
The term architect is a protected title in the UK. Only a person registered with the Architects Registration Board can be called an architect. There are more than 20,000 architects registered in the UK, but only a small percentage specialize in the repair of old buildings. The Royal Institute of British Architects (RIBA) keeps a register of such specialists and can supply you with a list of recommendations. You may also wish to consult the list of Architects Accredited in Building Conservation (RIBA/AABC), which is held by RIBA, or the lists of architects held by the Society for the Protection of Ancient Buildings (SPAB).

As well as RIBA, there are regional organizations you can turn to, such as the Royal Society of Architects in Wales (RSAW), the Royal Incorporation of Architects in Scotland (RIAS), who run their own accreditation scheme, and the Royal Society of Ulster Architects (RSUA). All architects are trained in building design, but those who specialize in working on older buildings bring specific expertise to the project. They have a broad knowledge of past construction methods, and should be skilled at blending new work with old. An architect can prepare all the documentation you need to apply for listed-building consent, planning permission or Building Regulations approval. If you wish, you can entrust on-site supervision and administration of the contract to your architect.

Building surveyor
Surveyors of this type can play a role similar to an architect's, but generally they are not trained as designers. Within the Royal Institute of Chartered Surveyors there is a building conservation group that maintains its own list of members accredited in building conservation.

Structural engineer
This type of specialist will carry out a structural survey of a property you are thinking of buying, or help you decide on the most suitable structural repairs for an old building. It is best to employ an engineer who has had experience of surveying older houses. The Institution of Civil Engineers (ICE) and the Institution of Structural Engineers (IStrucE) hold lists of engineers accredited in building conservation – the Conservation Accreditation Register of Engineers (CARE).

Quantity surveyor
For a large project, you might consider hiring a quantity surveyor who will deal with the financial control of the work and contractual issues.

Services engineer
Also known as mechanical or electrical engineers, these professionals can provide advice on heating, drainage, plumbing and electrics.

Project manager
This is someone you can employ either to coordinate a team of professionals or to act as your agent on a large building project.

Builder
Most architects or surveyors can help you find a suitable builder, but if you are running the job yourself it is essential to employ a builder who has the expertise and knowledge to work on an old house. Ask for personal recommendations, check up on references, and look at other jobs the builder has done in the past. Have a contract drawn up, which includes dates for starting and finishing the work. If possible, get a firm price, not just an estimate; but if certain aspects are difficult to cost in advance, establish with the builder how any additional work is to be costed. If at any stage you suspect a builder of serving his own interests by proposing unnecessary work, you should seek independent professional advice from an architect or building surveyor.

Specialist supplier
There is a wide range of suppliers who stock materials appropriate for repairing period houses – lime putty, plasters and renders, bricks and roofcoverings to match old stock, traditional paints, and so on. These suppliers can also give advice on how the materials should be used.

One useful source of such information is the website **www.buildingconservation. com**.

Conservation specialist
Materials and fittings used in building period houses are often vulnerable and could be irretrievably damaged by inexpert treatment. To find specialists for tasks such as the cleaning of masonry or paint, mortar analysis, or the installation of services in protected houses, try **www.buildingconservation. com**.

Conservation Officer
The Conservation Officer employed by your local planning authority is an invaluable source of technical advice on repairs and improvements, and can also give advice on proposed extensions and alterations to old buildings.

GRANTS
Although financial help is not widely available, grant schemes are operated by some local authorities. If your period house is listed Grade I or Grade II*, the work may be eligible for a grant from English Heritage as part of their Historic Buildings, Monuments and Designed Landscapes grants scheme. The grant application is more likely to be successful if it meets national and regional priorities, which are outlined in the application pack. The application must demonstrate that there is financial need for a grant and that the work will be undertaken within two years.

You may also wish to visit the website of the Funds for Historic Buildings (**www. ffhb.org.uk**). This provides a guide to funding for anyone seeking to repair, restore or convert a historic building and includes all the material previously contained in the Architectural Heritage Fund's Directory of Funding Sources.

GLOSSARY OF TERMS

A

Acanthus
Classical decorative motif based on the large deeply cut leaves of a plant native to the Mediterranean region.

Aggregate
Particles of sand or stone, mixed with materials such as cement or lime to make concrete or mortar.

Annealing
The process of removing stresses in a material, usually by heating.

Anthemion
Stylized floral motif derived from Greek and Roman architecture, widely used in neo-classical ornamentation. The most common form was based on honeysuckle flowers and leaves.

Architrave
A moulding that surrounds a door or window. *or* The lowest horizontal moulding of a classical entablature.

Arris
The sharp edge at the meeting of two flat surfaces.

Ashlar
Dressed and finely jointed stonework.

Astragal
Another term for glazing bar. *or* A moulding comprising a half-round raised central spine with a cove or square fillet on each side.

B

Band course
A square-faced horizontal moulding in stucco or stone.

Bead
A narrow strip of wood with a half-round profile.

Bevel
A surface that meets another at an angle of less than 90 degrees. See also CHAMFER.

Binding
A term used to describe a door or

hinged casement that is rubbing against the surrounding frame.

Bolection moulding
Wooden moulding used to cover the joint between members that have surfaces at different levels.

Bonding
A method of interlocking bricks or stone blocks in order to create a stable structure.

Bow
To bend as a result of uneven shrinkage – usually in reference to wood.

Brace
A diagonal member used to prevent a battened door from sagging.

Brushing out
Spreading paint finishes to avoid runs or uneven coverage.

Burr
A rough raised edge left on metal after cutting or filing.

Butt
To fit snugly against.

C

Cantilever
A projecting beam that is secured at one end only.

Capital
The topmost part of a column or pilaster.

Caryatid
A supporting column or pilaster in the form of a female figure.

Caulking
Weatherproofing a joint by sealing with a non-setting mastic.

Cement
A combination of powdered calcined limestone and clay mixed with water and an aggregate to make mortar or concrete.

Chair rail
Another term for dado rail.

Chamfer
A 45-degree bevel.

Clamp
A primitive kiln for firing, comprising a stack of unbaked bricks and fuel encased in a mound of old bricks and clay.

Compo
A mixture of materials such as whiting and glue used to fashion raised decoration on a frame etc.

Conservation
Work done to ensure that a building retains its historical or architectural character.

Console
A decorative bracket used to support a doorhood, soffit, etc.

Conversion
Altering the whole or part of a building to serve a different purpose.

Coping stones
Stone slabs laid on top of a masonry wall to shed rainwater.

Corbel
A bracket, usually of stone, brick or plaster.

Corbelling
A projection in masonry, formed by building successive courses outwards in a stepped fashion, one above the other.

Cornice
A decorative moulding forming a junction between the walls of a room and the ceiling. *or* The uppermost horizontal moulding of a classical entablature.

Cove
A concave moulding.

Cross grain
Wood grain that deviates from the main axis of a length of timber.

Cup
To bend, usually as a result of shrinkage. Cupping occurs across the width of a piece of wood.

D

Dado
A decorative or protective panel

applied to the lower part of an interior wall.

Damp-proof course (DPC)
A layer of impervious material that prevents moisture rising from the ground into the walls of a building.

Damp-proof membrane (DPM)
A sheet of impervious material that prevents moisture rising through a floor.

Dentil
One of a row of small toothlike blocks that form part of a classical cornice.

Distressing
The act of giving something an aged appearance by various measures, such as staining and denting.

Dormer
A structure projecting from a roof, usually housing a window.

Dressing
The act of cutting, shaping and finishing masonry or metal etc.

Drip groove
A groove cut in the underside of a projection such as a moulding or sill to cause rainwater to drip to the ground.

Dripstone
A moulding placed above a door or window opening to deflect rainwater. Also known as a label or hood mould.

Duo-pitched roof
A roof that slopes in two directions.

E

Edge grain
Grain (growth rings) running at not less than 45 degrees to the faces of a piece of wood. Also known as quarter-sawn timber.

Efflorescence
A white powdery deposit on masonry or plaster caused by mineral salts migrating to the surface as a result of evaporation.

GLOSSARY OF TERMS

Elevation
Side view of a building or other structure.

End grain
The surface of wood exposed after cutting across the fibres.

Engaged
Attached to a wall (e.g. an engaged column).

Enrichments
Decorative features, usually added separately to a cornice, frieze, etc.

Entablature
The band of mouldings near the top of a façade, divided into cornice, frieze and architrave.

Exfoliation
See SPALLING.

Expanded metal
A type of lathing for plasterwork made by slitting and stretching metal sheet.

F

Fabric
The material(s) from which a building or part of a building is constructed.

Façade
The exterior face of a building.

Facings
Weather-resistant bricks used for constructing exterior brickwork.

Faience
Glazed terracotta.

Feathering
Brushing out the edge of paint or other finishes.

Festoon
See SWAG.

Fettling
Cleaning up a casting by removing excess material.

Fillet
Strip of mortar used to seal the junction between two surfaces, such as a roof and a wall. *or* A

small square-section moulding, usually in wood.

Finial
A decorative spike or post set at the apex of a gable or on the point of a spire, tower, etc.

Flashing
A weatherproof strip (usually of metal) used to cover the junction between a roof and a wall or chimney, or between one part of a roof and another.

Frieze
The strip of wall between a ceiling cornice and a picture rail. *or* The central panel of a classical entablature.

Frog
The recess in the top face of a brick. Some bricks have a frog in the bedding face, too.

G

Gable
The triangular section of wall at the end of a duo-pitched roof. Also known as a gable end.

Gable roof
Another, commonly used, term for a duo-pitched roof.

Galvanized
Protected with an electroplated or dipped zinc coating.

Gather
The funnel-shaped smoke outlet leading to the flue above a fireplace.

Gauging
The mixing of a little cement or gypsum with lime mortar or plaster to hasten setting time.

Gesso
A mixture of plaster and size used as a base coat for gilding or painting.

Glazing points
Small triangular fixings used to hold window glass in a rebate.

Grounds
Rough strips of wood attached to masonry as fixing points for panelling, skirting, etc.

H

Hardwood
Wood cut from broadleaved (mostly deciduous) trees belonging to the botanical group *Angiospermae*.

Head
The topmost horizontal component of a casement-window or exterior-door frame.

Header
A brick or stone block laid so the end is visible.

Hingebound
A term used to describe a door or casement that cannot be closed properly due to a misaligned or poorly fitted hinge.

Hip
The external sloping corner formed by two angled faces of a pitched roof.

Horn
An extension of a sliding-sash stile that strengthens the joint between it and the meeting rail. *or* The extension of a door stile, designed to protect a new door from accidental damage during transportation.

Housing
A groove cut across the grain of a wooden component.

I

Indenting
Patching damaged masonry by cutting out a worn area and inserting new stone.

Intervention
Any action that modifies the fabric of a building.

J

Jamb
The vertical side member of a doorframe or casement-window frame.

K

Keying
Abrading or incising a surface to

provide a better grip for gluing or plastering etc.

Knapping
The process of shaping a flint by chipping flakes from its edges.

L

Laying off
Finishing an application of paint or varnish etc. with upward brush strokes.

Lintel
A beam supporting the masonry above a door or window opening.

Lipping
Protective solid-wood strip glued to the edge of a man-made board.

M

Maintenance
Regular upkeep of a building, to prevent it requiring major repairs.

Mitre
A joint between two pieces of wood formed by cutting bevels of equal angle (usually 45 degrees) at the ends of both pieces.

Modillion
One of a row of brackets, usually decorated with acanthus leaves, forming part of a cornice.

Mortar
A mixture of cement or lime with an aggregate and water for bonding bricks or blocks of stone.

Mullion
A vertical member separating two windows.

Muntin
A vertical member between panels (e.g. of a door).

N

Newel
A substantial post at either end of a balustrade.

O

Orders
The five classical architectural

GLOSSARY OF TERMS

styles that provided the basis for the proportions and detailing of neo-classical buildings.

Overmantel
A framed mirror surmounting a fireplace.

Overthrow
A decorative metal archway, often incorporating a lantern, spanning a gateway.

Ovolo
A quarter-round convex moulding.

Oxidize
To form a layer of metal oxide, as in rusting.

P

Pallets
Wooden plugs built into masonry joints on each side of a door or window opening to serve as fixing points for the frame.

Parapet
A low wall at the edge of a roof or balcony.

Pargeting
Decorative low-relief stuccowork. *or* Lime-mortar flue lining.

Paterae
Floral motifs, often alternating with modillions when used to decorate cornices.

Pediment
A triangular structure forming a gable on a Greek or Roman temple. Neo-classical doors and windows were often surmounted by a pediment.

Pilaster
A shallow square-section engaged column.

Pilot hole
A small-diameter hole drilled before inserting a screw to act as a guide for the thread.

Pin holes
Small holes caused by cutting into voids made by gas bubbles formed in cast metal during the casting process.

Pitch
The slope of a roof.

Plan
Top view of a building, room, piece of furniture, etc.

Planted moulding
A wooden moulding applied separately. Also known as an applied moulding.

Pointing
The act of shaping the mortar joints between bricks or stone blocks. *or* The mortar joints themselves.

Pontil
Iron rod used for spinning glass.

Poultice
An absorbent paste applied to masonry to draw out stains.

Preservation
Retaining a building in its present condition by retarding deterioration.

Pugging
The act of mixing and kneading clay with water to produce an even consistency. *or* Material inserted between wooden flooring and ceiling to reduce transmission of sound.

Purlin
A horizontal beam providing intermediate support for rafters or sheet roofing.

Q

Quarry
A square or diamond-shape pane of glass for a leaded light.

Quirk
A continuous groove in an architectural moulding.

Quoin
Masonry forming the outer corner of a wall.

R

Rafter
One of a set of parallel sloping beams that form the main structural element of a roof.

Raised grain
Roughening of the surface of a piece of wood, caused by the fibres swelling due to the presence of water.

Rebate
A stepped recess along the edge of a workpiece or component. Also known as a rabbet.

Reconstruction
The process of returning a building to a previous condition or style on the basis of documentary or physical evidence.

Relieving arch
A masonry arch built above a door or window to deflect the load away from a lintel.

Render
A mixture of cement, lime and sand (or lime and sand) used for coating the exterior of a wall. *or* To coat a wall with render.

Renovation
Making as new. Renovation usually involves more work than is required to repair the fabric of the building.

Repair
Work that is beyond the scope of regular maintenance, done in order to remedy defects such as significant decay or damage. Repairing involves returning a building to good order without significant alteration.

Repoussé work
Thin decorative metalwork raised in relief by hammering the metal from behind.

Restoration
Reinstating parts of a building to return it to its original appearance.

Reveal
The vertical side of a door or window opening, between the frame and the face of the wall.

Reversible
Capable of being returned to the present state or condition without any significant damage or alteration.

Ridge
The horizontal joint line at the apex of a pitched roof.

Ridge board
The horizontal beam to which the rafters are joined at the apex of a roof.

Roof cresting
A decorative ceramic or metal strip running along the ridge of a roof.

Rose plate
A backing plate for a door knob.

Roundel
A small circular piece of crown glass containing the pontil mark, used as a decorative element in leaded lights.

Rub joint
A joint made by sliding one glued component from side to side on another until suction causes the joint to stick.

Running mould
A template used for shaping stucco or plaster mouldings.

Rustication
Bevelled or chanelled joints between blocks of masonry.

S

Saddle bar
A metal bar used to reinforce a leaded light.

Sandblasting
The process of cleaning a surface (usually metal or masonry) with a jet of abrasive grit or sand. See also SHOT BLASTING.

Sapwood
New wood surrounding the denser heartwood of a tree.

Sash
A glazed frame forming part of a window, sometimes fixed but more often made to slide or to pivot on hinges.

Scribe
To mark and shape the edge of a workpiece so that it will fit exactly against another surface. *or* To mark by scratching with a pointed tool.

GLOSSARY OF TERMS

Scrim
Open-weave fabric used for reinforcing plasterwork.

Seasoning
Reducing the moisture content of wood.

Secret nailing
A method of securing wooden components with concealed nail fixings.

Selvage
The irregular untrimmed edge on each side of a length or roll of wallcovering.

Setting in
Making vertical cuts with a chisel or gouge to establish the outline of a motif carved in relief.

Sherardized
Covered with a protective coating produced by heating iron or steel in a container together with zinc dust.

Shim
A thin packing piece.

Short grain
This occurs where the general direction of the wood fibres runs across a narrow section of timber.

Shot blasting
A similar process to sandblasting but using iron or steel particles instead of sand or grit.

Show wood
Wood intended to be seen, often coated with a clear finish.

Sill
The lowest horizontal member of a window frame.

Skirting
A board used to cover the junction between an interior wall and the floor.

Soffit
The underside of a structure such as an arch, stair or beam.

Softwood
Wood cut from coniferous trees belonging to the botanical group *Gymnospermae*.

Soldiers
Vertical wooden grounds to which a skirting is fixed.

Spalling
Flaking of the outer face of masonry, often caused by expanding moisture in freezing conditions.

Spandrel
Panelling used to fill the triangular shape below a stair string.

Sprigs
Small cut nails used for fixing a window pane in a rebate.

Sprue
Excess metal left on a casting due to the metal solidifying in the channel through which it was introduced into the mould.

Stile
The vertical member on each side of a door or window sash.

Stippling
Applying paint or other finishes as spots, using the tip of a brush.

Straight grain
Grain (wood fibres) aligning with the main axis of timber.

Straightedge
A length of timber or metal that has at least one true edge – used for drawing straight lines or for scraping a surface level.

Stretcher
A brick or stone block laid so that one of its long faces is visible.

String
A board running from one floor level to another into which the treads and risers of a staircase are jointed. Also known as a stringer or stringboard.

String course
A horizontal strip of moulded stone or stucco (similar to a cornice but smaller in scale) that extends across a façade.

Stucco
A type of render used to imitate stone, often with details such as mouldings and cornices.

Stuck moulding
A moulding that is cut into a piece of wood. Also known as a struck or integral moulding.

Stud wall
An interior timber-frame wall sheathed with lath and plaster or plasterboard.

Studs
The vertical wooden posts within a timber-frame wall.

Swag
An ornamental motif depicting a hanging garland. Also known as a festoon.

T

Template
A cut-out pattern used to help shape a workpiece accurately.

Thixotropic
A term used to describe paints that have a gel-like consistency until stirred or applied, at which point they liquefy.

Throat
The narrow aperture at the base of a flue, designed to cause rising air and smoke to speed up.

Timber-frame wall
A wall composed of structural wooden components, sheathed on both sides or infilled with masonry or wattle and daub.

Transom
A horizontal rail separating a fanlight from a door. *or* A horizontal window-frame member.

U

Undercutting
Cutting away material from the edges of a recess to form a dovetail-shape cavity.

V

Valley
Trough formed at the junction of two sloping roof surfaces.

Vapour barrier
A layer of impervious material that prevents the passage of moisture-laden air.

Vermiculation
A form of carved surface dressing for stonework, composed of closely packed shallow recesses separated by wavy ridges said to resemble worm tracks.

Volute
A decorative spiral scroll found on column capitals, consoles, etc.

Voussoir
A wedge-shape member of a brick or stone arch.

W

Wainscoting
Wall panelling made of painted oak or softwood.

Wall plate
A horizontal wooden member placed along the top of a wall to support the ends of joists and rafters, thus spreading their load.

Wet-and-dry paper
An abrasive paper consisting of silicon-carbide particles glued to a waterproof backing, used to smooth new paintwork or varnish between coats.

Window guard
A low metal panel, grille or railing placed across a window at sill level on the outside.

Withe
A masonry partition dividing one flue from another in a chimney. Also known as a midfeather.

Work hardening
Increasing the strength or hardness of a metal workpiece by manipulation, such as stretching, bending, hammering, etc.

INDEX

INDEX

INDEX

INDEX

ACKNOWLEDGMENTS

The authors and producers are grateful to the following companies, organizations and individuals for their assistance in the production of this book.

Acquisitions Fireplaces Ltd
The Fan Museum
Aristocast Onginals Ltd
Artisan
BCM Contracts Ltd
Brighton Borough Council
Chris Blanchett
The Brooking Collection Trust
R. Bleasdale (Spirals)
Phillip Bradbury Glass
Brickmatch Ltd
Britannia Architectural Metalwork
   & Restoration
British Gypsum Ltd
British Society of
   Master Glass Painters
R. W. Brunskill
Building Adhesives Ltd
The Building Conservation Trust
Richard Burbidge Ltd
Barbara & Tony Burrough
C. D. (UK) Ltd
Constance & Jack Cairns
Capricorn Architectural
   Ironwork Ltd
The Carving Workshop
Cattles Precision Woodwork
Cement & Plaster Mouldings Ltd
Cico Chimney Linings Ltd
Pat & Jim Clark

Classic Designs
Classical Concrete Ltd
Clayton-Munroe Ltd
Clean Walls Ltd
Comyn Ching Ltd
Cookson Industrial Materials Ltd
Peter Cornish
County Forge Ltd
Crittal Windows Ltd
Anthony Cross
Crown Berger Ltd
The Department of the Environment
Barbara Doig
Exchem Mining & Construction Ltd
Feltham Glass Works
Geoff & Mareszka Fleming
Forgeries Ltd
The Georgian Group
Gray & McDonnell Ltd
The Hardwood Flooring Co. Ltd
E. J. Harmer & Co. Ltd
Harrison Thompson & Co. Ltd
Haslemere Design Ltd
Hayes & Howe
Tony Herbert
James Hetley & Co. Ltd
Allen Charles Hill
Hodkin & Jones Ltd
Ibstock Building Products Ltd
ICI Chemicals & Polymers Ltd

Jackfield Tile Museum
Jackson & Cox Architectural
   Restoration Ltd
H. & R. Johnson Tiles Ltd
K.C.C. Planning Department
Lamont Antiques Ltd
Langlow Products Ltd
The Lead Development Association
Warwick Leadlay
J. Legge & Co. Ltd
Luminaries Stained Glass Studio
Marflex International Ltd
Marston & Langinger Ltd
The Metalock Organisation
The Michelmersh
   Brick & Tile Co. Ltd
E. G. Millar (Plastering) Ltd
Mr & Mrs Scovell
Mumford & Wood Ltd
National Corrosion Service
Nero Designs
The Original Box Sash Window Co.
The Paint Research Association
Mr & Mrs Pery-Knox-Gore
Pilkington Glass Ltd
Plantation Shutters
The Post Office Archives
Protim Services Ltd
The Rainbow Glass Co.
Red Bank Manufacturing Co. Ltd

Rentokil Ltd
Ridout Associates Ltd
Dennis Ruabon Ltd
John Sambrook
B. C. Sanitan Ltd
The Society for the Protection
   of Ancient Buildings
Solaglass Technical Advisory Service
Stag Polymer & Sealants Ltd
Stained Glass Supplies
Staircase Solutions
Sterling Roncraft
The Stone Federation
Stovax Ltd
London Regional Planning, DOE
Thames Moulding Co.
The Tiles & Architectural
   Ceramics Society
Joseph Tipper Ltd
Jenny Todd
Top Knobs Ltd
Townsends (London) Ltd
The Universal Railings Co. Ltd
Hans van Lemmen
Vermont Castings
Webb & Kempf Ltd
Wellington Tile Co.
Westcombe Antiques
John Williams & Co. Ltd
Winther Browne & Co. Ltd

Owners of period houses may find the following sources of information useful.

National amenity societies

Amenity societies are a valuable source of information when repairing period houses. They produce many technical leaflets as well as organizing courses and lectures. Contact the following:

Society for the Protection of Ancient Buildings
www.spab.org.uk
Victorian Society
www.victorian-society.org.uk
Georgian Group
www.georgiangroup.org.uk
Twentieth Century Society
www.c20society.demon.co.uk
Ancient Monuments Society
www.ancientmonumentssociety.org.uk

Local authority guidance

Many local authorities provide guidance on historic buildings and the types of materials used in their area. Contact your local authority to see what services they can provide.

Conservation information available online

The internet is a rich source of information on conservation specialists and suppliers as well as useful technical information. The following websites are particularly useful:

www.buildingconservation.com
www.oldhouse.info
www.periodproperty.co.uk

Government advisors on heritage matters

Government agencies produce a wide range of publications on the historic environment. Some of this information is supplied free of charge.

English Heritage
www.english-heritage.org.uk
Historic Scotland
www.historic-scotland.gov.uk
Cadw (Welsh Historic Environment Agency)
www.cadw.wales.gov.uk
Environment and Heritage Service (Northern Ireland)
www.ehsni.gov.uk